DUDLEY PUBLIC LIBRARIES

The loan of this book may be renewed if not required by other
readers, by contacting the library from which it was borrowed.

CP/494

MARKY RAMONE

PUNK ROCK BLITZKRIEG

MARKY RAMONE

with Rich Herschlag

MUSIC
PRESS

First published in Great Britain by Music Press Publishing,
an imprint of
John Blake Publishing Limited
3 Bramber Court, 2 Bramber Road
London W14 9PB

www.johnblakepublishing.co.uk

www.facebook.com/johnblakebooks
twitter.com/jblakebooks

First published in hardback in 2015
First published in the USA in January 2015 by Touchstone,
a division of Simon & Schuster, Inc., New York

ISBN: 978-1-78418-640-1

British Library Cataloguing-in-Publication Data:

A catalogue record for this book is available from the British Library.

Design by www.envydesign.co.uk

Printed in Great Britain by CPI Group (UK) Ltd

1 3 5 7 9 10 8 6 4 2

Papers used by John Blake Publishing are natural, recyclable products made from
wood grown in sustainable forests. The manufacturing processes conform to the
environmental regulations of the country of origin.

Every attempt has been made to contact the relevant copyright-holders,
but some were unobtainable. We would be grateful if the appropriate
people could contact us.

To my Dipplo

CONTENTS

PUNK ROCK BLITZKRIEG

PROLOGUE

There were many reasons to come down to Florida. There was the weather, retirement, or just a vacation. My friend Mike came down for a kidney. Like me, he was from Brooklyn, but he had a rare genetic disorder and needed a transplant. His specialist told him that all the automobile fatalities in the Sunshine State made it the organ donor capital of the United States.

Dee Dee and I were in Florida for none of those reasons, even though a new liver, pancreas, or spleen probably would have done Dee Dee some good. The Ramones had just finished a show in front of a thousand screaming, moshing kids in St. Pete, and were set to drive across the state to do a show in Miami Beach the next day. But Mike, Dee Dee, and I decided we wanted to hang out in the Tampa–St. Pete area for another day and catch up with the rest of the band the day of the show.

Monte said it was okay. He trusted Mike to get me to the show, and he trusted me to get Dee Dee to the show. That meant a lot coming from Monte. To call Monte our road manager was to call da Vinci a painter. Monte had it all figured out, from A to Z. The last time I asked to stay behind, years earlier, things didn't work out so well. I never made it from Columbus, Ohio, to Virginia Beach, Virginia, and the Ramones had to cancel a show.

But that was then, and this was now. I had been sober four years going on five and was dedicated to my craft: professional drummer in the world's first and foremost punk-rock band, where if there was a dull moment, it was only because you were dozing. As for Dee Dee, he was a work in progress. Dope, coke, dust, and amphetamines had been replaced largely by lithium, Thorazine, Stelazine, and Buspar.

He hadn't found exactly the right combination yet, but he was still the iconic bassist and lyrical genius in that same punk-rock band. So, when Monte entrusted me to get Dee Dee to the show as well, it was like your parents leaving you in charge of the house and your kid brother. We promised to be good. Maybe we'd visit Busch Gardens or the Tampa zoo.

The next morning, we took off in Mike's Chevy Impala and headed south on Interstate 75 (I-75). It was about a 260-mile route that took us south to around Naples and then veered due east across the Everglades. We had the radio to help us kill time, and there was always lots of stuff to talk about – cars, girls, music. We had a new president elected a couple of weeks before, George H. W. Bush, and were heading into 1989 with a new album: Brain Drain. Dee Dee had written a song for it, 'Pet Sematary', in under an hour down in author Stephen King's basement, and it was also the title track for the forthcoming movie.

And, with all that to shoot the breeze, Dee Dee chose to rap his way across the state. With his now spiky hair holding pretty firm, he shouted out to central Florida that he was another James Brown and the baddest rapper in Whitestone, Queens.

Baddest in the Everglades, too. Dee Dee had practically invented punk rock. I wasn't so sure the world needed another rapper. What I was pretty sure we needed, though, was a mechanic. I had had more than my share of overheated cars for one lifetime, and I knew what I was smelling was not good.

I asked Mike to pull over to the grassy shoulder. There was nothing on this trip but grass, except for maybe a swamp off in the distance. Other than an occasional overpass, there was not much to distinguish one mile of highway from the next. I couldn't say I had any idea what town we were in. There were no towns. There were just wetlands linking one side of Florida to the other, plus saw grass that was now dry. Mike told me it hadn't rained for weeks.

Mike and I got out of the car, while Dee Dee, no longer rapping, sat in the back. When I dropped down and looked under the Impala, I could see the catalytic converter was extremely hot from the smoke coming off it.

'Dee Dee,' I said, 'you gotta get out of the car.'

'I'm not getting out,' he said. 'I just saw an alligator.'

I knew what he meant. The nickname for this stretch of highway was Alligator Alley. There were plenty of mosquitoes around, but no alligators. It was the Thorazine talking. Or the Stelazine. Or just Dee Dee. I smelled something else burning. It was the grass beneath the car. I yelled.

'Dee Dee, get out of the car! The grass is on fire!'

Dee Dee bailed out like a skydiver, alligators be damned. I put the gearshift into neutral, and Mike and I started pushing the car as Dee Dee joined in. We had a shot. The wind was blowing front to rear, so if we moved fast enough, we could keep the car from becoming engulfed. We rolled about twenty feet and felt the flames licking up our jeans from behind.

'Forget the car!' Mike screamed.

He was right. It was a lost cause. He didn't want us hurt on his account, and we didn't want him to wind up an organ donor. We let go of the car and ran down along the highway just ahead of the growing flames. The ring of fire stretched out around fifty feet and obscured both ends of the car. It was bye-bye, Impala.

I had been down this road before when my 1960 Cadillac Coupe de Ville went up in flames on Ocean Avenue in Brooklyn. That one wasn't my fault either, but it caused me to miss a rehearsal and was the beginning of a downhill run, and pretty soon it was bye-bye, Ramones.

In my mind, I already saw Monte's disappointment. Worse, I could see John's anger.

We jogged down the highway to maintain a safe distance. The brushfire was now covering an area equivalent to two city blocks. Mike understood the situation. He agreed to stay behind while Dee Dee and I hitchhiked. We would figure out the rest after the show, hopefully.

No matter where we were, we looked like Ramones. We had the T-shirts, sneakers, leather jackets, and the hair. We had the attitude. Sticking a thumb out on the Bowery would have stopped enough cars to snarl downtown traffic. But out here in the Everglades, Charles Manson had a better chance. And the inferno behind us wasn't helping.

At least a dozen cars, trucks, and minivans had passed us by. I didn't have Claudette Colbert's legs, and this wasn't It Happened One Night. But I knew the universal language, and it was greener than the burning grass. So I pulled out a small wad of hundred-dollar bills and began waving it around. Within a minute, a Ford F-150 pickup truck pulled up alongside us. The driver got out and walked around the front of the vehicle.

'Where you boys headed?'

He looked like a nice, hardworking, enterprising guy of about fifty. He had on a John Deere cap and was missing a couple of teeth.

'Miami Beach,' I said. 'We're musicians.'

'Okay, then,' he said. 'I'm going that way, and I have room in the cab.'

'Great,' I said. 'Thanks.'

Before I could reach over and grab the handle of the passenger door, something rolled off of Dee Dee's tongue. It spread faster than the grass fire and was harder to put out.

'Marc, how big do you think this guy's dick is?'

We all heard it loud and clear. No matter how much rapping Dee Dee had done along Alligator Alley, there was no rhyme to this. Or reason. Dee Dee was straight, married, and, like me, had a lot to lose if we didn't make it to Miami Beach on time. I saw the pickup driver's eyes go from Dee Dee to the money in my hand, back again to Dee Dee, and once again to the cash. Then it was settled.

'Tell you what,' he said. 'You boys are gonna have to make yourselves comfortable in the back of the truck.'

I nodded. I held out the cash, and he took it.

Late November in the Everglades can be chilly, especially when you're in the open air in the back of a pickup truck doing seventy-five miles per hour. I didn't bother to ask Dee Dee what he was thinking. I didn't want to know. I just kept staring at the two rifles mounted in the back window.

When we pulled up to the front of the theater, Dee Dee and I were huddled in the back like a couple of immigrants being smuggled across the border. The Miami Beach Ramones fans were already hanging out in front, and when they saw us stand in the back of the truck, a small cheer went up. I am always happy to sign autographs, but I was so cold, I didn't know if I could hold a pen.

The sound check was in ten minutes. I would have to hold sticks, and Dee Dee would have to hold a pick. And use them. So we ran into the dressing room to try to warm up quickly. John came by. He seemed a little edgy but mostly relieved.

'Marc, I was getting worried. We have a sound check.'

I had no doubt John was worried about us and about a possible lost payday. Joey came in next. He was the member of the band with an obsessive-compulsive disorder at times so severe that getting him to leave his apartment was an all-morning affair. But Joey had beaten us to Miami Beach by almost a full day.

'There was a huge fire on the highway,' Joey said. 'Alligator Alley. It was just on the news. Did you guys see that?'

'Yeah, we saw it.'

We were still shivering and not too talkative yet. But, when Monte walked in, he wanted to know everything. Who could blame him? How the hell I got here was a question I asked myself just about every day.

1

My father's father, Peter Bell, came to America from Holland in 1920 along with my grandmother. My father was born in Hoboken, New Jersey, on 11 August 1931, and christened Peter, after my grandfather. My grandfather was a chef at the Copacabana for ten years before becoming the head chef at the '21' Club. The Copa, as it was known, was located on East Sixtieth Street in Manhattan and was owned by mob boss Frank Costello. Jerry Lewis and Dean Martin made their debuts there. If you were a singer, bandleader, or comedian in the forties and fifties and made it to the Copa, you had made it, period.

My grandfather worked at '21' for eighteen years, right through its heyday. Established during Prohibition and located on West Fifty-Second Street in Manhattan, you could always spot the place thanks to all the painted statues of jockeys above the front entrance. Everyone who was anyone ate at '21'. My grandfather got to meet and hang out with stars including Humphrey Bogart, Jackie Gleason, and Judy Garland. These weren't just a bunch of tall tales – my grandfather had the pictures to prove it! Whenever we visited my grandparents' house, I would just stare at those photographs in awe that my grandfather actually knew the same people I saw on TV and in the movies.

In 1944, my father and his parents moved from Hoboken to Brooklyn. My dad went to PS 217 elementary school on Coney Island Avenue, and that's where he met my mother. My mother's maiden name was Gertrude Joest. Most people called her Trudy. Her mother, Johanna, was French, and her father, Julius, was German. They immigrated to America in 1923 and settled in Willoughby, Ohio. My mother was born on 10 September 1931 in her parents' home. Julius was an electrical engineer, and the family were middle-class, but most babies at the time were still delivered by a midwife instead of in a hospital.

When my mom was only two years old, her mother died. A few years later, Fredrick, my mom's older brother, died of pneumonia at the age of ten. Little Trudy and her dad moved to Cleveland for a few years before relocating to Brooklyn, New York. They lived on Ocean Parkway for a couple of years, and then moved to a four-story brick apartment building at 640 Ditmas Avenue, a few blocks south of Prospect Park. It was a solid working-class neighborhood made up mostly of modest private homes.

Mom and Dad were friends for quite a few years before they started dating when they were around eighteen. About a year later, on 15 December 1950, they got married at city hall in Lower Manhattan. On 15 July 1952, my twin brother, Fred, and I were born at New York Infirmary Hospital.

Our family lived with my grandfather Julius in a three-story brick walk-up, off the corner of President Street and Rogers Avenue in the Crown Heights section of Brooklyn. The buildings were all attached, usually with a little store on the ground floor and a separate stairway to the apartments above. Fred and I shared a room with bunk beds, which was fine with us because we got along really well.

My father was a card-carrying longshoreman, and my mother worked as a secretary. They sent Fred and me to a racially integrated nursery school in Bedford-Stuyvesant, a neighborhood just to the north. In the mid-fifties, most neighborhoods were segregated, but

Fred and I were happy to be with kids from different cultures and made friends right away.

One strange thing about our nursery school was the school bus. We didn't have one. What we had was a Cadillac hearse converted into a kind of station wagon minibus. It was big and black and came rolling up to the school as if there'd been a funeral to attend. When the kids saw the hearse coming up the block, we would all run to try to get into the backseat first. It was roomy and padded back there, and it was cool to think this same compartment was once used for dead bodies. I loved riding with the window down. We all loved looking out the back window and making weird faces at the cars behind us.

The only thing I really didn't like about nursery school was when they put us all down for naps in the middle of the day. I thought it was weird the way they set us all up on little floor mats and turned the lights out. There was plenty of daylight still coming in through the windows. I knew I was supposed to be quiet like everyone else, but it was hard. I knew there was no way I was going to fall asleep, so the best I could do was lie there with my eyes closed.

I daydreamed about doing anything else but taking a nap. There were toys put away on shelves all around the room – wooden blocks, a Slinky, Play-Doh, Mr. Potato Head, a Lionel train set – and they were begging to be played with. After our nap, the teachers let us play a little rough, especially outdoors, where we could just run around in the yard and make up our own games. To me, lying down on that mat and faking a nap was just a big waste.

In 1957, Fred and I turned five, and we moved along with Grandpa Julius back to the four-story building at 640 Ditmas Avenue, where my mother had lived when she was little. The bunk beds moved with us, so I still had to share a room with Fred. That was fine, because we still got along.

Dad and Grandpa Julius put their mechanical skills to work for Fred and me by helping us build a huge electric train set, which we played with for many hours. Dad also got us started building plastic models of cars, airplanes, and battleships. Fred loved making models of the

Universal Studios monsters – the Mummy, Dracula, the Wolf Man, and the Creature from the Black Lagoon. He painted them almost lifelike.

All the models required Testors glue, which had a very powerful smell that hit you sharply way up your nostrils. The smell was so bad it was good, and we got a little buzzed from it. That was the bonus of building models.

There were no more naps once we got to elementary school. PS 217 was the same place our parents first met. Mom packed our lunch boxes. We got to play in the schoolyard at lunchtime. I got along with the other kids for the most part but got into a fight here and there. One time some kid in the bathroom accused me of stealing his grape juice. Why the hell would I want some kid's grape juice? So we got into it right then and there by the urinal until one of the male teachers burst in and broke it up. It was just kids' stuff.

When Fred and I got home, our grandfather Julius watched us until Mom and Dad got back from work. The deal was we would usually get our homework out of the way before we played. If the weather was bad, we would watch reruns of *The Three Stooges Show*, *Abbott and Costello*, or *Adventures of Superman*. *The Three Stooges Show* was probably my favorite because they were out of their minds with the slaps, hits, and smacks, but at the same time they were a unit – a team. It was like three times as much comedy packed into a half-hour as anybody else.

Most days, I'd be waiting outside our apartment building for my father to come home from work. When I saw my dad, I'd run toward him to give him a big hug. I really looked up to my father. He was very relaxed about most things but firm when he had to be. My dad was six foot two and a half and 230 pounds, and he wore the thick, black-rimmed glasses that were popular at the time. He reminded me of Clark Kent. My mother looked like an actress. She was outspoken, and she was tough when she had to be. But my parents seemed to have a great relationship. I don't think I ever heard them argue, even once. If they did, it was never in front of us.

When the weather was decent, Fred and I would usually play punch-ball or stickball with our friends from the neighborhood. Stickball was basically street baseball using a broom handle. When that got boring, we moved on to more exciting things like climbing fire escapes or sneaking into boiler rooms. We got into fights with kids from other blocks in the neighborhood, usually because someone was on someone else's turf. We were just your average kids from Brooklyn.

On one particularly boring day, a friend had a cool idea to take a bunch of pillows and blankets, tie them together, and make a human dummy. We did a pretty good job considering we weren't pros. We carried the dummy up to the roof of our building and waited for a passerby.

Timing was everything. When someone was walking along the sidewalk about fifty feet away from our target, we would toss the dummy over the parapet wall and scream at the top of our lungs like someone jumped. It worked. When you had less than a second to look up and figure out what was happening, it really looked like a falling body. People flipped out.

One time we nailed a young couple carrying grocery bags. As the dummy plummeted to his 'death', the man and the woman both dropped their bags, and the groceries rolled all over the sidewalk and the street. Up on the roof we laughed so hard our eyes watered and our stomachs hurt. It was one of those laughs where you weren't sure you were going to be able to breathe ever again. If it wasn't for the parapet wall, I think we might have rolled off the roof and wound up like the dummy.

The dummy always lived to see another day, and we kept getting better at throwing him. One time we threw him way out to the middle of Ditmas Avenue in front of an oncoming 1955 Plymouth. The driver hit the brakes hard and skidded just short of running over the dummy's head. The problem was that the driver and the passenger both hit their own heads on the dashboard. The other problem was the size of the driver. He was huge. And he was pissed off. He stepped out of the car, looked up, and spotted us up on the roof. It didn't help that we were laughing, but we stopped laughing when he shouted he was coming up there to throw us into the street next.

We disappeared fast onto the rear fire escape, down the building stairway, anywhere to safety like a bunch of roaches scattering when the light comes on. There were places to hide in the basement. I came out when I figured it was safe. Whenever I thought about the stuff we did, I told myself that if you were a kid living in Brooklyn, getting in trouble was your *job*. Eventually the dummy got kind of beat up and the prank got old, so we moved on to other things.

I had a friend named Joel who lived in the building. He was a chubby kid. We hung out all the time, and Joel would do whatever the rest of us were doing. There was an empty lot close to our building where a bunch of us kids would go to have rock fights. One time I hit Joel with a rock and blood squirted out of his head like a fire hydrant. It was like a scene from a horror movie. One of the kids knew enough to apply pressure to the wound and stop the gusher. Amazingly, Joel didn't need stitches.

Another time Joel and I were in a neighbor's yard trying to squeeze between two one-car garages to get to another yard, but Joel's big belly got stuck and he started to cry. I wanted to help him, but I was laughing so hard I was pretty useless. As I stopped laughing, I told him maybe we'd have to get a crane and fish him out. Or maybe we'd have to demolish one of the garages. Or maybe he would just have to lose some weight. Finally, I got him to stop crying and relax a little, and we wriggled him out. The next day, he told me his mother wouldn't let him play with me any more.

Not long after that, I was playing in my room with a kid named Robert, whom I really didn't like that much. We were darting and jumping around the room and throwing whatever we could get our hands on. At one point I was on the top bunk and grabbed an old wooden milk crate off a shelf. I tossed it down to Robert, who tried to catch it and missed. One of the metal edges on the box caught him in the head.

Blood was everywhere. It was like the sequel to the horror movie with Joel – this time indoors with blood shooting all over the blankets and the walls. A few days later, I ran into Robert with a Band-Aid on his forehead, and he told me he wasn't allowed to play with me any more. This became a pattern in my neighborhood. Ten years old and I had a reputation. As far as I was concerned, it wasn't deserved. I didn't want to hurt anyone. I was just out to have some fun.

PS 217 was strict. In the morning we had to line up in the schoolyard and march into the building, grade by grade, like an army. Boys were required to wear a tie, a button-down shirt, and a sport jacket. For girls, the dress code was a skirt with dress shoes. The girls wound up looking like miniature versions of their mothers. Sneakers were forbidden for boys or girls except in gym.

In the classroom, seating was in size order with the short kids at the front and the tall kids in the back. The desks were made of old dark wood that looked as if it had been there from the day the school was built or maybe before. To get into your seat, you had to flip the desktop. There was a groove at the top for pens and pencils, and an inkwell with a brass lid. There were so many names carved into the desk that there were names carved over older names. Maybe if I looked hard enough, I could find Mom's and Dad's.

Every day started with our standing, placing our right hands over our hearts, and reciting the Pledge of Allegiance. Once we sat down and started the lesson, we were expected to remain silent unless called upon. If anyone made a sound or caused any disruption, they'd be punished. That usually meant standing in the corner and facing the wall. I had the corner memorized – the little crack, the missing paint chips. Usually the teacher would also call your parents and let them know you had behaved badly.

Once every week or two, a loud bell would ring, and we would do an emergency drill in case an atomic bomb was dropped. A few years earlier, the Soviet Union had developed its own atomic weapons, so we were expected to live on high alert. The drill was called 'duck and cover'. There was even a goofy civil-defense movie by the same name. The teachers marched us all into the auditorium and made us watch Bert the Turtle show us how to survive a nuclear holocaust. There were kids in the movie about our age, dressed neatly like us, who saw a flash of light in the sky. Instead of freaking out, they all calmly crawled under their desks, knelt down, and covered the backs of their heads and necks with their hands and shirt collars.

It was hard not to laugh. As if squatting under a table was going to do anything in a massive atomic blast! But we did what they did, because what we were afraid of was not getting fried by a radioactive shockwave but getting sent to the corner to look at the wall. If we ever did see a flash of light in the sky and knew what was coming, I doubt we would have been quiet or gotten under the desks. I mean, this was Brooklyn.

From the late fifties into the early sixties, things were pretty stable from year to year. That included our school, which stayed just about the same. The only thing that was changing was my attitude, which was getting more negative every semester. I was a hyper kid to begin with, so I had a really hard time sitting still. I'd bang on the desk, melt crayons on the radiator, and constantly disrupt the class. I was fidgety. I had a hard time paying attention, and my mind would drift off. The teachers called my parents in so often that it got to be a drill – as stupid as 'duck and cover'.

My father would sit me down and try to talk to me about my behavior. He'd explain how important education was and that it was something I'd benefit from later in life. 'It may not seem important now, but when you grow up, you'll understand.' He meant well, but it didn't have much of an effect once I was back in the classroom, bored and drifting off.

But there were still some cool teachers, even if most of them ended up yelling to get their point across. And I did like certain subjects. I liked to read, so I always got an A in English. Science was cool, too. Just like with the train set at home, I enjoyed trying to figure out how things worked. I was able to do well if I was really interested in something and was allowed to move at my own pace.

That was the reason I entered the fifth-grade science fair. I built a three-stage rocket out of wood and galvanized steel. It wasn't a working model, just my idea of what the inside of a spaceship might have looked like based on all the sci-fi movies and news stories I saw. My ship was split open in the middle, like a cross section, so anyone could look in and see the controls, the seats, and the living quarters. My dad helped, but I was the captain, and the project took first place. For the sixth-grade fair, I built a working telegraph system with wires, a tapping machine, and two large Eveready batteries. The telegraph was combined with a model train set to look more impressive. That project took first prize, too.

All of this made my parents very happy and made up for some of the other problems I was having. They knew I had potential. But it didn't always carry through the way they would have liked. I didn't care much for history, because as far as I was concerned, that was for people living in the past. I was more concerned about the present. Math was one of my least favorite subjects. I knew the basics, and that was good enough for me. I could figure out the change when I was buying candy, and I didn't think there would ever come a day when I would need to use a polynomial.

Sometimes I didn't need to worry about how much a Hershey bar cost because I stole it. We lived about ten blocks from PS 217. In the morning, on the walk to school, I'd usually stop at Maudie and Eddy's candy store, slip something small from a shelf into my pocket, and walk out. Until one day about three steps from the door, right near the newspaper stacks, Maudie grabbed me by the wrist. His hand was like a vise grip, probably from many years of moving boxes and stacking shelves. I knew Maudie wasn't about to let me go under any circumstance, so I punched him in the stomach and ran out of the store. I decided never to come back to the store, but really only to avoid Maudie. My mistake was getting caught. I saw other kids stealing candy all the time, so I didn't consider it a big deal.

One day in class, my friend Sandy Stock and I waited for the teacher to turn his back on the class and we nailed him with a couple of spitballs, which were small rolled-up paper balls soaked in saliva. The teacher wheeled around quickly, but we were even quicker. We did this a few times until he finally faked us out and caught us in the act. I was the head troublemaker, so he started yelling at me in front of the class. I thought the teacher would calm down after a minute or so, but he actually got louder, walked right up to my desk, and got in my face. I felt attacked, so I punched him in the stomach like I did to Maudie.

There was no running away this time. The teacher grabbed me by my arm and dragged me out of the classroom, down the hall. He opened the door to the science storage room, shoved me inside, and locked the door behind me. The room was a small concrete-and-steel prison cell filled with test tubes, which I started knocking off the shelves and smashing to bits, kind of like Frankenstein. When I got through with the test tubes, I moved on to throwing books, Bunsen burners, and anything that wasn't nailed down.

The storage room door opened, and the teacher stood in the doorway. I knew I had crossed a line and thought that might be the end for me at PS 217 or anywhere. Instead, the teacher asked me to step out into the hallway. He calmed me down, reasoned with me, and explained that we didn't have to go another step down this path. He said there was no reason the principal or my parents had to know anything about this. It would just be history and never happen again. I thought he was the coolest teacher who ever lived.

Record albums were too expensive for a young kid to buy, but I would scrounge together enough money once in a while to buy a single, which was a small disc that spun forty-five revolutions per minute. The first single I ever bought was Sheb Wooley's 'The Purple People Eater.' The song was about a Martian who came to earth and joined a rock-and-roll band. He was purple with a long horn on his head, which he used to blow out rock music. I thought that was a pretty cool story.

Since I was a big sci-fi fan, the lyrics and the story they told were as important as the music. I was also into all the monster movies I saw in theaters and on TV. On television, *Chiller Theatre* and *The Twilight Zone* were my favorites. On *The Twilight Zone*, there was always more than just a good sci-fi story. There was usually a real point to it. In one episode, a bookworm bank teller locks himself in the bank vault so he can read without being disturbed. While he's in there, an atomic bomb is dropped. When the teller steps out of the vault, he's actually glad that everything and everyone is gone so he has nothing but time and books. Then, as he begins to read, his glasses fall off and break.

For Christmas 1961, my parents bought me my first transistor radio. It may have been the happiest day of my life. I loved that radio. It was an RCA 3RH10 transistor. It was AM only, as FM was just getting started.

It was very basic – small enough to hold in your hand with one big dial in front for tuning. On the side was the volume control dial along with a small port to plug in an earphone.

A whole new world opened up for me. Murray 'the K' Kaufman was the big DJ on 1010 WINS. He was a real character, all over the place cracking jokes, playing sound effects, pulling pranks. In 1966, Murray the K worked at WOR-FM, one of the first progressive rock radio stations ever, and was still occasionally calling himself the fifth Beatle. It wasn't true in 1964, and it was even less true in 1966. There were dozens of people who might have laid one claim or another to that title – producer George Martin and, later, keyboard player Billy Preston and even John Lennon's controversial other half, Yoko Ono. Murray the K was not near the top of that list.

Bruce Morrow ('Cousin Brucie') and Dan Ingram were to the left on the dial over at 770 WABC, a very powerful station in terms of wattage and musical influence. The guys at WABC were fast-talking and clever, leading you in and out of a song as if they were part of it but without stepping on the lyrics. These DJs were smooth. They were breaking new, exciting groups like the Four Seasons and Jay and the Americans. The airwaves were like one big party.

In the summer of 1962, the song 'Monster Mash' by Bobby 'Boris' Pickett was released. Pickett sang the way Frankenstein's monster would have sung if he could. It was funny and catchy with a good rocking beat. Not only that, *Frankenstein* was my favorite monster movie of all time. I loved the way the monster was pieced together from body parts. I listened to my transistor every second I could that summer and into the fall hoping I would catch 'Monster Mash'. I also built a little radio holder for the handlebars of my bicycle. I was hooked.

At night, I'd listen to the radio under the covers in bed. If it was too loud and Fred was trying to sleep, I'd use the small plastic earphone that came with the radio. AM radio waves traveled thousands of miles at night. Sometimes I'd pick up a station from California, Texas, or even Mexico. I had the planet at my fingertips, so it was really hard to switch off the radio. Usually, I would fall asleep with the earphone still in my ear.

On 20 February 1962, our fourth-grade class along with all the other classes filed into the auditorium to watch astronaut John Glenn lift off from Cape Canaveral and try to circle the earth aboard *Friendship 7*. All eyes were on a black-and-white Zenith TV set not more than about twenty-five inches across. This was sci-fi come to life. When the countdown was through and the rocket launched, you could see and feel the power even on that little screen. As the ship passed through the thick part of the atmosphere, the normally calm newsman Walter Cronkite actually shouted out, 'Go, baby!' That's how exciting it was.

No American had ever been in space more than about fifteen minutes, and over the next five hours John Glenn circled the earth three times. Re-entering the atmosphere was not a sure thing. There was a real chance that the ship's heat shield would fail and *Friendship 7* would go up in flames. For about a minute or two – which seemed more like an hour – there was a blackout. There was no signal from the capsule, and you knew you might never hear from John Glenn again. When the ship came back into focus and you could hear the astronaut's voice, we all stood up and cheered. It was more than just a sigh of relief. It was a thrilling moment when we were all on the same team. You don't forget that feeling.

The summer of 1963 was special. My dad customized a Volkswagen camper to look like our kitchen at home. We drove that 'kitchen' cross-country. The engine was air-cooled and only 40 horsepower, so you couldn't push a Volkswagen camper over fifty-five miles per hour for too long. Including the stops we made in the Midwest, we took about two weeks to work our way across the US. We stayed at campgrounds, hiked, caught little fish in streams, learned the names of trees, and soaked in nature. I had my transistor radio with me, so no matter where I slept, I was still at home listening to all the latest hits.

When we stopped in town there were sometimes signs in store windows that said 'Whites Only'. But, for the most part, people were really friendly and happy to talk to us. I got a sense of how big America really was and how much there was to see outside Brooklyn. It was endless. I liked the road.

The road ended in San Francisco. The camper barely made it to California and needed major work if we hoped to make it back east. We didn't have the money to pay for an overhaul. But we did have the longshoremen. The union was very strong – a real nationwide community. We were able to stay with union friends for a couple of weeks while my father picked up a temporary job on the docks. In the end, the van was fixed, we took care of the bill, and we headed east again. For me, the change of plans and how we handled it wasn't a problem. It was an adventure.

On 22 November 1963, I was in my sixth-grade class when one of the other teachers walked into the room and told us that President John F. Kennedy had been assassinated in Dallas, Texas. Our teacher started crying and, when they saw her, a few of the girls in our class burst into tears, too. I was sure my mom would be doing the same thing. President Kennedy was a star – a young, brilliant man so many people connected with. Kennedy was not a typical president. He was always talking about the need for change. I felt sad, especially watching the girls around me crying. But it was one of those days, like most days, when I just didn't want to be at school. A thought popped into my head. *I hope we're dismissed early*. And we were.

When my parents got home late that afternoon, it was as if the president had been assassinated a second time. My mom and dad were big supporters of Kennedy. They believed in equal rights and equal opportunity and in the idea that America's best days were ahead. My parents were crushed. You could see it in their every step, and it stayed with them for a long time.

On Sunday evening, 9 February 1964, my mother called Fred and me into the living room to watch the Beatles on *The Ed Sullivan Show*. The build-up was going on all week with the Fab Four landing in New York and giving press conferences, imitating Elvis, and joking about their long hair – which wasn't even that long. When they appeared on the black-and-white TV screen in our living room, it felt as though things were changing right before our eyes. There was electricity in the air you couldn't exactly describe, but it was impossible to be sad. It took about two minutes to get through the first song, 'All My Loving', and the girls in the studio audience were hooked. The country was hooked. I was hooked.

The next morning, I started to comb my hair down in front the way the Beatles did. My brown hair wasn't long enough for real bangs – or fringe – but I figured in a few weeks it would be. John, Paul, and George were great, but I wanted to be Ringo. Sitting back behind the drums, pounding away, and giving the music all that power and rhythm was something I wanted to do. It was something I knew I *could* do.

There was no drum set in the house, but that didn't matter. At any given moment, I would be tapping my hands on the kitchen table, thumping on pillows, playing with a knife and fork as if they were drumsticks. My mom would constantly ask me to please stop banging. That would work for about five minutes. Riding on the subway, I would listen to the rhythm of the steel wheels on the tracks and tap along with it on my legs.

Around my twelfth birthday, my parents got me my first snare drum. It was a cheapo Japanese piece but better than a table and utensils. I persuaded my parents to take me for some lessons at a local place called Bromley's Music. Bromley's wasn't much of a music school. It was basically a drum set in the basement of someone's house. The instructor taught me how to hold the drumsticks military style and some rudimentary techniques such as flams and paradiddles. After about three months, I didn't think I was getting much out of the lessons and I stopped showing up. What I really needed was my own drum set.

A few weeks later, my parents took me to Milton Arfin's music store on Church Avenue, where they bought me a very basic drum set. The deal was they wouldn't get me anything expensive until they were convinced I was going to stick with the drums. The kit consisted of a bass drum with a single tom mounted on it, a hi-hat, and a ride cymbal. Of course, I already had a snare.

The new kit was a Zim-Gar brand with the logo printed on the bass drum head. That wasn't going to cut it, because Ringo used Ludwig drums. So I wrote to Ludwig and asked them to send me a large sticker.

When the Ludwig sticker came in the mail, amazingly, I immediately stuck it over the Zim-Gar logo. Right below it I spelled out 'The Beatles' in black electrical tape.

I spent almost every spare moment practicing the drums, which were set up in the small bedroom I shared with Fred. I had a small gramophone with only one speaker, and I would listen closely to the drum parts on my favorite songs. By concentrating, I could figure out the bass-drum patterns, off-time beats, rolls, accents. By the time the Beatles movie *A Hard Day's Night* opened in cinemas in the summer of 1964, I not only had maybe a dozen Beatles songs down on the drums but also was playing along with other British Invasion groups such as the Rolling Stones and the Dave Clark Five.

Fred's reaction to the Beatles and the British Invasion was to take up guitar. So my parents made another trip to Milton Arfin's and bought Fred a starter Harmony electric guitar and a small Fender Princeton Reverb amplifier. Fred's early favorite band were the Dave Clark Five. But Fred soon gravitated to the blues, which led him right to the Rolling Stones. Before they got into writing most of their own songs, the Stones were covering all sorts of old blues numbers. Fred also liked the surf-music pioneers Jan and Dean.

By this point, our room could barely contain the bunk bed, the drum set, and the Fender Princeton Reverb amp, let alone the noise we made – especially when Fred and I played together. So everyone in the family was really glad when we were able to move into a three-bedroom apartment. Even better, the apartment was on the ground floor of the same building we had lived in for years at 640 Ditmas. We were twelve years old, in junior high school, and needed our own space personally, and now musically, too.

My new room faced the alleyway on the side of the building where the super kept the garbage cans. It was hard to ignore the smell of tossed-out banana peels and grease wafting through the window, especially during the hot summer months. But it was a small price to pay for having my own room – my own *studio*. The more I played the drums, the less I noticed the stench.

Fred had a friend in the building who soon turned him onto the Blues Project, with Danny Kalb on guitar, and the Paul Butterfield Blues Band, with Mike Bloomfield on guitar. I was moving in a slightly different direction. In the spring of 1966, the Who released the album *My Generation*. An earlier Who single, 'I Can't Explain', was a tight, melodic four-chord song. But it was the title track of the album, 'My Generation', that really grabbed me. The chords came on fast, hard, and powerful. And drummer Keith Moon was doing things I had never heard before. Not even close.

The drumming style was manic and all over the place to the point where it was almost confusing. He added wild drum fills right over the top of the music and accents at parts of the verses and chorus no other drummer would ever have thought of. The weird thing was, it all worked. Moon's drumming made the songs more exciting but never completely took them over. I went right back to the drums and started experimenting with some of these techniques, putting in as many hours as I could.

As a thirteen-year-old self-taught drummer, I felt I was good enough to start a band. Kenny Aaronson was a bass player my age with a Fender bass and an Ampeg B-15 amp. He had the same musical influences as I did and was developing into a good player. The problem was, he lived twelve blocks from my building. But Kenny did what he had to do, carrying the bass in one hand and wheeling the amp in the other across streets and up and down curbs over a half-mile to get to my building. He became the other half of the rhythm section.

The guitar player lived a block or two away. The vocalist was my friend Steven Bakur. We would all pile into my room after school. Between the drums, guitar, and bass amps, and a separate amp for vocals, we were packed in, and the room got smaller once we cranked it up. Because we were on the ground floor, there was no one to complain in the basement below because there was no apartment there. The people above us weren't so lucky. We got a few complaints but not nearly as many as we thought we would. It had to be a pretty cool apartment building. My parents were very supportive, making sure we had enough to eat and letting us know when it was too loud even for them.

We called ourselves the Uncles, a tribute to the TV series *The Man from U.N.C.L.E.*, which was based loosely on the James Bond spy movies. Because we were getting ready for a show – our first ever – for the student government at Ditmas Junior High, we were allowed to rehearse a few times in the school auditorium after class. It was my first time on a stage, and it was a thrill. With no bodies in the audience to absorb the sound, it bounced off the walls and made everything louder. We weren't in my bedroom near the garbage cans any more.

At our first show, I was a little nervous, and I think the other guys were, too. As ten, twenty, fifty kids filed in, I knew rehearsal time was over. If we sucked, there would be nowhere to hide the next day. At the same time, we were excited, and as the show grew near, for the most part I wanted to show people what we could do.

Our set included 'My Generation' by the Who and '(I Can't Get No) Satisfaction' by the Rolling Stones. The rest of the set was mostly Top Ten hits from bands such as the Animals, the Beach Boys, the Searchers, and Jan and Dean. A few minutes in, I noticed that we had a tendency to speed up a bit. That was a natural reaction to the excitement of playing live. It could start anywhere, with a guitarist speeding up first, then the bassist, and so on. As far as I was concerned, it was up to the drummer – to me – to keep the song on track and lead rather than follow. I did it the best I could that day under the circumstances.

The kids at Ditmas liked us. It was not a typical experience for me. I could see right away there was newfound respect from the guys, the girls – and, yes, even some of the teachers. That included some of the tougher male teachers who had fought in World War II and were not your obvious fans of rock and roll. But drumming – whether it was jazz, big band, or even rock and roll – was a very physical thing that clearly took some real strength and coordination. It was something they could relate to. They looked at me a little differently from that day on.

The Uncles got to play a few of the dances at Ditmas and a few private parties around the neighborhood. Our home base was the Jewish Center on Ocean Parkway between Ditmas and Eighteenth Avenues. This was the same place where I went to Cub Scout meetings with Pack 27 when

I was eight or nine, with the same kids who were now coming to see the show. They were saying, 'Wow, look at Marc up there. He can really play.' I was very comfortable around the Jewish Center. There was such a rich history of entertainment in the Jewish culture. If you weren't a musician, actor, or comedian, you had an uncle who was.

We didn't play only the Jewish Center. We played wherever and whatever was available to us – churches, parties, people's basements. I was happy being appreciated for what I wanted to do, and I was always trying to develop. I was a big fan of drummer Hal Blaine, who was a member of the famous Wrecking Crew, a group of California studio musicians who always worked with Phil Spector and played on more Top Ten hits than anyone could count. If you were listening to Nancy Sinatra, Elvis Presley, the Beach Boys, the Ronettes, or Simon and Garfunkel, you were probably listening to Hal Blaine.

I got to the point where I could tell in under a minute if Blaine was playing on a given record. He had a very distinctive style with signature off-the-beat drum fills, and that style stood out even more at the end of a song. I was constantly committing these musical elements to memory and using them where it made sense.

Part of being in a band for me was looking the part. I grew my hair out like the Beatles. By 1965, that meant kind of shaggy hair with bangs. By 1966, that meant an inch or two longer. I wore Beatle boots, and suits that looked a bit Beatle-esque. I looked sharp for a kid in junior high school, which definitely helped attract the girls.

But my look had its downside, too. Some of the teachers at Ditmas gave me a hard time about it. My gym teacher, Mr. Gross, was an ex-marine in his late thirties. He picked on a lot of the guys in the gym class for any number of reasons, including not being able to drop down and give him forty push-ups. It was as if he had never left the marines. In his mind, he was still a drill sergeant preparing a bunch of fourteen-year-old string beans for the Korean War. Of all the guys, he really singled me out. I did every last push-up, sit-up, and chin-up he called out. But it was never enough.

One day, I was walking down the hallway wearing a tie loosely around my neck, when out of the blue came Mr. Gross, who was completely bald. He looked like Mr. Clean minus the earring. He grabbed me by the arm and marched me into his office. I thought fast about what it was I had done but honestly couldn't think of anything. Gross slammed the door, turned to face me from about a foot away, and started yelling at the top of his lungs. 'I've had it with you! You don't pay attention in class. You're disruptive. Do you think that just because you don't want to be here that you have the right to ruin things for the other students?'

'I'm not ruining anything for anyone. You're ruining it for *me*.'

I was ready to argue some more when Gross started poking me in the chest. I was surprised, and, when I pushed his hand away, he reached back and slapped me a couple of times across my face. I used everything I had to control my temper, but, when Gross's open palm made solid contact with my cheekbone, I lunged at him with my head down. The next thing I knew, I was seeing stars. He had hit me hard in the back of the head. It was all I could do to stay on my feet and pretend to listen to the rest of his tirade.

When I got home, I gave my father the blow-by-blow. He just sat and listened very calmly, asking a few questions here and there. I was not called into the dean's office the next day at school, and that was a relief. My dad was home from the docks early that afternoon. He had taken a half-day off to pay Gross a visit. In the same office where Gross had knocked me almost unconscious, my dad called him a sadistic bastard and said that if he ever laid a hand on me again, it would be the last thing he ever did.

Mr. Gross never bothered me again, but a few of the other teachers kept putting me down in class. It was my hair. It was my clothes. It was my attitude. Some of the other students went after me, too. There was tension between the kids who dressed like it was still the fifties and those of us who were changing with the times. I wasn't the only target. But I was target number one.

I was glad junior high school was almost over. The one thing that made the final few months livable was my first real girlfriend. Alyson and I started going out in April of 1967. I would walk her home every day after school, and we would hang out whenever we could. She came to some rehearsals. Just a few more weeks and I would not only be out of Ditmas Junior High but we would have the whole summer together.

Then she broke the news. For a moment, I thought we were breaking up. Instead, Alyson explained that her parents had a bungalow up in Connecticut and were making her spend the whole summer with them. That was better, but not much better.

The Uncles played their last show at a club on St. Marks Place in Greenwich Village called the Electric Circus. The club was situated in an old town hall and ballroom carved out of three very old four-story brick row homes. Just a few months before our gig, the place was taken over by new management, renamed, and decorated with a large modern dance floor, sofas, strobe lights, and projector screens all over the place. The four of us played our usual cover tunes okay, but we were definitely not the main attraction. On the screens, there were psychedelic images that were constantly morphing. The club had circus acts like jugglers, fire-eaters, and trapeze artists. It was hard to compete with that unless I was going to pour kerosene on my drumsticks and light them.

2

FROM DUST ...

The summer of 1967 was being called the Summer of Love. But my girlfriend was away, and my band were split up. Neither of those things changed what I loved: the drums. I had a lot of time on my hands to focus on learning more and getting better. There was an enormous amount of new and exciting rock music coming onto the scene literally every day. And the music was changing almost as fast as the screens at the Electric Circus.

The Jimi Hendrix Experience with Jimi Hendrix on guitar was unlike anything anyone had ever seen or heard. Jimi thrilled people with his wild look and playing guitar behind his back and with his teeth. At the Monterey Pop Festival in California, he lit his guitar on fire as if he were performing a sacrifice. But, when you closed your eyes and just listened, the real force of the music came through. It was blues and rock and soul reinvented, stretched to their absolute limits and beyond till they were transformed into almost a new kind of music. The guitar was a weapon or a divining rod as much as an instrument. This guy was so good that the Beatles and the Rolling Stones were his biggest fans.

But I was listening to the drums as much as the guitar. Maybe more.

Mitch Mitchell, a white guy from England, played with the soft touch of a veteran black American jazz drummer but provided a solid foundation for the power of Jimi's screaming guitar. Mitchell applied that light touch and offbeat fills to accent Jimi's raunchy guitar rather than compete with it. Listening closely during the summer and discovering new bits and pieces for myself was a great experience for me.

Cream were another three-piece band – a power trio – lighting up the airwaves. Eric Clapton came from a heavy-blues background with the Yardbirds and John Mayall's Bluesbreakers. But with Cream it was blues, jazz, and heavy rock creating memorable songs with great hooks and always a few subtle surprises when you listened a second, third, and fourth time. My ears were on the drummer, Ginger Baker, who was truly a full leg in the tripod. Baker played the drums as a complete instrument, with each piece of the set involved. You never got the idea that he was just keeping time, although he was certainly doing that, too.

Meanwhile, the Beatles reinvented themselves again, this time with *Sgt. Pepper's Lonely Hearts Club Band*, an album that was not a collection of songs but a concept album that told a bunch of stories of dealing with everyday life. With so much orchestration and so many complex arrangements, it was clear the band had moved beyond rock and roll. The Beatles stopped playing live, and you wondered if an album like *Sgt. Pepper* even *could* be played live. Ringo's drumming was in the mix but more as part of a percussion arrangement. Even the Beach Boys, known for clean-cut songs about love and surfing, had released an experimental but very successful concept album called *Pet Sounds*.

Out west in San Francisco, another scene was emerging. Bands like the Grateful Dead, Jefferson Airplane, and Quicksilver Messenger Service were performing free concerts in the street, where LSD was handed out and young people, dressed in togas and flowers, danced as if they were sleepwalking in a ballet. Any given song could go on for a half-hour, and the music featured weird guitar feedback and formless drum solos. The point of at least some of this music seemed to be to enhance the effect of the drugs rather than to create a song that was memorable on its own.

I wasn't into the whole San Francisco music scene. There were good songs here and there, but, in my opinion, the English bands had far superior musicianship. I couldn't understand how anyone could put LSD or any other hallucinogenic crap in their bodies and risk a nervous breakdown, brain damage, or suicide. I tried LSD once and wanted out less than halfway through my 'trip'. A beer, a shot of whiskey, or even a joint served a purpose: to loosen you up a bit and get you beyond just thinking about whatever was bothering you that day. Hallucinogens made you someone else.

What I did like about the San Francisco scene were the political beliefs. Sometimes it was hard to tell the difference between hippies going to concerts and hippies protesting the Vietnam War. With their freaky anti-military clothing and hairstyles, they were protesting the war just by going about their business even if they weren't actually attending a rally or sit-in. I did agree the United States was on the wrong track getting involved in a bitter civil war halfway around the world while millions of people here at home lived in poverty. As my dad said, the Vietnam War was being fought by America's poorest, who couldn't avoid the draft by going to college or hiring a lawyer. When all was said and done, win or lose, those American soldiers lucky enough to come home would still face the same poverty, lack of education, and discrimination. Many thousands, of course, would never come home.

The hippies out in San Francisco – and everywhere – were strong believers in the civil-rights movement. But that movement was led for the most part by Dr. Martin Luther King Jr., a Baptist minister who organized protest marches and spoke all over the country. The struggle for equal rights on behalf of black Americans dated back to the 1800s, and in some ways had little to do with the hippies. The fact was, there was so much unrest boiling over at one time that anyone taking a stand against the establishment seemed to be on the same side. The hippies' love of freedom was pretty much about their own freedom.

In Brooklyn, you could see changes in style, but that depended on who you were looking at. Miniskirts, bell-bottoms, and peace signs were everywhere, although definitely not on everyone. The greasers were dying out slowly but hanging on for dear life. In Brooklyn, they were known as hitters. They were tough-acting guys, some of them in gangs, who wore T-shirts and DA ('duck's ass') haircuts. They sometimes wore leather jackets and generally borrowed their style from Elvis or James Dean. In the summer of 1967, many of them held fast to that look while others gradually morphed, letting their hair grow a little longer, wearing sideburns, and adding a little color to their wardrobe. Musically, they might still be listening to Elvis, but they also might drift toward more modern, clean-cut bands like the Beach Boys, the Four Seasons, Jay and the Americans, or the Righteous Brothers. Sometimes they would let a hippie word or phrase slip: 'groovy', 'far out', 'dig'.

I wasn't a greaser. And I definitely wasn't a hippie. I updated my own look in a way that felt comfortable. The Beatles suits were long gone. I started wearing a leather jacket and jeans. I grew my hair a little longer. In September 1967, I entered Erasmus Hall High School in Flatbush. Erasmus was originally a private school and one of the oldest high schools in the state of New York. The building, in fact, looked as if it belonged to another age, with old-world Georgian architecture and a courtyard surrounded on four sides. Erasmus had more than its share of famous graduates: Barbra Streisand, Mae West, actor Eli Wallach, singer and songwriter Neil Diamond, and world chess champion Bobby Fischer, who actually dropped out in 1960.

I didn't want to drop out after having just dropped in, but it was a long haul to Erasmus from the Ditmas area. We lived in what was called a two-fare zone, which meant we took a bus, got off, and then caught another bus to the school. Then back home at the end of the day, day in day out. Some mornings I'd meet up with my friend and former Uncles bassist Kenny Aaronson, and we'd make the trek together. We always had things to talk about, not the least of which was music. The buses were usually crowded, and one morning one of them was so jammed that we rode on the rear bumper right down Flatbush Avenue. We used the fifteen cents each we saved on bus fare to go get a slice of pizza and decided that was worth doing again.

Kenny seemed to hate going to school even more than I did; our aversion gave us one more big thing in common. He mentioned that he might eventually be homeschooled. That sounded great, but there was no way my parents would ever go for that.

My problems were almost as old as Erasmus. My eyesight was never that good, and the outdated incandescent lights in the classrooms only made things worse. The letters spelled out in chalk on the blackboard never seemed really clear and bright, and it didn't help that I usually sat in the back. I wasn't looking to fail. I tried to pay attention in class, especially with a subject like Spanish that I could really use in a multilingual city like New York. But the teacher singled me out when she shared my most recent test score with the entire class. 'Marc Bell. *Muy estúpido*. The lowest score in the class. The lowest score ever at Erasmus. *Nada* – a zero. Congratulations.'

Before long, I was staying after school to make up work in the classes I was failing. I usually didn't get to leave the campus until dark. School was like a vicious cycle. During the day, I was bored, and all I could think about was being somewhere else – either playing drums or hanging out with Alyson. The more I thought about being somewhere else, the longer I had to stay after school, and the longer I had to stay after school, the less time I could actually be anywhere else.

Eventually, I started cutting out of school completely. I would usually leave at lunchtime and just not go back. My favorite destination was a local rehearsal studio. The guys playing there were a couple of grades ahead of me. It was a lot better than spending the afternoon bored under old lights, but it didn't last. My parents found out. Even if they hadn't, they would have known something wasn't exactly right when my report card showed I was failing every class.

On 4 April 1968, Martin Luther King Jr. was assassinated by a lone sniper in Memphis. Because Dr. King was loved by so many people and his approach to protest was always nonviolent, the moment he was gone, a lot of anger boiled over. For black people in America, it seemed that peaceful attempts at equality and freedom had failed and were doomed to fail again. Starting that night, riots broke out in Washington, DC, Baltimore, Chicago, Kansas City, and other major cities. In New York, Mayor John Lindsay spoke in Harlem and vowed to stay committed to fighting poverty and discrimination. That may have been the reason there were no major incidents in New York.

The next morning at school, someone threw a smoke bomb into the ventilation system, and the fire alarm rang. As the entire school filed out, the black students stayed on the school side of Flatbush Avenue, while the whites and other groups gathered across the street. We held our breaths to see if any fighting would break out. After a while, it seemed we were past the danger point. The black kids needed to show their solidarity, and they did. I thought, *More power to them.*

While I wasn't comfortable in the classroom, I was comfortable hanging out with black kids. The outcast in me could identify with them, even though I'd be kidding myself to think I understood what life was like for them. But, on 5 April 1968, that circumstance of my life was an advantage. I was concerned with what was going on at Erasmus, but whatever went down, I wasn't afraid.

I had one friend named Bruce, who was a keyboard player. I wasn't skipping school as much as I had been but was getting into Manhattan whenever I could. We had an older friend who drove a 1967 Oldsmobile Cutlass and gave us a ride sometimes. When we couldn't get a ride, we took the D train, which cut right through Greenwich Village. We had a friend named Charlie who worked as an usher at the Fillmore East. The Fillmore East was rock promoter Bill Graham's counterpart to the Fillmore Auditorium in San Francisco. Graham had both major and upcoming acts play one place and then fly across the country to play the other. Both rooms were usually packed.

We had an amazing thing going with Charlie. After the bands finished their sound checks in the late afternoon, he would sneak us through the back door. Getting to see Iron Butterfly, Led Zeppelin, Buddy Guy, and Jethro Tull for free – instead of paying $3 to $5 – would have been more than enough for us. But a few times Charlie let us take it to the next level.

'Are you sure?' we asked.

'Yeah, what the fuck, go ahead.'

So we walked out on the stage, took our spots, and played on the first band's equipment. With no one in the Fillmore to hear us, we were like trees falling in the forest. But we got to hear ourselves. We were loud. Not too loud, because we didn't want to pay for a busted speaker cone or have a seasoned roadie with a Hell's Angels tattoo come after us. But we were loud enough to feel the power of being onstage at a major venue. I thought, *In a couple of hours, Led Zeppelin's John Bonham is going to be sitting in this very same seat, pounding on the bass drum, doing monster rolls, and creating a huge wall of sound.* I shouldn't have been sitting there, but I was, and I loved it, and that was rock and roll.

There was normally a show at eight o'clock and a second show at eleven. Both shows were two sets long. The performances were usually amazing. First, whether he was there or not, on any given night you were playing for Bill Graham, an influential businessman who could book you well beyond the clubs he owned. Second, audiences in New York knew music. They generally weren't wearing love beads and dropping acid like the crowds in San Francisco, but they had grown up going to shows dating back to the beatnik coffee shops and the jazz clubs. Or they were kids who listened to the radio night and day and bought albums with whatever spare money they could pull together. If you could knock that audience off its feet, you could be proud of your band.

One school day when I was actually in school, I was bored as usual and looked out of the window. There, walking along Flatbush Avenue, was Bruce with Alyson. My first thought wasn't a good one, but I let it go. A few days later, as I walked out of the building, I saw the two of them together again, this time arm in arm. I asked them point-blank what was going on, and he said, 'She's my girlfriend now.'

I was shocked – both that it happened and at how matter-of-factly Bruce delivered the blow. For a moment I felt a little sick inside. But, a moment later, I was just flat-out pissed off, so I punched Bruce in the mouth. He came back at me with a hard right, and we went at it right in front of Erasmus. There was a police precinct around the corner, and two cops assigned to the school broke up the fight, but not before I got in a couple of good shots.

For whatever reason, the cops let Bruce go, but they dragged me into

Dean Gallo's office. One of the tough male gym teachers was there. I thought I was going to get a lecture on fighting and school policy, as if school policy was going to make any difference the moment your best friend stole your girlfriend. Whatever it was, I figured that, if I sat there and went along with the program, this would all be over in a few minutes, and I could go.

I was wrong. The taller cop told me to stand up. I did. He told me to face him and drop my pants to my ankles. I hesitated, but I did that, too. Next, they had me drop my shorts. My shirt followed. It was like being naked in the middle of a packed auditorium. But this was worse. These guys were ex-navy and ex-marine. They were in their late thirties and were threatened by my generation: how we looked, how we acted, and how we didn't buy into their program. The truth was, I had tried pot a few times, and that was it. Not only was I not on LSD, I couldn't afford it. But they assumed that the longer your hair was, the more drugs you did; the more drugs you did, the more you were looking to bury them, their culture, their identities. I felt their glare all over my skin.

The shorter cop went through my shoulder bag and then searched my shirt pockets. Nothing. He walked over to me, put his hand in my hair, and shook it. Nothing. He told me to open my mouth and then looked inside like a narc dentist. He knelt down and went through my pants pockets. His hand brushed the inside of my calf. I thought about punching him. But this wasn't Maudie at the candy store, and that would have been the last thing I did for a very long time as a free man.

I figured there was no place left to search, but I was wrong about that, too. The shorter cop ordered me to turn around and spread my cheeks. Yeah, *those* cheeks. I put one hand on each and pushed outward. I didn't know when it would end or how far it would go. But nothing fell out of my ass, and I heard one of the cops say to pull up my pants.

When I told my dad that night I had been strip-searched, he flipped out. I spared him some of the details because I didn't want my father to serve time for manslaughter. The next day, I didn't take the bus into school. I rode in by car with my father and his two brothers. My uncle Ronnie was eight years younger than my father. Uncle Johnny was a change-of-life baby and was only five years older than I was. They were both rough working-class guys, especially Uncle Johnny. At one time, he was in a gang and was still a real greaser. The only thing he would have liked more than kicking the shit out of a teacher was kicking the shit out of a cop.

My father did all the talking. Dean Gallo and the gym teacher stood in the same office where the day before they'd treated me worse than a lab rat, and now they looked as though they wanted to hide somewhere. Their shoulders slumped. They could barely maintain eye contact with my dad, who wasn't an angry or violent guy but saved it for the few times in life it was called for. My dad told them he would have trouble ever forgiving them for subjecting his son to that kind of degradation. That it was sick, immoral, and illegal to boot. And that, if it ever happened again, he and his brothers would take both men outside in front of the school and make an example of them.

I could see my uncle Johnny hoping for a wrong move or a wrong word, but the dean apologized. He explained they were being overrun with drug incidents and were trying to look out for the welfare of the entire school. The gym teacher added they were very wrong about Marc and that it would never happen again.

'Hopefully not to him,' my father said. '*Or to anyone.*'

I appreciated what they did, but having my dad and uncles come in to fight my battles didn't exactly do wonders for my ego. Neither did losing my girlfriend, especially the way I had. I was devastated. Some part of me actually thought Alyson and I would be together for ever, so it felt like the rest of my life was ruined. But another part of me said that now I would have more time for music. At least, I hoped.

By tenth grade, I was going to night school to stay on track. If I didn't do well enough at night school, I would have to go to summer school to make it to eleventh grade. I had less free time than before, and going to the Fillmore East was now out of the picture. That's when I started hanging out at Parkside a lot.

Parkside was a small plaza at the southeast entrance of Prospect Park in Brooklyn, at the intersection of Ocean and Parkside Avenues. The Parkside subway station entrance was across the street. At the entrance to the park was a sitting area with two large canopies and masonry columns. Over time it became a meeting place for musicians and music lovers. I had gone a few times in ninth grade.

On warm weekend nights, it wasn't unusual to have seventy, eighty, or even more people on hand. Some people brought their acoustic guitars and got into spontaneous jam sessions. Other people just talked music. Acoustic versions of songs from Jimi Hendrix, Cream, the Who, and Led Zeppelin filled the air. It was a freeform singalong. Most kids wore tie-dyed shirts and bell-bottom jeans.

Pot, beer, red wine, and LSD made their way around as if they had a mind of their own. If you were tripping more than just casually, it was a good idea to venture deeper into the park to avoid the cops on patrol. There was a lake about a hundred yards in. Some kids having a massive trip would just disappear into the night.

By tenth grade, I was jamming regularly with two guys I met at Parkside. Scott Fine was about my age and a solid bass player. Scott dressed simple: jeans and a T-shirt. The other guy, a guitarist and vocalist, was Velvert Turner. Velvert dressed over the top: velvet pants, paisley shirts and vests, and a large hat with a colorful scarf wrapped around it. There was a buzz surrounding Velvert, but not because of his musicianship or even because of his wardrobe. Velvert was a friend and protégé of Jimi Hendrix.

According to rumor, Hendrix was teaching Velvert everything he knew about playing guitar and music in general. Supposedly Velvert even got to hang out at Jimi's apartment on West Twelfth Street in the Village. A tall, lanky black guy with a big Afro, Velvert looked the part. By being a little brother to the one guitarist we all really worshipped, Velvert was a god. You wouldn't have known he was only about a year older than I was.

At this point, Velvert wasn't a great guitar player. Scott was actually better. The three of us would get together on and off at a rehearsal studio called Baggie's off of Canal Street in Chinatown. Velvert showed up in full Hendrix regalia, including the white Fender Stratocaster. But the Strat didn't sing like Hendrix's. Probably no other Strat did, and Velvert seemed image-conscious above all, as if he needed a full-length mirror in the rehearsal room. I locked in with Scott's bass playing, freeing Velvert to do whatever he did over the rhythm section. We weren't a real band. We didn't have a name. It was all about drinking a little beer, smoking a little pot, and having a good time.

One night the three of us went to a club called Salvation on Sheridan Square in the West Village. Hendrix had played there as a relative unknown a couple of years earlier. Now, as a celebrity, he hung out at the club and had invited Velvert to meet him there. Salvation had a reputation as a gay hot spot and was reportedly run by the Mob. So there was just about nothing you couldn't find at Salvation.

The inside was all red, like the eyes of most of the customers. The dance floor was circular, with seats surrounding it completely. Velvert led us over to a round table where three guys were drinking and smoking: Jimi Hendrix, Buddy Miles, and Jim Morrison. I had never sat down with a single celebrity before, and here I was with three of them.

Jimi was in his element. The Experience had split up recently, and Buddy Miles was his new drummer. Miles, just twenty-three, was once a child prodigy whose aunt nicknamed him after his idol, Buddy Rich, maybe the best jazz drummer who ever walked the earth. Miles had met Hendrix in the early to mid-sixties when they were both sidemen for several blues and R&B legends. Hendrix still owed an album to the record company, and along with Miles and bassist Billy Cox was working on a live project called *Band of Gypsys*.

Jim Morrison was not just the lead singer and poet of the Los Angeles-based band the Doors. He was a cultural icon and troublemaker who liked to provoke audiences. The Doors produced records that mixed rock, blues, jazz, and the surreal into memorable songs that actually got a lot of airplay. But you never knew what Jim was going to do onstage. One minute he was writhing around on the floor, the next he was stopping the show cold in the middle of a song just to see how long it would take the audience to rebel. At Salvation, Jim's drink of choice was Jack Daniel's, of which he drank shot after shot. He was bloated and looking kind of heavy.

I sat at the table just taking in the whole scene. I didn't have a lot to say. I watched and listened to them talking about this song, that girl, and the other kind of grass. I thought it was weird that they kept getting up one at a time and heading to the bathroom. After a couple of beers, I got up and went, too – because I had to. There in the men's room was Buddy Miles by the sink offering me a snort of cocaine. I passed and watched him do a few lines before we both went back to the table. I left around one in the morning, and it looked as if Jimi and friends were just getting started.

The next day at school, I told my friends where I had been and who I was with. They sort of believed the where. As for the who, they thought I was bullshitting, tripping, or both.

The summer of 1969 was famous for the Apollo 11 astronauts' landing on the moon and a half-million kids landing on Max Yasgur's farm in upstate New York to be part of the concert phenomenon known as Woodstock. Most of my summer of 1969 was spent in summer school. But I hung out at Parkside every chance I got. The rehearsals with Velvert and Scott had fizzled out, but I was getting into new things. The talk of Parkside that summer was a band called Dust. Bands typically played cover songs, but Dust wrote and played originals. They were a heavy-rock band along the lines of Cream but with a darker edge. Dust's songs were usually faster and the lyrics darker.

Dust was Gary Woods on lead vocals, Richie Wise on guitar and vocals, Anthony LaTorre on drums, and my old friend and bandmate from the Uncles, Kenny Aaronson, on bass. Anthony was a friend of mine, too. We would cut out of school, go back to his apartment, and play drums. He had a double-bass setup like Ginger Baker's. Dust also had another thing most local bands didn't have: a manager. Kenny Kerner wasn't just a guy hanging around Parkside. He worked for the music business trade magazine *Cashbox*. And he, along with Richie Wise, wrote lyrics. We all thought Dust was going somewhere.

Parkside was like a club with no rules. We were all friends and sometimes traveled around the city like a pack of hungry musicians. For a fare of fifteen cents, the guys from Dust, myself, and a few others loved to take the subway to Forty-Eighth Street in Manhattan. Between Sixth and Seventh Avenues were about a dozen music stores, one after the other: Manny's, Sam Ash, Alex Musical Instruments, We Buy Guitars. It was as if we'd died and gone to rock-and-roll heaven. We would stare at all the new equipment in the windows and try not to drool. There were drums from Ludwig, Slingerland, Rogers; amps from Vox, Ampeg; guitars from Fender, Gibson, Hagstrom. There was enough equipment on those couple of blocks to outfit every band in North America.

When you walked into any of the stores, you usually heard a half dozen guys sitting down trying out a guitar or a bass and playing the one riff they were comfortable with over and over again. The better musicians played various riffs and put on a mini-concert. The store managers were cool. They let all the noise happen at once even if nobody was actually buying anything. That was part of what made Forty-Eighth Street special.

From there, we would usually get a hot dog with everything on it from one of the street vendors and then walk uptown to catch a live concert at the RKO 58th Street Theatre. These shows were hosted by Murray the K.

But the shows he put together at the RKO were fantastic. They usually started around ten or eleven in the morning and went all day. As many as a dozen bands would be on the bill, with dance contests held between sets. Some of the bands were there because they had a current hit on the radio. Other bands were more established acts. Once, during Easter 1967, Cream and the Who were on the same bill. I was not quite fifteen years old at the time and sat in the audience in awe. Both bands were making their American debuts. They got to do only three songs apiece, and then were off the stage.

But it was enough to change my life. Ginger Baker of Cream and Keith Moon of the Who taught me in a few short minutes the outer limits of what drumming could be. Whenever I went back to the RKO, like my friends, I stayed through the very last show. You never knew when you were going to see the next Ginger Baker or Keith Moon.

One day I was practicing the drums in our apartment on Ditmas Avenue, and my mother stepped into the room to tell me I had a phone call. If you've ever tried to tell a drummer in the middle of drumming he has a phone call, good luck. This call, however, was good luck for me. It was Kenny Kerner, who explained that Richie Wise felt that Anthony LaTorre's drumming wasn't cutting it. Kenny asked me if I would be interested in coming down to audition, and I said yes.

Even though Anthony was a friend, I didn't feel terrible about possibly taking his spot. If you were in a band and hoping to get anywhere, you had to have the best musician available on each instrument. There were exceptions to that, but rarely on drums. When you heard a band, and the drumming wasn't up to par, even if you didn't know much about music, you would say something was missing: excitement, professionalism – something. There was no hiding it.

The other element that excited me about the audition was the opportunity to play original music. As much as I liked playing Hendrix, Cream, and Who songs, I needed to grow, and one great way to grow was to have to come up with your own parts while fitting in with the overall sound. It wasn't automatic for everyone.

The audition was a challenge. Dust songs had a lot of parts and transitions. One of my audition songs, 'Chasin' Ladies', was a good example. There were several time changes, triplets, quadruples, and double-stroke rolls all in about four minutes. The drumming had to be on the money and powerful enough to stand up to the heaviness of the rest of the music without taking over. There were sections where the drum part was like a lead instrument and other sections where it was supporting the bass, guitar, and vocals. The drumming needed to move through all these phases seamlessly. But I had the advantage of knowing the songs from the shows and from generally having practiced my ass off. I thought I nailed it.

Kenny Kerner called the next day and asked me to join the band. I had to learn the rest of the songs fast because we had a gig the following weekend. I thought we sounded good overall, but, a couple of days later, Kenny Kerner told me that Gary Woods was asked to leave the band. That made sense to me. Richie Wise had a great voice, could pull it off while playing guitar, and was co-writing the songs. So Dust became a power trio in the spirit of Cream, Grand Funk Railroad, and Blue Cheer.

We played a few shows at the Flatbush Terrace, a private hall we rented out ourselves, right around the corner from Brooklyn College, where my mother worked. We were so loud, she could probably hear us from her office. Maybe the most exciting thing about those first few shows as a trio was how much tighter we were getting musically. We could hear a definite difference from performance to performance. Rehearsals are a must, but when you know individually and as a band that you don't have the option of stopping and going back over a part, you have to rise to the occasion.

Scott Muni was a popular DJ with a distinct, deep voice who could be heard every day on WNEW-FM, another New York radio station setting the tone in progressive rock for the rest of the country. When Scott asked Kenny Kerner if Dust would play a free show for WNEW at the Prospect Park Bandshell, it was like being nominated for a Grammy and having homecoming rolled into one. The band shell was a short walk in the park from our home base, Parkside.

The Prospect Park Bandshell was built in 1939 and had a postmodern sci-fi look to it: a white concrete shell within a shell within a shell. At the center of all of it were the three of us, ready to perform for a couple thousand Brooklynites. For all we knew, this was the top of the mountain. My brother had a good friend with a Super 8 movie camera. Fred stood a few rows back zooming in and out as we did our sound check. The film was color, but the camera silent. That was fine. We knew what the songs sounded like anyway, and it was going to be a thrill to have a visual record of this big event and get to see what we actually looked like playing.

I had a basic kit: bass, floor tom, snare, ride, crash, hi-hat. I wouldn't need any more. All the pieces were painted red. I was in a sleeveless vest with no shirt underneath. My hair was now very long and flew all over the place when I did a big roll. Kenny Aaronson and Richie Wise also wore their hair very long. It was amazing how 'long' became 'not long enough' in the space of only about two or three years.

We played for about half an hour and came off great. There was no problem for me, playing in front of so many people. I was consumed by the drums and what I was doing. There was not much opportunity to sit up and look around. The music was that challenging. But, when I did manage to take it all in, what I heard was a band quickly coming into its own.

I had known Kenny Aaronson for years and always respected his ability to hold down the rhythm on bass. But somewhere along the line – maybe only in the past few weeks – he started playing lead bass. At times I thought I was listening to John Entwistle of the Who. You had to be talented to fill all those open spaces in a three-piece band tastefully, without smothering the music. But you had to have something else, too: confidence. That confidence was developing right before our eyes and ears.

As for Richie Wise, he was about eighteen going on twenty-eight. You could hear that what I was trying to do on drums – soak up playing from the best out there and make it my own – Richie was doing successfully on guitar. When you closed your eyes, you could hear a wail from Jimi Hendrix, a measure from Jimmy Page, a bluesy arpeggio from Eric Clapton, a power chord from Pete Townshend. And he did all that while singing like a slightly higher-pitched version of Grand Funk Railroad's Mark Farner. Doing either was a triumph. Doing both was a miracle.

After the Prospect Park Bandshell, Kenny Kerner booked us aggressively at clubs in the Village at venues including Cafe Au Go-Go and Cafe Wha? These were obviously much smaller shows in terms of audience size but in some ways even more important. These clubs were where it was all happening. Cafe Wha? was a seedy little corner place that already had a rich history dating back to when Manny Roth founded and ran the club. Allen Ginsberg was reading his Beat poetry there in 1959, when the idea of a gay man talking frankly about his sexuality would have sent the average American running for the hills. In the early sixties, Bob Dylan played long, thoughtful acoustic sets at Cafe

Wha?, sometimes singing lyrics he had written down on a notepad just an hour before.

As for Dust, we wanted to blow the doors off the place. The room looked like the sixties, with black lights and groovy Day-Glo psychedelic posters. And it smelled like the sixties, with pot smoke coming out of every crevice in the place. But musically we were pushing into the next decade.

No one was pushing their way into the show. The place was about half filled. That was okay. We delivered the goods on 'Stone Woman', 'Goin' Easy', 'Love Me Hard', and a few of our other originals. By the last song, everyone in the room was standing. They loved 'Loose Goose', and we did an encore.

As we broke down our equipment, individual members of the audience came up to us, patted us on the back, told us we rocked, and offered us beer, pot, or whatever we wanted. One of those guys was John Cummings, who told me he was a guitar player from Forest Hills, Queens. He was in his early twenties and thought we were about the same age as he was. When I told him we were actually a few years younger, he couldn't believe it. He thought the musicianship was incredible. To top off our night, we were paid $30 each, which was a lot for a club gig.

My paternal grandfather retired in 1969, and he and my grandmother decided they'd had enough of the cold New York winters. When they moved to Florida, instead of selling their house in Brooklyn, they let my parents take it over. The timing couldn't have been better for me. Dust was newly formed, and we needed a place to rehearse. My parents, as always, were very supportive and told me we could play in the basement during the day, when they were at work.

We literally moved into the basement. Unlike in a rehearsal studio, where you usually paid by the hour and had to use whatever beat-up amps and drums were already there, Dust got to customize our new home. Kenny brought in two Acoustic bass amps. He was more than welcome to keep them there, but sometimes he chose to wheel them both back to his apartment, which was twelve blocks away. Richie brought in two full 100-watt Marshall stacks. Pete Townshend of the Who was the first guitarist to start stacking Marshall cabinets one on top of the other to provide a kind of crunching sound. Just about everyone followed, and stacking Marshalls became the centerpiece of the new hard-rock sound and a point of pride for bands everywhere. The more the merrier – and the louder.

In the basement, I set up every piece I had, perfectly arranged, so that I would want to be down there every opportunity I had, whether the rest of the band were there or not. It wasn't a very large basement, and part of the space was taken up by the boiler and the hot-water heater. We were crammed into a twenty-foot-by-twenty-five-foot area, with enough gear to play a small auditorium. By the time we were done rehearsing, my ears were always ringing. One time when we were bringing up Kenny's equipment, we noticed a fine white powder coating the hood – or bonnet – of my parents' car parked in the driveway. We realized it came from the stucco from the exterior of the house. We had played so loudly, we brought the house down, literally.

We didn't always play at maximum volume. When we wrote new material, it was critical that we could hear every part clearly and stop to go back over something. Usually Richie would strum the basic chord progression at low volume and sing over it. If he didn't have lyrics written, he would just make up whatever he needed to develop the idea. I would just hit the snare to keep time. Once there was a song structure, Kenny would quickly follow the chord changes and come in on bass.

Each time through the song, there was a little more detail, a little more sophistication. We would try different tempos. We knew the right one when we didn't have to think about it any more. As our familiarity with the song grew, I would add accents, and Richie would extend the guitar solos where it felt needed. It sometimes took less than an hour to have the full song polished. We had chemistry.

In the late spring of 1970, Kenny Kerner told us the band were ready to be shopped to record labels. That would require a good demo tape. We didn't have a lot of money to go to a professional recording studio, so we set up a studio in the basement. A friend of ours, Daffy, lent us his mixing board and a reel-to-reel tape recorder. Everything was done in-house. Kenny Kerner and Richie served as our producer and engineer.

They placed a single microphone in the room to get a preliminary sound. We played our instruments individually and then together. Kenny and Richie would check the sound on headphones and each time move the microphone this way or that: closer to the Marshall or further away. Closer to the bass drum or back it off. This took a couple of hours. When something was miked closer, you got more power but also more distortion. Kenny and Richie had a certain sound in mind and worked well within the obvious limitations.

Kenny hit 'record', and we ran through a song. If it felt good, we would listen back. If it didn't, we would go right to another take. If a take was obviously no good, we would rewind and go back over the tape. There was no point in wasting tape. When we did a great take, we all knew it. But sometimes Kenny Kerner would have us do one more just in case we hadn't 'peaked' yet.

The tape sounded surprisingly powerful considering it was done in my grandparents' basement. I expected to hear a combination of rejections along with maybe a few comments on what the labels were looking to hear. But Kenny got the tape into the hands of Neil Bogart at Kama Sutra/Buddah Records, and Neil really liked what he heard. We were offered a record contract for two albums. I was just shy of my eighteenth birthday.

3

...TO DUST

Kama Sutra had been started in the early sixties and was known more for lighter music and bubblegum rock. The Ohio Express, with 'Yummy Yummy Yummy', and the 1910 Fruitgum Company, with 'Indian Giver', were typical of that category. But the label also had great bands like the Lovin' Spoonful. What Kama Sutra did not have was a single hard-rock band, or anything, for that matter, sounding remotely like Dust. But we didn't give it much thought. We were three kids from Brooklyn who made a tape in the basement and ended up with a major label recording contract.

Our advance was small by record-industry standards but big by the standards of three guys looking to buy equipment on Forty-Eighth Street they had been drooling over for years. The advance was to pay for recording expenses, but the band could keep money left over. We spent our leftover money up front.

Richie bought more Marshalls, effects pedals, and better guitars. Kenny bought a few more Acoustic bass amps. When I hit Forty-Eighth Street, I was truly a kid in a candy store. I bought a whole new Ludwig kit with an oversized bass drum. John Bonham of Led Zeppelin was using a twenty-six-inch-diameter bass drum, which helped give him that massive bottom sound that felt a combination of a war drum and an earthquake. In the spirit of one-upping the best in the business – at least on the equipment side – I had a twenty-*eight*-inch bass drum custom made. To go with it, I bought two twenty-by-eighteen-inch floor toms, a fifteen-by-fifteen-inch rack tom, and a small arsenal of Paiste crash cymbals and hi-hats. I was ready to roll with the best of them. But my grandparents' house would probably be declared a disaster area.

We also got to hire our own roadies and technicians. These were friends from the neighborhood who had helped us move gear for free, set up for shows, and break down. It was a thankless job, and now we got to say thank you. J. R. Smalling was the guitar tech for both Richie and Kenny. He could straighten out the neck and get the string action perfect as if he'd been born to do it. My drum tech was Max Blatt. Most people don't realize that a drum set has to be tuned like any other instrument, except with drums it's a lot harder. All the pieces in the kit have to sound good together.

We started recording our first album in September 1970 in Bell Sound Studios at 237 West Fifty-Fourth Street in Manhattan. Even though the studio sounded as if it had been named after me, I was more at home in the basement. The building was an old industrial loft structure. The interior of the studio was very old and beat-up, with scuffed wood floors and peeling ceiling paint.

One of the first things I noticed was the studio drum set, an old white shot-to-hell Rogers kit. Using my finger, I tapped at the toms, which were covered with a few strips of duct tape. They sounded dead. For a moment, I thought about bringing in my own customized set – the one I had just bought with the record company's advance. But then I figured the people who ran the place had to know what they were doing, and who was I to start messing with it? Legends including Ray Charles, Buddy Holly, and Del Shannon had recorded here at Bell, and apparently it was good enough for them.

With our limited budget, we used Kenny Kerner and Richie Wise as

our producers. Harry Yarmark was the engineer. I adjusted the heights
of the drums and cymbal stands but not much else.

We had sixteen separate tracks going to two-inch-wide Ampex reel-
to-reel tape. Five or six mikes were on the drums, two on the guitar, two
on the bass. With a guitar or bass, one patch cord would go directly
from the instrument to the board, while another channel was fed by the
amp mikes. That way, the engineer could work with a clean signal plus a
signal with a lot of overdrive and live feel. The balance between the two
got worked out during the mixdown. There was also a microphone set
up far from the instruments just to get the overall ambience of the room.

Right off the bat, Harry had a problem with Richie's and Kenny's
volumes. Ray Charles and Buddy Holly never pumped out anything like
that. Of course, I was used to going part deaf for an hour here and a
day there, but Harry looked shell-shocked. He told us we had to turn
it down. We weren't used to that – not in a club, not in the basement,
and not even in the old apartment on Ditmas Avenue. 'We have to play
loud,' Richie explained. 'We're a hard-rock band.'

Harry told us we could push the volume later when we mixed the
tracks but that we couldn't have so much distortion on the original
signal. The microphones just couldn't handle it, and we wouldn't be
able to work with it later. There was some bickering back and forth,
and we finally settled on a volume that was too soft for us and too loud
for Harry.

Things rolled along better once we actually started recording. All
the rehearsing paid dividends. Given the sixteen tracks, we could have
afforded to make mistakes, but we didn't make many. When we did
the initial tracking, because I was the drummer in the band most of the
weight was actually on my shoulders. The focus was on getting one
really tight drum performance all the way through. Guitar, bass, and
vocals could be overdubbed, or punched in, afterward, but that was
usually not the case for the drums, which flowed continuously through
the song and were recorded by multiple mikes. Of course, we wanted to
get a live feel and not rely too heavily on studio tricks, so there was some
pressure on Richie and Kenny as well.

I was also very conscious of not speeding up or slowing down while playing a song. The tendency to speed up a bit during a live performance was sort of acceptable in that situation as the band and the audience got more into it. Not so for a record, which is for keeps and should be professional. But there was an extra complication for me: some of our songs were actually supposed to increase and decrease in tempo.

A good example was the song 'From a Dry Camel', a ten-minute epic that provided the mood for the album and could have wound up the title track. 'Camel' began eerily with an extended huge gong crash followed by a drum intro. The song started with a 6/8 time signature then launched into a super-heavy three-minute sonic assault in 4/4 time. There was no metronome in the world to play this track to. *I* was the metronome. We were the metronome. I loved playing 'Camel' for the sheer challenge.

Another favorite of mine was 'Love Me Hard'. This was more of a standard rock song based on a relatively simple hook. But there was a lot of space within the hook for percussion and anything else we wanted to put in. The transitions were more about variations in the hook than in time changes, but this song was still a workout for me. I did long double-tom rolls and provided a strong percussive thread – more like a percussive *rope* – throughout the four-minute-plus piece. There was no letting up.

No matter where you record, there are some universal elements. As in the basement demo that got us the record deal in the first place, at Bell Sound we would listen back to three or four initial takes of a song and pick the one that had the best feel. There were technical terms to describe what you were looking for, but in the end, you took the version that made you want to get off your ass and shout. On a really tight take, you didn't hear individual instruments so much as one unstoppable, driving musical force. Once you had that, you had the foundation on which to build the rest of the recording.

I knew the members of my band the way I knew my own drum set, but Kenny Aaronson still managed to impress me. In addition to playing bass guitar, he overdubbed parts for steel guitar, Dobro, and bottleneck guitars. These contributions gave the recordings a more diverse and sophisticated feel. The greatest bands in the world – from the Beatles to the Stones – routinely brought in top session players. We didn't need to. Our session player was already in the band.

We worked quickly. By the beginning of the third week, we were mixing down. The mixdown can sometimes take longer than the recording. Every instrument and vocal has to be balanced against everything else. We would listen over and over to a track and know that something was a little 'out', yet not know exactly what it was. Kenny Kerner and Richie had good instincts for knowing when to make a background vocal softer or bring up the hi-hat. The problem was that once you've listened to a song eight or ten times, you get numb and might not hear the song as a whole any more. In that sense, it's like anything else – you have to know when to take a break and walk away for a half-hour.

The last step in the process was mastering. Mastering is a series of sonic treatments that bring out the treble and bass more. It gives the recording a sheen, like taking a car to a car wash. More to the point, mastering makes the song radio ready. With any luck, that's where our music was headed.

The Beatles were so huge that they could put out an album with a blank white cover and watch it sell millions. A start-up band from Brooklyn didn't have that option. We needed a cover that grabbed people's attention and became one of the first bands to use skulls for this purpose. We used a stark brownish photo of three genuine skulls taken from the Mexican catacombs. The bodies attached to the skulls were fully dressed as if they had been left in the desert to waste. It was riveting and a little comical. The back cover featured a band photo shot by our friend Daffy. I had on my leather jacket and jeans. There was also a photo of a camel walking across the desert sands, a reference to our anthem 'From a Dry Camel'.

We now had an album 'in the can'. But there was little time to celebrate because I still didn't have my diploma. Graduation for the rest of the class was in June. As it turned out, you couldn't get extra credit for landing a record deal, so I didn't go to graduation. Between recording sessions, I was going to summer school, and, after we mixed and mastered, I had to keep going, learning the stuff I was supposed to have read ages ago.

I wasn't exactly thrilled when I found out I would have to keep going to class right through September. I finally picked up my diploma in October 1970 in the principal's office. It wasn't much of a ceremony. I returned all the textbooks I owed, and they handed me the sheepskin. I didn't feel cynical walking out of the principal's office. I went home, framed the diploma, and hung it on my bedroom wall. It wasn't a Grammy. But I was proud of it.

Our self-titled album, *Dust*, was released in January 1971. Seeing it in the window of the independent record store across the street from Erasmus was a surreal moment. Even more surreal was the first time I heard it on the radio. Kama Sutra decided to release 'Love Me Hard' as the first single. It was short and powerful, so it made sense. But, when I heard it in my bedroom on WNEW-FM, it all started to hit me. It didn't sound like me and my friends in a room putting together something to see what would happen. It sounded like a monster rock band booming out over the air. I thought about how many other people might have been listening across the New York metropolitan area at that very moment and had one more thought: *Life couldn't get any better*.

Then it did. To promote the album, Neil Bogart got us some shows opening for Alice Cooper. Alice's third album, *Love It to Death*, was released just after ours and was climbing the *Billboard* charts. The song 'I'm Eighteen' was all over the radio and was Alice's first big hit. The main riff was a slow, deliberate ascending scale in E. The lyrics were direct and simple and included, 'I'm in the middle without any plans / I'm a boy and I'm a man / I'm eighteen.' I was eighteen. And I liked it.

Alice Cooper's tour was mostly midsized arenas: four, five, six thousand. To us, it could have been Woodstock. The venues were nearly packed, and we delivered about a thirty-minute set while some people were still filing in or were out at the concession stand getting a beer. We played near the front of the stage, because behind us in the dark was all the gear and special effects for Alice Cooper's outrageous stage show. But lots of people in the audience stopped what they were doing and watched. The applause and cheers grew louder after each song. We were not just a commercial on TV providing a chance to go to the fridge and get a sandwich. We were worth listening to and were winning over the fans gradually.

It would have been worth playing those shows just for the opportunity to see Alice Cooper. Rock was changing, and with Alice it was happening right before our eyes. Alice Cooper was theater. With his wild hair, dripping black makeup, and long frocks, he looked like he had stepped out of a horror movie. He would walk out midset with a boa constrictor wrapped around his neck. One wrong move, and the blood supply to his brain would be cut off, but, from the looks of it, the snake may have been afraid of him.

There was press all over the place. If there was any theater in rock before Alice, it was connected mostly with British bands. The British had a long tradition of theater, and it showed up in seminal albums like the Beatles' *Sgt. Pepper* and the Who's rock opera, *Tommy*. The song 'Fire', recorded in the UK by the Crazy World of Arthur Brown, was usually performed with the frontman in a devil's costume and horns literally in flames. But theatrical rock wasn't an American thing, until now, and Alice Cooper was taking it to a level meant to shock. It definitely worked.

By the time we got off the road for a short break and went back to Brooklyn, the *Dust* album had made it to the *Cashbox* Top 100. The kids I went to school with were either still in school or were living in the neighborhood. And now they all wanted to be my friend. Guys who used to want to start a fight with me to prove a stupid point to themselves – or to their parents – now wanted me to sign an album cover. Or they wanted tickets to a show. Or to find out what life was like opening up for Alice Cooper. I dug it. I talked to everyone, including the ex-greasers. But I did draw a line.

One day on Flatbush Avenue, I ran into one of my old teachers. He wasn't the worst teacher I'd had. More like average. Unfortunately, average meant busting my chops from time to time over the usual things: my long hair, my jeans, and my inability to focus in class. He loved making me climb the ropes to see me burn my hands on the way down. My hair was longer now than ever, but apparently it wasn't hard to recognize me.

He shook my hand and congratulated me. I said thanks. He was beaming and knew all about the album hitting the charts and our opening for Alice Cooper. He actually named cities we played. It was as though he'd stopped reading *Popular Mechanics* and got a subscription to *Rolling Stone*. That was flattering and a little amusing, so I opened up and told him how we were going back on the road soon and that I managed to get my diploma at the end of the past summer. Without skipping a beat, he asked me if Dust would consider playing a benefit concert to raise money for the school. I did consider it. It took about two seconds.

'Why should I do anything for this school after the way you all treated me for years?'

He just turned and walked away. I didn't feel a pang of regret. Not a day went by in school when at least one teacher didn't single me out for being different, a weirdo, or a bad student. They might have thought – *he* might have thought – the putdowns were part of the job, but they never considered the effect any of it had on me. It made me uncomfortable, angry, and even less inclined to work hard at school.

Maybe even more important, not one of the teachers believed in me or encouraged me to develop the real talent that I had. Any time I told one of them my goal was to play music professionally, all they could do was roll their eyes and tell me it was never going to happen. So coming back to do a benefit was like making a statement that it was all right, and it really *wasn't* all right.

When I thought about it later without getting agitated, I wondered what life would have been like if they had built me up instead of knocking me down. Maybe I would have been a better student and an even better musician. I definitely would have played the benefit.

Sharing whatever success we had felt better, and that's what we tried to do. Our roadies started out as our friends. Coming back from Philadelphia or Wilmington, Delaware, on the bus back to Brooklyn, we partied all the way up I-95 as the sun rose. These were guys who helped us for nothing when there were twenty or thirty people in the audience. Now they got paid with two or three thousand people in the audience.

Kama Sutra also hired a young photographer named Bob Gruen to document the band before, during, and after a few of our shows. Gruen had followed the Grateful Dead and a few other well-known bands in the past year or so and was starting to make a name for himself. His specialty seemed to be black-and-white shots that captured the band in its natural element. We were definitely in ours.

The next big leg of our 1971 tour was the Midwest. It wasn't a set line-up of bands every night. Different-label acts were crisscrossing the country at any given time, and tour managers along with the record companies were always making phone calls to get their band a good slot here or there. Sometimes you got a date at the last minute because another band had to cancel.

Typically, we played on bills with other rising hard-rock acts such as Wishbone Ash and Uriah Heep. Sometimes we played with an older, more established act such as John Mayall, who with his band the Bluesbreakers in the sixties had catapulted some of the greatest young British guitarists into the mainstream. One of them, Eric Clapton, had just finished recording a sort of reunion album with Mayall, *Back to the Roots*.

We were stunned when we found out Dust would be headlining at Cobo Hall in Detroit. No bus – the record company flew us in. Cobo held twelve thousand people, probably more with festival seating. It was a large, circular concrete building along the Detroit River. With Windsor, Canada, right across the narrow river, it was the closest we had ever come to playing another country. More important, it was like a coming-out party for Dust. The place was packed, and we could feel as much volume coming from the fans as we were putting out.

When you're headlining, you get the full benefit of the best lighting and the best sound the venue has to offer, so, if you don't deliver as a band, you can't fall back on excuses. Fortunately, we got to do two encores. The hall lights went dark, and many of the fans flicked their lighters and held up the flames. The arena looked like a sea of lights, and the crowd chanted 'Dust! Dust! Dust!' After the second encore, arena management turned on the big houselights, which meant no third encore. We were a little relieved. We were starting to write songs for a second album, but most of them weren't ready yet. We were running out of material.

We were like celebrities in both Detroit and St. Louis. After the shows, the hotel was party city. Hotels that booked a major rock act knew what they were getting. The band had multiple rooms together on the same floor. Adjoining rooms usually had doors that opened from one room to the next. Members of other bands, fans, groupies, and press people flowed freely from room to room, as did beer, pot, and harder drugs. Dust stayed away from dust. And cocaine and heroin. We avoided the hard stuff but couldn't control what other people did. Food fights would break out, and a couple of TVs magically found their way down to the sidewalk below. The hotel just submitted a bill to the tour manager and called it a night.

In the morning – or more like the early afternoon – we would meet with the press or visit with the top local FM-station DJs, who talked up the band, had fun with us in the studio, and ran contests giving away tickets to people who called the station. We were treated like royalty. There was a buzz. The Midwest was definitely Dust territory. It was impossible to know exactly why, but this part of the country seemed to go for hard, loud, and musically challenging rock.

It was in Detroit that well-known rock critic Lester Bangs caught up with Dust for an interview. Dust was just getting known, but Lester's reputation preceded him. Bangs was maybe the one and only person writing about rock who was bigger than some of the acts he covered. Not only wasn't he afraid to skewer a band in print, he seemed to enjoy it. He called Black Sabbath a pathetic Cream wannabe. He called Paul McCartney a snob. He called Jefferson Airplane a bunch of radical capitalists. Even the MC5, a proud product of Lincoln Park, Michigan, and a unit known for being on the cutting edge of both politics and hard, raw sounds, Lester Bangs cut to shreds. What chance did three kids from Brooklyn have?

It turned out that Lester Bangs loved Dust. More than that, he was a fan. He told us so. He could quote 'Stone Woman' and 'From a Dry Camel'. He compared us to a couple of literary figures I had failed tests on in school. From what I understood, Lester Bangs hated anything pretentious, especially in rock and roll, which was supposed to be the answer – young people's answer – to anything and everything in the world that was fake. Dust, to him, was the real thing. It was honest. It was three guys dressed as themselves, being themselves, putting out a huge, raging sound, and saying if you don't like this, it's not our problem, 'cause we like it. He called us *three young punks*.

Lester Bangs was actually a nice, down-to-earth guy. But he had no style, was overweight, and needed a shower badly. He must have seen a little of himself in us, because we got a three-page article in *Creem* magazine saying we were the next big thing. Rod Stewart was on the cover.

Touring wasn't all about headlining, encores, and rave reviews by world-famous critics. One night between shows, Kenny Aaronson and I figured we would get back to the hotel room a little early and actually get some sleep. When we opened the door, a putrid smell hit us in the face. It was like someone died in there, but, as far as we remembered, everyone the night before left the room alive.

We had been out getting a few beers and we were pretty buzzed. Too buzzed to feel like combing the room for the source of the smell, but not buzzed enough to ignore it for long. So we looked around: the bathroom, the closet, the garbage pail. Then Kenny hit pay dirt. Someone had made a shit right in one of the dresser drawers. We laughed. Sometimes you just had to take some shit.

In the late summer, we had some time off, and I had the phone number of a nice girl named Jill, someone I'd met when we played St. Louis. She told me to go and visit her when I had the chance and that her mom's house was huge with plenty of room. So I booked a flight out of JFK

Airport and flew to St. Louis. She drove me back to the house, and we got settled in. I hadn't eaten much that day, so we thought it would be a good idea to drive over to the nearby supermarket to pick up some beer and food.

We were halfway down the bread aisle when a voice came crackling over the store's PA system. It wasn't for a special on Twinkies. It was the manager informing the patrons that a tornado was reported heading in our direction. He instructed us to lie facedown on the floor. Everyone else in the store, including Jill, did it immediately without complaints or confusion. They seemed used to it. It was their 'duck and cover'. In Brooklyn, we had blackouts, gang fights, and sanitation strikes, but no tornadoes.

I was down on the floor staring at the sawdust, with only Jill to hang on to. As the wind picked up speed, I looked up and noticed that both doors and all the windows were wide open. I thought about getting up to shut them all, but then I thought again. The wind suddenly picked up, and not by a little. It was tenfold. Cans, bottles, and boxes flew off the shelves like in a horror movie. Glass shattered on the floor, and we covered our eyes while getting pelted with Ding Dongs, Rice Krispies, and Crisco. Ceiling tiles flew like paper plates, and a fan came crashing down. We covered our heads with our arms. I hoped we didn't become a couple of the items getting swept away into the Midwest plains.

The wind died down and then disappeared almost as fast as it started. The whole episode felt like an hour, but, when I looked at the Coca-Cola clock that, miraculously, still hung on the wall, it had been more like three minutes. I was shaken, while Jill and the other customers got up and brushed themselves off matter-of-factly. The aisles were piles of rubble and Cheez Doodles. No one seemed hurt, and Jill suggested that we find a store that wasn't directly hit to pick up the beer. As we walked out, I asked her why the store owner left the doors and windows open. She explained that was to let the wind pass through the building instead of allowing pressure to build up inside the store. If they remained closed, the building might have lifted right off its foundation. Everyone who lived there knew the drill.

As we drove off, we could see the tornado heading toward the horizon, receding from us like a pillar of fire in the movie *The Ten Commandments*. The sky was a combination of dark purple and black. Out of all the strange sights I had seen on tour, this was the strangest.

Back in Brooklyn, Dust were outgrowing my parents' basement. It didn't seem to us that we were playing louder than before the tour, but maybe Cobo Hall had made us deaf. The doctor who lived next door complained to my mother, and my mother told us to turn it down. We did, but the volume slowly crept back up, and the doctor was getting sick of it. Meanwhile, my mother found a marijuana plant growing in the backyard. Since I never planted it, my guess was that someone else did it as a prank. The plant was near the fence, and someone must have tossed the seeds through the chain links. Whoever did it, my parents had had enough, and we had to find another place to rehearse.

Neil Bogart wanted us to start work on the second Dust album, so in late 1971 we loaded into A&R Studios in Radio City. The less-than-satisfying sound qualities of the first album were stuck in our heads even as we roamed the country playing to large audiences. It wasn't as if we bitched and moaned about the sound the whole time. It was just a stray comment here and a thought there about a guitar sound on this song, or a snare sound on that song. We had a running checklist, and we really wanted another crack at it.

Going to A&R Studios was a great start. Located in Manhattan on the corner of Fifty-Second Street and Seventh Avenue, A&R was founded in 1958 by Jack Arnold and legendary producer and product of Brooklyn Phil Ramone. The original studio was a few blocks away on West Forty-Eighth Street. Much of the recording equipment there was put on wheels so it could be relocated quickly from room to room. It was in the old building that Ramone produced Frank Sinatra, jazz great Stan Getz, and folk standouts such as Peter, Paul and Mary. It was also in the old building where in 1963 Bob Dylan sang 'The Times They Are a-Changin''.

The new home of A&R was a large, brick, four-story, square building.

In the few years since relocating, it served as the studio for Paul Simon, Aretha Franklin, Rod Stewart, Stevie Wonder, James Taylor, and countless other superstars of the music world. The Allman Brothers had just recorded there over the summer. Compared with Bell, A&R was much nicer, better equipped, and more professional-looking. The performance room was a lot larger, and, once we were loaded in and started getting our sound up, we discovered it was also a lot more alive sonically, with a brighter, more powerful tone.

There was no excuse for doing anything less than a stellar job on this album. We had a bigger budget. We had more rehearsal time beforehand and had developed great chops not only from practice but also from all the priceless experience playing on the road. Kenny Kerner and Richie Wise were producing again and had spent weeks riding around on the tour bus ignoring the beer, pranks, and distractions in favor of discussing how they would approach the second album. We even had photographer Bob Gruen documenting the entire album-making process.

Just as the times were a-changing in 1963, they were changing again as we moved into 1972. Politically, the outcry to end the war in Vietnam reached a peak. Women's rights, gay rights, and all sorts of human rights were at the forefront. Musically, things were changing rapidly as well. Rock was getting extremely diverse, breaking into subgenres, each with a record label or two or three trying to cash in on it. Lester Bangs had warned us that corporate people already had a complete takeover planned.

As for Dust, we had been like a sponge, traveling around, playing, listening, meeting people, and soaking in just about everything that was going on around us musically – then putting it back out through our own fingers, feet, and throats. That became even more apparent as we began listening to the initial tracking.

'Learning to Die' featured fast riffs and even faster guitar leads, with playing at moments that sounded a bit like Alvin Lee of Ten Years After. 'All in All' was influenced by the new Who album *Who's Next*, with power chords, funky breaks, and Kenny Aaronson doing a good

John Entwistle, with the bass taking the lead at times and blowing the doors off. 'Suicide' was Black Sabbath-influenced, based on a heavy riff. 'Ivory' was an instrumental in 5/4 time, with a thunderous drum intro launching into a sonic exploration that reminded some people in the room of the Edgar Winter Group. Kenny's bass prowess allowed him to match Richie's guitar licks on this run or that.

But it was on the tracks 'I Been Thinkin" and 'How Many Horses' that you really heard the changes and diversity. If not outright country songs, both were heavily country influenced. We didn't sit down one day and say we had to write country songs. It was just in the air. The Byrds had drifted in this direction, and former members Gram Parsons and Chris Hillman took it a step or two further in the band the Flying Burrito Brothers. Crosby, Stills, Nash and Young were probably half country. The second side of *Led Zeppelin III* was a twenty-two-minute, largely acoustic folk experiment that left a lot of critics pissed off that they didn't get to hear the next 'Whole Lotta Love'.

We were happy with what we heard coming out of the Altec Voice of the Theatre studio monitors. I made sure to use my own drum set with absolutely no tape over any of it. As producers, Richie and Kenny had moved from feeling their way around the recording process to having set techniques that clearly worked. There was a nice mix of clean and powerful on the individual tracks. The music sounded crisp rather than muffled. Kenny and Richie were able to jump from hard rock to country mixes and back again fairly easily, taking notes all over the place on the sound levels.

The project was a tour de force for Kenny Aaronson, who not only had risen to the top of his game as a bass player but also, at the age of nineteen, handled the steel guitar parts like a seasoned professional. Somehow, he just kept getting better.

The album took four and a half weeks to record, a little longer than the first album but still relatively quick in an era when budgets were expanding and timelines were getting dragged out. The album was titled *Hard Attack*, which described some but certainly not all of the music within. The cover art was a painting called *Snow Giants* by artist Frank

Frazetta depicting three Vikings swinging large blades at each other high atop an icy mountain.

That trio on the icy mountain weren't Richie, Kenny, and I. We got along fine. But *Hard Attack* did not come out of the gate strong when it was released in September 1972. Neil Bogart was looking for an immediate hit, and there was none. We played a few shows to support the album, but there was little of the momentum and buzz from the first LP, and we could feel the wind going out of the sails.

The relationship between the label and the band was strained, but that strain wasn't routine. Changes were happening at Kama Sutra, and they actually involved members of the Dust team. Neil Bogart was planning to start a new label and was talking to both Richie and Kenny Kerner about producing some of the bands he was working with. One group were the already-established Gladys Knight and the Pips. Another comprised four ambitious guys from the outer boroughs who wore makeup and called themselves KISS. They played shows in the New York area but were unsigned as of yet. Meanwhile, Kenny Aaronson was starting to work with other bands and doing session work.

Dust never officially broke up. There was no formal meeting or conversation. It just ended. It made sense. There was no pressure to support a record that didn't produce a hit. Kenny Aaronson had emerged as a prodigy. We could see that Richie Wise and Kenny Kerner had talents that went way beyond the ability to make one or two records with a single band. Meanwhile, I had, along with everyone else, learned a lot since the summer of 1969. But I had to figure out what was next for me.

4

A few years had passed since my friend Bruce and I had come to blows over Alyson in front of Erasmus High School and I wound up being strip-searched. It seemed like even longer than that. At the time it felt like getting knifed in the back. By 1972, with recording, touring, and now a band breakup under my belt, I saw the whole episode for what it really was: a short break in my sex life, and the kind of thing that happens every day to friends in high school. Bruce was still dealing hash and assorted other substances, but he had a legitimate day job as a bike messenger.

Bruce and I talked about the past and decided to bury the hatchet. After we hung out a few times, it was as if the whole thing had never happened. We both wanted to move out of our parents' houses and decided to split a small basement apartment on Avenue O and East Nineteenth Street in Brooklyn. The apartment had a separate entrance along the side of the building, down a ramp, and right next to a couple of big green garbage bins. It was just like home.

The rent was $100 a month. Not only wasn't I sure what I was going to do with the rest of my life, I didn't know where I was going to get

57

my monthly $50. There were no royalties coming from Kama Sutra. Apparently, sales from the two albums were not enough to pay back the advances. So Bruce got me a job as a bike messenger in Manhattan. To make it worthwhile, we would pick up multiple packages at the main office and try to deliver to as many places of business as we could in one run. It was chaotic on the streets of New York. If you biked in the middle of the street, you could get hit by a moving car. If you biked nearer the curb, you could get creamed when someone opened the door of a *parked* car. You had to run red lights and avoid buses, pedestrians, hot-dog carts, and insane cabdrivers.

But I liked it overall. It was good exercise, unsupervised, and paid okay on a good day. Conditions were horrible when it rained, but I stuck with it. Then winter approached and the job became unbearable. Biking into the wind at thirty miles an hour on a thirty-degree day meant a wind-chill factor of about zero degrees. And when it snowed the job went from unbearable to impossible. So, after a few months, I hung up the bike.

My next job was stock boy at the Waldbaum's supermarket on Ocean Avenue and Avenue Z, which was near the apartment. The salary was around minimum wage, so, while I could just make the rent, I rarely had money for food. Some days I ate just one meal. Other days I didn't eat at all. I was down to 140 pounds – just 10 stone – and looking gaunt.

I was looking for a band with a hard edge, hopefully one that was doing something a little different from the mainstream. I knew the New York Dolls from hanging out at Nobody's, the most happening place on Bleecker Street in the early seventies. It was basically one big room with a bar and large tables in the back. There was no VIP room. Everyone was welcome, but at any given moment, rock gods might walk in: Jimmy Page, Robert Plant, Pete Townshend, or anyone else you could think of. During the summer, the action from Nobody's spilled out onto Bleecker Street at all hours of the night. The club was kind of a home base for the New York Dolls.

The Dolls wore makeup, high heels, and women's clothing, as the name suggested, and were tagged as a pioneering glam band. If you closed your eyes and listened, they sounded a little like a rough New York version of the Stones. The blues and R&B influences of performers like Muddy Waters and Sonny Boy Williamson were front and center. The lead singer, David Johansen, made sure of that. Throw in the girl-group sound of the sixties, and you had the Dolls. Their first gig was Christmas Eve 1971 at the Endicott Hotel, a homeless shelter. Their first big break came in 1972 when Rod Stewart flew them out to open for him at a concert in London. But while overseas, the Dolls' drummer, Billy Murcia, passed out and drowned in a bathtub due to mixing drugs and alcohol.

When the band got back to New York, Marty Thau became their manager, and the Dolls got a deal from Mercury Records. They were getting ready to record their first album, and all they needed was a drummer. My girlfriend, Fran, was also friends with the Dolls. She told me David Johansen and guitarist Johnny Thunders wanted me to audition. They liked my playing in Dust and thought there might be a fit. I thought so, too.

There were only two auditions that day. Jerry Nolan was the other one. I was asked to go first. The first song was 'Personality Crisis', which opened with a sort of Jerry Lee Lewis piano part and a straight-ahead beat. It had the feel of a Stones song like 'Live with Me'. The song 'Pills' was a Bo Diddley cover with a walking bass line, 4/4 time, and a rockabilly feel. The final song was 'Trash', which wasn't by Bo Diddley but had a bit of the Bo Diddley beat, like a fast shuffle. There were also background vocals suggestive of the doo-wop era and David Johansen wailing on the harp when he wasn't singing.

The song – all the songs – had a raw feel and a tough attitude. Life wasn't a beautiful dream but a hard reality, and you'd better figure that out fast. There was little or no polish on the chords, the leads, or the words. The songs were also short. The band got in your face for two and a half or three minutes and then got out.

I thought my audition went well. I stayed to watch Jerry Nolan try the same three songs. He played very straightforward: few fills, no rolls, and not a lot of crashes. I kind of kicked myself because I realized that's what the songs called for. The next day, Fran told me that Jerry got the gig.

One night Bruce and I went to a party at friend's house. We were up most of the night hanging out, drinking, and smoking pot. I was glad to have a few things to munch on, but pretzel sticks did not make a meal. Around five in the morning, Bruce and I decided to head back to the apartment. Avenue O was dead quiet except for an occasional car. Bruce was just as hungry as I was. We passed in front of a grocery store. It was obviously closed, with the solid metal gate at the front pulled down and padlocked. Leaning against the gate were about a dozen large paper bags filled with freshly baked loaves of bread. A couple of feet away were a few stacked crates filled with bottles of milk ready for the morning rush.

We looked up and down Avenue O and upward at the dark windows of the apartment above the store. Then we grabbed a few loaves of bread and a bottle of milk each. It was hard not to start filling our stomachs till we got back to the apartment. We were about two blocks from the store when Bruce took the first bite. From that day on, we were up at the crack of dawn looking for milk and bread delivered to local grocery stores, whether there'd been a party the night before or not.

We had to improvise phone calls, too. Bruce and I had a friend who worked for the phone company. He lent us a special handset that was used to test the phone lines but which anyone could use to tap a line. The handset was basically a telephone receiver and a small dialing pad with a couple of alligator clips. There was an old gray interface box in the basement hallway connected to every phone in the building. This friend showed us exactly what to do. Pick a phone line and connect the red alligator clip to the red wire and then the green to the green. Once you hear the tone, you're ready to dial. To get a clear connection, it was important to clean off the screws on the line.

For incoming phone calls, we had our friend Joel on the fourth floor. Joel was a few years older than Bruce and I and was a Vietnam vet. He had seen heavy fighting as a marine and was someone you would never want to mess with. You could see the suffering in his eyes. But he was a friendly guy and great to have around. He wore his hair long and had crossed over to the peace side.

One night Bruce and I were going out and asked Joel to come along. We liked to start our night with a lime rickey, a homemade carbonated drink, at the corner candy store. The husband and wife who owned the store were Holocaust survivors in their fifties. We saw the serial numbers branded on their forearms the first time we ever walked into the store, and we knew enough never to mention it. The couple took a liking to Joel, Bruce, and me. They never judged us by our looks.

On that night, Joel told Bruce and me to go on ahead, and he'd join us at the candy store a little later. Bruce was drinking his lime rickey, and I was sipping on cherry phosphate, another special from the soda fountain, when we heard a car without a muffler pull up to the curb. The sound vibrated the store window. Two guys in their early thirties with long overcoats walked in. They reminded me of greasers from Erasmus but a little weathered and down on their luck.

They looked around, and one of them deliberately closed the front door behind them. I knew they were going to rob the place. I just hoped they weren't carrying guns under those coats. The guy farther from the door said to the wife, 'Don't go near that fucking phone. And don't fucking move.' Both the husband and wife were behind the counter. I can't say they looked afraid. They had probably experienced things so horrible it would make this scene look like a party.

One of the guys moved toward the register. Bruce had been learning karate, and I could see he gave a thought to taking matters into his own hands. I could also see he thought better of it. No matter how quickly you learned, a few months of training wasn't going to stop a bullet. Meanwhile, I couldn't understand why these guys would not only drive up to a robbery in a car without a muffler but also why their driver would keep the motor running. The only answer I could think of was that they were complete amateurs. Or, worse, they were complete morons. Right when I thought the guy near the register was going to pop it open, he looked at me and Bruce and said, 'So I guess you guys are a couple of real fucking hippies.'

'I guess,' Bruce said.

'Why do you wear your hair like a fucking girl?' the other one asked.

'Does it matter?' I said.

'Yeah,' the one at the register said. 'Why don't you tell us, faggot?'

This went on for about a minute. Suddenly Joel walked into the store. He might have known that something was wrong from the roar of the car downstairs. The guy near the register glanced at Joel and then looked back over at me and Bruce and said, 'Look, another hippie freak. He must be with yous.'

'I must be,' Joel said.

'You got a name?' the other one said. 'What's your fucking name, Flower Power?'

'My name's Joel.' He walked toward the center of the room and looked at the owners, and then at Bruce and me. 'What's going on?'

'It looks like these guys want to rob the store,' I said.

Joel turned slightly toward the counter and spoke to the owners. 'Are these people causing you any trouble?' Neither the husband nor the wife said a thing. When Joel lifted his right hand, it might have been to make a point, but we would never find out. The guy farther from the counter lunged at him. Joel grabbed his arm and twisted it behind his back. As the guy folded like an accordion, the guy near the counter tried to choke Joel from behind and was smashed in the mouth with an elbow. As he went down, the guy on the floor tried to get back up, and Joel clocked him in the head with his boot.

The whole thing took about ten seconds. As a commando, Joel was trained to kill. In the candy store, there was no desire whatsoever to kill. Joel was more like a puppeteer, and the show was over. It could have been a horror show. As the two guys squirmed on the floor with their coats open, we all saw that they were both packing .45s. Joel had them both disarmed in another few seconds. At that moment, we heard the car without the muffler pull away. Now the guys were without their pieces *and* their ride.

We waited for the police to come, and, once they did, the three of us left. From that day on, every lime rickey and cherry soda was free – even for Bruce and me, though all we really did was pick our friends wisely.

One day down in the basement apartment, we got a knock on the door from a lady who lived on the third floor. It was a good thing Bruce answered the door because his friend at the phone company had prepared him for a moment like this. I could hear she was upset, and she began interrogating Bruce. Worse, she really wanted to talk to me. It was my voice she recognized that evening when she picked up her phone and probably heard me talking to my manager from Waldbaum's. It made sense. I had probably spoken to her a couple times in front of the building, and as she grilled Bruce, I recognized her voice, too.

Bruce claimed the phone company told us it was an open line we had tapped, and we really tried to use it only for emergencies – that we had no idea it was hers or anyone else's, for that matter. She calmed down quickly and let us slide. After that, we made sure to tap the other lines and leave hers alone.

Sometime later Joel came knocking on our door to say the band Estus were trying to get in touch with me. I had never heard of Estus. Nobody had, at least not in New York. I was told they were a country-rock band from Missouri who were recently signed to Columbia Records and needed a drummer. There would be an upfront fee of $5,000 to record their studio album, plus $300 a week. I said yes immediately, and the following morning skipped getting up at dawn to scavenge for bread and milk.

Estus consisted of brothers Tom and John Nicholas – John on bass, Tom on guitar and lead vocals – and Harry Rumpf on lead guitar and keyboards. The musicianship was very good. All three sang, and their harmonies were top-notch. But, as I listened to the demo in producer Andrew Oldham's office, I knew it wasn't really my type of music. I liked music with a harder edge. Record companies were scouring the US for the next big singer-songwriter or soft-rock band. Millions of dollars in album sales were pouring in from Carly Simon, Joni Mitchell, Carole King, James Taylor, the Eagles, and America. The songwriting in Estus wasn't anything near what those seminal acts were producing, but many of the lesser groups were making money, too.

What really sold me on Estus, aside from the money, was Andrew Oldham himself. Oldham discovered the Rolling Stones and produced and managed them from 1963 to 1967. He was really more of a manager than a producer. As a savvy nineteen-year-old kid working for a Mod designer on Carnaby Street in London and with no real musical experience, Oldham got the Rolling Stones a record deal with Decca, the company that had, regretfully, along with others, passed on the Beatles.

Once signed, Oldham cultivated an anti-Beatles image for his new group, generating provocative PR slogans like 'Would you let your daughter marry a Rolling Stone?' He encouraged Mick Jagger and Keith Richards to write their own songs and retained ownership for the Stones of their master tapes. Later, after a falling-out with the Rolling Stones, Andrew Oldham started one of the first independent record labels in England, Immediate Records, and worked with top artists including Eric Clapton, Jimmy Page, Jeff Beck, the Small Faces, John Mayall, and Rod Stewart.

Andrew Oldham was an eccentric, but he was an innovator and a legend. Throw in the fact that the engineer for Estus was Don Puluse, who had worked with Chicago, Janis Joplin, and Al Kooper, and there was no way I wasn't jumping on board.

I had my father's friend, who was an attorney, look over the contract. My father looked it over as well. His goal was to study law and eventually leave the docks, and he already knew a lot more than most people about contracts. But there was nothing that wasn't standard in this one. I also gave my parents about half of the $5,000 signing payment to hold for me. After Dust, I didn't believe in gravy trains, and I needed dental work from time to time. My teeth always gave me trouble.

Rehearsals went well. John was kind of morose and introverted, but we locked in instantly on bass and drums. Tom was a bit less subdued than his older brother but still pretty serious and mature. At only twenty-one, he already had a wife and a baby. Harry was the extrovert of the three. He'd walk around all day, guitar in hand, trying to turn on anyone who would listen to a new lick.

Recording began in December 1972 at Columbia Records Studio B at 49 East Fifty-Second Street in Manhattan. The advance for the album was a substantial $100,000, much of which, it appeared, would go to Andrew's fee and to any extra production costs. Oldham was known for lavish production and at one time had formed the Andrew Oldham Orchestra. The orchestra featured top London session players and recorded numerous instrumental versions of already well-known pop tunes. Oldham idolized the legendary American producer Phil Spector, so I could imagine where Estus were headed.

The studio was the largest recording space I had ever been in. When I walked into the room, the first thing I saw, next to the mixing console, was a gallon jug of Almaden Rhine wine. As I worked on getting down the drum parts for a hippie-country number called 'In the Morning', I noticed Andrew, wearing dark sunglasses, constantly sipping the wine from a glass. After a couple of hours, I noticed the jug was half empty, though I couldn't recall seeing anyone else in the room taking even a swig. But Oldham didn't seem the slightest bit drunk.

As a rule, I didn't drink before or while playing. But, by the end of the third session, I was sharing some wine with Andrew.

Andrew was a very laid-back producer. He was interested mostly in whether the live tracking had a nice, tight feel. If he asked us to do it again, he was never bossy or arrogant about it, and we rarely had to go beyond a third take. Based on his personal accomplishments, which included helping to spearhead the British Invasion, Oldham could have been full of himself, but that was far from the case.

By the end of the first week of recording, Andrew and I were in a pattern of going downtown to the Village and having a few drinks at some of the clubs. I did more listening than talking. Andrew was a character who could talk endlessly. He'd lived by his wits in London before the Stones and then went on to produce song after great song: '(I Can't Get No) Satisfaction', 'Get Off of My Cloud', 'Mother's Little Helper', 'Time Is on My Side', and 'As Tears Go By'. Whether he shaped the songs directly or, more likely, was simply in the room sipping booze and adding ambience, it was all mind-blowing to me that I was his new drinking buddy.

Pretty soon I was past the wine and on to Bacardi 151, which I drank straight up. As the name says, the proof is 151, which translates to an alcohol content of just over 75 per cent. When I borrowed Andrew's 'torch', he might have thought I was going to light up a cigarette, but I didn't smoke. I poured some 151 into an ashtray and lit it. The flames shot up to eye level, and I quickly killed the fire with a small glass of Coca-Cola.

'There goes my chaser,' I said. We both laughed and drank some more.

During the third week of recording, Andrew took me to a party at someone's apartment in the East Fifties. It was all men and exactly one girl, who was pretty hot. Andrew made a point of introducing me to her. She and I shot the shit for a little while over a few drinks and then made our way to the bedroom. We threw a half-dozen winter coats off the bed and started fooling around. I had her shirt off and my pants off, and she was on her back. I stopped for a moment and had the strange sensation that someone had walked into the room. As I thought about how to ask whoever it was to kindly leave us the fuck alone, I looked up and saw Andrew standing by the side of the bed.

Before I could think of anything to say, Andrew approached the bed. That was all for me. I sprang up and was back on the floor as if the bed were on fire. As I tried to jump into my jeans, I said, 'Well, you know, I'm not really into that, but definitely go ahead without me.' I never found out if they did, because I bolted from the room and then the apartment in a matter of seconds.

I was barely out of my teens and was freaked out by what had happened. I had headlined at a major arena and been backstage where things got wild, but I never saw that coming. As I walked up Broadway, I tried to make sense of it. All men. One girl. Andrew's friends. It seemed as if Andrew Oldham, who had orchestrated so many songs, had tried to orchestrate a threesome. But I refused to follow the chart. I really didn't care about his preferences – or anyone else's, for that matter. Sex for me was straight up, like my drinks, with the one exception being a vodka martini.

The next day, I felt incredibly uncomfortable when I walked into Studio B and saw Andrew sitting there with his gallon jug of wine. I said nothing, avoided eye contact, and sat down at the drums to work on a sappy song called 'B.M.D.'

Neither of us mentioned it. No one else apparently knew a thing about it. By the end of the day, the situation seemed back to normal. We didn't go out drinking that night, but we did the next night, and it was like nothing ever happened. Well, almost. I knew that in a few weeks the sessions would be winding down, and I would really miss Andrew. By the following week, I was no longer showing up most days because I didn't need to. With all the basic tracks down, Andrew was adding the orchestration he was known for. Violinists, cellists, and clarinetists were flocking to the studio every day, but that was the producer's job, and I had other places to be.

One of those places was Shaggy Dog Studio in Stockbridge, Massachusetts. I had gotten a call from the owner of Biograph Records, asking me to play on a new album with the Delta blues artist Johnny Shines. Shines was American blues royalty. When he was growing up in the 1920s in Memphis, his mother taught him how to play guitar. By the mid-1930s, he was touring with the blues legend Robert Johnson. They split in 1937, and a year later Johnson was dead.

While the legend of Robert Johnson grew and grew, the career of Johnny Shines was stagnant for decades. He made a living in construction while continuing to play in bars. He recorded several tracks for Columbia in 1946, but they were never released. Six years later, an independent label released an album, but sales were modest. It wasn't until 1966, when Vanguard Records asked Shines to play on the third volume of its series *Chicago/The Blues/Today!* that his career took off. From then on, he recorded albums regularly and toured with the likes of Willie Dixon and Big Walter Horton. These two master artists were a huge inspiration to many, including John Mayall, Eric Clapton, Jeff Beck, and Led Zeppelin.

Biograph was owned by Arnold Caplin, who put together a great band for the album, titled *Johnny Shines & Co*. The 'company' included notables Jay Ungar on the fiddle, Peter Ecklund on trumpet and cornet, and David Bromberg on guitar. Bromberg, who was also producing the album, was a Columbia University graduate and an in-demand player of blues, bluegrass, jazz, and almost any type of music you could think of. Over the past few years, he had played on albums by Bob Dylan, Richie Havens, Carly Simon, and Willie Nelson, to name just a few. I was thrilled to be in company like that.

The studio drum set was a standard-size Fibes Vistalite, unmistakable since they were made from clear acrylic. Shines, Bromberg, and the whole band were easygoing. Bottles of Jack Daniel's and Old Grand-Dad were making their way around the studio, but I waited till the end of the session to party along with these old pros. I had all thirteen drum parts done within two days. Caplin, Bromberg, and Shines himself listened back and were all happy with the basic tracks. At that point, the drinks really started to flow.

One day when I visited the Columbia Records Studio to check in with Estus, I got to see a sample of the album cover. Back in December, the art director had the four of us show up at a Park Avenue address at five in the morning. It was predawn on one of those early-winter days in New York when the freezing rain hits the ground and melts into slush puddles, but not before chilling you right to the bone. The idea was to do the shoot when no one else was around and the streets were empty. They were empty for a reason: no one wanted to be there.

Now as I looked at the album cover, I felt almost as cold as I did on that nasty December morning. There the four of us stood in the middle of Park Avenue, looking soaking-wet, groggy, and dejected. There were frowns and hands in pockets. I was on the right, looking down at the pavement. We were four drenched guys who looked like a major label had just dropped us. If this was the best shot out of a half-dozen rolls of film, I would like to have seen just how bad the rest of them were. Hopefully, rock fans didn't judge an album by its cover.

A dry version of Estus began touring in advance of the album release. There was no orchestration in the live shows other than the sounds the four of us put out. We played small and midsized venues and opened for

Aerosmith, Quicksilver Messenger Service, and B. B. King. I was getting paid, so I was happy. But then I was told the band wanted to focus on its new music and was relocating from New York City to Rosendale.

Rosendale was a sleepy rural town of about five thousand located ninety miles north of the city, just off of the New York State Thruway. The town was a bit south of Kingston and a little north of New Paltz, a college town. Rosendale's claim to fame was a cement plant. Flush with record company money, Estus rented a twenty-room mansion with a swimming pool in the back. When I got there, I thought maybe I had the wrong address. I had my pick from among several bedrooms and took one that could have fitted the whole apartment I shared with Bruce. There were no garbage bins within sight or smell.

Tom, the lead singer, had bought a Jaguar XKE, which was parked outside. His brother, John, not to be outspent, bought an Austin Healey sports car, which he liked to park next to the Jaguar. We were usually flown to gigs, but, in case there were no good flights, we had a twelve-passenger Ford Econoline van in the garage. Alongside it was a truck for the roadies and equipment. The four of us in the band were still on salary and were given a $100-a-week raise. All this overkill was nothing unusual. Record companies were throwing money at bands with a shot at being the next Three Dog Night. If you didn't climb the charts, you were dropped and used as a tax write-off. It was all just business.

I was bored out of my mind. There are only so many laps you can do in a pool, test-drives you can take around the block, and conversations you can have about where you're going to put your Grammy for best album. The one place I felt at home was a bar in town, about three miles from the mansion. Bartenders at the Well gave us free drinks because we were local celebrities and practically the house band. We did our warm-up sets at the Well before hitting the road to tour.

For a modest place, the bar had a real presence on the circuit. While we were there, Muddy Waters, Buddy Guy, Junior Wells, and several other prominent blues artists stopped in and performed for food and gas money on their way down to New York City. But, even on a good night, the place closed around two o'clock, and then the whole party usually relocated to the Estus palace. I would normally wake up in the afternoon and find dozens of locals – having partied with us the night before – asleep on couches and in deckchairs and otherwise empty bedrooms.

But the well was beginning to run dry. The Estus album was dead on arrival. Sales were weak, it didn't make the *Billboard* 200, and you could spin the FM radio dial all day long and not hear any of the songs. It was the summer of 1973, and other forms of music were taking off, including glam rock and disco. My friends from Dust were part of it.

Kenny Aaronson played bass in a band called Stories, who covered a song called 'Brother Louie', about a white guy dating a black girl. It went to number one in the US and stayed on the charts for eighteen weeks. Kenny probably played more notes in a few measures of any Dust song than he played in the entirety of 'Brother Louie', but the bass part he laid down gave it a funk-soul feel that helped put it over the top.

The self-titled album *KISS* was scheduled to come out on Neil Bogart's new Casablanca label in early 1974. Kenny Kerner and Richie Wise were the producers. The band's stage makeup was more pronounced now. More important, they were beginning to get some media attention and a fan base.

I was restless by the late summer of 1973 but glad to play a show with Estus on my home turf at the Academy of Music on East Fourteenth Street in Manhattan. The New York Dolls, who over the past year had become the center of attention on the New York scene, came down to watch the show. Their self-titled album – the one I was almost a part of – made it to 116 on the *Billboard* 200. It was produced by Todd Rundgren, former guitarist for the Nazz, a psychedelic and garage-rock band from the sixties. Rundgren was driven half crazy by the Dolls' overall sloppiness and wound up taking a hands-off approach to the sound and mix.

The Dolls' reckless attitude, both onstage and off, led to extreme reactions. In a 1973 *Creem* magazine poll, they were voted both the best new group and the worst new group. Robert Christgau in *Rolling Stone* raved about the Dolls, while Ben Edmonds of *Creem* called them 'the most walked-out-on band in the history of show business'. Everyone, more or less, had a good point.

The Dolls' second album, *Too Much Too Soon*, had been out for just a couple of months. Shadow Morton of Shangri-Las fame produced it, and the evidence was all over the album. Morton had produced mid-sixties teen hits such as 'Leader of the Pack'. Production on the second Dolls album was not as raunchy as the first. There were cute sound effects used here and there and a lot of female background vocals. While debate about the band's merits raged on, *Too Much Too Soon* was too little too late. The album barely cracked the *Billboard* 200. Johnny Thunders was on heroin, and Jerry Nolan wasn't far behind.

Johnny was a very nervous person when he was not high. Once he was high, he seemed calm, collected, and focused. Almost a normal guy and fun to be around. It was an impossible dilemma.

I liked to think that the dope explained some or all of Jerry's behavior around me. After the Dolls passed on me, I remained friendly with the band, but Jerry and I had a love/hate relationship that was heavier on the hate. One night I went to the Dolls' loft to jam with Johnny Thunders and their bassist, Arthur 'Killer' Kane. The drum set, of course, was Jerry's, and I noticed the skins were extremely worn. About four songs in, the snare skin broke. The next time I ran into Jerry, he demanded, 'Where's my money?'

'Wait, did you lend me money?' It had been a while, and I had no idea what he was talking about.

'You broke my skin, and you're gonna pay. I want my money, or next time it's gonna be just you and me.' Jerry had a reputation as a tough guy, but he was about average for almost any neighborhood in Brooklyn. The thing was, if he hadn't threatened me, I might have paid for the skin. It was only a few bucks.

'That skin was ready to break the next time someone breathed on it. So guess what, Jerry: I ain't paying for shit.'

I didn't feel we were going to mix it up, but at the same time there was always that small chance. Whenever we ran into each other, we were both a little wary.

Now at the Academy, as I slogged my way through the set with Estus, I looked over at Johnny Thunders, who was watching from the side of the stage. Johnny looked right back at me and shook his head as though he knew what I was thinking: *I'm wasting my time.* The Dolls had practically every problem under the sun. They were a train wreck. But, when they took the stage, it was chaos and energy, the way rock and roll was meant to be. When Columbia Records pulled the plug on Estus a few weeks later, it felt like a mercy killing. The guys in the band decided to move back to Missouri to play shows and work on their next album independently. They still needed a drummer and still wanted me, enough to offer $400 a week plus any American car I wanted. I thanked them but told them I didn't want to relocate to the Midwest. I couldn't see myself living in Missouri. I could barely stand Rosendale. I was looking to take the first bus back to New York City.

My head popped up early the next morning. I threw all my belongings into a pillowcase and started walking toward the outskirts of New Paltz college to find the nearest bus stop. Because of the college, there were buses going back and forth to the city all the time. As I walked off the front lawn and into the street, one of Estus's roadies drove his car alongside me and rolled down the window. He wasn't surprised I was calling it a day, because everyone in that house knew I was miserable. But he gave it one last shot, telling me the fans in the Midwest were great. He was right about that. But I knew I had to get back to New York City.

While I was living in Rosendale, Bruce started seeing a girl who owned a small house in Brooklyn on Twenty-Eighth Street and Avenue D. There was no point to staying in that dingy basement apartment when you had a beautiful woman and a nice home somewhere else. So he took his stash along with a bag of clothes and moved in with his girlfriend.

When I got back from Rosendale, I spent one night in the apartment alone and realized not only couldn't I afford the $100 a month in rent, but also I didn't want to even if I could. No one else did either. I couldn't find a roommate, and, after spending my summer in a mansion, I wasn't thrilled about sleeping on a mattress in a cold, empty shithole. When

I told Joel upstairs about my situation, he offered to have me move in with him. He had a second bedroom, and I could pay him the same $50 a month I paid downstairs with Bruce.

Moving in with Joel was paradise compared with the basement. No more garbage bins. I had a regular key to a regular bolt lock instead of a padlock. There was heat, and not just the excess heat from a boiler down the hall. And, although we didn't have an ocean view, we had a view of Ocean Avenue. Joel was cool with my friends coming over, even if we threw firecrackers and ash cans off the roof.

Joel would smoke a little pot to take off the edge but was not into anything hard. Heroin addiction ran wild among American forces in Vietnam. Tens of thousands of vets were returning unable to function without shooting up daily. I was glad Joel avoided that fate. But it wasn't as if he'd escaped clean.

Some nights I awoke to the sound of long groans, which usually morphed into bloodcurdling screams. It was Joel in the next room having flashbacks of fighting in the jungle. I would always get up, walk over to his door, and ask him if he needed anything, and he would always tell me no, thanks.

5

PUNK, PAIN, AND WAYNE

Max's Kansas City was the happening place in New York in the early to mid-seventies. The club was located on the ground floor of a narrow five-story, turn-of-the-century commercial building on Park Avenue South just a couple blocks north of Union Square Park. The club really had two incarnations. When Mickey Ruskin first opened the place in 1965, it quickly became the haunt for artists and writers, including Allen Ginsberg and William S. Burroughs of the so-called Beat Generation.

Soon after, Andy Warhol and his crowd followed, which transformed the club into an important rock venue and hangout. Lou Reed, Iggy Pop, Alice Cooper, David Bowie, and Aerosmith all played to intimate but wild audiences. If you were there on New Year's Day 1974, you would have seen Bob Marley and the Wailers kick off a world tour by opening for an up-and-coming Columbia Records artist named Bruce Springsteen.

By 1974, when I started hanging out there a lot, you could argue that a third incarnation of Max's had begun. New groups with a different sound – different from what came before and even from one another –

were in and around the club, onstage, in the back, outside, wherever. The Dolls were the first and most obvious band on the list, having been around since 1971 and releasing two major label albums. But even the shortest list had to include the Patti Smith Group, Television, the Heartbreakers, and Blondie. Deborah Harry, the striking bleached-blonde lead singer of Blondie, was a waitress at Max's. And no shortlist of the new bands could possibly be complete without the Ramones.

I had first met John Cummings when he turned up at Cafe Wha? to see an early Dust show. Now he called himself Johnny Ramone, after the band he had helped form. All four members took on the same stage surname as a tribute to Paul McCartney's pseudonym, Paul Ramon, back from when the Beatles were the Silver Beetles. They were all from the nice middle-class, largely Jewish, neighborhood in Queens known as Forest Hills.

With all the single-family homes and upscale apartment buildings going up since World War II, there wasn't much forest left, but there were still a few hills. In Brooklyn, we thought of Forest Hills as the suburbs. It was the home of tennis's US Open and to luxury European-style condominiums built in the 1920s along the Long Island Railroad to cater to the fat cats busy making a killing on Wall Street before the crash of 1929. Musically, there was something in the water in Forest Hills, but until that point, you couldn't say the water was hard. Burt Bacharach, Paul Simon, and Art Garfunkel grew up there, but they didn't look or sound anything like the Ramones. No one did.

In 1974, the Ramones started playing clubs in the New York area including Max's and, especially CBGB. CBGB stood for country, bluegrass, and blues, but there was less of those types of music at CB's in 1974 than there was heavy metal in Burt Bacharach's backlist. The musician and promoter Hilly Kristal had opened the club the year before and had the vision to just let it become what it wanted to become.

When the Ramones took the stage, there was no bullshit. It was four seemingly street kids in jeans and T-shirts. Their hair was long, but not like a hippie's. Their songs lasted two minutes – maybe two and a half. There was no milking it between songs. Just a few words, then,

'One, two, three, four!' and on to the next. The songs were kicks to the chest, with straight-ahead pounding drums, fast downstroke power chords on guitar, and a driving bass. The vocals were fifties rock on speed, sometimes with an English accent. There were harmonies but no shrill screams or falsettos. The lyrics told simple stories of beating up a neighborhood brat, sniffing glue, being afraid to go down in the basement. A whole show was fifteen, maybe twenty minutes, and if that was too short? Fuck you.

But the band needed work. They were not exactly trying to be polished, but at times they were flat-out disorganized. The songs could have been tighter. Sometimes they would make a mistake near the beginning of a song and start the count over again. Sometimes they would argue with one another onstage. You got the feeling you weren't watching a performance so much as a rehearsal.

The bassist, Doug Colvin, was known as Dee Dee Ramone. Dee Dee was very friendly and outgoing whenever I ran into him. He started out as the lead singer and bassist but had trouble doing both at once. The original drummer, a tall gawky-looking kid named Jeffrey Hyman, called himself Joey Ramone. Joey was more introspective. Like Dee Dee, he also had trouble playing and singing, so he became the lead singer. While auditioning drummers to help out the band, their friend Thomas Erdelyi realized he was the right guy for the job and became Tommy Ramone.

The third incarnation of Max's Kansas City didn't have an exact date or a formal name, but some people began to call it punk rock. Or simply punk.

One night in 1974, I was having a few drinks at Max's, and Wayne County stopped by my booth. I had never actually met him, but everyone knew Wayne as the house DJ at Max's. He had one hell of a backstory.

He was born Wayne Rogers in Georgia and moved to New York City in 1968 as a young man looking to meet the boys. He was a regular at the Stonewall Inn and was part of the famous riot in 1969, when the police raided the place for no valid reason, and the modern gay-rights era began. He plunged into stage acting and was cast by Andy Warhol in *Pork*, which had a successful run in New York, then in London. His stage name became Wayne County, a tribute to Detroit.

Back in New York, Wayne formed and fronted a campy rock band called Queen Elizabeth. With a transvestite lead singer, Queen Elizabeth may have been a first. My old friend and nemesis Jerry Nolan was the drummer. David Bowie was a fan of Wayne's and got him signed to his management company, MainMan Artistes. They put together an elaborate stage show, but there was no album to show for it.

And here was Wayne County sitting across from me as I drank a vodka martini and wondered what the occasion was. He was in outrageous attire, but the male sort: denim from head to toe and a big pimp hat with a wide brim. He told me he was putting together a band called Wayne County and the Backstreet Boys, and they were looking for a drummer. By the end of my vodka martini, I was a Backstreet Boy.

The other Backstreet Boys in the initial line-up were Jeff Salem on lead guitar, Michael Geary on rhythm guitar, and his brother, Eugene Geary, on bass. Wayne was still signed to MainMan, which was run by Tony Defries along with his close friend and roommate, photographer Leee Black Childers. The guys in the band, myself included, were happy to be with management just to eat. None of us ever had any money, and MainMan had a running tab at Max's. That tab ran a marathon.

MainMan also paid for Wayne and Leee's duplex apartment on Fifty-Eighth Street right off of Second Avenue. That location was prime all by itself. But, because of the girl I was going out with, it was even better. I'd first met Marion about eight years earlier when I was fourteen. Fred and I used to go to our friend Paul Baxter's house near Church Avenue and Beverly Road in Brooklyn to jam with Paul and his brother, Michael. The Baxter brothers played guitar and organ, so they were a good match for the Bell brothers on guitar and drums.

The Baxters had a little sister in the fourth grade named Jodie. Her best friend was a cute redhead named Marion. Jodie and Marion were our fan club. Any chance they got, they watched the Baxter-Bell four cover Beatles, Stones, and Who songs. When they got old enough to take the subway, they would come out to see Dust play at the Flatbush Terrace.

Jodie's parents were progressive. Marion's family were traditional Irish Catholic and sent their daughter to Catholic school. In those days, when people met other people, they would ask, 'What are you?' They didn't mean Democrat or Republican, Virgo or Capricorn, Mets or Yankees fan. They were asking for your religion or ethnicity. When Marion met Jodie and asked her what she was, Jodie didn't know what she meant. They became friends and stayed that way.

Marion's parents had a certain perception of entertainers. They were friends with Sammy Spear, Jackie Gleason's orchestra leader. The story they heard through the grapevine was that musicians were very nervous people who drank and did drugs. So they didn't necessarily want their daughter going out with a guy who was not only a musician but also older. On top of that, they thought I was Jewish.

Marion and I remained friends for several years. We liked the same music and had the same taste in clothing. We always got along. By 1974, with Marion graduating high school, we became an item.

Jodie became the governess for a wealthy family who lived only a couple of blocks away from Wayne and Leee's duplex. The family would spend weekends, holidays, and summers at their home in the country. They knew that, while they were away, Jodie would have Marion and me stay over to help watch the house. They just didn't know the full extent of our activities. We had the run of the house. Wayne, dressed in his everyday straight clothing, would arrive about ten minutes after the family left. Some of the Backstreet Boys would usually follow. We would empty the liquor cabinet and then work our way down to the wine cellar.

Marion and I would hole up in the master bedroom. Fortunately, Marion was about the same size as the lady of the house, so when we went out to a club or restaurant she had a large walk-in closet's worth of designer outfits to choose from. One night Marion tried out a sable fur coat, and when we walked into CBGB, Hilly pulled me aside and said he wasn't thrilled to see rich girls like that slumming it at his club.

He was dead serious. But the biggest problem with house-sitting was transportation. It was difficult to choose which car to test-drive: the Bentley or the Rolls-Royce.

The backyard was a private landscaped communal area the size of a city block in a city where Fortune 500 companies had to share blocks. When we took our party out back, the well-off neighbors never seemed to mind. They took a liking to Wayne and the rest of us, but especially to Marion and Jodie. They were a pair of cute, sassy Brooklyn girls, and the neighborhood royalty couldn't seem to get enough of them.

For a well-off couple the owners were very cool, especially as parents. When they were home, Wayne came over sometimes to play with the three kids, who were eight, ten, and twelve. Wayne was a natural, telling them stories, playing board games, and horsing around. The kids loved Uncle Wayne.

Band rehearsals were almost always a good time. It was hard keeping a straight face when Wayne came in and read us whatever new lyrics he had come up with. One of my favorites was Wayne's torch song, 'Man Enough to Be a Woman', which had a psychedelic sixties garage-rock feel.

MainMan paid for studio time so we could record a six-song demo, which consisted of 'Man Enough', 'Wonder Woman', 'Queen Age Baby', 'Midnight Pal', a cover of the Stones song 'Tell Me', and 'Max's Kansas City'. 'Max's Kansas City' sounded like an alternate version of the Velvet Underground's 'Sweet Jane', but the verses introduced many of the regulars at the club by name: the New York Dolls, Patti Smith, Iggy Pop, Lou Reed, Blondie, and Dee Dee Ramone. It was a Who's Who of Max's.

Stage shows were even more fun than rehearsals. Wayne wore a massive blonde wig that looked as if it had been stolen from Dusty Springfield. He would take a couple dozen condoms, blow them up, pin them all over his hair, and tie them all over his outfit. When we did 'Toilet Love', he looked menacing waving around a plunger. MainMan seemed happy with the demo and was actively shopping it. A&R people came down to the shows, hung out with us afterward, and told us they loved what we were doing. We thought a record deal was right around the corner. But there were no offers from the record companies.

The apparent reason was Wayne's outrageous cross-dressing combined with the risqué subject matter of the songs. My father came down to one of the shows. Even as a very liberal guy, he thought I was crazy associating myself with Wayne. He said there was no future in the mainstream for a transvestite singer. But David Bowie was already sexually ambiguous, and the next logical step seemed to be Wayne County.

So I went to plan B. I gave a copy of the demo along with a band photo to my old friends Richie Wise and Kenny Kerner, who by this time had gone platinum with Gladys Knight and the Pips and just completed their second KISS album. I thought I would have two sets of sympathetic ears, not to mention sympathetic eyes. KISS's makeup was now well established and over the top. It wasn't exactly feminine, but it was outrageous by any standard. Kenny's ears were into Wayne County. He liked the music. As for his eyes, not so much. In his opinion, the masses were ready for Gene, Paul, Peter, and Ace, but not Wayne. That could take many years.

MainMan had their own plan B. They shot two different promo photos of the band-one with Wayne dressed as a man, the other as a woman. The more liberated showcases would get the cross-dressing Wayne shot. That worked for Mother's on Twenty-Third Street and KISS's old stomping ground, Coventry, on Queens Boulevard. The blue-collar clubs would get the straight Wayne shot. When the band actually showed up, both types of clubs got the cross-dressing Wayne, and eventually that became a problem.

We were booked at a club in Newark, New Jersey, that got the straight Wayne shot. The night of the show, Wayne looked ravishing in a corset and black fishnet stockings. As I looked around the room from behind my drum kit, I felt very far from the hip New York scene I was used to.

The guys who ran the club were Old World. They were in their late thirties and older, with a cigar here, a gold tooth there, an eye patch over there. They seemed like they fitted in more with my dad's longshoremen's union than a rock club. In fact, they looked like the guys who ran the union. They watched the front door, the back door, the room, and everyone coming in and out of it like hawks. Every few minutes one of these guys would emerge from the backroom, and then someone else would return. It became obvious that this was a Mob-run club.

But the kids who packed the place that night were New Jersey glammers. They wore glitter, blush, tight pants, and a little eye makeup. They weren't exactly Bowie knockoffs. They were knockoffs of Bowie knockoffs. They weren't ready for Wayne County, but they were glad as hell to see him take the stage. He was the real thing. As we launched into 'Toilet Love', they pushed up to get a closer look at the he/she covered in condoms. They danced, swinging their arms and bobbing their heads, and they hardly ever took their eyes off Wayne.

The powers that be were not happy. You could imagine how they got into this situation. They were running a business. They usually hired local rock-and-roll bands, which worked out okay and wasn't all that far from the doo-wop of their day, especially when they took into account the cash coming in at the door and the bar. But they thought they could do even better by venturing out and getting a more modern act – even a glam act if they had to – from across the Hudson River. The publicity shot looked passable. But what they got was a freak show. A disgrace.

The fourth song we played was 'Man Enough', and the old guard had had enough. A huge bouncer who looked as if he had a day job as a bookie's debt collector walked over to our manager, Peter Crowley, and told him something that made his eyes widen and his nostrils flare. As 'Man Enough' ended, Peter turned and walked up onstage.

'That's it. They want us out of here. Now. Let's break everything down and get out.'

I figured that was that. What were we going to do but cooperate? The roadies started to break down my drum set. Wayne said something nasty, but the microphone was cut, and I was relieved. Then I saw Peter walk back over to the bouncer, who was now with a couple of the club managers. I caught a glimpse of an argument, and almost that fast, they had Peter on the floor and were punching and kicking him.

We hustled to get out of there, with roadies working double time and wise-guy types surrounding us to make sure we didn't straggle. In the parking lot out back, Wayne took off his wig and bitched, and I saw Peter walk out the door with his hand over his eye.

The story of Wayne County and our manager almost getting whacked in Jersey made its way back to the city and created a buzz. Shortly after, we got a recurring gig at 82 Club on East Fourth Street, just off Second Avenue in the Village. The club had been around for forty years and for much of that time was a legendary drag cabaret. But very recently, 82 had reinvented itself as a gay disco bar with live bands. The place was run by two butch lesbians and a bouncer named Jimmy, who looked like Chuck Berry as a disco queen. Wayne County and the Backstreet Boys fitted right in. When you threw in the roast-beef and turkey sandwiches they served on Sundays, free to the band, it was our home away from Max's.

The neighborhood was not great. On the corner was a bodega with a cashier inside a Plexiglas booth. The Plexiglas was about an inch thick and bulletproof unless the assailant happened to have an AK-47. Customers purchasing Slim Jims, plantains, and Miller beer passed money and received change through a movable tray that allowed no human contact. To get to 82 Club you had to open a battered steel door and walk down a rickety staircase to the basement. The coatroom and kitchen were to the right, the dance floor and tables behind a curtain to the left.

One night as Marion and I were getting ready to leave, I went to the coatroom to get my jacket and ran into my friend, photographer Bob Gruen, who was just coming in. Bob had been documenting the nightlife at CBGB, Max's, and the emerging music scene in Lower Manhattan. He had also been working with John Lennon, photographing him and Yoko Ono throughout the city. I thought of asking Bob if he had seen Lennon lately, but as soon as the thought hit, there he was.

John Lennon stumbled out of the coatroom. He was wearing sunglasses, a long blue coat, and a newsboy cap similar to the one he wore in the movie *A Hard Day's Night*. For some reason, he looked taller in person. Not for long, though. Lennon stumbled, and Bob grabbed him under the shoulder. Lennon had tripped over himself. He said something resembling thanks to Bob, but that and whatever came right after were heavily slurred.

John Lennon, who urged us to give peace a chance and asked us to imagine a better world, was too drunk to stand on his own two feet. I was a little disappointed to see a boyhood idol of mine staggering around out of control, but at the same time, I tried to understand the constant pressure of being who he was. Bob held up John Lennon with two hands and guided him over to a seat.

A few weeks later Marion and I were at 82 Club on an off night for the band, just hanging out sitting in the main room having a couple of drinks. The sound system was blasting 'Rock the Boat' by Hues Corporation when a few of the customers burst out from the other side of the curtain and ran in different directions. It was hard to hear anything over the music, but within a few minutes a story made its way back to us. A guy with a gun was chasing another guy across Fourth Street, and the guy being chased ran randomly into 82 Club and down the stairs. He was gunned down at the bottom of the staircase. We never heard the shots.

A minute or two later the music was cut as police and paramedics swarmed through the curtain. One of the officers announced that the doors would be sealed until everyone in the building gave a statement. It took three hours until they got to me and Marion, and our statement was the simple truth: we saw and heard nothing. They took our names and addresses and let us go. On the F train platform at sunrise, commuters were just starting to slink into Manhattan.

One evening a few weeks later, Marion walked into her parents' apartment in Brooklyn and found her father waiting with a letter in hand from one of the detectives at the Ninth Precinct in Manhattan. It was a standard interview follow-up letter from the police asking if there was any new information regarding the murder. The letter mentioned 82 Club.

It wasn't easy for Marion to tell what upset her father more – that his daughter was considered a witness to a murder or that she was in a sleazy drag bar. Marion explained that 82, like so many clubs downtown and elsewhere, had reinvented itself, and while it wasn't exactly the Harvard Club, lots of middle-class white kids from Brooklyn and Queens went there all the time to run into former Beatles.

There was a third item that Marion couldn't explain away so easily: the fact that she was going out with an older guy who played in a band fronted by a tranny and who took her to dive bars. Other than to tell her father that Marc was a good guy, there wasn't much of an answer for that one.

When our bass player Eugene Geary left the Backstreet Boys, I got my old friend Kenny Aaronson to fill in for a few gigs, including one at 82 Club. Kenny liked what Wayne was doing and loved the scene. But it was understood that Kenny was just keeping the seat warm. He was in demand for both live situations and studio work for well-known acts and was basically just passing through.

Wayne County at this point wasn't a very stable situation. There were rumors going around that MainMan kept Wayne on their roster only so Bowie could cop ideas and styles from him. Personally, I thought that was bullshit. After Ziggy Stardust, Bowie had his own good thing going on. Even if for some reason David Bowie was starved for ideas, he wouldn't have to hire someone and have them at arm's length to steal from them. There were new ideas, trends, and fashion for the taking on display every night in clubs up and down Manhattan. But the fact remained that we weren't getting any bites from the record companies, and MainMan was taking less and less of an interest in the band.

When we played CBGB in March 1976, it was almost an act of defiance. Still no record contract, more neglect from MainMan, but we packed the place anyway. Dee Dee and Joey from the Ramones were there. Their band were getting tighter by the month. David Johansen and Johnny Thunders were there, though the Dolls were as good as broken up. Bob Gruen was there with his camera. The atmosphere was charged.

You could spot CBGB by the large white awning with red letters along the Bowery. The room was narrow and very long, with the stage at the back. When we got up to play, we were surrounded on three sides. Wayne was dressed a little differently tonight from his usual stage persona. There was no corset or fishnet stockings. The wig was black instead of blonde. His shirt was the usual white, but the tie and pants were white, too. This was the more masculine but still outrageous Wayne. It was also the more hyper Wayne. The guys in the band all knew that he had taken some speed before getting onstage.

A couple of songs into our set, Richard Manitoba pushed his way to the front of the stage. Richard was the vocalist for the band the Dictators. He began shouting at Wayne and taunting him. Wayne was used to getting heckled. His persona was meant to be provocative. But this went on for a few songs and seemed to be getting to Wayne. With the volume of the music and the crowd, it was hard to hear what Richard was saying, but I heard a few scathing words here and there. Every once in a while I caught a glimpse of Wayne's face. He was agitated and pissed off. He called Richard a 'stupid fucking asshole' a few times, but that just seemed to get Richard and the crowd even more riled.

Richard finally stepped onto the stage, which was only about a foot high. Wayne was in the middle of 'Toilet Love' and snapped. He slammed the heavy steel microphone stand down on Richard's shoulder. Wayne then jumped on Richard, who was writhing in pain and clutching his shoulder. They rolled around onstage, with Wayne getting in some good punches and furiously kicking the overweight singer all over his body. They fell off the stage and onto the beer-soaked floor of CB's as the crowd parted like the Red Sea.

The place was going wild. I stood up and grabbed a cymbal stand, prepared for whatever might come next. Wayne's wig was off and so were the gloves. Blood sprayed all around as Wayne and Richard wrestled. It took only about fifteen seconds for Hilly and his friend Merv to push their way to the stage area and grab Richard. By this point, blood was pouring out of the side of his head.

When Wayne got back onstage, his white shirt was covered in Richard's blood. Wayne looked at the audience and asked them if they wanted to quit or if they still wanted some rock and roll. 'Rock and roll!' they screamed. 'Rock and roll! Go Wayne!' Fittingly, we launched into 'Wash Me in the Blood of Rock and Roll' and finished the set. Afterward, someone told me a couple of his bandmates took Richard to St. Vincent's Hospital.

Richard had a broken collarbone. He claimed the only reason he stepped onto the stage was to make his way to the hallway, which led to the bathroom. He filed assault charges against Wayne, and there was a warrant out for his arrest. Normally one of the easiest people on the planet to spot, Wayne started keeping a low profile, but he was arrested a few days later wearing a fake mustache. Even though he was not in drag, the police put him in a special cell with a cross-dresser to protect him from some of the homophobes who were locked up that night.

People in the scene took either Wayne's side or Richard's side. But more people seemed to be on Wayne's side. Danny Fields, the Ramones' manager, spoke to the press on Wayne's behalf. Debbie Harry and Dee Dee Ramone helped organize a benefit at CBGB for Wayne's legal defense fund. Eventually, the case was thrown out of court. For a while, the Dictators were banned from CBGB, Max's, and some other clubs.

Wayne County and the Backstreet Boys were still welcome, but Wayne took off for London, making the brawl at CB's my last gig with the band. As good as we were, none of us believed the band were going to gain acceptance outside of hip New York City, at least not in the States. In London, Leee managed Johnny Thunders and the Heartbreakers. Wayne and Leee put together a new band called Wayne County and the Electric Chairs. Greg Van Cook and Elliot Michaels both played guitar in the band and were both friends of mine from Brooklyn.

It was a small world, and the world of rock and roll was even smaller. At the same time, the larger world was beginning to catch on to the punk sounds and sensibilities of New York and London. And I was looking to catch on again somewhere.

6

In April 1976, I started hanging around Cynthia Whitney, who was known as 'Roxy'. Roxy lived a life of luxury and sleaze. She was a sharp-witted trust fund baby from a Chicago family. Roxy came to New York to be in the middle of the rock scene – one that seemed to be evolving constantly. The check from her trust fund came in the mail every month like clockwork, and that was about the closest she got to being normal. Since she had no need for a real job, she was free to look for excitement, and she usually found it. She would work on and off as a topless dancer in the seedy clubs around Times Square. Just walking down the street showing off a tight dress with a plunging neckline was a performance for her. Roxy was an exhibitionist.

Roxy's old money paid for a nice apartment in SoHo on Thompson Street just south of Houston Street. It was a first-floor mini-loft in a renovated five-story walk-up building. The apartment was only about twelve feet wide, but it ran the length of the right side of the building and had everything we needed.

Roxy's tip money paid for the booze. Roxy and I liked our booze. Until Roxy came along, I didn't have a friend who was into drinking as I was. I would hole up in her apartment for days on end drinking whatever she had around. It wasn't just me. The apartment was party central. On any given night, members of the Dolls, the Ramones, and Blondie would stop by. There was always plenty of pot and pills to go with the alcohol.

My contribution to the apartment was a top-of-the-line stereo. At all hours of the night, the stereo blasted out a mix of Bowie, Roxy Music, and Sparks. Also on the playlist was the Ramones' self-titled album, which had just been released. It was 'Blitzkrieg Bop' till four or five every morning. When the upstairs neighbors pounded on the door and complained around midnight, our concession was to wind it down around two or three. Our friends without a reason to get up in the morning eventually got up in the afternoon and got more pot, pills, and booze, and it all seemed routine. Then one night Roxy introduced me to Richard Hell.

Richard was a wiry guy with thick, wavy dark hair. He had been a major part of the New York scene for a couple of years. From a well-educated family in Kentucky, Richard met Tom Verlaine in a Delaware boarding school in 1969. The two left school and headed for New York, where they formed the Neon Boys. Richard played bass and sang. Tom played guitar. When they held auditions for a second guitarist, Chris Stein (later of Blondie) showed up. So did Doug Colvin, who later became Dee Dee Ramone. But Richard Lloyd got the job.

The Neon Boys changed their name to Television in 1973. They had a very original sound. The guitar was melodic, but the chording and progressions were a bit dissonant. The vocals were weird, poetic, and a little screechy, but they somehow sat just right in the music. It was Richard Hell and Tom who persuaded Hilly Kristal to build a stage for bands at CBGB. It was that stage where people started to tune into Television, Talking Heads, Blondie, Patti Smith, and the Ramones.

Television had a record deal, but Richard and Tom were not getting along. Tom, Richard told me, took complete control and wouldn't put any of his songs in the set or on the forthcoming album. In any case, Television's debut album, *Marquee Moon*, was being recorded without

Richard Hell. For a short while, Richard joined forces with ex-Dolls members Johnny Thunders and Jerry Nolan to form the Heartbreakers.

The Heartbreakers' most popular song was 'Chinese Rocks', written mostly by Dee Dee Ramone. As the story goes, Johnny Ramone refused to record a track obviously about shooting heroin. So Dee Dee took it to Richard, who added a couple of verses. But there was some sort of competition going on in the band between Johnny Thunders and Richard Hell, and Richard's time in the Heartbreakers lasted just a little longer than a good fix.

When Roxy introduced me to Richard one night at her apartment during a hell of a party, he was in the process of putting together a new band and looking for a drummer. He invited me down to Daily Planet rehearsal studios on West Thirtieth Street in Manhattan, and I decided it was worth checking out. At bare minimum, Richard was an interesting-looking guy. He wore his hair kind of spiky. I didn't know if it was intentional or just the result of not shampooing much. His jeans and T-shirt were old and falling apart and held together by a bunch of safety pins. It was either the end of a wardrobe or the beginning of a new look.

When I got to Daily Planet the next day, I met the guitarist, Bob Quine. Bob had a reputation as a very original and creative musician, and he didn't waste any time showing me what he and Richard were cooking up.

Bob played like someone from another planet. The chords and scales were bizarre. I heard something like rock and roll but filtered through a futuristic time warp. I would hear a blues chord but with one note in a strange place. I would hear a blues progression but with a strange detour. The leads contained notes that almost belonged, but by the time you started really thinking about it, he was on to some other strange experiment. Bob's playing was surreal, like the sonic version of a Salvador Dalí painting.

I wasn't told to listen to a demo tape and copy something some other drummer had conceived. Instead, I sat down right there on the drum set in Daily Planet, on planet earth, and started playing along with Bob's guitar, helping fill in a partially blank canvas. In fact, the song was called 'Blank Generation'.

I had never heard the song before. Considering where I hung out and performed it with them, maybe I should have. Richard Hell had written it with the Heartbreakers. It wasn't on an album I could go out and buy, and I didn't recall hearing it at CBGB or Max's, and even if I had heard it, it was probably lost somewhere between the stage and a vodka martini. So I followed along. It was a simple descending chord progression – C, B, G#, G – with a loose shuffle feel.

As much as I was concentrating on getting the right time, attitude, and accents that make the difference between an okay song and a good song, I was actually struck by the lyrics. This didn't happen to me every day. In a lot of situations, I was back there doing my thing, hopefully doing it really well, and barely concerned with what was actually being said. But these lyrics said something. They spoke for me. I spent my childhood trying to escape the rigid ways of the World War II generation. But I wasn't really part of the Woodstock generation, either. I was somewhere in between. I couldn't exactly claim to have a plan in life. And I could imagine a lot of my friends feeling the same way.

Richard's voice wasn't what a vocal coach or a music critic would consider polished. He sometimes half-sang, half-spoke, and both halves were as uneven and spiky as his hair. Singing was not even what he was shooting for. It sounded more like a lament. But he wasn't just some guy complaining that he couldn't pay the rent or there were too many muggers roaming the streets of New York. It was a poetic lament. It was intellectual. What he had was *punk intellect*. He was a punk Bob Dylan.

After a few minutes, Bob, Richard, and I launched into another chord progression Bob was working on. This one had no history. We could make it into absolutely anything we wanted. What struck me at that point – more than the mastery Bob had over his Fender Stratocaster and the whammy bar he used the way a fine sculptor uses a knife – was that this wasn't an audition. Even if it had been, it was over. We were a band working on songs. Sparks were flying.

What also struck me was Bob's maturity. He had lost a lot of hair, and if I was twenty-three, he might have been thirty-three. But that wasn't what caught my attention. Bob seemed more like fifty. He was composed and focused. Without having to state it, he was the adult in the room. In the circles I traveled, there were plenty of rooms but very few adults.

Bob's chords went way up the neck of the Strat. Everything I had absorbed about rock and roll told me that after the third or fourth ascending chord it was time to go back down and resolve the phrase. Bob's progressions kept going up. It produced kind of a manic, out-of-control feeling, and I pushed the already driving beat in the spirit of the thing. Meanwhile, Richard started singing some lines he had already written for the song when he was with the Heartbreakers. I couldn't make out all the words, but the title was unforgettable: 'Love Comes in Spurts'.

After the first rehearsal, Richard came up with the name Voidoids. I liked it right away. It was different and worked well with the bizarre sound. Not to mention the theme of a song like 'Blank Generation'. The three of us continued rehearsing at Daily Planet, and sparks continued to fly. But after a few rehearsals, Richard thought the band could use a second guitar player. It had nothing to do with Bob not cutting it. Bob was cutting it into fine pieces.

Richard simply thought a second guitarist could make things even more interesting. It was also possible that a second guitarist would take some weight not only off Bob but also off Richard himself. Richard's bass playing was solid and minimalist. He never played one more note than the music called for. Still, he had to do that and sing at the same time, pretty much the same burden that pushed Dee Dee out of his early role of lead singer in the Ramones.

We ran an ad in the *Village Voice*. The *Voice* was the first successful alternative weekly in the country. It covered the cultural revolution of the sixties from the trenches and served the gay community before anyone ever heard of Stonewall. Our friend from the Dust days, Lester Bangs, was one of dozens of well-known writers from the ranks of New Journalism who wrote for the *Voice*. The paper covered the emerging New York punk scene front and center. Meanwhile, the back of the

Voice was famous for having hundreds upon hundreds of sex ads and musical notices, and ours that week was spotted by the right musician.

Ivan Julian was the first person to respond and the first to audition. He was a young guy with curly hair. When Ivan walked into our room at Daily Planet, Richard was nodding off in a corner. I was guzzling vodka out of a bottle, and there were two girls hanging out by the drums. I didn't know either of their names. Bob was the only normal-looking guy in the room, probably because he *was* the only normal guy in the room.

Bob immediately took charge of the audition. Watching Ivan was a little like watching myself weeks earlier. Bob spent a few minutes with Ivan showing him the guitar parts. Bob was calm, patient, and methodical about it. The noise from two guitars woke up Richard, and soon he and I joined in.

Ivan's playing had more of a straightforward rock approach than Bob's artsy one. Ivan would play the same chord but in a standard position, often lower on the guitar neck. There were rarely any strange notes and no whammy bar. There could have been a sonic conflict, but there wasn't. As it turned out, the two styles complemented each other. By a happy accident, there was a kind of off-color harmony. Ivan's playing was anchored to my drums and Richard's stripped-down bass, with Bob free to fly circles around the ship. With Ivan on board, Richard Hell and the Voidoids were complete.

After experimenting with a few songs, we took a short break and talked about music. Richard had been taken by the rawness of the MC5 and the Stooges. Lyrically, he was influenced by Jack Kerouac and the Beat Generation that began to emerge with the publication of Kerouac's *On the Road* in 1957. He also loved surrealist art and the decadent movement poems of Arthur Rimbaud and others from the late nineteenth century. He was born Richard Meyers, but, when you mixed all that together and stirred it with Bob Dylan's attitude, you got Richard Hell.

Bob listened to jazz and blues. The way it all oozed out of his Strat was his own invention. Ivan was from the Washington, DC, area and favored a lot of heavy rock. His eyes lit up when I told him I was once in a band called Dust. He had actually seen us play a few years earlier near his hometown. Oddly, Ivan remembered the local radio commercial promoting the concert, daring the audience to come see and hear the biggest bass drum in rock. And all this time, I thought they came to see the band.

Over the next few weeks, we got into a rhythm of rehearsing, writing, sleeping, and doing it all over again. I would usually start the day with a few shots at Roxy's place and then walk over to Bob's apartment on St. Marks Place off Second Avenue. Bob's seniority expressed itself in various ways. First of all, he had a real apartment. Other musicians either had no official residence, or they had a rat-trap hole-in-the-wall filled with milk crates and roaches, both the crawling and marijuana kinds. Bob had real furniture where we sat and listened to Dave Brubeck and Miles Davis.

Bob's drug was Valium. I understood that. He had a real intellect, a real analytical mind. I could tell there was a lot of experience, disappointment, and misgivings pent up inside him. He released that by playing guitar, but he couldn't play guitar all the time. So a couple of Valium and a side of Stan Getz would get him through whatever his Stratocaster couldn't.

On an ambitious night, Bob and I would walk to rehearsal on West Thirtieth Street. The other nights we would take the R train. After rehearsal we usually took it back to Richard's apartment on Tenth Street between First Avenue and Avenue A in the East Village. Richard had a musician's apartment. The place was on the edge of Alphabet City, for many years the poorest working-class neighborhood of the Lower East Side, but now mostly an area for the wayward and drug-addicted seeking low-rent shelter.

Richard's rent was $55 a month, or $45 less than what Bruce and I paid to live in a Brooklyn basement storage compartment and steal phone service. It was worth every dollar of the fifty-five. Gangs roamed outside. After walking up four flights of stairs to the top floor, you entered the battered metal door of the rear apartment. The front room was a narrow kitchen, and the first thing you noticed was an old cast-iron, claw-foot bathtub. You could almost see and hear a bunch of unwashed little kids from the 1880s sitting naked in the tub while their mother poured water from a large kettle heated on a coal stove.

The floors were raw, unvarnished wood that creaked when you walked them. There were enough cracks and holes in the plaster walls to make you think someone had started to demolish them but then for some reason stopped. Behind the kitchen was a narrow living room with cardboard boxes housing Richard's numerous books and albums. Off to the side was a closet with a toilet in it. In the original apartment, it was a chamber pot, but someone in the 1920s had decided to modernize. Richard's bedroom consisted of a bare floor with a mattress and a bass guitar usually lying on it. For good measure, the Beat poet Allen Ginsberg lived downstairs, maybe close enough to hear the thump of Richard's bass when he messed with it.

There was a second, tiny bedroom with a bunk bed in it. That was where Ivan and I would crash whenever we couldn't make the walk back to wherever. It was a little like sharing a bunk bed with my brother, Fred, staring at the ceiling and falling asleep to the sound of music in my head. Here on Tenth Street, the apartment faced the interior lot and was high above the rear yards. There was strangely some peace and quiet and a nice breeze running through, in the middle of chaos.

One night at CBGB, Richard introduced us to Terry Ork. Terry was a fun guy with a beard and mustache. We all knew who Terry was and how he figured into the birth of the new music scene downtown. He started out making silk-screen prints for Andy Warhol and hoped to follow in his footsteps by grooming the next Velvet Underground. Terry helped Tom Verlaine and Richard Lloyd when they formed Television and ultimately managed the band, which, for a while, had Richard Hell in it. As the band got its act together, Richard learned to play the bass. Terry promised CBGB owner Hilly Kristal he would make good money at the bar if he let Television play there, and he made good on that promise. After that, Terry effectively became the booking agent for CBGB.

Parlaying his presence in the New York punk world, Terry now ran a small independent label called Ork Records. He and Richard, of course, had some history, and he asked Richard if we'd be interested in recording a single – two songs – with an A side and a B side. Richard quickly bargained him up to a three-song extended-play, or EP, record. Without much time together as a unit and not having played our first gig, we now had a small but very real record deal.

Ivan more or less moved into Richard's apartment. It wasn't as if he didn't know what he was getting into, but there were always new surprises. Sometimes Ivan walked into the kitchen and found Richard asleep in the bathtub. At least once Richard had been in there all night through to the morning and was slumped over with his mouth wide open and an arm dangling out haphazardly. He looked comatose. There were empty bags of heroin on the floor, so death was not out of the question. Ivan shook Richard, who barely awoke just in time for Ivan not to call 911.

When Richard wasn't nearly drowning in it, the kitchen bathtub served as a table. With a few pieces of scrap wood laid across the top, it was perfect for sitting around and cutting up meat, potatoes, or smack. The people doing the cutting were Johnny Thunders, Jerry Nolan, Heartbreakers guitarist Walter Lure, and Dee Dee Ramone. The real Hell's Kitchen was a neighborhood of tenements and mobsters in Manhattan's West Thirties and Forties. But this Hell's kitchen gave it a run for its money.

We recorded the EP at Plaza Sound, on the eighth floor of Radio City Music Hall. I was hyped up, not only about the opportunity but by our producer, Craig Leon, who only months before had produced the first Ramones album. I hadn't recorded in a while and was a little anxious. Roxy was with me and slipped me a Valium. It was a 2.5-milligram white pill. I never drank before playing and wasn't sure this was the right time for my first-ever Valium. It was like spinning a roulette wheel. But it got me loose, took the edge off, and most importantly didn't ruin my focus. I felt great. It was like taking a page out of Bob Quine's book.

We worked on 'Blank Generation', 'Another World', and 'Gotta Lose'. The studio drum set was a 1967 blue-sparkle Ludwig with Paiste cymbals, and I felt right at home. Craig let the band do what we wanted to do. He just went with what sounded good to all of us. The constant rehearsals paid off. We finished all the basic tracks in one day.

We sometimes partied at Terry's apartment, a huge loft on East Broadway in Chinatown. Richard Lloyd had once lived in the small front room. One night the whole band were there, and Ivan got really drunk. He staggered to the toilet, first pulling his pants halfway down to pee, then realizing he had to throw up. He knelt down before the porcelain god, as they say, and let the booze out the way it came in. If there is one thing everyone has in common in that situation, it's lingering there a while to see if the episode is really over and just to catch your breath.

Before Ivan could do any of that, he felt a pair of hands around his belt pulling his pants the rest of the way down. It was Terry, the master of the house, trying to get into the Voidoid. Sick as he was, Ivan sprang to his feet screaming. When I saw Ivan stomping through the living room trying to wipe his mouth and pull his pants up at the same time, I knew I should leave with him and talk him down. He had his pants up by the time we hit the sidewalk on East Broadway.

'He fucking tried to bugger me! What the fuck?'

'Look, you can't blame the guy,' I said with a smile. 'He gave it his best shot.'

It was a long walk back to Richard's apartment on East Tenth Street, and that was good. Ivan was a liberal guy, not at all a homophobe, but he was in shock. It was a combination of being dazed to begin with, the surprise element, and wrapping his head around exactly how to think of Terry from now on. But by the time we got to East Tenth Street Ivan started to see how funny the whole thing really was.

Terry Ork was about business, too, and his place of business was just that. Cinemabilia was a store devoted to old movie books, posters, and magazines. It was a place where the radio and TV nostalgia king of New York, Joe Franklin, would have felt at home. Cinemabilia also served as home office to Ork Records. Terry could easily have afforded an expensive Marantz stereo for the office. Instead, he had a cheap hi-fi he bought at a discount store on Fourteenth Street. He wanted to listen to his product on the same sort of sound system most of his customers did.

The phone on Terry's desk was ringing off the hook lately. The five thousand copies he had pressed of the Richard Hell and the Voidoids EP sold out almost immediately. Terry also had a distribution deal with Stiff Records in England. Stiff was a new label dedicated to punk that distributed British acts such as Nick Lowe and the Damned. One of Stiff's slogans was 'If it ain't Stiff, it ain't worth a fuck'.

Our EP was selling well in the UK, too. It was nice to know we were worth a fuck.

Meanwhile, Terry did better for us than just book us at the club he always booked. In the spring of 1977 he got Hilly to pay us $4,000 a show for two shows at CBGB. We didn't have to do much publicity. There was strong word of mouth about the band. Between Richard's time in Television and the Heartbreakers and my stint in Wayne County, there was a carryover effect. CBGB put out its usual flyers and advertised the shows in the *Village Voice*, but that was customary for every headliner. Fortunately, both shows sold out and the crowd loved us. So Terry booked additional shows, one per month. Four thousand dollars was serious money. It could keep Richard's rent paid up until at least the eighties.

On a day when I didn't have to rehearse or do a show I would usually get up at Roxy's around noon. Around two or three in the afternoon, we'd grab a pint of vodka and share it. Sometimes Johnny Ramone would show up in the middle of the afternoon. There would be a knock on the door, and I'd usually be the one to answer it. I would say, 'Hey, John,' and he would say, 'Hi, Marc.' And that was pretty much it. We were like two ships passing in the day.

About half an hour later, they would head out the door, John in his jeans, T-shirt, and leather jacket, Roxy in a red patent-leather miniskirt and black bondage latex. Lately she was bleaching her hair white and putting on a ton of black eyeliner and bright red lipstick. On a superficial level, you could see why the two of them hit it off. The Ramones were the big fish in the sea, at least south of Fourteenth Street. Roxy hadn't come to New York to catch minnows. She was a wealthy and wild girl who dressed to kill. She looked like an S&M fantasy chick. I thought she was more S than M.

I supposed John was the masochist here. He was married to Rosana, his high school sweetheart. She was very personable and happened to be built like Sophia Loren, John's idea of the perfect woman. Who could ask for anything more? *John.* He and Rosana had an apartment in Forest Hills, which was in another borough, not on another continent. It seemed as if John was setting himself up for a fall. But it was none of my business. I was seeing Marion and had my own life to deal with.

When it was time to go out in the evening, I would drink a beer or two to get loose and then make the rounds – 82 Club, CBGB, Max's. Everyone gave me free drinks because I played there. It was my circuit.

Friday nights my circuit included the Roosevelt Hotel on East Forty-Fifth Street in Manhattan. Marion worked the front desk on weeknights from three to eleven, which was great for going out and staying out late. But she usually volunteered for the early shift Saturday, which was seven thirty in the morning till three in the afternoon. When you worked a night shift into a day shift, the hotel gave you a room overnight so you didn't have to commute back and forth.

I would show up at the front desk Friday afternoon, and Marion would hand me the key as if I were a regular anonymous guest. I would then go upstairs to the room whose number was printed on the key, let myself in, then sleep and watch TV all day. Just past eleven in the evening, Marion would join me for a nightcap. It was mahogany furniture, color television, plush carpet, and room service. For a nice Brooklyn girl still living at home and a struggling musician, it was the high life.

One off night, I was at Max's with friends just drinking. Around three in the morning, either I decided I'd had enough or someone else did. My brother, Fred, my friend Elwood and I all left together and started walking downtown. Elwood told us he was working as a roadie for KISS, but I didn't entirely believe him. A friend and roadie in Dust, J. R. Smalling, who was now KISS's tour manager, had never mentioned

Elwood. In any case, KISS had just finished recording their new album. Elwood was carrying a large black road case with metal corners.

We started to walk along the Park Avenue side of Union Square Park. Just inside, at the center of this small park, was a huge statue of George Washington on a horse. Lucky for them, neither could smell the faint odor of urine always in the air. Near the north entrance to the park, we came across two white guys fighting. They were wailing on each other. It wasn't one of those bullshit movie fights where each sweeping roundhouse punch gets its own camera shot. It was a blizzard of rabbit punches.

The custom was to let two guys who were fighting keep right on fighting. The polite thing to do was to walk away instead of hanging around and watching. But there was something not right about this fight. One guy was much bigger than the other – literally a foot taller. So I walked over and pushed my way between them. They both froze. I yelled at the big guy, 'Hey, don't pick on this fucking little guy! Look at the size of him!'

Out of nowhere, the little guy lunged at me. As I stepped back, I saw there was a knife in his hand. I felt it slice the underside of my left arm, through my leather jacket. As soon as I grabbed my arm, both the little guy and the big guy bolted, heading south along the sidewalk. Fred and Elwood were right behind them. The big guy got away, but Fred tackled the little guy, and Elwood clocked him over the head with his road case.

As I took a few steps in their direction, I started getting nauseous and light-headed. I looked down and saw a puddle of blood on the ground. If I was drunk enough to break up a fight between two assholes, I was apparently also drunk enough not to realize just how badly I was stabbed.

A few seconds later, a patrol car pulled up near the curb and two cops got out. There was always something shady going on in the park, so the cops circled it regularly. Another patrol car pulled up a moment later near Fred and Elwood, who stopped beating the little guy long enough to explain to the cops what had happened.

There was no time to call an ambulance, so the patrol car doubled as one. They put me in the back with one of the cops. They cuffed the little guy and put him in the front. The officer driving told us the first stop was Bellevue Hospital on First Avenue. The second stop was the precinct. There was blood all over my jacket, shirt, and pants. *My* blood. The cop next to me said, 'Hey, don't mess up the backseat. How about sticking your finger in the cut to slow it down?' He was joking, sort of. I needed a paramedic, but I wasn't one, so I just squeezed my left arm with my right hand.

I felt light-headed again as the patrol car rolled past the wrought iron gates at Bellevue. As I was wheeled into the ER, a nurse asked me if I had been drinking, and the answer was on my breath. Because of the alcohol, they couldn't give me a general anesthetic. I was drifting in and out as they laid me out on the operating table. I didn't get a good look at what they were doing and I didn't feel a thing. Maybe that was because they gave me a local anesthetic. Maybe it was because of the shots I did at Max's. I smelled burning skin and figured it had to be mine. They must have been cauterizing the wound.

Roxy heard I was stabbed and showed up at the hospital. My father showed up right after. In the recovery room, I couldn't tell which pissed off my father more – what some lunatic had done to his son or how his son practically handed out an invitation to be stabbed.

'So much for being the Good Samaritan, Marc.'

'Hey, I just saw it as this big guy picking on this little—'

'You can't assume anything. You don't know these guys or what was happening a minute before you got there. I'm just glad they didn't have a gun.'

My father also wasn't happy that we'd be going to court, but he would definitely make sure we were prepared.

I found out in the morning that one of my main arteries had been cut. The attending physician wanted me in the hospital for a full week. I felt like crap, so I didn't argue. After two days, though, I was feeling a lot better.

On the second morning, I was feeling stronger and tired of eating Jell-O and watching soap operas. I asked to be discharged. But the attending physician refused to sign me out. So I took matters into my own hands. I rolled out of bed, stood up, and took off the long hospital robe I was wearing. My left arm was throbbing with pain, so I mostly used my right arm. My street clothes were in a bag in the corner. I put them back on slowly, dried blood and all. But I couldn't find my sneakers. I looked down and saw the stupid smiley-face slippers the hospital had issued me and figured, *What the hell!* Who knew if I could tie my sneaker laces anyway? So I ducked out and hit First Avenue in the smiley-face slippers.

I called Elwood from a payphone and told him I was on my way over to his apartment. He told me I was fucking crazy but come on over anyway, he'd be there. It was about a ten-block walk. Elwood greeted me with a bottle of vodka and a promotional copy of the new KISS album, *Destroyer*. I put the bottle to my lips and Elwood cranked up the record. The airwaves lately were filled with mediocre arena-rock bands turning out corporate hits for the music industry. But *Destroyer*, no matter how many times it might eventually go platinum, was not really part of that world. It rocked. For a guy who narrowly escaped being stabbed to death and was now released into the wild, the album was like the soundtrack of freedom. The song 'Flaming Youth' seemed to be speaking directly to me.

The wound to my left arm hampered my drumming for a little while, but I did what I had to do. If you have a rehearsal to go to or a show to do, you find a way to push through it. The pain actually didn't compare with the aftermath of some of the root-canal work I had been through, and there was always booze around to take the sting out. Within about two weeks, I was pretty much healed.

In the late spring of 1977, along with everyone else in the downtown music scene, I was listening to the Sex Pistols. I bought the single of 'Anarchy in the U.K.', with Johnny Rotten proclaiming himself an Antichrist, and I heard for myself the rage of English youth loud and clear in a way mainstream music was incapable of expressing. But when I picked up a copy of the British music newspaper *Melody Maker* and saw a photo of the band, I had an entirely different experience. The

Sex Pistols looked like Richard Hell. They wore dark sport jackets that didn't exactly fit, ripped T-shirts with safety pins, and spiked hair.

It was ironic. Richard had started the look by accident years earlier, before I knew him. The look had made its way across the Atlantic and was now crossing back again as an export, as something original. In reality, it was derivative. The Pistols' manager, Malcolm McLaren, was also a fashion designer and owner of the London boutique, SEX. He had done for the Sex Pistols what Brian Epstein had done for the Beatles except in reverse. McLaren had dirtied up his boys and given them a complete image to go with their snarls. Looking at *Melody Maker*, I felt like I was in on some kind of inside joke. I hoped Richard looked at it the same way.

We couldn't be sure he would. There was a narcissistic side to Richard Hell, and the attention he got from women tended to reinforce it. The wildcard in all of it was the heroin. We never knew which Richard we were getting. At times he was hyper. Other times he was level, even sedate. The smack could cause his anxiousness or resolve it. We never knew for sure, and we were never on solid ground around him.

Sometimes backstage after a show, when everyone else was celebrating a good performance, he would sit somewhere isolated and barely acknowledge anyone else. Now that Richard was the missing link in a transatlantic phenomenon, there was every chance it would go to his head – or into a vein.

A few weeks later, Fred, Elwood, and I had to appear in criminal court on Centre Street a few blocks from city hall in Manhattan. The district attorney had pressed charges of assault and reckless endangerment against the little guy, who was now neatly dressed in a little gray suit. I was put on the stand and asked to point out the assailant plus answer a few simple questions. The judge gave the little guy one year's probation.

My father wasn't happy, and he had a lot more insight than most of us. After putting himself through night school, he had recently graduated from Brooklyn Law School, all while still working as a longshoreman. 'Is that what attempted murder gets you in New York these days?' he said. 'A slap on the wrist?' But, by the time the doors of the Criminal

Court building closed behind me, I had much better things to think about. We had just landed a deal with Sire Records.

With the Ork EP selling well on both sides of the Atlantic, Richard Hell and the Voidoids caught the attention of Richard Gottehrer, along with Seymour Stein, the cofounder of Sire Records. Gottehrer got his start in the business as a songwriter and producer in the famous Brill Building with such hits as 'My Boyfriend's Back', 'Hang On Sloopy', and 'I Want Candy'. More important, Sire was the home of the Ramones, Talking Heads, and the Pretenders, so it was the right home for us, too. Recently, Sire had begun using the term 'new wave' rather than 'punk' to describe the new music scene. All we cared about was getting our music right and getting it out there.

7

LONDON CALLING

My piece of the advance was put to good use, eating real meals instead of living off bread, peanut butter, and the kindness of friends and club owners. I bought nice new clothes including a leather jacket, plus a few good pairs of Keds sneakers to replace the ones worn through crisscrossing Lower Manhattan. I picked up a really nice boom box on Forty-Eighth Street.

I even got a few more of my teeth fixed. The dentists we went to as kids did the best they could, but they were more or less patching things up. As a result, over the last few years a filling would pop out here and a crown there. I knew I needed a root canal, and I was getting by in life practically OD'ing on Anbesol, which slowly formed a little hole in the inside of my cheek. My dental plan was basically to get work done every time I got a record deal.

We started recording the Voidoids album in the late spring of 1977 in Electric Lady Studios on West Eighth Street in the Village with Richard Gottehrer producing. Jimi Hendrix and his manager Michael Jeffery had originally bought the building with the idea of reopening the Generation Club, but the plans morphed into a studio that would be world-class.

Ironically, Hendrix recorded at Electric Lady only during what would be the final days of his life. But the studio remained and became part of his legacy. The round windows, multicolored ambient lights, and the huge spacey mural wrapping around the hallway between Studio A and Studio B were all still in place. The twenty-four-track mixing console, tape machines, and effects were all topflight.

The Voidoids sessions were pretty grueling. We would start in the late afternoon and finish up around sunrise. The level of performance expected was high – the bar was raised. It wasn't like the EP session, where we did a good job and were in and out. There were mighty ghosts in this room. Good was no longer good enough, and this fact was getting to Richard Hell. When Gottehrer or Bob would listen back and suggest we try another take, Richard would usually brood or get pissed off.

That was a problem for the whole band but especially for me. Richard wasn't just our singer and frontman. He was our bassist, and the drums and bass had to work together like the gears in a clock. I couldn't have him doing another take on bass in a disaffected state of mind. If his heart wasn't in it, his fingers wouldn't be either. We needed Richard to save the screeching and complaining for the vocals. But I didn't want to confront him when he stepped over the line. So I kept reminding him that we were a unit and he should remember that. *Cool off, Richard. Cool off.*

Strangely, he did, and it didn't have much to do with anything I said. The drugs probably kicked in. Suddenly it was Richard Hell wanting to do another take or getting a burst of genius. At the end of the funky-psychedelic anthem 'Another World', Richard began to cough. That was understandable, because eight-plus minutes of wailing and barking is a lot for anyone, punk or not. But Richard wanted it in, and we realized that was the perfect ending to this lovesick fantasy.

I was happy with my own playing and with the trashy drum sound Gottehrer gave me. Meanwhile, Bob's playing was outrageous. He rose to the occasion from what was already high ground. The song 'Betrayal Takes Two' was a punk ballad, which sounds like an oxymoron. 'Betrayal' had a bluesy feel, and, when the break came, Bob nailed it to the wall. We thought he might actually be channeling Jimi Hendrix. The punk version.

When the album was mixed and mastered, Richard gave us Hell. Upon reflection – in exactly what state of mind we didn't know – Richard decided that about three-quarters of the album had to be redone. This is the last thing in the world a record company with an album in the can wants to hear. But Richard must have thrown his best tantrum ever, because Sire caved.

On 13 July 1977, around nine thirty at night, Richard Hell and the Voidoids were in Plaza Sound on West Fiftieth Street in Manhattan. We were listening back to our latest recording of 'Blank Generation'. Counting the EP and the Electric Lady sessions, it was the third version. Or maybe the tenth. We could take it or leave it each time. But this time, the tape slowed down, making Richard's high-pitched wails sound almost normal. And then the machine stopped completely and the lights went out.

As in any studio, there were usually several people who smoked, so the butane lighters came out as if at the end of a concert. We went to the window facing West Fiftieth Street and it was almost completely dark out there, too. Windows, storefronts, street lights – all dark. The only thing illuminated were the headlights of cars moving eastwards along West Fiftieth. They looked like two-eyed zombies, and they were moving at zombie speed.

There are plenty of things to do in the dark in plenty of places, but there is not much to do in a recording studio. Ivan and I were the first ones out. We took a couple matchbooks and made our way to the stairs and down and out onto the street. We were like kids in an amusement park. It was sweltering hot, and we wanted adventure. We decided the place to be was Max's. It was a long walk from Fiftieth to Eighteenth Street, but it wasn't like taking the subway was an option.

While Midtown was filled with moviegoers, theatergoers, and tourists bewildered and polite, things got a little more dicey with every block south. On Forty-Eighth Street, there were a couple of looters running out of an electronics store carrying stereo components and laughing.

At Forty-Second Street, a crowd were looting a men's clothing store. These weren't professional criminals. These were everyday pissed-off New Yorkers who saw an opportunity.

There was glass everywhere. Faces were shadowy except when a car drove by and exposed everyone in their natural state. Once in a while, a bolt of lightning shot across the sky and for a second or two people were looting in broad daylight. Menacing voices bounced around corners, answered by other menacing voices who wanted to know where the getting was good. The victims were inanimate objects, not people. It was like a sci-fi movie about the end of the world. I felt alive and free.

July 1977 in New York was also the summer of the Son of Sam. A crazed gun-toting killer was roaming around blowing away couples making out in parked cars. Unemployment ran high. Inflation ran higher. Sanitation pickups were optional and subway cars were canvases for graffiti. The future looked bleak. Blank. Scary. The people in my crowd wrote songs about it. But the strange thing was, here in the dark and the chaos, there was a sense of camaraderie that was normally missing.

They had to let me and Ivan in at Max's. Of course, they weren't letting just anybody in. Max's was now in survival mode. So what was normally a club in the entertainment sense was now a real club – either you belonged or you didn't. The bouncer's name was Moose, and of course he knew us. Moose was about six-foot-six and 240 pounds – or a little over 17 stone. Moose was an ideal defense against looting, and there was no rule against looting a club that was trendy. But Moose had help. Inside Max's were the usual crowd, sitting in candlelight, drinking beer that was slowly warming. If you were a looter and managed somehow to get by Moose, you would have to go through these punks, too.

We had a couple of beers at the bar. Someone with a portable radio told me that the lightning storm earlier in the evening had knocked out a couple of electric substations, and from there it was like a domino effect. The whole city was out with the exception of southern Queens, which got its power from the Long Island Lighting Company instead of Con Edison. The looting in the South Bronx and in poorer Brooklyn neighborhoods like Brownsville and East New York supposedly put the Lower Manhattan ruckus to shame. In the more dangerous neighborhoods, helicopters were flying overhead and viewing what looked like multiple blocks consumed by fire.

But at Max's, in a way it was business as usual. The club was usually open till almost dawn, at which time the blackout chaos would mostly vanish. So all Max's had to do was push closing a little later and they were out of the woods. I could drink to that.

Ivan and I left Max's for Richard's place around three in the morning. Facing Union Square Park, not far from where I was stabbed, was a Chase Manhattan Bank. The festivities were still going strong, and I wanted to be part of it the same way a kid in Coney Island wants to go into the fun house. I didn't know how to crack a safe, but I knew the first step had to be getting into the bank. So I picked up a rock and threw it at the plate-glass window. It bounced off without leaving a scratch.

I picked up another rock, a larger one, and threw it with the same result. Next, I grabbed a piece of two-by-four I found in a trash can, ran up to the building, and started slamming the window. Nothing. It was like whipping a mattress with a pillow. The bank guard on the other side of the plate-glass window stood up from his chair and waved me away. That's about all he could do. There was no chasing in Manhattan tonight.

As Ivan and I walked away, I thought about how, given the right circumstances, almost anybody could do almost anything. My parents didn't raise a vandal. But their son felt a lot of pressure and welcomed a release, even if it took a riot. I thought about how I probably couldn't live this way for ever. It was now 14 July. The following day, I'd be twenty-five.

If the record industry lived in a truly punk world, the *Blank Generation* album would have been released quickly. But Sire Records saw punk booming in the UK and was negotiating a major distribution deal with Warner Bros. Records. Deals took time. Meanwhile, Sire was sending us over to Britain to tour with the Clash, who were the new rage over there. We were thrilled to be a part of that. But we thought it was crazy and self-defeating to make the trip without an album to support. It was like showing up at Christmas empty-handed.

The British Airways flight over was hell for Richard. He wasn't used to going seven, eight hours or more without shooting up. It should have been a glorious trip. Instead, we watched Richard in withdrawal dashing to the bathroom and wondered when he was coming out.

Our tour manager picked us up at Heathrow Airport, London. Richard was antsy in the car, and not because we were driving on the left side of the road. When we got into the heart of London and stopped at a red light, Richard jumped out and hailed a cab. He told us he was going to meet Johnny Thunders and Jerry Nolan and would catch up with us later. We all knew that meant he was going to cop.

The Clash, the Sex Pistols, and the Damned were singing about downtrodden Britain, and they weren't lying. Cities and countries don't go downhill overnight, but we could see that's where they were headed. Countless thousands of unemployed workers were on the dole. There were beggars on the street. Muggings and even random attacks were happening every day. There was a general bleakness. We could see it in the way people dressed and the way roads and bridges were slowly falling apart.

We didn't stay in London long. The tour would go for about three weeks and would trace a route that looked like a crescent on a map of the UK. The first leg would be the longest – getting all the way north to Scotland to play Dunfermline, Glasgow, and Edinburgh. From there we would work our way south through industrial cities such as Leeds, Newcastle, and Manchester in northern England, and then down through towns in the south including Bristol and Southampton before ending the tour with two nights in London.

Punk attitude and all, we weren't thrilled on day one when our driver picked us up in a rented Volvo station wagon. The driver, Richard, Bob, Ivan, and I made five, and Richard's habit made six. All our equipment was with us. Whatever we couldn't fit in the back wound up on our laps. The Clash were somewhere in a legit van. After all, they were headlining.

We had our first clash with the Clash in Dunfermline. As the opening act, we got to do our sound check first. The roadies set up my kit on the drum riser, and we worked out the sound levels. But somewhere between the Clash's sound check and our first song, the Clash's manager, Bernie Rhodes, told us we couldn't use their riser any more. I understood it from a technical standpoint. Once you and your roadies had a kit set up perfectly during a sound check, you didn't want to move it off and back again. Sure, you could tell yourself you were setting it back up exactly the way it was during the sound check, but it was never the same under those rushed conditions.

But, from a personal standpoint, it pissed me off. It was not in the spirit of what we were trying to accomplish. It was more in line with the egomaniac rock acts we were rebelling against. In any case, I was relegated to a spot in front of and below Nicky 'Topper' Headon's kit, but I played my ass off, anyway.

Just when we were dug in for a long, harsh, thankless tour, it turned into a blast. The kids in the audience loved our music and who we were. They seemed thrilled to have a real American punk band in their hometown, and they showed it by screaming, thrashing around, and moshing in front of the stage. We didn't get the sense of being an opening act, like when some band with one song on the radio goes out there before Led Zeppelin at Madison Square Garden, and everyone's getting a Coke and taking a leak. These kids were with us at the beginning, middle, and end of every song. They went wild for 'Blank Generation'. The fact that they couldn't go out and buy the album the next day felt like a kick in our collective crotch.

It turned out the Clash loved us, too. They weren't backstage doing lines with groupies. They were watching, listening, and learning. We tried to do the same. Once we showed the United Kingdom what we could do – that we were the real deal – the tour became a caravan. The Clash and almost everyone in their scene were more into Americana than most Americans.

The fans wore eagle and US pins on their leather jackets, as the Ramones did. They loved James Dean, Jimmy Cagney, Humphrey Bogart, and the whole Warner Brothers movie catalogue of tough guys.

They wore Clint Eastwood button badges that said, 'Do you feel lucky? Well, do you, punk?' They had their own tough guys, of course, such as the notorious Kray twins from London. But, as far as they were concerned, no one could touch the Gambinos, Luccheses, Columbos, and Genoveses of New York. All this somehow made Richard Hell and the Voidoids that much more authentic, and who were we to argue?

The Clash were practically satirizing their own American obsession with the song 'I'm So Bored with the U.S.A.' It was like any addiction – you couldn't live with it, you couldn't live without it. But the depth of that addiction didn't fully register with me until I heard the opening measures of the Clash's song 'White Riot'. When I closed my eyes and listened to the fast, heavy downstroke, I thought I was at CBGB listening to the Ramones. Especially the 'One, two, three, four!' before each song.

It was no accident. When the Ramones played at Dingwalls in London on 5 July 1976, members of the Clash, the Sex Pistols, and other upstart English punk bands turned out to take notes. Most of the guys left feeling discouraged. The Ramones blew them away with their overall tightness, attitude, and aggression. That was the same band, ironically, I had seen a couple years earlier having a more or less public rehearsal onstage. Now they were schooling British punk wannabes on English soil. It was the British Invasion in reverse. The Brits left Dingwalls that night vowing to work harder, and they did. Hearing those stories gave me a sense of pride.

There was incredible energy when we took the stage in Manchester on 29 October. Manchester was a rowdy soccer town, and on this night the volume was funneled into the Apollo. The moshing and stage diving were almost out of control. The attitude seemed to be split. A lot of kids looked like they were just there to have a good time. But a lot of them were almost warlike. You couldn't blame them. All those years of school and no job. Then you're trying to find an identity somehow, to come into your own. So you put on military boots, leather jackets, and studs only to find the establishment has gone from not caring about you to putting you down. So you dig in deeper. You mosh harder. You scream louder.

In the middle of 'Love Comes in Spurts', it did. The Manchester kids started spitting at us. It wasn't just one or two spits: it was a spitfest. And these kids had serious range. We had seen other crowds do it to the Clash, and we knew it was out of appreciation. But we didn't like it. In New York, spitting at someone could get you killed. In Brooklyn, it could get your whole family killed.

When a big British glob of saliva splattered on Bob's bald head, the American Revolution was on. Bob yelled and jumped offstage and into the crowd, swinging his long, heavy Fender Stratocaster guitar. No amount of Valium could stop him. He was like Davy Crockett out there splitting logs. The three of us kept playing, hoping the tour and our careers would somehow continue. The strange thing was that while a few of the punks up front cut and ran for their lives, the crowd as a whole ate it up. They cheered as if their soccer side had scored a goal. Bob made his way back onstage, and, as a tribute to his sheer balls, the spitting stopped.

After Manchester we had all birthed some real punk folklore together, and everyone on the tour became even more like a band of brothers. Bernie Rhodes and the roadies would get drunk with us in the hotel lobby on Newcastle Browns. We put away boilermaker shots and had beer-drinking contests. One afternoon in Birmingham, we climbed up the fire escapes of some row homes and hopped from roof to roof. As a rule, I stopped drinking a few hours before stage time, but, after the show, I picked up where I left off.

I always had a great time with Joe Strummer, Clash guitarist and vocalist. We would hang out in his hotel room and listen to *Rocket to Russia*, the Ramones' third album, plus anything by Bob Marley or Peter Tosh. Joe took a liking to my Converse sneakers, so I yanked them off my feet and handed them over. I already had a few pairs of British sneakers in my travel bag. Joe and I would both leave the tour believing we were more punk than when it started.

The bass player, Paul Simonon, always carried two fake .45 Colt revolvers with him. We liked to duel in hotel lobbies, backstage, wherever. We stood about ten paces apart, counted down, and drew. I won about two-thirds of the time, but, as an American kid growing up in the fifties and sixties, I had the benefit of seeing all those Westerns.

As the tour drew closer to the end, I minded the location of my drums less and appreciated Bernie Rhodes more. He was a good businessman and was old-school, hands-on. He was with the band from the beginning, and you got the sense he would be there at the end. He wasn't some kid with a rich dad and connections. In that sense, Bernie reminded me a little bit of Led Zeppelin's Peter Grant, someone who could be your best friend or worst nightmare. If you got in the Clash's way, you would pay. He wasn't just a fanboy.

Rock critic Lester Bangs traveled with the Clash. It was where he belonged. After bemoaning the massive sellout of stadium rock bands – with their insufferable guitar triplets and ten-minute indulgent drum solos – to the lecherous money-grubbing formula-driven major labels, Lester took up the punk cause. In an article titled 'Free Jazz/Punk Rock', he wrote, 'I don't give a good goddamn if somebody can barely play their instruments or even not at all, as long as they've got something to express and do it in a compelling way.'

Bangs thought it was fortunate, even a privilege, that he got to see musicians evolve musically from hard rock and heavy metal to this new music and actually make a go of it doing what he liked – what we both liked.

The truth was, we all felt privileged. That included even Richard, particularly after shooting up. We didn't really care who wore what pin first or figured out that a voice cracking at the right time can be cool. We liked a good song, and we liked to make a statement whether it was simple, funny, sarcastic, or outrageous. Uncool as it sounded, we were really happy to be making a living for the time being with these little quirky bands we started in basements and rat holes. And we were excited to see people digging it.

In London, back where we started the tour, we were now better off. We were part of a fraternity. Not a fraternity that took pains to exclude people – one that took in everybody, especially if they had a problem with the way things worked, or didn't work. And with that very sensation coursing through our veins, Joe Strummer and I walked into Bob Quine's hotel room. Bob was older and liked to get to bed earlier than the rest of us, so he bunked alone. On either side of the Atlantic, there was no rule in the rock-and-roll tour manual against opening a door that wasn't locked. But there should have been.

Bob was on the edge of the bed with his pants around his ankles, getting a blow job from a groupie. She couldn't have been more than eighteen. In the light and the moment, Bob looked downright middle-aged. Joe and I had an honest reaction, which is not to say it was an ideal one. We laughed our asses off. 'Bob Quine' and 'blow job' were not phrases we thought we would ever use in the same sentence. The whole thing looked more like an experiment than a sexual act.

The more we laughed, the more the girl screamed, ending the blow job not just for the night but for the tour and for all time. Bob's reaction was to throw anything he could find – shoes, socks, keys, loose change – at us. We were lucky he didn't play his Strat while getting blown.

We played the final night of the tour on 15 November at the Music Machine in London. The building, a three-story Victorian constructed at the turn of the century, was at one time called the Hippodrome. It had a long and great history of English entertainment and now we were part of it. Johnny Rotten of the Sex Pistols was in the audience and made a play for some hometown applause by jumping up onstage with us to sing a cover of the Stones' 'Ventilator Blues'. The plodding, growling R&B number was right up his alley. But Johnny was like the guys in the Clash: well studied in the art of being pissed off in public but very well-mannered in private.

The London crowd loved it. We did an encore and the spitting started. Even Bob took it. What were we going to do? We had a good thing going. We just needed to get home, get some sleep, and get some airplay.

Blank Generation was released in late November 1977. The first time I heard the title track on WNEW-FM 102.7, it was sandwiched between 'Cold as Ice' by Foreigner and 'More Than a Feeling' by Boston. It sounded like a bunch of punks had broken in and taken over the station, then got busted. Or maybe Scott Muni's spike-haired nephew was hanging out in the studio and pulled a little prank.

Or maybe the program directors were reading the reviews. *Record World* called it 'the future of American rock', adding, '"Blank Generation" serves as the anthem of new wave on both sides of the Atlantic.' A poster advertising a show at the Village Gate called the song '. . . a unifying lifeline for a scene that has been divided and disrupted much too often'.

The album cover was a photo of a vacantly gazing Richard whipping open his black sport jacket, exposing his bare and fairly ripped chest. Written across his pecs in black ink were the words: 'YOU MAKE ME _____'. As a dedicated drummer, I made him responsible. Definitely not all by myself, but I helped. With his heroin habit, Richard made me uneasy. He made me guess. He made me wonder.

When I got back to the States, I moved in with Fred, who had a spare bedroom in his apartment on Ocean Avenue in Brooklyn. It was just a couple of blocks from the basement apartment I once shared with Bruce. After a few weeks, Fred did the same thing Bruce did: moved out to live with his girlfriend. Maybe I had that effect on people. Suddenly, I had two very important things to think about that I never expected to have to think about at the same time: what was next for our influential major label act and where my next meal was coming from.

There was no money left and no money coming in. The album was loved but not in heavy rotation. We were young legends in New York and London but barely known beyond. Punk itself hadn't taken hold outside these two hip cities and maybe a half-dozen others. Still, we could have patched together a tour. I was ready to go back on the road and needed the money. Richard, on the other hand, wasn't going anywhere. His focus was on writing songs for another album. I wasn't the only person around him who tried to explain reality – without serious touring to promote the first album, there might never be a second one.

Richard reasoned it all out like some rambling character from a Jack Kerouac novel, but we knew the unspoken truth. The road made him dope-sick. Copping in Westminster Abbey was a bitch, but copping in New York was like taking a drink at a water fountain. So we rehearsed at some rundown Canal Street loft owned by a friend of Richard's. He was a junkie, too. We were moving backwards and not even in a straight line.

The food Fred had left behind in the cupboards was almost gone. But I had my resources. I didn't go back to stealing bread and milk at dawn from bodegas. Whenever friends dropped by the apartment, I would tell them to bring something. And a bottle of wine with it. I would drop by Marion's family's apartment, where she still lived. That was a meal here, a meal there. The candy store two blocks away was still owned and operated by the holocaust survivors who still made me a free cherry phosphate in return for a favor someone else had done.

I had a friend in the neighborhood named Richie. His father had just passed away, and his mother was lonely. Richie's older brother had moved out. So there was an empty chair or two, and I fitted into one of them. Richie's mother would cook for us at least once a week. She was a wonderful Jewish lady who made amazing chicken soup and latkes. She smoked Pall Malls like a four-alarm fire at a cigarette factory. I had great stories from the road, and I made her laugh. I couldn't thank her enough. And I couldn't eat enough.

Another friend, Steven, the lead singer of the Uncles, lived upstairs from me. He and I went way back, to Ditmas Junior High. Like everyone else, it seemed, he was moving, but his new landlord wouldn't let him bring his dog. So he was finding a new home for the dog and leaving the dog food behind. I told Steven I would take it, and he asked what for – I didn't have a dog. I told him I was going to eat it, and he thought I was absolutely full of shit.

It was a brand called Iams – health food for dogs and cats and pet owners who liked to kid themselves. But as I dumped a few ounces into an old charred black frying pan, I had to admit it looked better than your average crap. There was no cooking oil left, so I used butter. I had no food in the house but plenty of condiments – salt, pepper, oregano, pickles. I stirred it all in and kept one simple thought in mind: I wasn't going to bed hungry. It wasn't that bad.

It wasn't that good, either. No matter what I had masked it with, it definitely wasn't for human beings. But it was dinner, something millions of people didn't have, even with Christmas coming.

A few days into the New Year, I had a resolution and all my unpaid bills in my hand as I walked through the door of Richard's apartment for a band meeting. There were roach clips and empty bags of smack on the board over the kitchen bathtub, but what pissed me off a little was the new bass guitar and amp I spotted. With Bob and Ivan sitting in the kitchen, I turned to Richard, put the stack of unpaid bills on the board over the tub, and said, 'Are you gonna pay these, or what?'

'No,' he said. 'That's your business.'

'Richard, you gotta come through for me here.'

'Look,' he said, 'I'd love to. But first Sire has to come through for *me*.'

'How exactly is that going to happen?' Bob said. 'You're suing them. Remember?'

'Well that's my fucking point!' Richard said.

'Richard,' Bob said, 'why don't you stop copping for a day and help Marc? He's the fucking backbone of this unit.'

I could see the torment in Bob's eyes. The Valium wasn't going to help much. If you were lucky as a musician, there was always one other member of the band who totally appreciated your playing, right down to the beats you *didn't* play. For me, that person was Bob. And there was nothing he could do.

'Sorry,' Richard said. 'Sorry.' He stared in my general direction – blankly.

'Well,' I said, 'fuck this.'

I slammed the door behind me. As I walked westward on a cold, bleak East Tenth Street, the different versions of why I was doing what I had just done took turns in my head. Each version came with a justification, and each justification came with its own anger. But only one version, one justification, and one kind of anger stuck. I knew as full of himself as he sometimes was, Richard didn't realize the talent he really had or how close we were to going over the top. The truth was, he could barely manage his own life. The drugs were supposed to hide the truth, but they just made it worse.

8

Every time I ran into Dee Dee at CBGB in the winter of 1978, he told me I ought to join the Ramones. As if you could just do that, like joining the Y or the ACLU. He said the band were having trouble with Tommy, their drummer, and I was actually a little upset to hear that. I didn't want the original line-up of the Ramones to break up. *I was a fan.* But I didn't put much stock in what Dee Dee said. He was a nut and known to exaggerate.

It takes a nut to be involved with two psychotic women at once. About a year before, he was living in an apartment with Connie, a violent stalker, prostitute, and drug addict. Dee Dee was also having a fling with Nancy Spungen, the schizophrenic girlfriend of the Sex Pistols bassist Sid Vicious. When she came home to find Dee Dee in bed with Nancy, Connie grabbed an empty beer bottle, smashed it, and stabbed Dee Dee in the ass with the jagged edge.

But, when Johnny Ramone asked to meet with me about joining the band, the whole proposition turned real. I arrived at Max's with Marion, and we took seats across from John and Roxy in a booth up front. I was impressed with John. He seemed to have a handle on the

Ramones' business matters and a vision of how to get the band through this difficult transition. Joey wasn't exactly up to it, and Dee Dee would have sent the whole thing into the toilet.

John laid down some rules. Maybe they were more like guidelines. Whatever they were, the Ramones didn't get high before playing. *Me neither.* Dress on and off the stage was leather jackets, jeans, and sneakers. *I was already wearing all that and had been for ever.* Dee Dee always counts off the songs. *Definitely. I know.* We don't go away on tour for more than a month. *Sounds good.* We travel together, and girlfriends are welcome. Marion can come. *Thanks.*

The only confusing thing was the audition. There would be one at the Ramones' rehearsal studio. But John discussed the rules and regs as though my being a Ramone was already a done deal. Then I thought, *Whatever they call it, I'll blow it away.*

On our way out of Max's, Marion and I put our heads together. We had heard through the grapevine that the Ramones already auditioned several drummers, maybe more. Marion's take was the Ramones knew from the start that I had the experience they needed, but in the back of their minds they preferred a nobody they could boss around. It was hard to get all that in the same package, so over time they realized I was their man.

From what I had heard, Dee Dee wasn't the only one rooting for me. Tommy was, too. In fact, Tommy was the one who first suggested me. Beyond whatever had happened between him and the other Ramones, Tommy still loved the band and wanted it to continue. What better way to do it than with an experienced professional drummer who knew the ropes?

When I walked into Performance Studios on East Twentieth Street in Manhattan and sat down, Tommy was sitting at a drum set behind the set I would be using. It was an unusual way to run an audition, a show, or anything musical unless maybe you were in the Grateful Dead. I asked him what all this was about.

'Don't worry about it,' Tommy said. 'Just in case you need a little help.'

'Thanks,' I said. 'I got it.'

I shot Tommy a little smile. I really did have it. The songs 'I Don't Care', 'Sheena Is a Punk Rocker', and 'Blitzkrieg Bop' were on the jukebox at CBGB, on my stereo, and in my world. I had listened to them again before coming down, and that was enough. It wasn't like learning 'From a Dry Camel'. But they were great songs, and I was like Sheena and her friends – all hopped up and ready to go. Even so, I appreciated Tommy's concern. He literally had my back.

Dee Dee counted, 'One, two, three, four!' and we launched into 'I Don't Care'. It was one of the purest rock-and-roll songs written after the year 1962. With a deliberate, powerful beat underpinning a progression based on E, F, G, A, it was a song a novice could learn on but never tire of playing: not caring about the world or the girl was the entire message served up in two lines, repeated over and over like a punk mantra.

The song clocked in at a minute forty seconds. We were locked in as a band within the first ten of those seconds. Thirty seconds in, the audition – if there ever was one – was over. We were relaxed and smiling. Rehearsal had begun.

I had my work cut out for me. Recording for the new album, *Road to Ruin*, was set to begin in less than three weeks. We'd be doing shows immediately after. We were scheduled to do fourteen songs for the album, and the Ramones' live set was twenty-four songs. So I had almost forty songs to learn, minus the three for the audition, in about the length of a honeymoon. The Ramones handed me a pair of cassette demo tapes with all the songs. I stopped in at Sam Ash on Forty-Eighth Street and picked up a set of drum pads. When I got back to the apartment on Ocean Avenue, I hooked up a pair of headphones to the boom box I had gotten with the Voidoids advance. Right next to it, I set up the pads. And that's where I spent most of the next eighteen days.

My favorite song on the *Road to Ruin* demo was 'I Wanna Be Sedated'. It was catchy and huge even in stripped-down form on a cheap cassette tape. It was pop but without sacrificing hardness. Lyrically, being sedated could mean any number of things, but at its simplest level it was about needing a drink. The song captured being on the road just about perfectly. Of course, I had never been on the road with the Ramones, but I would be finding out what that was like soon enough.

I also really liked 'I Just Want to Have Something to Do' and 'Go Mental'. 'Mental' was faster than most Ramones songs – and faster than most songs, period. It felt like what it was about: sitting in a hospital bed and losing your mind. The album's one cover song, 'Needles and Pins', was written by Jack Nitzsche and Sonny Bono back in 1963. The original single was done by Jackie DeShannon, but the Searchers had more success with it the following year, giving it an early-Beatles feel. The chord changes and subject matter – heartbreak and holding back tears – were right up the Ramones' alley.

We recorded at Media Sound in Manhattan. I was prepared, but everyone there totally expected that of me. I understood my role from the get-go. I was not a ringer, mercenary, hired gun, or session player. I was a member of the band who could nonetheless deliver what a ringer, mercenary, hired gun, or session player could deliver. But I wanted to take it a step further. I wanted to help take the band's sound to the next level.

There was a lot of heavy competition out there. Not so much from the punk bands. I considered the Ramones the originators of punk, so in that sense there was no one to compete with. But the Ramones were a punk-rock band with the emphasis on *rock*. In rock, there were a lot of big boys with heavy drums: AC/DC, Black Sabbath, Aerosmith, and Van Halen. Van Halen were the new kids on the block, and someone the Ramones might not even have considered. Yet their self-titled album had just come out and it was worth considering.

Van Halen stood out from the corporate rock clones being churned out monthly by the music industry. Eddie Van Halen loved Page, Beck, and Clapton but squeezed his influences out of his black-and-white-striped red Charvel with a new, wild hammer-on style of playing that was melodic, smooth, and raucous all at the same time. Alex Van Halen's drums were huge, sounded huge, and were locked in perfectly with his brother's playing as well as bassist Michael Anthony's. The band didn't take itself very seriously. They were kind of campy, thanks especially to lead singer David Lee Roth, who brought his Las Vegas A-game to the show. The album was a fun listen and made me think.

The idea for *Road to Ruin*, I thought, was not to be Van Halen or anyone else. The idea was to be a heavier Ramones. We had our fans and would keep aiming to please them. And we had our punk/new wave competition – the Clash, the Police, the Cars. But there was no harm in letting the metalheads and all their cousins know that the Ramones could rock a stadium if they needed to.

To begin with, I tuned my snare a lot tighter than Tommy's and used larger cymbals. I wanted to get more projection and impact from the sound. There were a bunch of other factors involving microphone placement, levels, and even the way I struck the kit that would give the songs a bolder, more muscular feel. The beauty of the situation was that I had a great producer who worked closely with me to get that sound: Tommy. He hadn't just passed me a golden baton. He was clearing the track for me. Tommy was there alongside me every step of the way.

The very first song we tracked was 'Sedated'. I speeded up the tempo a bit from the demo. The song itself didn't feel right sedated. It had to be manic and *in need* of sedation. I added a few fills here and there that helped distinguish the parts, plus a critical fill in the break. It sounded nice when we did it. Then it jumped out of the monitors and had all of us smiling.

During recording, I noticed Joey had a funny habit. He would touch a spot somewhere – the mixing console, a chair, a microphone stand – and then touch it again. And again. And again. It didn't matter. His vocals were great, and he didn't need to do them again and again and again. It was just a little weird.

I got to meet and talk to the full Ramones entourage, including Seymour Stein of Sire Records. Seymour was already my boss from the Voidoids, but he especially loved the Ramones. He appreciated the way they took the chord changes and vocal approach of the doo-wop era and spit it back out as their own – harder, faster, and a little warped. Seymour was knowledgeable, easygoing, and quiet.

His wife made up for the quiet part. Linda Stein was a short, loud, opinionated, outgoing quintessential New Yorker. She started out as a schoolteacher – probably one you would never want to be caught throwing a spitball at. She learned the music business from her husband, and the Ramones were lucky to have her managing *their* business.

Danny Fields was the other half of the Ramones management team. Danny had started out doing publicity for the Doors and later was instrumental in signing the Stooges and MC5 to Elektra. In 1975, he brought the Ramones to the attention of Sire. Danny was the hands-on manager for the group, plying connections at rock magazines, booking venues, getting the band radio interviews. Together, the Steins and Danny Fields spearheaded a professional organization behind what looked like four punks in street clothes.

It was this professional team that asked me about changing my name. I was off to a good start, but we weren't going to be Marc Bell and the Ramones. My new last name was a done deal, but I needed a first name that ended in a long-*e* sound. Rocky Ramone was either too suggestive of the Sylvester Stallone movie or made me sound like a gangster. Timmy, Jimmy, and Willie Ramone and a dozen others made me puke. And just adding a *y* to Marc came out as Marcy, which was not only a girl's name but happened to be the name of the discount store Marcy's, across the street from Erasmus High School. The fewer reminders of high school, the better.

So I said, 'Let's go with Marky, with a *k*.' My grandmother called me Marky as a kid, and the name was made famous by Marky Maypo. In the fifties and sixties, Maypo was one of the big three hot cereals, along with Farina and Wheatena. Mickey Mantle was a pitchman for Maypo, literally crying if he didn't get a bowl of the stuff. Marky Maypo was the goofy, whinny, cartoon mascot wearing a cowboy hat. For the sake of nostalgia, I could live with that. So Marky, like the cereal, stuck.

There was no need to change my name legally. My bills would still come to Marc Bell. And so would my paychecks. The Ramones team let me know that I would be receiving a nice check every week, on time, from our accountant Ira Herzog. The check would come whether we were on the road or off. When we toured, there would be extra *per diem* payments based on the shows we did. This was all a load off my mind and off Marion's. Moving into Manhattan was on the horizon.

Rehearsals for live shows were mostly just Johnny, Dee Dee, and me. Joey showed up a couple of times. Joey had health problems, and the band thought it was better to save his energy for the shows. There was a hidden advantage to doing things this way. Although Dee Dee would sing where necessary, we weren't using the vocals as a crutch to know where we were in the song. When a band used that crutch, there was sometimes a bit of uncertainty and a slight wavering when a change came in. This way, with no one to lean on but ourselves, there was no choice but to become a well-oiled machine.

After rehearsal one day, I learned a little more about why Tommy pushed the eject button. In the beginning, he was the manager and, in that sense, an authority figure. When the real management team were brought in, Tommy was reduced to just a member of the band, and the other three Ramones seemed to rub salt in the wound. Tommy was an unimposing guy, and they taunted him – maybe good-naturedly, but it didn't feel that way to him. Also, there was a fair amount of bickering among the other band members, and what seems kind of funny at first gets really old when you're on the road for weeks on end.

The last straw was more like a last cigarette. John was the bully of the group. His bark was usually worse than his bite, but still, John laid down rules of the road. One of them was no smoking cigarettes in the van, which was a problem for Tommy, who smoked. But, on a trip to Chicago, John took a plane out early to be with Roxy, who was visiting home in the Windy City. Tommy was relieved to be able to smoke on the long ride west in the van, but what he didn't count on was Dee Dee and Joey taking mushrooms as they pulled out of New York. The two of them were hallucinating heavily for a few hundred miles on Route 80. While Dee Dee was counting pink elephants, and Joey was counting clouds shaped like Superman, Tommy was counting the days till he got out.

Tommy impressed me. He had barely ever picked up a pair of sticks before joining the Ramones but gave them what they needed. He helped create a blueprint for three successful albums, hundreds of performances, and, most important, a new sound. He laid down a foundation, and I was grateful for the opportunity to build on it.

On 29 June, the Ramones' fifteen-passenger Ford Econoline van picked us up around noon in front of artist Arturo Vega's loft on East Second Street in Manhattan, where Joey was living. We were headed to Poughkeepsie, New York, for my first gig with the band. John was very insistent that Marion and I sit in the second row. John and Roxy sat in the first row behind Monte Melnick, the driver and road manager. Dee Dee sat behind us, and Joey sat in the very back.

It was a nice way to break in, because the trip up the Taconic State Parkway to Poughkeepsie was only about an hour and forty minutes, barring traffic. Still, between tokes on a joint, Dee Dee kept asking if we were there yet. John was speechifying on how Nixon never should have had to resign four years earlier. Joey was in the back quietly twiddling his long hair.

The Chance was a theater in downtown Poughkeepsie built in the early part of the century. It was empty and full of ghosts when we did our four-song sound check. It held about a thousand people and had a very historic feel. There was no concrete anywhere. The floorboards were oak. The seats were also wood and probably hand-carved. The mezzanine had decorative façade work. The place looked as if it belonged more in the old South than upstate New York.

Before the show, Danny Fields came by to take a photo for the back cover of *Road to Ruin*. The four of us sat on the stoop at the rear exit. Dee Dee and Johnny sat on the lower step at opposite ends. Joey and I sat in the middle on the upper step. Joey's long, skinny legs reached all the way down to the brick pavement with length to spare.

It was 'Hey Ho, Let's Go!' from the first song. The theater was packed to the point where I looked around for the fire exits just in case. The kids screamed and jumped. Our sound was upbeat, loud, and heavy, and the set started to fly by. There were no mistakes halfway in, and I knew there wouldn't be the rest of the way through. When there was even a hint of drifting off the beat or missing a change, I would look at John, or he would look at me. Upon eye contact, I knew what he was doing, and he knew what I was doing. Mistakes were never allowed to develop. We weren't on automatic pilot, but it sounded that way.

The history in the room was personal now. It was my initiation. I wasn't nervous, because I learned early on that it was only about doing what you had to do. At the same time, I became aware of the pressure only because it was gradually disappearing. There was a series of firsts for me: the so-called audition, the first rehearsal, the first recording. But the first live show was the biggest. If that didn't work, what was the point of all the other firsts?

Backstage after the show, Joey, Dee Dee, John, Marion, Roxy, Monte, Danny Fields, Linda Stein, and everyone who made the transition a reality were on the same page as me. There was a sense of security in knowing that the machine known as the Ramones could continue. Dee Dee was the first to come up to me and pat me on the back.

'It was great playing with you,' he said. 'You're my bunny now.'

'Thanks. Thanks a lot.' I really appreciated that.

The set wasn't the most complex music I had ever played live, but it was maybe the most demanding in its sheer energy. It was not a marathon. It was more like a very long sprint. I was drenched in sweat. So was the rest of the band. When I walked into the dressing room, Joey had already begun changing and had his shirt off. He had a big nasty scar on his back that looked like an upside-down letter *V*.

'Hey, how'd you get that?' I said.

'Shark bite,' Joey said.

Sharks were on people's minds with the movie *Jaws* cleaning up at the box office three summers earlier and then again with the sequel that had just come out. But Joey was the last person on earth I figured for a shark-bite victim. First of all, you had to go swimming fairly far out in the ocean. Joey had spent time in the hospital on more than one occasion for a variety of anxiety disorders. A hospital room is where he wrote the lyrics to the forthcoming song 'Go Mental' on *Road to Ruin*.

So I didn't picture him at six-foot-six, 190 pounds, in a Speedo, swimming out past the buoys at Rockaway Beach as the lifeguards blew their whistles and gave chase. On the outside chance that he ever managed to pull that off, the odds of his swimming back safely to shore with blood gushing from his torso seemed even closer to zero.

John explained to me a little later that Joey was born with a parasitic twin. It was a malformed Siamese twin growing out of his back. The twin was incomplete, a threat to the life of the newborn, and so it was surgically removed. I could understand why he used the shark story.

When we piled into the tan Econoline for the ride back to New York, Marion and I were about to climb into the front row when John stopped us and explained that we all had assigned seats and had to stick with them. I asked why, and he said that's the way the Ramones had done it for years. So we climbed into the second row.

John continued his pro-Nixon harangue on the ride back.

'The thing is, the liberals were out to get him from the fucking beginning. Watergate was bullshit. The whole thing should never have happened.'

I didn't really mind having to sit with Marion in assigned seats, but there was only so much I could take.

'You know what?' I said. 'The whole thing *did* happen because Nixon ordered it and then covered it up. He doesn't have anyone to blame but himself. He was the president, and he fucked up. And he resigned because he knew he was wrong.'

'Bullshit!' John said. 'Do you think a tiny, insignificant fucking security break would have meant shit without the liberal press looking to screw him?'

'If it was so insignificant, why did he bother covering it up?'

'Because he knew they had it in for him.'

'Why do it in the first place?'

It was surprising to see a rock musician, or any musician, for that matter, defend Richard Nixon, but that seemed to be as much a part of John as the scar on Joey's back was a part of him.

The summer was a blur. We did two dozen shows scattered across the East Coast and the Midwest. Bands usually liked to settle in, especially when playing multiple dates in a city or in quick succession in cities close by. That was not happening with the Ramones. Not if they could help it. They were homebodies. They liked their own pillows, their own mattresses, and their own leftovers in the fridge. If it was possible to make it back to New York City by dawn, we were there.

Destinations such as New Brunswick, New Jersey; Greenwood Lake, New York; and, of course, Poughkeepsie, were no-brainers. They were truly local. But it seemed neurotic to play Boston three nights in a row with a 450-mile round trip on I-95 in between two of the three shows. There were a lot of Holiday Inns with empty beds along the way. It wasn't like stumbling back from Max's through Union Square Park.

But there was also a practical side to taking the redeye van back to New York. The Ramones were running a business. The pitfalls of the road were too many to list. Countless bands convinced themselves they were having fun and supporting an album, but when the album didn't produce royalties and the shows didn't produce take-home pay, the fun quickly disappeared.

The Ramones' solution was to economize. Why travel in a huge gas-guzzling luxury bus when a van will do? Why pay for a bunch of hotel rooms you didn't need? All the money you saved one week was money in the band's pocket the next.

Besides, not much sleeping went on in hotel rooms. When we got off the stage at, say, midnight, we were buzzed on adrenaline. There was not going to be any sleep happening for three or four hours, anyway.

Being in a van at all hours of the night gave me a chance to learn a lot more about John than when he dropped by the apartment in SoHo to pick up Roxy. His dad was a blue-collar guy. John's parents sent him to military school for a few years, which explained his routine in the dressing room. A normal rock musician would leave his street clothes anywhere. Let alone a punk musician. John would fold his pants and shirt neatly, perfectly. He lined up the seams of the pants symmetrically. The shirts were folded as if to be ready for reshelving. He could have worked at the Gap.

John was about four years older than I. After he graduated from

Forest Hills High School, his father got him work as a pipe fitter. One of his jobs was working on the World Trade Center, which in the late sixties was slowly forming a shadow above Lower Manhattan. The centerpiece was the Twin Towers, a pair of office buildings destined to rise 110 stories and with pumps so large they were normally used to supply water to cities of a half million people. But even with hundreds of miles of pipes to fit, there were occasional distractions.

One afternoon while the Vietnam War was raging, a large group of young protesters showed up at the site. A bunch of the union guys on the ground confronted them, and it quickly became a classic hard-hat-versus-hippie battle complete with name calling, shoving, and hair pulling. Up on the eleventh floor of Tower 1, young John Cummings was taking a break from welding the joints of ten-inch-diameter cast-iron soil stacks and looked out the window. Most of the hippie freaks were assembled together. John had a clear shot. He took small bags of sand and started tossing them out of the window. They were not lethal, but they stunned on impact and made little clouds when they broke. The hippie freaks scattered. It wasn't napalm, but it made a statement.

'What do you fucking mean how could I do that? These hippie assholes have such a good deal in America, and they don't even appreciate it.'

'Appreciate what?'

'What the guys fighting in Vietnam did for them.'

'What did they do for them?'

'Protected their freedom.'

'Their freedom to have sandbags thrown at them?'

'Hey, fuck 'em.'

John probably didn't realize those same hippies fought for his right to wear long hair one day. And somebody somewhere fought for his right to play in a rock band.

All these rides back and forth to New England and elsewhere, day in day out, seemed efficient, on one hand. But, on the other, they invited delays. Waiting for Joey to emerge from Arturo's building was a show in itself. We couldn't leave the motor of the Econoline running unless we wanted to fill the tank a second time before leaving the five boroughs.

We would try to buzz Joey down, but after about five minutes, Monte would go upstairs and help him get dressed. Meanwhile, Dee Dee continued smoking pot in the van. There was an oil crisis going on, but no marijuana crisis other than paraquat.

Once he was done tapping the door saddle in the bathroom, Joey would step in and out of the door to the loft thirty, maybe forty times. Once that was done, he would walk down the one flight of stairs. Then back up. Then down. Then back up again. This would go on ten or twenty times before Joey finally came out of the building. We were lucky he didn't live on the ninetieth floor of the World Trade Center.

Once we hit Youngstown, Ohio, we were out of range for even the most extreme Ramones definition of local. Driving across Pennsylvania alone was three hundred miles, and we had Lansing and Flint, Michigan, next. It was a long ride out to Ohio, and John made sure we were still in the same seats from Poughkeepsie. He also made sure we knew the only reason John F. Kennedy was ever elected president was his good looks.

Monte booked our rooms ahead of time, and not long after we got to Youngstown, I found out why. Dee Dee, John, Monte, and I would all get rooms on the same floor, while Joey would get a room on a different floor. When I checked out his room on the fourth floor, Joey was opening and closing the door again and again. Just like home. The band preferred getting some sleep to hearing their lead singer come and go nowhere all night. Hopefully, Joey's new next-door neighbors were insomniacs.

Mornings were fairly normal. We would get up in time to check out, get some coffee and breakfast downstairs, and meet in the lobby. If Joey wasn't there on time, we usually sent Monte up to his room to escort him down. Joey not only had trouble getting out of his room: he had trouble getting out of the shower. It wasn't easy for him to get in in the first place. At six foot six, he was too tall for the shower nozzles, so he had to squeeze underneath to wash his hair, taking care not to smash his head against the plumbing. Getting out of the shower wasn't much easier. And then the excruciating repetition began: getting in and out a dozen more times. Sometimes Monte had Joey skip the shower altogether just to avoid triggering his compulsion to repeat the showering process umpteen more times.

Dee Dee had no problem getting in and out of the shower or the tub. He would take four or five baths or showers a day. It was not easy to cram in all that bathing activity, but he managed: a bath when we checked into the hotel; go do the sound check; come back and take a shower; another bath before the show; a shower after. Then there was the bedtime bubble bath. All the way across the Keystone state, Dee Dee talked about the luxurious bubble bath he was going to prepare that night. Passing steel mills, cement plants, and coal mines, Dee Dee never lost focus on his big date with Mr. Bubble.

Dee Dee was not only super-clean, he was super-shaved. He liked to shave the hair thoroughly off his chest and arms, and, when that was done, pluck out the stray hairs with a tweezers. You never knew if he was getting ready for a rock show or a walk down the runway.

Dee Dee was revolted by the smell of Joey. Dee Dee would freak out sometimes when he got a whiff. He would complain to Monte that he needed to wash Joey's clothes and get him some cologne. If only Dee Dee could have taken a shower for Joey, they could have solved the Ramones' entire hygiene problem.

Joey was cool onstage. I thought that when I watched the Ramones at CBGB early on and I thought that now from behind my drum kit. He stood in one place the entire set, clutching the microphone stand. John, meanwhile, moved around like a spinning top, bending his knees a little and stroking his guitar rapid-fire like an AK-47. Dee Dee was bouncing all over the place. But Joey's position looked like someone taking a stand. Like James Dean. He had something to say and wasn't going to budge. He was going to protect his turf.

The truth was, Joey was frightened to leave his turf. Once he found his spot onstage, he was afraid to vacate it, like a shower or an apartment. We were just glad he didn't turn the microphone on and off seventy times.

Our trip across the heartland of America was filled with racism, but not from Midwesterners. It was from John. We saw blacks, Puerto

Ricans, and Asians. Johnny saw spades, spics, and chinks. Somewhere between Columbus and Cincinnati, we learned that spades were too lazy to put out a fire in their own bedroom. Somewhere between Madison and DeKalb, we discovered that spics were too crazy about roaches to kill them. Somewhere between Kansas City and Springfield, we found out that every accident between Kansas City and Springfield was caused by a Chinaman carrying around a phony learner's permit. John was rock and roll's Archie Bunker.

We really didn't know if John was an out-and-out racist or if he was doing it to get a rise out of us. Probably a combination. He didn't draw the line at anti-Semitism. Even riding cross-country in a van with a Jewish lead singer and road manager. Johnny called Joey and Monte rabbis. The things Johnny did to save money were smart. The things the rabbis did to save money were 'cheap'. Johnny was so over the top and in their faces with this shtick that Joey and Monte didn't have much choice but to roll with it. And if it wasn't simply anti-Semitism, it was masking other emotions that weren't all that great either.

We could drive halfway across a state – or a time zone – without John looking at Joey. There was usually no conversation or eye contact. You could explain it away by saying they were just oil and vinegar. That John was the jock and Joey was the shy, sensitive poet of the band. But I got the sense that there was more to it than that.

With every hotel we could barely check out of because of Joey's tapping, touching, and endless in-and-out routine, we were all obviously aware that he had problems. John, however, seemed disgusted with those problems and with Joey himself. And to a degree, that attitude colored John's comments and the ride. When you're all great friends, ethnic slurs don't cut the same way, even when it's your ethnic group. But calling Joey a rabbi when it's a rabbi you won't even look at or talk to is no longer a sign of affection – especially when that guy is alone in the back of the bus. The rift grated on me. I wanted everybody to get along.

So while John was at the front of the van telling Monte the Yankees were going to come all the way back from fourteen games behind the

Red Sox, I was turning around and talking to Joey, not just to make him feel better but because I enjoyed it. We talked about which songs sounded great or not so great from the night before and maybe switching the order. About Blondie, the Cramps, the Sex Pistols, and Cheap Trick – one of Joey's favorites. About a pretty girl in the audience. It kept our wheels rolling and was better than letting Joey count the number of stitches in the seat of the van.

At the same time, I had to give John credit. He went about things in a professional way, for the most part. He had quit shooting dope years earlier. There was no rehab as far as I knew. He just understood he was going down the road to ruin, which is fine as an album title but not where you wanted to be as you pushed thirty and had a chance to make your dreams a reality.

For most people in entertainment, being in a movie was one of those dreams, even if it was a B movie on a shoestring budget. We were back in New York 11–13 August to showcase the band for the director of a movie called *Rock 'n' Roll High School*. Linda Stein and Danny Fields had been talking to a young guy named Allan Arkush, who directed independent teen-oriented comedies for the producer Roger Corman.

There had been talk about calling the movie *Disco High*, but, even with the countless millions made the year before by *Saturday Night Fever* with John Travolta, a lot of people both in show business and out were over it. Someone in A&R at Warner, which distributed the Ramones for Sire, told Arkush he should check out the Ramones. So he did.

Arkush flew in from California, and Danny and Linda slapped us on the bill at Hurrah. Located on West Sixty-Second Street not far from Columbus Circle, Hurrah was not a typical venue for the Ramones. Aside from being in Midtown, the club was more of a new-wave place and had television monitors all over the club showing music videos. We were on a bill with the avant-garde European singer Klaus Nomi and Lance Loud. Lance became louder than life in 1973 when he came out to his parents on the pioneer reality series *An American Family*.

Arkush was a good guy. He was a little surprised to see us rehearse a few of the songs unplugged before the show, but that's what worked for us. Tina Weymouth, the bassist from Talking Heads, was there, and so was Lester Bangs. Bangs was shooting the shit with Tina and being his usual no-holds-barred self, and Arkush seemed to be in awe, taking notes like he was a student in the New York campus of a Rock 'n' Roll high school.

I didn't think Bangs had gotten a listen yet to *Road to Ruin*, but I hoped he liked it half as much as he liked my last band. Bangs had written, 'The first real-deal punk-jazz mix I heard around this town came from the recently disbanded Richard Hell and the Voidoids, and mainly from their lead guitarist Robert Quine.'

The unplugged rehearsal must have worked, because Arkush loved the show. We all went to CBGB afterward and then to Arturo Vega's loft around the corner. Arturo did the lights and sold Ramones merchandise before and after every show.

There was a big buzz in advance of the movie *Animal House*, about a bad-boy frat house battling the asshole preppy frat on campus. The movie starred John Belushi of TV's *Saturday Night Live* and stood to rake it in at the box office. Allan Arkush was looking to capture some of that lightning in a small bottle. He told us he needed a band that had a defining look and sound that kids in this fictional high school could identify with. The plot involved one girl's love for a band and her attempt to get them to listen to a song she's written for them. When the band finally rocks the school, the conflict with the prudish principal escalates to the point where the police come in and the building is blown up. John heard this and said, 'So, we gonna make this movie or what?'

In September, *Animal House* debuted in movie theaters across the country, and people lined up around the block. *Road to Ruin* came out, too, opening at 103 on the *Billboard* 200. Not as strong out of the gate as the previous album, *Rocket to Russia*, but the reviews were promising. Writing for *Rolling Stone*, Robert Christgau said, 'Like any great group, this one is always topping itself . . . "I Wanted Everything," "I'm Against It," and "She's the One" are as good as any they've ever done.'

I thought the cartoon by John Holmstrom on the cover, showing the four of us with leather jackets and very blue blue jeans against a backdrop of amps, drums, and a gritty city skyline, was good. But Joey and Dee Dee didn't like it. They objected to being depicted as cartoon characters because they thought it suggested the band itself was a cartoon. They complained the drawing was amateurish. But there was no reason to argue about it. The cover, like the album, was a done deal. The album was going over big in Europe, and we were booked for a twenty-two-city tour of the Continent.

9

A LONG WAY BACK TO GERMANY

Joey counted squares on the flight over to Helsinki, Finland. The fabric on the back of the seat in front of him was patterned in squares, and while most of us read a magazine or tried to get a little sleep, Joey had to know the number of squares. Then check it. Then check it again.

The trip out to JFK Airport was, in some ways, like the start of any Ramones tour, whether one show or a dozen. Monte called Joey around eleven in the morning and told him it was already one in the afternoon and he'd better get his ass moving or we were going to be late. This was standard operating procedure. If Joey could tap everything in the loft with a sense of extreme urgency, we might only be forty-five minutes late instead of an hour and a half.

Monte's time upstairs getting Joey ready was a pain in the ass for most of us but a window of opportunity for Dee Dee. Once the van was parked, Dee Dee had time to walk a few blocks to Ninth Street and Third Avenue to cop. The dealers stood on the sidewalk in plain view.

A tour bus met us in Helsinki. It was 5 September. Around two in the morning, there was a glow in the eastern sky otherwise known as sunrise. Joey almost needed the sunglasses he always wore. The latitude was about 60 degrees north, and, even though we were more than a month past the summer solstice, there wasn't much darkness at any hour. The air was a little cool and very crisp. We were about as out of New York as you could be. I felt energized, but it was time to go to sleep.

In the early afternoon, we drove around Helsinki, which is a sparkling flat town of both modernistic concrete buildings and four-hundred-year-old log houses. We picked a restaurant, and I was the only Ramone not complaining about the food. I loved exotic food, especially if it was well prepared. I loved to cook whenever I had the chance. So I ordered some of the standard things on the Finnish menu – cabbage rolls, smoked fish, and mushroom soup – and I dived right in. Dee Dee had at least half a clue, having spent most of his childhood in Germany. John called the cuisine weird Nordic crap. Joey just stared and nibbled on a meatball. 'Hey,' John said. 'Do they have a McDonald's in this town, or what?'

If the Finnish kids were any indication, we were headed for a great tour. Helsinki punks spoke better English than some of the New York punks and hung around the hotel. Just outside, two spike-haired guys in their late teens pulled off their leather jackets and asked Dee Dee and me to autograph their arms. They wanted the autographs large and clear and explained that by the end of the day the signatures would become permanent tattoos. As we signed, more kids came over, including young women with features too good for a mosh pit. We signed albums, T-shirts, more arms, and a few breasts, and would have done it till the sun went down, which wasn't till about ten.

The venue held about two thousand people and was packed. I felt the same boost in energy as during the Voidoids' visit to the UK a year earlier, only double. It was ridiculous how many Ramones songs these kids knew the lyrics to. It wasn't just the first three albums. They knew 'Sedated', 'Something to Do', and 'I'm Against It'. These songs had been out all of a few days. Like the kids outside the hotel told Dee Dee and me, they were starved for a new Ramones album and now they had one. They were glad we were still doing what we were doing and not watering it down or going disco like a lot of other bands.

There were a few minor changes. *Road to Ruin* had a couple of small lead guitar parts. But we weren't jumping on anyone else's bandwagon except our own.

We did an encore of 'Sheena', and then another one of 'Rockaway Beach', and that was it. But Joey had as much trouble leaving a stage as he did leaving a room. As in most venues, a curtain separated onstage from offstage. We had all exited through it, but now Joey was re-entering, just barely. He poked his big head of hair and sunglasses through the opening in the curtain, then a long skinny jeans leg. It was just part of an endless ritual for Joey, but the Finnish wanted another big finish. There would be no third encore. Two of our roadies, Big Matt and Little Matt, grabbed Joey and started breaking down the stage. Next stop: Stockholm.

We flew into Sweden for three dates and then to Germany for two more. But, once we landed in Hamburg, we had a bus for the cities on the Continent. That was what the contract with the promoter called for. The bus driver was friendly and the bus was like a punk party on wheels. At the same time, the driver warned us about the different checkpoints between countries, and some of those weren't as friendly.

We went through lots of those checkpoints on the way to West Berlin. One was controlled by the US. Another by the Soviet Union. Another by East Germany. We were driving along a no-man's-land known as the Helmstedt–Berlin autobahn. It was hundreds of miles long and surrounded on both sides by fences, walls, hills, and basically anything that would make you think twice before trying anything funny. There was no tour guide, but every one of us was a baby boomer who sat through endless hours of high school history classes teaching us about the aftermath of World War II. We were now driving through that aftermath.

When the war ended and the Allies and Soviets split up Europe, the great city of Berlin became an island. Germany was divided into East and West, but Berlin remained free even though it sat far to the east of West Germany, deep in the heart of what was now Communist-controlled East Germany. In between West Germany and this last outpost of freedom was the road we were on now, stretching like an umbilical cord of rock and roll. At the other end of it, we were told, and, crazy as it sounded, were thousands of Ramones fans.

It wasn't a lie. They were out in throngs. Berlin – the west part, at least – was festive. It was like a remnant of the Weimar Republic, with cafés and little opera houses still surrounded here and there by the ruins of war. The young Berliner Ramones fans had invaded the hotel. There was beer, pot, grimy streets, and leather-jacketed punks. For us it was like home. For Dee Dee, it really was home.

Dee Dee was born in Fort Lee, Virginia, but grew up in Germany until the age of fifteen. His father was an American soldier stationed in Germany after World War II. Dee Dee's mother was a German woman who might have met her GI Joe husband in a bar or a dance hall. The couple moved around a bit, but Dee Dee spent most of his childhood in Berlin. Unfortunately, his father's alcoholism led to his parents' divorce, and Dee Dee, his sister, and his mother immigrated to the musical Mecca of Forest Hills, USA, in 1966.

We didn't know much about Dee Dee's German childhood. Evidence of it would pop out at odd times, like when he counted off a song. Most of the time it was 'One, two, three, four!' but once in a while it was 'Eins, zwei, drei, vier!'

That came out of his mouth randomly, and it wasn't as if the curiosity was going to make us stop playing 'We're a Happy Family' to ask, 'Why now?'

Dee Dee's childhood was like a riddle. Sometimes the answer was another riddle. No one could make complete sense out of 'Blitzkrieg Bop', but the image painted by the words 'shoot 'em in the back now' was as dark and SS as the title suggested. The song, with its cry of 'Hey Ho, Let's Go!' by now laid claim to being a global punk anthem. It was a bit unintelligible and ran on like Dee Dee's everyday thoughts and sentences. Meanwhile, the *Road to Ruin* song 'It's a Long Way Back' asked more questions than it answered. The storyteller sat waiting, perhaps in Germany, for a phone call that never came. It was a single haunting verse repeated. It said a lot. It said a little.

Dee Dee hated the Nazis. That didn't make him unique among American citizens, but neo-Nazis, like any insane radical group, will believe whatever they want to believe. The afternoon before our Berlin show, a local TV reporter was interviewing Dee Dee in the lobby of the hotel. Dee Dee transitioned from English to fluent German and back again as if it was verse-chorus-verse. It freaked us out. The reporter kept asking him about his time in Vietnam until Dee Dee put a stop to it like the Tet cease-fire.

'I can't talk about it. It's too painful. But, you know, we'd like to sell some albums over there and do a tour.'

Dee Dee had never been there. But the reporter was duped and relentless. Instead of jumping to the next topic, he did a blitzkrieg. 'This was, of course, a completely immoral war perpetrated by America. That is no longer a matter of debate. That is an established fact. So as you wear US military pins, how in your mind do you justify America's involvement in that atrocity known as Vietnam?'

Marion's eyes nearly rolled out of her head, and we all shot the reporter a glance as if he was a moron shooting a howitzer in a glass house. I had to say something.

'So, how do you justify the German involvement in World War II?'

'Yeah, you guys were like . . . satanic,' Dee Dee said. 'You were practically the Antichrist.'

The show was a lot easier to get through than the interview. The German youth, born in the fifties and sixties, were there to have a good time, and they had it. There were about fifty thousand American soldiers still stationed in West Germany, and there could have been five hundred at the show. Throw in about fifteen hundred screaming, dancing, stomping, beer-guzzling German kids, and you had the real 'Blitzkrieg Bop'. There was sweat dripping off the ceiling. Dee Dee counted off in German and threw in a few slogans in the mother tongue. We didn't know what he was saying, but the crowd did and went crazy. Dee Dee could have milked it a lot more, but that wasn't what the Ramones were about, in any language.

The spitting was getting out of control. It was like Normandy without the bloodshed. The German punks were accurate to the point where I could no longer hide behind a Paiste cymbal. They were launching wet V-2 rockets. The promoter in Ronneby, Sweden, had given us T-shirts that said 'No Spitting – we're Americans', but we weren't wearing them, and, if we had been, they'd be drenched in saliva. So Joey told the crowd, 'Come on, fucking cut it out.' Most of them listened. We earned that. The rest of them stopped when Dee Dee said something in German. It was a good time to give orders.

And to follow them. *Mehr! Mehr! Mehr!* We understood the concept of more as much as Dee Dee did. The spitting was as forgiven now as the Battle of the Bulge. Our third and final encore was 'It's a Long Way Back', which brought the house down the way the Allies took down the Axis. As a band, we had nothing left. It was a long way back to the hotel.

We had the next day off before we'd have to get back on the bus and head to Belgium. Dee Dee and I were in the hotel lobby getting ready to do some sightseeing while John was giving the promoter a hard time in a way that only John could. He was a big collector of miniature Nazi soldiers and a huge autograph collector, and no autograph outside of Moses or Jesus was a bigger score than Adolf Hitler's. The day we checked in, John asked the promoter if he could help him get the Führer's signature. The answer was '*Nein.*' The promoter looked at him as if he wanted to line up John in front of a firing squad. Germans didn't deal in the memorabilia of bad memories. Weapons were one thing, but some things were *verboten*. So, on this morning, using an American weapon John had mastered, he needled the promoter.

'Can you get it, or what? I told my friend back home I was getting it, and he's gonna raise a furor!'

Dee Dee and I walked along Tiergartenstrasse. He had exactly four things on his mind: copping, drinking, German prostitutes, and Nazi weapons. He rambled about all of them almost interchangeably. When he talked about being a child and picking out artifacts from rubble-filled lots in this same city, I knew he wasn't talking about the prostitutes.

He would sift through bricks and shards of glass and find bullet shells, knives, medallions. They all had a place in his collection.

As we walked, I noticed Dee Dee's posture. It was very straight with his head up and shoulders back. It didn't jibe with being a rock-and-roll musician. It didn't jibe with very much of anything Dee Dee did or said. When I met his father at a show back in New York, I saw the same pose, and I saw it now as American soldiers passed us right here on Lennéstrasse. Like the shells, knives, and medallions, it was part of Dee Dee's inheritance – a hodgepodge of stuff rolled up into a true American character.

Part of the Ramones' legacy was people all over the world thinking we'd fought in Vietnam. It wasn't just the reporter in the lobby. You could see where they were coming from. We looked rough, wore bits of military hardware, and took a tough stance in some of the songs. Most important, we were all draft age at the time. That was the situation for all our friends born in the late forties and early fifties. We just got lucky.

I wasn't the luckiest or the unluckiest. My draft lottery number was seventy-seven – not low enough to get called first, not high enough to sleep easy. My dad and I had talked about it. He was against the war, which was not a typical position for a longshoreman, but very little about my father was typical. His reasoning was clear: the best way to fight communism was to provide good jobs and opportunity at home, not to overrun a small country halfway around the world. Besides, he had two sons who could get killed.

I didn't get called until 1973. A bus from the army induction center stopped in front of my building on Ocean Avenue at five in the morning, and a sergeant came pounding on my basement door. I had been asleep for only about two hours, and it wasn't even good sleep. How could it be? The last person I spoke to before crashing that night was my friend Joel from upstairs who was going to coach me on avoiding Vietnam. He had friends up in Canada.

Whether Joel could or couldn't help, no one could keep me off that bus. As I boarded, I spotted a half-dozen guys I had gone to Erasmus High School with. None of the guys I spoke to had traveled much beyond

Brooklyn in the three years since graduation, while I was glad I had the opportunity to see the country with Dust. Touring was fine as long as it wasn't a tour of duty. One of the guys was talking about how we could still beat the Vietcong and how much he wanted to get over there and get a confirmed kill. 'Great,' I told him. 'You can take my spot.'

They took us to the armory at Fort Hamilton, a hundred-and-fifty-year-old building off the Belt Parkway. I was in good condition and passed the physical with no problem. That was thanks in large part to drumming. Drumming was my life, and now drumming could get me killed. But the months afterward went by without my getting a draft notice. Fewer and fewer men were getting called. American involvement in Vietnam was winding down. We began pulling out that year, and by 1975 were out completely. I guess I was lucky enough.

I didn't have all the details on the other Ramones. Joey's situation, though, was obvious. He was a 4-F poster boy. Dee Dee could have talked his way out of the draft, whether he was trying to or not. As for John, his lottery number was high, and so he was probably not called. We all knew that, even if he had been, he would have found a way out of it, no question. For all his rah-rah jingoism bullshit, he would have come up with a limp, a phobia, a hangnail, a doctor's note, or whatever it would have taken to stay out of the jungle. John talked the talk, and that's where it ended.

Berlin's inheritance from World War II was still in evidence: building lots here and there that remained piles of rubble even after all this time. War was the gift that kept on giving. Buildings, like people, were created painstakingly one at a time and then obliterated all together in a few mindless hours. Kurt Vonnegut wrote about carpet bombing in Dresden so intense the heat melted stone clock towers, marking the moment the temperature took its toll. Superheated air rose up in a column, sucking in cars, people, and trees, feeding the fire still more. With a history like that, no one could expect Berlin or Dee Dee to avoid residual damage.

The Kaiser Wilhelm Memorial Church was maybe the best example of a monument to ruin. We walked around the building, which was badly damaged in a 1943 Allied bombing raid and left largely as is. There were bullet holes, charred masonry, missing stones. The belfry had been replaced by a modern-looking one, but the various spires were no more. It looked kind of macabre, like a naked torso with its arms and legs cut off, left to die.

As Dee Dee and I approached the Brandenburg Gate, we realized that was as far as we were going to get. We couldn't get to the famous structure itself because it was on the other side of the Berlin Wall. But there was plenty of activity on our side. There were street vendors selling a wide variety of Nazi daggers, and Dee Dee had a field day. He was thrilled to pick up a dagger made especially for members of the Third Reich. The Nazi Party logo was right there on the brown handle. But the big thrill was the etching on the ten-inch-long carbon steel blade: *Alles für Deutschland*. Everything for Germany. The dagger, however, was only a hundred deutschmarks.

A few steps to our left, Dee Dee spotted a Hitler Youth dagger with the etching '*Blut und Ehre!*' ('Blood and Honor!'). The blade was short and compact – something thoughtful for that growing young Nazi in the family. 'Yeah, why not?' he said. 'One for the road.'

After dark, we found a stretch of the Berlin Wall with stairs. We followed the stairs up to the top of the wall. From that location, we were able to peer through the barbed wire and see the other side, into East Berlin. The difference was stark. East Berlin was bleak. It was a black-and-white and gray world across the road below, just five hundred feet from where we were standing. The buildings were large, repetitive, boxlike structures, colorless, looking as if they all came from the same mold. The closest thing we had in America to these buildings was prisons. Even the air that drifted across the wall from the east side seemed sterile and ominous.

The wall at this spot was wide enough to walk along. But as soon as we did, a bunch of searchlights from the other side lit us up, practically blinding us. We picked up the pace a little and the searchlights followed us. It was eerie. Whoever they were, they could see us a lot better than we could see them. To us, they were faceless communists existing in a kind of hell right here on earth. To them, we were targets. It was time to get down off the wall.

We kept walking and found a bar a few blocks away. It wasn't a touristy place. It was filled mostly with middle-aged men who looked as if they worked for a living, probably in the trades. Dee Dee and I took a small table and ordered a couple of beers. He was excited we would be in Amsterdam in a couple of days. Most drugs were legal there, and what the Dutch lacked in daggers they easily made up for in hashish.

As he rambled on about how he wanted to get high there and go watch some freaky movies, I noticed Dee Dee's facial expression turn a little annoyed. He seemed distracted, stopped talking for a few seconds, and glanced back over his shoulder.

'These guys are talking shit about us,' Dee Dee said. He was referring to a group of six men sitting at the table next to us. They were blue-collar guys in their forties with a couple pitchers of beer on the table. We looked American and were speaking English, so they had no idea Dee Dee understood every last word they spoke in German – probably better than they did.

'What kind of shit?' I asked.

'They called us a couple of American faggots,' Dee Dee said. 'They said you liked to go on top and me on the bottom.'

'Yeah? Anything else?'

'Well, we should take these US pins we're wearing and shove them up each other's ass.'

'Why would we want to do that?' I said.

I was a little pissed off but not exactly trembling with rage. Sometimes you just had to laugh it off and let it go. But then Dee Dee stood up and turned around to face them. He ranked on them in German. It was as though he were fourteen again, not missing a beat between a Berlin schoolyard a dozen years ago and this very moment. I couldn't understand what he was saying, but the harshness of the German language worked well in a barroom confrontation. I did understand one word Dee Dee used: 'arschloch'. In the fatherland it meant asshole.

The looks on the faces of the Germans were mixed. There was anger over the German obscenity-laced tirade Dee Dee was shoving up their collective rear ends. But there was also a strange look of something like betrayal. The deal was supposed to be they got to say whatever they wanted to say as if they were making fun of characters on a TV screen. But Dee Dee stepped out of the screen. And I stepped out with him.

'Fuck you guys!' I said. 'Fuck you all!'

It wasn't exactly German, but it was universal. Although the wiry guy in the denim vest stood up first by a hair, they all stood up within a second or two and we heard that also universal sound of a bar table sliding around as beer glasses fell to the floor. A burly German in a wool sweater cursed us out in a booming voice about two octaves lower than Dee Dee's. Dee Dee's voice didn't match his looks. He looked like a tough kid on either side of the Atlantic, but he sounded like a Long Island version of Liberace. That alone got the Germans out of their seats, and it got me out of mine.

The wiry guy pushed his chest up in Dee Dee's face and Dee Dee chested him back, cursing the whole time. '*Arschfotze! Arschgeige! Blonde Fotze!*' I moved toward a German in a wool cap who shoved me with his hands. I shoved him back. All other activity in the bar stopped cold. That was another universal: bloodthirsty silence before the massacre. We all knew the exact same thing. Shove and curse all you want. Once a single punch was thrown, all hell was going to break loose.

Suddenly, the bartender appeared to my right. He was as large as the big guy at the table, and from the looks of his nose, which had been broken at least twice, he didn't just break up fights. He broke the people in them. He smacked a long black billy club hard into his open palm, and we knew he had no problem swapping the palm for an open skull.

The Germans backed off, and Dee Dee and I turned and walked out through the door. The bar patrons looked very disappointed. There wasn't going to be an encore at this show. As we walked along Altonaer Strasse, Dee Dee translated everything he'd said and they'd said. I didn't really need to know that Dee Dee told the wiry guy we were going to have sex with his mother and sister while he watched, but it was entertaining.

I was relieved we were out of there. We could have hurt somebody. So could they. We didn't need a headline in the *Berliner Zeitung* saying 'Ramones Blitzkrieg Bop!' We had shows coming up and dozens of people who made a living from those shows. So we headed back to the hotel to drink Jägermeisters the rest of the night. As I hoisted my first cold one, I remembered something and had a moment of clarity – we were lucky tonight we left the daggers back in the room.

Next stop: Amsterdam. Dee Dee was in heaven. Drugs were legal. The Dutch government had decided that spending a big chunk of the gross domestic product to throw people in jail for smoking weed or shooting dope was a total waste. Instead, substances were controlled and sold by licensed establishments, like booze in the US. Kids came from down the road and all over the world to Amsterdam for the drugs. When we walked along the canals – which were laid out in circles – we saw boatloads of those kids clustered around benches, steps, and statues, looking dazed and confused. If we didn't have to leave the next day, Dee Dee would have been one of them.

Our show was at the Paradiso, a well-known rock venue on the edge of the Leidseplein, a square packed with nightlife. The Paradiso was a three-story brick building originally built as a church but occupied in 1967 by hippies looking for a place to party. Although the hippies themselves got kicked out by the police, their plans for the building eventually became a reality, which said a lot about Amsterdam.

Partying at the Paradiso started with the upper balcony. There was Coca-Cola, beer, popcorn, pretzels, and all the usual vending way up above the stage. Plus the pot vendor. Just another guy making a living, except this guy had a line running almost to the exit. Marion and Dee Dee's wife, Vera, were near the front of that line. When it was their turn, they asked the vendor what he had and he said pot and hash. Marion said they'd take everything and the vendor looked puzzled. He dealt in little bags of five or ten dollars and tins of twenty.

'What do you mean everything?'

'We mean everything you have. All of it.'

The vendor explained that would cost two thousand guilders, which was roughly eight hundred dollars. Fine. No problem. Marion pulled out about half and Vera the rest. The kids in line behind them, at least the ones close enough to witness the transaction, were pissed off. But we had a lot of mouths to feed and brains to fry. The bus rides were long, and big fat joints made them shorter.

The vendor must have called in his supplier for more. Either that or most kids walked in with their own, because by the time the lights went up and we launched into the show, the place smelled like a drug den. Combined with a bar. There was a full house of about fifteen hundred, every one of them stoned and amped up. The smoke was so thick it seemed machine-generated, but the only machine was the collective lungs of the Dutch youth.

We noticed that, for whatever reason, the kids in Holland were physically large – larger than the Swedes, Germans, or Belgians. From where we were it looked like an audience of giants and not just because we had a contact high. Maybe there was something in the bong water. Or the hash brownies sold next door at the Melkweg. When these oversized punks moshed and stage dived, it was brawnier and beefier than in the rest of the Continent. The kids shook the old church ghosts out of the walls.

The spitting at the Paradiso was bigger, too. The Amsterdam punks started spitting out mouths full of beer onto the stage and the band. Then the spraying started. They would shake a can or a bottle of beer and pop it open in our direction. The range was incredible, like a bunch of fire hoses shooting Amstel and Heineken. It was hard to tell what had more distance, cheeks or containers. If I was getting sprayed behind the drums, Joey, John, and Dee Dee were getting soaked. It would take a thousand bubble baths for Dee Dee to stop smelling like a brewery. Joey tried to appeal to reason.

'Cut that fucking shit out, guys. I mean it. You're gonna electrocute us. This is not a fucking joke.'

All it took was enough ale to create a ground between a hot wire and a Ramone and there would be no fifth album. The last thing we ever sniffed would be fried hops and barley. Joey took his life in his hands every time his lips neared the microphone. And he thought the shower was dangerous!

The storm subsided, maybe because they listened to the band, maybe because Amsterdam was running out of brew, maybe both. But the party went on. It was a loony bin in a brewery.

After playing Arnhem in the Netherlands, we were headed to Paris by bus, through Belgium. This was a big problem for Dee Dee, because cannabis and all other street drugs were illegal in both Belgium and France, and Dee Dee was carrying enough to get an entire embassy stoned. But, when it came to illegal substances and international intrigue, Dee Dee was as resourceful as James Bond.

Dee Dee made friends with the bus driver, which wasn't hard to do because the driver was a good old European soul. When we stopped just outside the Dutch–Belgian border to exchange guilders for francs, Dee Dee walked around to the back of the one-story brick customs building, and I followed him. He looked around a bit at a concrete planter with some shrubs and poked at the dirt with his hand.

'What do you think?' he said.

'I think you're fucking crazy.'

That was good enough. Dee Dee picked a spot between the second and third shrubs from the left and started digging with both paws like a beagle burying a bone. Once he got about a foot deep, he pulled two large clear plastic bags out of his jacket and placed them in the hole. Then he filled in the hole and patted it down. This wasn't a first time for Dee Dee. He had buried pot, dope, and pills all over New York. Some of it was still there. He also hid stuff in the backs of speakers, under floorboards, and in the hollow bodies of acoustic guitars. If you knew Dee Dee, you might be holding some of his junk and not even know it.

'Yeah, all right. Perfect.'

He took one last look before we headed back to the bus. It was never as simple as it seemed. For mission accomplished, three things would have to happen. First, he would have to persuade the bus driver to cut back through the same route and stop at the same customs office. Second, no other dope fiend could spot him. Third, Dee Dee would have to remember exactly where he buried it. The last one might have been the hardest. Maybe that's why I was there.

The Palais des Congrès in Paris was like a burlesque theater. The stairs to the stage were a huge climb, so we were looking down at most of the room, basically the opposite of the early CBGB. The Parisian kids were very different from the kids up north. We did 'Sedated' and they already were. Not that they didn't like the music and even bounce around. But they were cooler, like sophisticates at an art gallery. They were taking it all in. We didn't complain. The place was sold out, and we weren't covered in spit and beer.

As we passed back through the Netherlands on the way up to the UK, the bus driver stopped at Dee Dee's one-story brick customs building, though there was no currency to exchange in the middle of the night. I followed Dee Dee around the back as he walked up to the spot between the second and third shrub from the left. He was 'on' in Paris and he was on in this little parking lot.

He dug quickly and efficiently, and when he pulled out the first bag, he eyeballed it closely. He did the same thing with the other bag. Then he smiled and loosened up a little, cradling the two bags. If I didn't know how fucked up Dee Dee was going to get once we got back on the bus, I would have been almost touched. It was like watching a family reunited after the war.

We landed at JFK Airport in Queens on 9 October. I was jetlagged. Given the flight back from Scotland, my body thought it was midnight, even though it was six in the evening. But I was excited to be home, and home was about to get better with the loft on John Street that Marion and I would be moving into.

Monte got our van out of long-term parking and picked us up at Terminal 4. We cut around the south tip of Brooklyn along the Belt Parkway to try to miss the remains of rush-hour traffic. Still, it took about an hour and a half to finally pull up in front of the loft on East Second Street in Manhattan. As Monte looked over his shoulder and parallel-parked in what was probably the last open spot in the East Village, Joey spoke his first words since we'd left the airport.

'Monte, we gotta go back.'

'What happened?' Monte said.

'I left something at JFK,' Joey said.

'What did you leave, Jeffrey?' John said. 'Your fucking brains?'

John was pissed off. He thought Joey was doing this to break our balls, but we really all knew better. Joey couldn't help it. The thing was, this was taking it to a new level, at least on my watch. We had just returned from a transcontinental flight where our lead singer counted every seat, every overhead light, and every emergency air supply button. He had actually used the bathroom twice but returned dozens of times to tap the soap, touch the seat, and flush the toilet. Now he was headed back across the river to JFK without his band.

We pulled our luggage off the van and scattered. Marion and I jumped into a cab to go back to Brooklyn. Monte would have to drive solo with Joey. What else could he do? He was the driver. Joey couldn't have enjoyed it much either. The only consolation was he could move up to John's seat if he wanted to.

The following afternoon I heard from Dee Dee by phone. Dee Dee had spoken to Monte. Monte and Joey had pulled up to British Airways at Terminal 4. Joey got out, walked a few steps and tapped the curb with his foot. Then they headed back to Manhattan. At least they didn't have to fly back to Glasgow.

10

WE'RE NOT STUDENTS – WE'RE RAMONES

Once Marion and I had our own place in Manhattan it was easier to visit Joey, and I made a point of doing so. We had some time before our next tour, which would focus on the Northeast, take another break, and then head south. As I got out of a cab at East Second Street just off of Bowery around four in the afternoon, I had a couple of beers in me but my stomach was growling.

This was the center of the Ramones' universe. CBGB was around the corner, and a hundred or so feet down East Second Street was Arturo Vega's loft. I opened the old metal door and pressed the buzzer. A few seconds later the buzzer sounded and I pushed open the wrought-iron security gate, then started my way up the narrow staircase. The door to the loft was already open and I walked through. The door was usually open to let out the fumes when Arturo was painting. I could, in fact, smell a combination of acrylic and oil, but it looked like Arturo had left. Joey sat on a leather couch and was scribbling something on a notepad.

'Hey, *Merk*.'

'What's up, Joey?'

It was a factory building built in Manhattan's industrial days, and the brick walls and high ceilings were pretty much unchanged except for Arturo's neo-psychedelic art hanging everywhere. Aside from a long table where Arturo had been silk-screening Ramones T-shirts, the place was very neat and uncluttered.

I walked over to Joey and asked him if he had anything around to eat. He said yeah, but instead of showing me to the refrigerator he led me to his bedroom, and I felt that I had to follow. Joey's 'bedroom' was a small area behind a freestanding bookcase toward the rear of the loft. Behind the bookcase, on the floor, was a mattress covered with mounds of records and tapes that spilled out onto the surrounding floorboards. There were T-shirts, jeans, sneakers, books, and magazines that looked as if they had just been shipped from Birchwood Towers in Forest Hills and dumped from a suitcase. But Joey had lived here at least three years.

Joey pointed to a milk crate just beyond an empty pizza box. Sitting atop the crate was a hamburger with a side of fries and a large pickle. Hungry as I was, I was about to step around the mattress, reach down, and take a bite, but I froze for a moment. Something was wrong with the picture but I couldn't put my finger on it.

Actually I *could* put my finger on it. I leaned over carefully and touched the top of the burger roll with my index finger. It was rock hard. So were the burger, the pickle, and the fries. Everything was as dried out as instant coffee, but this food was never going to be brought back to life. It looked like one of those plastic replicas of a meal you sometimes see in the window of a Chinese restaurant. Except this food was harder.

I looked back over at Joey and didn't want to ask him. His whole cluster of neuroses was a very touchy subject for all of us. If I was going to question him I didn't even know where to begin. Why didn't you want to eat this when you ordered it? Was something wrong with it? Why didn't you throw it out? Why didn't you wrap it up and put it in the fridge or the freezer? Exactly what kind of long-term plans did you have for this meal? Have you touched it lately? Have you tapped it? Have you tried hitting it with a hammer? Why did you offer it to me? Exactly how long has this been sitting here? A week? Two weeks? Since before the European tour?

'You know what?' I said. 'I could really go for some Indian food.'

We headed down the narrow stairway to East Second. Actually, I headed out and then watched Joey go in and out a few times before joining me on the sidewalk. East Sixth Street was where all the great Indian restaurants were. We were just a few blocks away and started walking east. At the next corner I made a left turn to go north on Second Avenue and Joey said, 'No, no. Let's go this way.'

Joey wanted to continue walking east on Second Street. That didn't make any sense. If we made the left on First Avenue, that was the long way. If we made the left a block after, on Avenue A, that was even longer.

'This is the fastest way,' I said. 'I'm hungry. Why do you want to stay on Second?'

'Well, you know,' he said. 'God's on this block. I gotta stop in and see God.'

He smiled a little. He knew he was being nuts. That was a good sign. So I followed him east on Second. Chicken vindaloo tasted even better when you had to wait for it.

When our tour headed south through Richmond, Virginia, and Raleigh, North Carolina, we were out of local range – that is, Ramones local range – and began staying in hotels again for the first time since Europe. I didn't mind the hotels or taking the same seat as always for the long rides down I-95. I didn't even mind hearing John talk for an hour at a time about how the Yankees had won the World Series against the Dodgers after being fourteen games behind the Red Sox at one point. What I did mind was that some of the band's problems were getting worse.

Dee Dee's use of every drug under the sun was becoming a loaded weapon aimed at himself and anyone who cared. Whenever Vera opened the door to their bedroom in Whitestone, she hoped her husband was in there breathing. If he was, the next hope was that he hadn't turned blue. She had dialed 911 so many times the operators knew her voice.

Meanwhile, Roxy was on perpetual thin ice with John. I had shared plenty of bottles with Roxy back before the Ramones, and I was no angel. I liked to have a drink or two or three when it didn't interfere with playing. But it seemed like Roxy had been on a bender since about Amsterdam.

Her MO was to pop open a can of Tab, empty it out, and fill it with vodka. That allowed her to drink without apology everywhere – in the van, at rest stops, in supermarkets, just walking around. She could no longer hold her liquor. Her speech was slurred and her legs were wobbly. She started stupid arguments with John. John tried to keep her away from the band, but on a tour that was next to impossible. So he went to plan B.

We could often hear John pushing and smacking Roxy around in their hotel room. We would hear her stumbling, bouncing off a thin wall, and then falling onto a bed and shrieking. It didn't go on for ever. Usually it was a minute or two. There was no excuse for it. Like every kid of my generation and all the ones before, I was taught never to hit a girl, and this routine made us all a little sick. *But a routine was what it became.* John did it, at least in part, to calm Roxy down. And it worked. We all wondered why she stayed with him. In some horrible way, it worked for her, too.

By Atlanta, things got so bad that John locked Roxy in the dressing room before the Ramones took the stage. Most *dogs* got better treatment. At least she was in there alone.

We had another problem in Atlanta. On 13 November, we were at the Omni opening for Van Halen and Black Sabbath. More accurately, we were opening for Van Halen, who were opening for Black Sabbath. I liked both bands, especially the old Black Sabbath albums, which laid the groundwork for all future heavy metal, both good and bad. But we were all wary of how their audience would react to the Ramones. The promoters billed the show as 'Punk vs. Metal'. Metal had been around a lot longer, so we knew we were getting fed to the lions.

Black Sabbath had problems of their own. The whole band were heavily into drugs and alcohol to the point where they were just going through the motions. Ozzy Osbourne was a raging alcoholic and had already quit the band at the end of 1977. He came back to record the album *Never Say Die*, but, when they saw the record's poor sales, some people were at least *thinking* die. Van Halen had been opening for Sabbath throughout the fall of 1978 and were by all accounts putting the old guard to shame. David Lee Roth was doing karate kicks all over the stage while Ozzy looked as if someone had just kicked him in the gut.

When the Ramones opened with 'Blitzkrieg Bop', it felt as though we'd had crashed someone else's party. The Omni was packed with around sixteen thousand people, but half of them were getting food, while the other half stared at us as if we were some kids who had walked into the wrong classroom. 'Blitzkrieg' was our anthem, so, if they weren't stirred, you knew it was only going to get worse.

It did. By 'Sheena', a lot of the kids were yelling out, 'Black Sabbath!' By 'Something to Do', the projectiles were flying: soda cans, beer bottles, hot dogs, peanut shells, and anything else they could get their hands on. Joey was getting pelted left and right. Normally, a lead singer gets it because he's out front, but Joey was even more of a sitting duck because of the way he stayed glued to one spot. I was a sitting duck, too, even though I was sitting in the back. The cymbals shielded me from a popsicle, but some wet ice cubes got through and hit me on the shoulder. It sucked. We would have taken European spitting over Southern inhospitality any day.

The seventh song in the set was 'I Don't Care', and we didn't. John was the first to unstrap his guitar, and the rest of us were right there. We weren't going to be humiliated. We gave the crowd the collective finger and walked off. I saw pockets of kids here and there clapping and waving as if they didn't want to go along with the masses, but they and we were overwhelmed.

Backstage, no one argued with our decision. Monte and the crew said we should have walked off earlier. The promoter's people knew the situation. If one of the Ramones got hurt in their venue, they would have gotten sued and would have lost.

We looked on the bright side. We actually played well and may have made a few new fans with the metalheads, even if some of them were afraid to admit it in public. Every show couldn't have a Hollywood ending. But our year was going to have one.

We checked into the Tropicana Motel on Santa Monica Boulevard on 6 December. The Tropicana was a low-rent Hyatt House, nicknamed the Riot House. There were plenty of riots at the Trop, too. They just cost a little less to clean up.

The building was a two-story horseshoe structure with access to the rooms by outdoor staircase and walkway only. It was a classic-looking motor lodge built in the late forties, when the country was putting World War II in the rear-view mirror and hitting the highway for fun and sun out west. Celebrities and wayward folks both frequented the Trop, with a steady stream of pimps, hookers, and junkies coming and going. The establishment had a reputation at the time for delivering on even the kinkiest of a guest's demands.

In the sixties, Jim Morrison would get drunk in the bar across the street and stumble into the Trop for some shuteye. According to rock-and-roll lore he wrote many of the Doors' most famous songs in any number of the interconnected rooms. Just as rock and roll itself was contagious, so was the Trop's reputation as a rock hotel. Over the years, rooms had been trashed by Johnny Cash, Led Zeppelin, the Clash, the Runaways, the Stooges, the Beach Boys, and a long list of less renowned boys and girls who liked to check out leaving the place worse than when they checked in.

The room I got with Marion on the first floor was more like a little apartment – sort of a glorified efficiency. There was a living area with a TV in the front room and a kitchenette at the rear. Down the hall to the right was a bathroom, and to the left was a bedroom with two double beds. As always I asked for a room between the roadies' rooms on either side. That way my partying wouldn't disturb the other Ramones. It was sort of a buffer zone. It was a buffer for the regular guests, too. We were an unusual-looking bunch of people and we did get a few strange stares from some of the everyday folks staying there. But, when you were filming a movie called *Rock 'n' Roll High School*, anything short of a *Rock 'n' Roll Hotel* wasn't going to cut it.

Partying, however, was for the end of the day. Making a movie is all work and waiting, with one part work, four parts waiting. We would get up around seven in the morning so Monte could pick us up in the van and drive us to the location. Whether they're in a rock band or not, there aren't many people who like to hear screaming and yelling at close range in a cramped moving vehicle before nine. But Joey's new girlfriend, Cindy, was doing just that.

She was a brunette who seemed nice enough until she opened her mouth. Then the rest of us were subjected to Cindy's ranting about Joey's morning routine, which was a lot like Joey's afternoon and evening routines. Except that, in a motel, there are a lot of doors to touch and steps to count. I felt bad for Monte, who had to hear all this twice.

'Joey, why should I have to get up early for you? Why don't you get some professional help?'

'Why don't you shut the fuck up?' John snapped. John had problems of his own with Roxy, who was already blitzed at a quarter to nine. The Trop was ground zero for alcoholics, and Roxy was off to a fast start. But at least she was quiet on the way over.

Our main location for the movie was Mount Carmel High School in Los Angeles. Two weeks before Christmas, schools in Los Angeles are still in session, but not this one. We had it all to ourselves. Mount Carmel was a Catholic school with a classic Spanish-American stucco look, but it was closed in 1976 because of a shift in demographics and lack of enrolment. In fact, it was slated for demolition. Roger Corman, Allan Arkush, the Ramones, and company were there to make sure it went out with a bang.

To no one's surprise, the Ramones didn't go much for makeup. We took just enough powder not to get too shiny under the klieg lights. There were no dressing rooms in a condemned Catholic school, but there were plenty of empty classrooms. The Ramones were given one on the west wing of the first floor.

On this given day, we were going to be filming a climactic scene where the four members of the band push the two SS-like hall monitors in a laundry cart down the hall and out a second-story window. We were looking forward to it, since none of us ever liked Nazis or hall monitors very much. But that was in the afternoon. In the morning, we basically had to wait. It would have been a perfect time to lip-synch 'I Just Want to Have Something to Do', but even that had to wait. For most of us, sitting and waiting in a classroom felt eerily like detention.

As with school back in the day, we made the best of it. We talked with other cast members who were not at that moment shooting a scene. We read the script and got a better idea of the plot and where we fit into it. Vince Lombardi High School, the story goes, gets a new principal who is a hardline, old-fashioned, eccentric schoolmarm looking to make a name for herself and is ready to steamroll anyone who gets in her way.

Riff Randell, a hot-looking girl and the world's number one Ramones fan, gets in Principal Togar's way from the beginning. Randell's goal is to get to Joey at a Ramones concert and give him a song she wrote for the band. Randell's forged absence notes claim a dead mother, a dead father, and a dead goldfish. Principal Togar smells a rat and declares war. The war concludes with the Ramones and the kids taking over the school and blowing it up. The band always liked happy endings.

Principal Togar was played by Mary Woronov. In person she was nothing like the insane tyrant in the script. Woronov had been one of Andy Warhol's well-known actors and made her debut in the relatively successful experimental flick *Chelsea Girls*. Mary was really cool and friendly, but when Allan yelled 'Take!' she became an insane tyrant.

P. J. Soles was long past her teen years but was still making a good career playing one in the movies. She was in the Stephen King thriller *Carrie*, the horror movie *Halloween*, and the dorky TV movie *The Boy in the Plastic Bubble*, starring John Travolta. She was injured on the set of *Carrie* during the prom scene. While all the spoiled brats who tortured Carrie got fried in a gymnasium inferno, PJ got her eardrum ruptured by a fire hose. More happily, she had recently finished filming *Our Winning Season* and married its star, Dennis Quaid.

We were excited in the early afternoon to finally be pushing the laundry cart down the hallway. We blocked out the scene, which was really divided into multiple shots, each one of which had to be done right. The camera and cameraman were on a dolly being pulled by two grips. We ran through it a few times to make sure the Ramones were properly in the frame and we were all moving at the same pace.

Once the kinks were worked out, we filmed the sequence a couple of times. Allan made sure we looked like we were doing it for the first time instead of the fifth or sixth, which is one of the keys not only to acting but also to music. Even though it was a teen comedy being shot for about $300,000, it was important to look as if we were really pissed off at the hall monitors and sending them to their doom instead of just going through the motions. Thinking about being strip-searched at Erasmus worked for me.

Before we did a bunch of close shots, it was time for a short break, so we did what any overgrown, ageing school kids would do: hit the schoolyard. It was like any schoolyard, concrete pavement with a chain-link fence around it. The difference was that it was lined along the outside with Ramones fans. Los Angeles was a city with celebrity whereabouts coursing through its veins. Word of mouth was the lifeblood. If they cared enough, they knew where you were and when you were there. The only unknown was when the director would yell, 'Take five,' but these kids seemed to have all day. And some other things, too.

We approached the fence ready to sign autographs, but something else was going on between the albums and pens being waved around. A few of the fans, typical California guy and girl punks and mall rats, were tossing pills and packets over and through the fence. Since they put in the effort to show up, they were probably big enough Ramones fans to know only one Ramone was interested in free drugs. Sure enough, Dee Dee was down on the pavement picking up random nickel bags, capsules, tablets, and anything else hitting the concrete that looked potentially mood altering. It was like watching an amateur gambler on the floor of a casino after pulling all triple-bars on a slot machine.

'Dee Dee! Dee Dee! Acapulco Gold! Right here!'

'Dee Dee! Valium. Five milligrams, baby! Come to mama!'

Our bassist stuffed some of this in a jeans pocket and some of that in a coat pocket. And then some of the other things in his mouth. I wasn't sure which pills he swallowed or how many. *Eins, zwei, drei, vier* – it was past counting in any language. And beyond understanding. Vera watched it. I watched it. It became like the fight I saw in Union Square Park – you eventually just learned to let it happen.

'You girls happen to have any more of the red?' Dee Dee smiled as he stood up and walked along the fence toward a girl of about sixteen who had sort of a Farrah Fawcett thing going on. 'Come on, more red. I was invited to a party tonight, and I hate showing up empty-handed.'

I would drink after the shoot to wind down. My two main drinking buddies were Dee Dee and Phil Spector. But I could drink with only one at a time. Phil didn't like Dee Dee. He was all over the place and made Phil nervous. Phil was already nervous enough as it was. Phil liked to talk to me and Joey about music and anything related to it.

I had just met Phil myself, but we hit it off. We had a sort of Bronx–Brooklyn crosstown mutual respect. We both hated bullshit – giving and receiving. And I loved the girl groups, the Beatles stuff, and just about everything Phil Spector had anything to do with. Phil was remixing two songs for the movie soundtrack of *Rock 'n' Roll High School*. The Ramones were getting scale for the movie, but there were big perks: free rooms, all we could eat and drink, and royalties on the soundtrack. For me, the biggest perk of all was working and hanging out with a legend.

On the way to my room, I passed by the pool at the Trop. Dee Dee was poolside hanging out with the Dead Boys' lead singer Stiv Bators and various local punk luminaries. There was a brief winter in Southern California, and this was it. It was overcast and in the mid-sixties Fahrenheit, or what New Yorkers called spring and fall. But there was no way any of our crew was jumping into the Trop pool in any season.

The water was always dirty. It could barely have passed as bong water. If you were brave or crazy enough to jump in, you might swim into a syringe. The pool was kidney-shaped and a leading cause of renal failure. The Astroturf on the surrounding deck was not green like your typical fake grass. It was black. No one knew what sort of mold, blood, or fecal matter the turf might have been camouflaging at any given point, and no one wanted to know.

Dee Dee and his punk entourage were heading over to Stiv's room, and I told them I would be along later. Or not. Phil Spector was due at my room in about a half-hour. I really didn't know how Dee Dee was holding up after swallowing half the pills in Los Angeles County, but he had probably built up the same tolerance to drugs that we had built up to him.

The knock on my door came at nine sharp. It was Phil Spector, dressed flamboyantly as always. He had on a frilly shirt, a cape, and Beatle boots. I saw his brand-new 1979 Cadillac Seville in the parking lot, and I knew his bodyguard, George Brand, was waiting in the driver's seat. George was licensed to carry firearms. So was Phil Spector. He was carrying now. I could see the bulge under his jacket.

Phil was also carrying a bottle of Manischewitz kosher grape wine. That did not require a license, but it should have. I associated Manischewitz with all my Jewish friends celebrating Passover. It was way too sweet for me – an acquired taste I would never bother to acquire. It seemed worse than wandering forty years in the desert. But Phil loved it, and who was I or anyone to question Phil Spector's taste?

I poured Phil a glass of his best and myself a shot of vodka. We talked for a minute or two about the soundtrack, and then Phil launched into a tirade.

'What they did to him was a crime! A capital offense! And this was our government. *My* government. *Your* government. *Our* government.'

He was angry about his good friend Lenny Bruce. Bruce had died of a morphine overdose in 1966. We were now just days away from 1979, but Phil Spector sounded as if he had just that morning bought the police photo of the comedian Lenny Bruce, collapsed and deceased with a syringe on the bathroom floor, to keep it out of the newspapers. Phil was capable of being the best friend you ever had, even after you were dead.

'You're right,' I said. 'Once you questioned Vietnam or anything else the establishment was pushing, you were public enemy number one.'

'Not only that,' Phil said, 'but he didn't back down. He believed in what he was doing. The police came to every show he did waiting to bust him for saying one wrong thing. And he found a way to say it, more often than not, without actually saying it! Do you know what I mean?'

I nodded.

'He was a genius at that. A genius! But in the end it killed him. They killed him.'

Phil Spector was probably the best producer who ever lived. With hit record after hit record, he created a wall of sound that jumped out of the speakers. On that basis alone, I believed everything he was saying, at least for the moment. On some level, I even believed that all Phil Spector had to do was talk about the police and you would hear the police. But, as the sirens got closer and closer, I realized they were real.

We opened the door to my room and looked to the left along the first-story concrete deck. Two black-and-white LAPD patrol cars were parked in no particular spot below. One officer was waiting by the car and one was on the deck right outside Stiv's room. A few of the punk partiers had spilled out onto the deck, and there was a lot of yelling and banging. A moment later, two cops came out with Dee Dee. His hands were cuffed behind him, and the cops led him by either arm past the railing. Vera followed them and shouted, 'Okay? You got what you wanted!'

Phil saw this, turned to me, and said, 'Can I ask you something? What the fuck is wrong with that guy?'

Later that night when I got back from hanging out at a club with Phil Spector, Marion told me that, after they took Dee Dee away, he started turning blue in the patrol car and slumped over. The car never made it to the station and instead went to Cedars-Sinai Medical Center, where they pumped Dee Dee's stomach. The police called Monte, and Monte called Vera, who went to the hospital. A full recovery was expected. Everyone said Dee Dee was like a cat with nine lives. But, actually, he was on his third or fourth cat.

The next day, Allan and the crew shot around the Ramones, who were missing their bassist. Dee Dee was being kept for observation – which, if it was going to be done right, would have taken a year or two. But the following morning Dee Dee was at the van bright and early and was apparently okay until the next batch of pill-pushing groupies showed up at the schoolyard. The only trace of his latest near-death experience was the plastic hospital bracelet still on his wrist.

The problem this morning wasn't Dee Dee. It was Joey's girlfriend, Cindy. We were getting ready to board the van and she was pushing Joey's buttons.

'We're not staying in that classroom all day. No way. I'm not doing it. I'm not gonna be cooped up all day like a prisoner. You have to say something.'

'Come on, gimme a break,' Joey said. 'I don't run the set.'

'You don't run anything!' Cindy said, getting hysterical. 'Why don't you try running your own life? You might enjoy it!'

With that, John slapped Cindy in the face. It was a right-handed, open-palm blow across her left cheek that landed cleanly. The sound of the smack was almost good enough for a Hollywood movie. The sound editor might not have needed to dub in an effect.

'What the fuck . . .'

'You're not getting in the van!' John said. 'You're off! Do you hear me?' Cindy backed off and backed down immediately. The hot air was out of her sails. She had met Joey's alter ego. Where behind the sunglasses there was softness and compassion in Joey's eyes, there was blue ice in John's. Cindy had done everything in her power to provoke Joey, but the reaction came from someplace and someone else. Cindy turned and walked away stunned. The rest of us boarded the van. Monte closed the doors and we pulled out.

The ride to Mount Carmel High School was quiet. Joey's silence said a lot. If his relationship with Cindy wasn't over when he got up at dawn, it was definitely over now. Joey might not have known how to handle the situation on his own, but the problem was he would never have the opportunity to find out. John took that from him. Joey brooded and glared at John from the backseat while John looked ahead and told Monte what exit to get off at on the 110.

Nothing could stop John from navigating the van or steering the band. It was his ship, and he had no trouble throwing off excess baggage. The problem was, he had excess baggage of his own. For Roxy, California was one big open bar. They sold booze in 7-Elevens and bodegas. She was drunk at the Trop and drunk on the set, and it was getting on John's nerves. When we were shooting a scene, it was her chance to get away, so she would ask Marion and Vera to walk her off school grounds and around the corner to a convenience store. Sometimes she could barely make it back.

Marion had told me in Europe about Roxy's exploits in hotel rooms. When we got to Paris, it was Marion's first time there, and she wanted to see everything from the Louvre to the Arc de Triomphe. She wanted Roxy to come along, but Roxy's only goal was to stay in the room and clean out the minibar. As if that wasn't bad enough, she didn't want to pay for it. She had her minibar rip-off MO down to an art form.

Roxy would take a small bottle of Scotch or wine or rum and carefully remove the aluminum wrapping at the top like a surgeon. Next, she would unscrew the cap like a watchmaker. The easy part was drinking what was in the bottle. That she did like a fish. Then she would fill the bottle with tap water and restore the cap and foil like a liquor mortician. All this from a trust-fund baby who could have bought the entire hotel a round without blinking. Roxy's habits at the Tropicana were not much different. And, even though it was all on the house, the thrill of getting shitfaced was rivaled only by the idea of getting something for free.

We didn't have time for boozing, lovers' quarrels, or random pill popping today. For us, this was probably the busiest day of the movie shoot. In the story, Riff Randell and the Ramones have just taken over the school and mayhem ensues. But mayhem looks a lot different when you're shooting it one short scene at a time.

In the most ambitious scene, the students and the Ramones joyously parade down the hall while singing 'Do You Wanna Dance?' The lip-synching had to be on the money, and the look had to be loose like a party. My part presented maybe the biggest challenge. I was playing the drums on a wheeled drum riser pushed by members of the football team. Allan Arkush was calling the signals, and we were getting ready for the first down.

This was the moment Roxy picked to lose her balance and stagger a bit. It was right in front of the cast. As the day wore on, she would get progressively sloppier, and, while we weren't even at halftime yet, Roxy was clearly in the fourth quarter.

John shot Roxy one of his vintage laser stares. This was no longer a teen comedy. John looked as if he'd come straight out of *Village of the Damned*. His looks could kill, but he had to save them for the movies. So he grabbed Roxy and dragged her into the nearest empty classroom. Roxy had on a pair of hard, high-heeled, backless shoes called mules, and they clipped and clopped all the way to the classroom door, which John slammed behind them.

Action on the set came to a standstill. For the time being, real life trumped the silver screen, and John was giving Roxy a full dose of it behind closed doors. The clip-clopping of Roxy's shoes continued but sounded like the footsteps of someone struggling to stay on her feet. There were grunts and smacks and the sound of desks and chairs sliding around a linoleum-tile floor, sometimes toppling over.

There wasn't much screaming or yelling from either John or Roxy, which made the near silence of the people out in the hall that much more deafening. John, Roxy, and the Ramones knew the drill, but, to the rest of the cast and crew, it was a pre-talkie horror movie. There were unwritten rules in the world, and this display was breaking at least a few of them. But by the time anyone in the hall had figured out what they were, John appeared in the doorway looking ready to do a take.

After a day like that, I needed more than just a couple of drinks, and nothing soothed the savage breast better than eating at Duke's. Duke's was a coffee shop built into the Trop at the motel's right side, tucked under the first floor at street level. They had the world's best bacon, sausages, pancakes, and fresh-squeezed California orange juice. The portions were huge but never enough. Heaven was a perfect breakfast eaten at night. Everyone's mood was suddenly sunshine. Seating was family style. There were feuds going on in this family, but they seemed to melt like fat pads of butter on rye toast.

Later in the evening, I walked to the liquor store down the block with

Phil to get some more Manischewitz. I picked up a bottle of Bolla red wine. We drank our respective bottles back at my room and then we went out. Phil could have sat up front with George, but he preferred to sit in the back and feel chauffeured. He asked me to sit up front with George. The plan was to hit a few clubs – the Whisky, the Rainbow, the Troubadour, etc. We pulled up to the Troubadour first.

I had walked into a lot of clubs with a lot of well-known people, but this was a new experience. Maybe five foot six in heels, Phil Spector and his aura seemed eight feet tall. I wasn't sure exactly why we were going to these clubs until I witnessed this coronation. They didn't serve Manischewitz at the Troubadour, but the Red Sea still parted as we made our way back. In the crowd that lined the hallway two kinds of face immediately lit up: those in the record business and those that *wanted* to be in the record business. In Los Angeles, that was everyone. They noticed me, too. I was a Ramone. I was a moon orbiting Jupiter.

We sat in the back. There was not much else in the world I would rather be doing than talking with Phil Spector about echo chambers, how to build up recorded sound without cluttering it, and what it was like working with the Beatles. In truth, there actually was one thing: recording with Phil Spector. In a life filled with more success than I could ever have imagined banging away at my first cheapo snare drum, it was looking more and more like I was going to get my wish. Phil had been talking to his old friend Seymour Stein about producing the Ramones' next album, *End of the Century*.

As George pulled up to the front entrance of the club with the Seville, Phil for whatever reason talked about the civil rights movement.

'All the true sacrifices were made in the late fifties and the sixties,' he said, wagging a finger. 'This is lazy time out here. Someone else paved our way. I was there.'

While he talked, he kept turning around very quickly as if someone were tapping his shoulder. But no one was there. He was so convincing, he had me wheeling around to look a couple of times.

'Phil,' I said. 'Whatsa matter? What are you doing?'

'Oh, you know,' he said. 'The first time you don't look, that's when they really start following you.' It was going to be interesting having him and Joey in the same room.

We had exterior shots to do the next day, which included most of the lines the members of the Ramones would get to speak in the movie. That wasn't many. We were there to put on a show, take over the school, and provide comic relief, but we definitely weren't students of Stella Adler. For a guy who wouldn't shut up, Dee Dee never met a line he didn't flub. Joey was shy off camera. On camera, he played a shyer version of himself. John could say a line correctly, but he came across as stiff. He was much more at home playing guitar or talking baseball.

Outside the front entrance to the school, they were setting up a bonfire of Ramones albums. They were all there: *Ramones, Leave Home, Rocket to Russia,* and *Road to Ruin.* There were enough of each to stock all the Tower Records stores in LA. For the authorities to burn your book or album, you generally had to be pretty good. Also sprinkled into the pile for good measure were a few legendary albums. I spotted Bob Dylan's thoughtful face on *Highway 61 Revisited* and the tight blue jeans on the cover of the Rolling Stones' *Sticky Fingers.* At least in one sense we were all burning up the charts.

The four Ramones rolled into school in the open-top pink Cadillac with our battle cry license plate – 'Gabba Gabba Hey'. The plate proudly read New York. We would be going back the long way. We had a couple more days on the set, then three shows to film in one day at the Roxy for the movie. At that point, anyone outside the band might guess we were scheduled to fly back to New York, but that wasn't the case. We would be touring California for a week or two, spending New Year's Eve in San Jose, then making our way east in correct van seating formation, hitting every viable venue between the two oceans. It was a formula for burnout, but the money was starting to get really good.

Joey was not going to receive an invitation any time soon to the Actors Studio, but, as we walked on camera toward the bonfire, he delivered, flawlessly, one of those rare lines that go down both in comedic and rock-and-roll history: 'Things sure have changed since we got kicked out of high school.' John's place in the history of cinema was secured moments later when Principal Togar mistook us for students. 'We're not students. We're the Ramones.' The line was delivered flatly, and I thought it would have been even better without 'the' in it, but with the Ramones you took what you got.

What I got was the chance to stick a piece of loose-leaf paper on Togar's back that said 'Kick Me'. But, as we walked into the school, Mary Woronov got the best of all of us when Principal Togar shouted, 'Do your parents know you're Ramones?'

Part of a director's job is to make sure the actors understand their motivations in any given scene. That's even more critical when the scenes are shot out of sequence, which is just about always. Especially when you're doing a low-budget independent movie, the producers have to group together scenes by location to keep costs down. So here we were in a school office, but supposedly backstage after the big show at the local theater that we hadn't actually played yet. Dee Dee's big moment had arrived.

'Hey, pizza!'

Those were his words as he walked into the room with a half-dozen soggy pizza cartons. At least he got it right. They were already carving his name into a best supporting actor award at the Academy. Next, resolving a major subplot, Riff Randell walked in and handed Joey her sheet music for 'Rock 'n' Roll High School,' a song actually written by Joey and Dee Dee. In the real world, she could have given them acting lessons in return for songwriting lessons, but this was Hollywood.

The pizza should have been paid scale, because it saved the scene. There was a close shot of Dee Dee staring down an oily, gooey slice and wondering whether or not to put it in his mouth. This after swallowing dozens of pills off the playground floor. John threw a slice across the room. Joey started to eat his slice, but our sleazy manager, played by Herbie Braha, had other ideas.

'How many times do I have to tell you, no pizza for you, Joey! More wheat germ and riboflavin! Organic alfalfa!'

Herbie began stuffing Joey's mouth with alfalfa sprouts. Joey the actor made Joey the character cooperate and chew. For Joey the real person, it was shock treatment and would have to work itself out in the coming weeks with thousands of sidewalk taps and doorknob touches. At least the sprouts were fresh, rather than the kind left out on the kitchen table for weeks.

The only Ramone on the set who ate the pizza without a fuss was me. So, for at least a moment, art imitated life. All that was left was for Joey to tell Riff and her music teacher he'd take a look at the song. Easier said than done. The teacher, Mr. McGree, was played by Paul Bartel, a Brooklyn guy who got the acting bug many years before and headed west. Now, looking like a horse with the oats almost cleared from his mouth, Joey spoke.

'If we like 'em, we'll come and pay you and Mr. McGloop a visit.' Allan yelled cut.

'Who the fuck is Mr. McGloop?'

'I don't know,' Joey said. 'I think I was thinking of Mr. Magoo.'

'That's great, Joey. Now try thinking of Mr. McGree.'

We tried it two more times and got two more Mr. McGloops. So Allan decided to leave it in. What the hell! One day, we figured, 'McGloop' would be the answer to a punk-rock trivia question. Meantime, we wouldn't be holding our breath for our Screen Actors Guild cards to come in the mail. It was good we didn't have many lines, or the movie would have been finished around the end of the century.

Back at the Trop, Dee Dee was hanging out with two LA girls by the pool. There were many people around the hotel and around the world who would have identified these two as 'groupies'. I tried never to do that. To me they were fans. They were people who bought our albums, came to our shows, and enabled us to spend our lives doing what we loved instead of wiling away our time at a desk or on a dock. I introduced myself as Marky and shook their hands.

These fans, however, were handing Dee Dee little orange pills, which I identified as speed. I had known Dee Dee for years and really didn't know he was into that. Then again, he wasn't the most discriminating drug user. I walked over to my room. I didn't know where Marion was – maybe out with Vera getting something at Los Tacos, down the road.

Phil Spector wouldn't be coming by tonight, so I thought it would be a good idea a little later to check in on Dee Dee.

When I did, I got another surprise. One of the girls was in the living room smoking a joint. She told me Dee Dee was in the bathroom. Given his activities lately, I thought it wasn't a bad idea once in a while to see if our bassist was alive. The bathroom door was open and I poked my head in.

'You okay, Dougie?'

'Yeah, great. Come on in.'

Dee Dee and the other girl were in the bathtub. She was naked. Dee Dee was, too, except for underwear. It wasn't his. He was wearing what I figured were the girl's underpants – a frilly satin pink Frederick's of Hollywood number with a red heart on it.

'Do you know if Marion's with Vera?' I said.

'I dunno,' Dee Dee said.

'Dee Dee, what the fuck exactly are you doing?'

'This young lady needed a bath,' Dee Dee said. 'Just a bath. Look, I'm still dressed!'

Craziness, like everything, had different levels. Some people thought pushing the limit with your dedicated, loving wife was crazy. Others thought popping amphetamines or wearing some girl's kinky underwear in a motel bathtub was crazy. But doing all of it at once when your wife could walk in the door any minute was Dee Dee.

The scene at the fictitious Rockatorium was one of the last exterior shots. Riff was camped out waiting to buy tickets in front of what was actually an abandoned movie theater in downtown LA. In the real world, people were walking to work on a typical weekday morning. Commuters at traffic lights were honking and little coffee shops and diners were cooking breakfast. You could literally smell the ham and eggs. In our make-believe world, cordoned off with wires and security ropes, the Ramones were being chauffeured to the venue on the day of the big show. Our chauffeur was Rodney Bingenheimer.

Rodney Bingenheimer was a well-known DJ both inside and beyond Los Angeles. He didn't take the normal route: tinkering with ham radios, getting a communications degree, and doing the graveyard shift at a 100-watt jazz station. In the sixties, he was a moptop chameleon. He looked so much like Sonny Bono that he almost fooled Cher, who became a close friend. Bingenheimer also got the job as the stand-in for Davy Jones on the TV series *The Monkees*. Eventually, Bingenheimer looked and sounded enough like a disc jockey to become one. On KROQ, he was one of the first in the country to play the Ramones, Blondie, and the Sex Pistols. He loved us and gave us the airwaves. The spot in the driver's seat was like a small token of our appreciation. Really, *we* should have been chauffeuring *him*.

After being let off at the curb, the four Ramones walked on camera lip-synching 'I Just Want to Have Something to Do'. I didn't have the luxury of strutting along the sidewalk with a guitar or bass like John or Dee Dee. The drums stayed in the open-top Cadillac. The only props I had were a pair of drumsticks miraculously creating this monster rock sound. I felt ridiculous.

'Cut!'

Allan wanted me to be a little more animated. I needed to play along, dance, act out the music. Click the sticks to the beat. I asked how two sticks without a kit could sound like drums. Something about 'suspended disbelief'. When we did the next take, I clicked and bobbed and weaved and shook. I pointed the sticks at screaming fans. It was goofy. Goofier than even Mr. McGloop. And it was a wrap. The only problem was, one day I would have to watch it back on a large screen.

On 14 December, we played the first of three consecutive shows at the Roxy on Sunset Boulevard in West Hollywood. The movie would feature five live songs with a screaming audience. To keep the screaming fresh, we would play to three separate audiences and use the best footage. Cast members would stay in the front all three shows for continuity. They included Clint Howard and Vince Van Patten. Clint was the younger brother of Ron Howard, Richie from TV's *Happy Days*. Vince was the son of Dick Van Patten from TV's *Eight Is Enough*. In Hollywood, good lineage never hurt.

The lineage of the Roxy was everything you could have hoped for.

Originally a strip club, it became a rock club in the early seventies. Not simply a venue for top acts, the acoustics at the Roxy were ideal for live recordings. Artists including Bruce Springsteen and the E Street Band, George Benson, Frank Zappa and the Mothers, and Bob Marley and the Wailers had each recorded all or parts of live albums here. Even the name had lineage. During John Lennon's long 'lost weekend' in 1974–5, Lennon, Harry Nilsson, Keith Moon, and Alice Cooper all partied regularly at the bar above the club. The Ramones brought along their own Roxy, Johnny's girlfriend, to continue the tradition, and she could drink Lennon and friends under the table.

The Ramones were a young band but had already spawned countless disciples of their own. Some of them were at the Roxy on this night. Black Flag had a raw guitar sound evidently influenced by the Ramones but with a far more guttural vocal approach. The band had just released a four-song EP with a total running time of five minutes and twenty-three seconds. Forget leads: there was barely time for a chorus.

The Germs featured the very talented chord-shredding Pat Smear on guitar and the manic, self-destructive lead singer Darby Crash, who usually delivered on the last name. The band X were probably the most talented of the bunch. Songs like 'White Girl' were offbeat in theme and featured inventive melodies along with terrific vocal harmonies. When Doors keyboardist Ray Manzarek agreed to produce X, you had a notion of what he heard – a distant legacy of the strange LA tales his own band used to weave.

But the truth was, these LA punk bands could barely find a place to play in a California baked in soft rock, lite rock, commercial rock, and corporate rock. As eager as the Ramones were to break through in a still bigger way than we had, we were, simply by being on this famous stage with lenses trained on us – enjoying success that the LA disciples could only dream of. The dues were a bitch. I could only hope that our being in the limelight for the moment would encourage these bands to keep pursuing their artistic vision no matter how many times they were spit on – or worse still, not spit on.

We ripped through 'Blitzkrieg', 'Teenage Lobotomy', 'California Sun', and 'Pinhead' before closing with 'She's the One.' It felt good not to be lip-synching. To be bashing away for real and having the crowd's energy flood the stage. I still felt the heat of the pyrotechnics from the final school scene we had shot the day before, when Riff and friends pushed the plunger and detonated the building. It blew out windows and forced up massive plumes of smoke.

But once Riff yelled, 'Hit it, Marky!' I had to sit there in my leather jacket, play along to the title track, and not look back like Lot and his wife in the Old Testament. It wasn't about turning into a pillar of salt. The stakes were larger – we could blow up the school only once. So I tried to ignore the heat on the back of my neck, grimaced a bit, played through a little anxiety, and took one for the team.

Before long, we would be back to record an album with Phil Spector. In rock and roll, there could hardly be a better legacy. I hoped the pyrotechnics were behind us.

11

WALL OF SOUND

We were back at Los Angeles International Airport waiting for our baggage to slide down the ramp and swing around the carousel. I knew what everyone's stuff looked like more or less, and the Ramones' luggage wasn't on the first cart unloaded. A situation like this one required patience, and Dee Dee didn't have any. He edged up to the carousel and eyed a particular red American Tourister suitcase that had already circled around once, unclaimed.

The suitcase looked as if it had taken a beating over the plains states. The handle was busted and the zipper was broken. Clothing was sticking out. As the bag swung around for lap two, Dee Dee positioned himself to intercept it. He yanked it off the belt using the broken handle and began rifling through. A white silk blouse caught his eye. So did a gray cashmere sweater. Dee Dee had excellent taste in stolen women's clothing at the airport. He slipped the items under his jacket and continued the treasure hunt.

I smiled and looked at Marion in disbelief. She smiled back and rolled her eyes. There were a hundred and fifty witnesses and basic rules of civilization, and none of them seemed to mean anything to our bassist. But the middle-aged white lady now yelling in Dee Dee's face caught his attention.

'Excuse me! What are you doing with my clothes?'

'Oh, this yours? Sorry.'

He didn't seem sorry at all other than that he was caught. He pulled the blouse and sweater out from under his jacket and sheepishly handed them over to the lady.

'What is wrong with you?'

We were all still trying to figure that out and really didn't expect a breakthrough here in baggage claim at LAX. The lady folded her garments and tried to put Humpty Dumpty back together again as Dee Dee gazed back down the carousel for the next victim. I hoped our luggage was coming soon.

There were turrets on either side of Phil Spector's Beverly Hills mansion. As we stood outside the wrought-iron gates waiting to be led inside, I wondered whether Phil Spector himself was up right now in one of those turrets looking out on me, Dee Dee, Joey, John, and Monte. It was kind of the same creepy feeling Dee Dee and I got walking along the Berlin Wall and getting lit up by searchlights, except the East Germans weren't looking to deliver the Ramones a platinum album.

It was less a house than a compound. There were a lot of warning signs. Do not enter. Do not touch gate. Beware of attack dogs. The signs looked pretty amateurish, and that made them more rather than less imposing.

George Brand let us in the front gate, past the fountain, and in through the large wooden entrance doors. The furniture was mostly red velvet from the mid-seventies, which was recent history but receding fast. George led us to the living room, where behind a grand piano sat Phil Spector.

'Ramones! You ready to make the best album of your lives?'

'Yeah, yeah, ready.'

Sitting on the love seat was Grandpa Al Lewis. Lewis would for ever be connected to the role he made famous on the sixties TV show *The Munsters*. But I loved him even before that as Officer Schnauser in *Car*

54, Where Are You?. It was surreal seeing him in Phil Spector's living room – or anyone's living room, for that matter. And the next surprise arrived when Grandpa stood up. He was well over six feet tall. In the cowboy boots and ten-gallon western hat, he looked closer to seven feet.

Phil walked us toward his billiard room. On the way there I looked through to the gigantic kitchen and saw a massive St. Bernard chained up in the corner. He looked big enough to drag the mahogany cabinets and marble counters with him if he really wanted to. If a visitor for some reason tried something unwise and somehow got past George, Phil's guns, and Phil's karate, the dog would maul whoever it was and make them wish Phil or George had finished the job.

Phil Spector had a lot to be proud of, but he was proudest of his billiard table. Right here the legendary pool player Willie Mosconi had given Phil lessons on how to sink balls like a champion. Mosconi had once sunk 526 in a row. He could make one billiard ball jump over another and then strike and sink a third ball. Mosconi had coached Paul Newman during the filming of the 1961 movie *The Hustler*. Phil Spector was no Paul Newman, but, when it came to producing a record, he was Marlon Brando.

He had big plans for *End of the Century*. The Ramones' fifth studio album was going to be big in both the sonic and sales senses. Seymour Stein was paying Phil Spector on the order of a quarter million dollars to produce it and put the band over the top.

Phil led us back to the living room and explained how his Wall of Sound would meet the Ramones' wall of sound and create wall-to-wall sound. For that to happen, we had to all listen to him and put our confidence in him. He told us how much he liked the new songs, including 'Do You Remember Rock 'n' Roll Radio?', which he said had a classic fifties feel and should become a huge anthem. He had high hopes for 'Danny Says', which was an airy ballad and a major departure for the group.

The cover song he wanted to do was 'Baby, I Love You', which he had co-written back in 1963 for the Ronettes. Phil emphasized how important it was for Joey to get the right feel on the vocals for 'Baby', and that if he did, there was no stopping us. The song had been a hit before and could do it again.

Although I loved the song, I wasn't sure it was right for the Ramones. But it wasn't as if I was going to question the judgment of probably the greatest producer who had ever lived. In any case, Phil Spector was comfortable with old friends, whether they were songs or people. It was easy to see why Grandpa Al Lewis fitted into that category. Lewis's politics were, like Phil's, radical and to the left. There in the living room, with his cigar and classic New York accent, Lewis argued for the abolishment of New York's harsh Rockefeller drug laws and the establishment of universal healthcare. John wasn't into it.

'You give these lazy immigrants something free like that and you'll never get rid of them.'

'Who wants to get rid of them except you?' Lewis said. 'They built the country.'

'People like my father built the country,' John said.

'Do you know how many Chinese immigrants died pounding out the Union Pacific Railroad, my friend? Hundreds!'

I had to laugh hearing John warn us about immigrants taking free stuff. All his T-shirts came from the band's merchandise. We would get plain T-shirts in bulk so that Arturo Vega could silk-screen the Ramones logo onto them for sale after the shows. Before the logo went on, John would skim a dozen black shirts, a dozen blue ones, and a half dozen of whatever color. Those were the shirts John wore to every occasion including interviews, bar mitzvahs, and wakes. He never under any circumstances bought underwear or socks. His mother always bought him a ton of them for Christmas and that was all he ever needed. John's yearly wardrobe budget was zero dollars and zero cents.

Grandpa Al was more than a left-winger. He was an eccentric and one with a delusion here and there. He told us he served on the legal defense team of the 1920s anarchists Sacco and Vanzetti. There was no doubt Grandpa would have if he could have, but he was about eleven years old at the time – or an infant, depending upon which birth date you believed. He also informed us that in the sixties he met Charles Manson, who babysat his sons. 'He was a gentleman!' Grandpa said. Hearing this, Dee Dee started talking about his own sons, who didn't even exist, and about his fictional days fighting the Vietcong. Someone should have grabbed a tape recorder, because *this* was an album.

When we walked into Gold Star Recording Studios on 1 May, Phil, my new buddy, stopped me.

'Take it off. Take it off! I'm not spending the fucking day staring at a picture of my ex-wife!'

I was a Ronettes fan. It was as simple as that. That's why I was wearing a T-shirt with Ronnie Spector and the other two Ronettes on it. It was not to annoy Phil. If anything, it was a tribute. For a second, I didn't know what to do. On one hand, I didn't take shit from people, including the guys in my own band. On the other hand, I wanted things to go smoothly, especially now. We didn't need to start the album of our lives with a confrontation. But, on the first hand again, I didn't have another T-shirt with me.

So I took off the shirt, turned it inside out, and put it on again. Now Ronnie's gorgeous eyes were staring at me, not him. I thought I saw Phil smile for an instant. It wasn't much – just an upturn of one side of his mouth and done. I had shared wine with Phil many times and felt equipped to deal with him. If everyone in the room took the same approach, there was no reason it shouldn't be smooth sailing.

There wouldn't be many people in the control room. Those were Phil's rules. It would be just Phil, his longtime engineer Larry Levine, the three other Ramones and myself. No wives and girlfriends allowed, and no crew. Monte had driven us to Gold Star from the Tropicana and would drive us back later but was content to sit in a chair just outside the control room. He had other things to worry about and had taken enough shit from us on the road to last a dozen rock-and-roll lifetimes.

The women at this point were Marion, Vera, Roxy, and Linda. Linda was Joey's girlfriend. We discovered that fact when filming for *Rock 'n' Roll High School* wrapped and Linda boarded the van to continue with the Ramones on tour. Joey hadn't stepped inside yet, and Linda took a seat in the front row. John turned around and busted her in one second flat.

'No, no, no, honey. You sit in the back.'

'What do you mean?' Linda said.

'We have rules here,' John said. 'You're with Joey. You sit in the back.'

'Not for long,' Linda said.

Even as she got up and moved to the rear, Linda was defiant. John was speechless. He opened his mouth halfway as if a string of words coupling rage and disbelief were on their way out, but their sum total was silence. He shook his head and looked around as if to point out that we were all witnesses.

She was short, pale, and rail thin. But that's where the similarities ended. Linda had a big mouth. She had an answer for everything. Joey seemed to love that about her. Shy and nonconfrontational as Joey was, Linda had enough chutzpah for the both of them. And, when she went to battle with John, it was as if Joey went to heaven. Still, she sat outside in the studio lounge with the other women. Butting heads with Phil Spector was out of the question.

Just hanging out in the lounge at Gold Star was an honor. This was where it all happened – if not literally all, at least most of it. Phil Spector and Gold Star made magic together. The Ronettes recorded a string of Top Forty hits within these walls. Phil Spector gave birth to the Righteous Brothers' 'You've Lost That Lovin' Feelin'' here. John Lennon, George Harrison, Leonard Cohen, Ike and Tina Turner – the list was long and the space on the walls too small to fit all the gold records produced within them. Gold Star's résumé was largely Phil Spector's résumé.

It was also Larry Levine's résumé. Larry was Phil's engineer. He was there for the whole ride. When you heard the strings and horns blend in perfectly at the beginning of the Crystals' 'Then He Kissed Me', it was Larry Levine's finger on the fader. When you heard the pounding bass guitar on Ike and Tina's juiced-up version of 'Proud Mary', it was Larry Levine mixing the miked speaker sound with the direct signal.

Someone not only had to know exactly what Phil Spector meant when he shouted 'Give me more bottom!' but had to actually give it to him. And fast. When Phil Spector created a wall of sound by cramming forty musicians into a tiny room, someone had to make sure every brick in the wall was where it was supposed to be. Like any good soldier, Larry Levine deserved combat pay once in a while, whether or not he actually got it. Like only some good soldiers, Larry was very gracious and professional. We were lucky he was here for the whole Ramones ride.

The doorway leading to the Gold Star echo chamber off to the side was narrow. The walls in the main room consisted of thick cement plaster with heavy isolation forms. As we set up the drums, I was conscious of Phil Spector's preferences. He leaned away from cymbals and hi-hats. He preferred to get his trebly percussion sounds from tambourines, maracas, or any other percussive instrument he could better control in the studio. Particularly with a cymbal, once there was a big crash on the drum tracks, the 'wash', or fade, of that crash overlapped everything and could easily get in the way of other sounds. The cymbal was next to impossible to scrub out when you were going back to work on the tracks.

For that reason, Phil Spector would physically remove Wrecking Crew drummer Hal Blaine's cymbals. In the back of my mind, I thought about the trouble that approach would cause the Ramones. We had a style. I had a style. That style could be tinkered with but not sabotaged. Going to the crash cymbal was automatic for me. It was automatic for the band. When it felt right, I reached for it like a runner taking a deep breath. Fortunately, the issue never came up. Phil's main suggestion was to put a towel over my snare drum to get a dry sound, and I agreed.

I played to a click track, as I always did in the Ramones. I never did it with Richard Hell and the Voidoids, because that music was largely about rhythmic feel and included multiple changes in time signature within a given song. Sophisticated programming would have been required to match a click track, and all that effort would have hurt the songs anyway. But Ramones songs were perfect for the click track: 4/4 and 2/4. I knew if I could play along perfectly with the click, the band would sound that much more solid and tight. Phil Spector agreed. And John liked the savings in studio costs.

I played the songs one after the other. Through the glass I saw Phil pound the console a couple of times, but it was no big deal. I couldn't hear any of it in the headphones, just as I couldn't hear what looked like Phil's occasional yelling at Larry. Other than my own drums and the scratch tracks, all I heard most of the time in the cans was Phil hitting the 'talk' button and saying 'Try it again.' Usually, by the third or fourth take, he would yell, 'That's it! That's the one!'

Usually I knew what he meant. The difference between a passable take and a keeper was often just a matter of energy. That was a subtle difference on some songs. On 'Chinese Rock', the heroin saga Dee Dee had written with Richard Hell, it wasn't too subtle. Phil Spector pumped his fist into the air at the end of the second take, and all I had to do was let the microphones record the quick natural fade-out of the hit on the snare.

Phil listened closely and agreed when I suggested we use Rototoms on 'I'm Affected' and 'This Ain't Havana'. Rototoms could actually be tuned – by rotating the head – which I thought would work well with the big sound Phil was looking for. There were certain pitches that resonated more depending on the degree of echo. It wasn't like *Road to Ruin*, where the bottom heads of the drums were off and I was just looking for a big thud.

Day five was nothing like days one, two, three, and four. Phil had a concept in mind for the opening chord of 'Rock 'n' Roll High School'. The opening chord to the Beatles' 'A Hard Day's Night' was an F with a G added, played on a Rickenbacker 12-string electric guitar. Producer George Martin had George Harrison strum the chord hard and let it ring out for a few seconds. There was incredible sustain on those notes, and it became probably the most famous, identifiable chord ever to introduce a rock-and-roll song. The very first time the world heard that chord, everyone knew that whatever followed was going to be great. In that vein, Phil wanted John to let his opening chord ring. John wanted to wring Phil's neck.

We lost count of how many times Phil had him play it. We lost track of time itself. It had probably been over an hour. But, as with Chinese water torture, an hour could seem like a lifetime. The drip-drip-drip of this torture was consistent enough to cause madness. John would stroke down on the G and stand there scoffing while it rang. He looked down at his Keds sneakers, then rolled his eyes up toward the ceiling.

Meanwhile, Phil shook his head, pounded the console, and motioned with his finger to do it again. He did a shot of Manischewitz and tossed a Dixie cup into the garbage can. Phil muttered a few things, but he wasn't yelling. Neither was John. That was too bad. The silence was deafening. It was a cold war, and we all wanted someone to fire a harmless little shot to break the tension. Even better, we wanted Phil to yell, 'That's it! That's the one!' But it never came. It was hard to know for sure, but it seemed like Joey enjoyed it.

Phil reached for his gun. Dee Dee sat up straight. Joey stopped grinning and put down his Coke. We knew what we knew, or at least we thought we did. Phil had pulled a gun on Leonard Cohen in this same room. Phil had fired a shot off in the studio during the recording of John Lennon's album of classic cover songs, *Rock 'n' Roll*. Now he would have Johnny Ramone make history even if he had to kill him.

I didn't believe it for a second. Phil walked a few paces to his right and laid his .38 down on the wooden end table alongside the console. The .45 came out next. The firearms were even less likely to send anyone to rock-and-roll heaven on that end table than they were in their holsters, but the other Ramones apparently didn't see it that way. Dee Dee looked at me as if to say, 'Should we run for it?' I shook my head back as if to say, 'Give me a fucking break.' John was frozen on the other side of the glass. But Phil walked back toward Larry and gave John the signal to play. The faucet was dripping again.

The water torture itself had the sustain John's chord lacked. Something was needed to stop the insanity, but what? A power failure like the one during the Voidoids sessions during the summer of 1977 would have been nice, but blackouts rarely came when you needed them most. Maybe Larry Levine would come up with a technical solution. Maybe John would break a string and we would move on to something else. *Anything* else.

Relief came as it often does: in the form of two LA prostitutes. They walked in one after the other, following George Brand. One hooker was a bleached blonde wearing red spandex and a tight, low-cut silk blouse. The other had dark hair and an olive complexion with a body wrapped in denim so tight that, if you opened a button, she might pop like a balloon. Both hookers wore fur coats. It was eighty-two degrees Fahrenheit on this May afternoon in Southern California.

Our producer followed George and LA's finest out the control room door. Phil's drill was to disappear into a side office and return ten or fifteen minutes later as if he had been to the men's room. We didn't know exactly what to call this kind of break, so we called it lunch. The control room door flew open. It was John.

'You all saw that. He was going to fucking shoot me.'

'Yeah, right,' I said. 'In your dreams.'

'Well,' John said, 'let him shoot me. It'll be better than going through this shit any more.'

'You saw him pull out those guns, Marc, didn't you?' Dee Dee asked.

'You're overreacting,' Joey said. 'He didn't point them at anyone.'

'He was getting ready to use them,' Dee Dee insisted.

'Remember, those are heavy guns,' I said. 'You expect him to carry them around in the studio all day?'

At that point, Dee Dee told us the same story he had told us several times over the last few days. While we were at the Beverly Hills mansion, Phil had a talk with Joey in a room upstairs. Dee Dee and John thought Phil wanted to take Joey away from the Ramones and produce him as a solo act. That didn't make any sense, especially with Seymour Stein paying Phil Spector a lot of money to produce the group. More likely, Phil was interested in getting the best and biggest vocal sound possible on the album and wanted to give Joey kind of a pep talk.

In any case, Dee Dee, who like the rest of us was drinking all afternoon, wandered upstairs to find Spector. According to Dee Dee, at that point Phil, maybe thinking Dee Dee was an intruder, burst out of the room with his .38 drawn. Dee Dee claimed they had a few words and then Phil pointed the gun at Dee Dee's heart and told him to go back downstairs to the living room.

It wasn't impossible that it happened this way, but I didn't actually see it, and it was unlikely. And I had to consider the source: Dee Dee, who fantasized the way other people breathed. It didn't make him a reliable witness, but it made him a great songwriter.

In the control room, after hearing this, I told the other guys not to obsess over the guns, the yelling, the pounding, or the retakes. We were going to walk away with a great album. I also told them to remember where Phil was coming from and not to take it personally. When he was in high school, he was grabbed by a bunch of bullies and beaten severely, after which he swore he would never be a victim again.

'He probably fucking deserved it,' John said.

Phil was in a good mood when he walked back into the control room. The LA hookers were worth their weight in gold. Maybe platinum. Phil was very cordial with John and had Larry adjust the guitar amp setup in the echo chamber to do tracking for 'Rock 'n' Roll High School'. Phil, John, and Larry got a lot done over the next thirty minutes or so until the door to the control room opened and Monte walked in. I saw Phil's mood sour a little right away. Monte wasn't supposed to be in the room except at the end of the session, when it was time to drive us back to the Tropicana.

'I need to talk to John for a minute,' Monte said.

'We're in the middle of something.' Phil shot Monte a nasty look. But Monte proceeded into the main recording room and fished John out. They left together through the control room. Phil was now visibly angry. Whatever personal triumph there was for him in working smoothly with John for a short while had now dissolved to disgust, and Larry was right in the line of fire.

'Don't ride the fader! Don't ride the fader unless I tell you to!'

'Okay, Phil. I got it.'

'Not okay! What part of "Don't ride the fader" do you not under-stand?'

The control room door opened again and Monte stepped in. I was braced for Phil to savage Monte for sending him into a tailspin.

'I have some bad news,' Monte said. 'John's father died.'

We called it a day.

John's father had died of a heart attack. It was a complete shock. He was only sixty-two. It was obviously very sad. He had recently retired and moved with John's mother to Florida. There was such a thing as the American Dream, and there was also the American nightmare. The nightmare was to spend your entire adult life doing hard labor in return for a few golden years and then get short-changed. I had seen it many times before, and it wasn't going to be me if I could help it.

When we saw John in the lounge a minute later, he was pale, numb, and shell-shocked. One bookend to his life was John Wayne, and the other was his father. He idolized his dad. He was always trying to please him, to prove himself. Even in the Ramones. And now he was on his own.

John was gone for a few days. He had to fly from Los Angeles to New York to see family, then from New York to Florida for the funeral. Phil used the studio time to work on bass parts and vocals. Working with Dee Dee seemed to stress out Phil even when the bass sounded great. The annoyance jumped a couple of notches when we worked on 'Chinese Rock'. I thought the song was coming out okay. Joey liked it. Dee Dee, of course, loved it. And Phil went through a lot of Manischewitz and Dixie cups.

When John came back, he looked worn out and not just from jetlag. He had flown a triangle around the country to put things in order, comfort his mother, and be strong for everyone who came to the funeral. He had no time to even begin sorting out what his father's passing meant to him. But beneath the bags under John's eyes was a little smile, which he explained to us. Linda had gone along with Monte a few days earlier to drop John off at the airport. And today she had also gone with Monte to pick him up.

All of this was anything but expected. Not only was Linda Joey's girlfriend, she and John seemed to be in perpetual conflict. Whatever the dynamics, John was touched that someone would care enough about him to go along, especially with no obligation to do so. John seemed to believe he had alienated the rest of the band, and of course there was some truth to that. So Linda's gesture meant even more.

We weren't sure if it had something to do with John's return when the following day Phil Spector asked us all to enter the control room at Gold Star to hear the playback of 'Rock 'n' Roll High School'. The most unusual aspect of the request was that it included everybody – wives, girlfriends, and crew. Maybe it was Phil extending an olive branch. Maybe he just wanted to prove to us how great the album was turning out under his direction. Whatever the case, we were glad to get a chance to hear progress.

The couches in the control room were stuffed with bodies. Monte sat next to John Markovich, our sound man. The control room was usually off-limits to both of them. The last time John Markovich had stepped inside, Phil shouted, 'Who the hell is he? Get him out of here!' Phil Spector didn't seem impressed when we told him repeatedly Markovich's vocation. If anything, it got him more pissed off. As for Monte, he was allowed entrance only to inform band members of a parent's death. And even then . . .

Phil hit the 'play' button on the main tape machine. We heard John's one-chord intro, which sounded not quite up there with 'A Hard Day's Night' but pretty good nonetheless. Next, we heard the drums, then guitar, a bit of Joey's vocals, and then Phil stopped the tape and rewound. We figured there was a technical problem. Phil hit 'play' again and let the tape run before stopping at about the same spot and rewinding again.

Phil said nothing, and we asked nothing. He went through the cycle a third time, then a fourth, then a fifth. I looked quickly at Marion, who, with Phil's back turned, shook her head a bit. I knew that look as well as I knew anything. It meant, What the hell is going on here?

I really didn't know. It seemed a little hostile, maybe toward John. Maybe Phil was trying to point out how the chord needed still more sustain. Or maybe he was showing us that all the hard work had paid off. I wasn't sure. The only thing I was sure of was that I wanted to hear the whole song and so did everyone else.

'Well, you don't need me here.'

It was just a whisper from Monte to John Markovich. It wasn't meant for anyone else's ears, especially not Phil's. But Phil had the best ears in the western hemisphere, so, if we heard it, so did he. It might as well have been said in the echo chamber. Still, Monte lifted himself up off the couch and tried to slink out of the control room.

'What the fuck do you think you're doing?' Phil Spector was pissed off.

'I'm leaving,' Monte said. 'You don't need me here.'

'You're damn right we don't need you here,' Phil said. 'We only need the keys.'

'The keys?'

'Are you deaf? The keys. To the van. Hand them over.'

'C'mon, Phil,' Monte said. 'What are you doing this for?'

'What do you think, you're going to go back to the Tropicana and take a nap? Fine. Take a cab!'

'I'm responsible for the van,' Monte said. 'The insurance is in my name. I can't just leave it with you, or with anyone, for that matter. If something happens to the van, it's my ass.'

'I got news for you,' Phil said. 'It's already your ass. Van or no van.'

At that point I felt bad for Monte. He seemed to be fighting back the tears. No matter how many gold records Phil Spector had on his wall, there was no way the Ramones were going to fire Monte. Not over this. On some level, Monte had to know that. On another level, Phil had us all so agitated that anything seemed possible. Someone from the band should have jumped in at that moment on Monte's behalf. But no one did. We were paralyzed. Monte was between a rock and an echo chamber.

I felt even worse when I considered the way we endlessly pranked Monte. Earlier in the year, on our way from Chicago to Detroit, we all had to take a leak and the next rest stop was at least a half-hour away. So we pulled the van off to the service road of Route 90 and took our turns. Each of us would pee facing the van, so that the vehicle would shield us from the passing traffic. I went, then John, then Dee Dee. Joey was holding it in.

When it was Monte's turn, John took the wheel, and we waited till Monte's fly was open. At that point John put the van in gear and pulled up about fifty yards, leaving Monte exposed to the world. His reaction was the normal one. He panicked and ran to catch up with the van with his schlong still hanging out. I let John know Monte was coming, and when he got close, John stepped on the gas and pulled the van forward another fifty yards.

And here we were at Gold Star, leaving Monte exposed all over again. This time it was no joke. Monte walked out of the control room and into the lounge, all the while hoping Phil wouldn't follow him, but he did. John, John Markovich, and I followed behind. Phil wasn't going to let it go. Where were the LA prostitutes when you really needed them?

'I'm coming back later to pick everybody up,' Monte said. 'Okay?'

'No. Not okay. Don't come back.'

'I am coming back,' Monte said. 'It's my job.'

Monte made his way out the exit. No personnel were fired. No shots were fired. Phil shook his head and walked back into the control room muttering.

'Stupid schmuck.'

I looked at John, who was also shaking his head, and offered the only two words that popped into my head.

'Welcome back.'

John had another concern. Phil had told him earlier in the day that we were going to move to a different studio the following day, but Phil wouldn't tell him where. I told John that was because it was nowhere. There was no way we were relocating. This was the place where all the magic had happened going back to when we were still kids listening to Darlene Love. Maybe Phil was just kidding around with John. Or fucking around with John. Either way, I felt the urge to get away from it all. I thought about renting my own car and heading up into the hills.

I was glad about one thing: that, no matter how close he had come to blowing a gasket, Monte ultimately did not give in to the great Phil Spector. In a sense, Monte had earned his own gold star.

But this was no way to make an album. We all knew it. So the four of us put in a call to Seymour Stein. Seymour was one of the all-time class acts and had sunk a fortune into the Ramones more out of belief than out of financial sense. So we weren't going to tell Seymour Stein what to say or do or think. We just had to clear the air. We were at a boiling point. We never knew what to expect when we walked into the studio. There was happy Phil, and there was down Phil. There was understanding Phil, and there was maniac Phil. We needed producer Phil.

That night, when Phil Spector knocked on my door at the Tropicana, he seemed fine, and I certainly wasn't going to recap the day's events or tell him we had complained about him to the guy who was paying all the bills. Phil enjoyed my company and had obviously calmed down. He probably had a few drinks between then and now, and, if the bottle of grape Manischewitz in a brown paper bag was any indication, he was about to have a few more.

Fortunately, there was always other stuff to talk about, especially with Phil. The nuclear plant at Three Mile Island in Pennsylvania had nearly melted down earlier in the spring, sending the eastern part of the United States into a state of fear and alert. The crisis was averted, but Phil was convinced it actually got much closer to a catastrophe than the government ever admitted, and more radiation got out than we were being told. I agreed. A meltdown was a terrible thing on either coast.

The next morning on the van ride over to the studio, John told us he had heard from Linda Stein the night before. Seymour had called Phil and asked him to cool it. It was fine to do whatever he needed from a production standpoint, but the confrontations had to stop. That included confrontations with the Ramones crew who, like Phil Spector, were just doing their job. There was no argument. Seymour was paying him, and that was the way it had to be.

Phil was calm when we got to the studio. He had never been abusive directly to the band members, but now he was far less edgy and more businesslike. Dee Dee looked ready to bounce off the walls as Larry set up his microphones and Phil watched. We were working on the bass sound for 'I'm Affected'. The bass guitar introduced the song and had to be big.

Phil had Dee Dee run through the song a few times before recording. Larry had three or four microphones on the bass cabinet at different distances and angles. Phil told Larry repeatedly to leave the faders up, but Larry kept bringing them down a bit.

'How fucking badly do you want to ruin this song?' Phil said. 'That was the sound I was looking for, and you went and fucked with it.'

'Phil, there was too much distortion on the bass. I couldn't record it.'

'You mean you have the balls to sit there and tell me something you've done – something *we've* done a thousand times – you suddenly can't do.'

'We never recorded with that amount of distortion,' Larry said.

'What's distorted is what you're telling me! What's distorted is your fucking brain!'

It struck me that, no matter how good the album might turn out or how many copies it might sell, the experience of making it wasn't going to get much better than this. Phil wasn't giving less shit. The shit was just running downhill.

The next day, Monte told us we had the day off. He had gotten a call from Gold Star Recording Studios saying that Phil wouldn't be in today. It was kind of a relief, but John and I didn't want to waste the day. So we had Monte drive us to SIR, a rehearsal studio on Sunset Boulevard in Hollywood.

'Us' consisted of John, Dee Dee, and me. Although my tracks were already down, we wanted to make demos of a couple of songs that still needed guitar and bass, starting with 'I Can't Make It on Time', and 'All the Way'. We took one of the medium-sized rehearsal rooms in the back as opposed to the large production stage at the front. About half an hour in, I had to go to the bathroom, so I excused myself and walked to the men's room down the hall. After finishing and washing, I figured I would get a fresh pair of sticks from my shoulder bag. As I unzipped it, I saw that my wallet was open and my money was gone.

It was $150. I knew I had packed it. I remembered putting it in that morning just before walking out the door. I challenged my memory. Maybe I thought about putting it in the bag but didn't. No, I definitely had. I remembered putting it in the billfold and even remembered the denominations – six twenties, two tens, and two fives. I turned my head and saw Dee Dee sitting on a stool and fiddling with his bass. As I looked up from the floor, he looked down at me. If it was an awkward moment, it was awkward for me only. When John walked back into the room a moment later, it was game on.

'What are we going to do, John? I said. 'My money's gone.

'You sure?' John said.

'Of course I'm sure,' I said.

'Okay, come on, Dougie,' John said. 'Start with the pockets. Come on.'

'Seriously?' Dee Dee said.

'Come on, Dee Dee,' I said. 'I gotta check you out.'

Dee Dee didn't put up a fight. He just shrugged and emptied his jeans pockets. Out came room keys, a few dollars, roach clips, and a rainbow assortment of pills. That wasn't going to be good enough. I had him hand me his leather jacket, and I went through that. Then John told him to take off his pants entirely. John knew I didn't want to pat Dee Dee down. I didn't want to relive being strip-searched at Erasmus even if I was the one doing the searching. It was bad enough I had to see Dee Dee almost naked. If management or another band walked in, they would have thought the Ramones were rehearsing for a porno instead of an album.

It was amazing how many drugs one man could slip and shove into his clothing if he put his mind to it. Dean Gallo would have lit up like a Christmas tree. But my money was still missing. I knew one thing: if Dee Dee had it up his ass, he could keep it.

I looked at one last suspicious area and then looked at John. John nodded.

'C'mon, Dee Dee,' I said. 'You gotta finish with the socks.'

Dee Dee was now sitting on the floor. He put one foot up on his knee, pulled off a white Champion athletic sock, and turned it inside out. I nodded, which in universal strip-search language meant, C'mon, the other one, too. Dee Dee took off the other sock, and the money came right out. I picked it up and counted it: six twenties, two tens, and two fives.

'Don't look at me,' Dee Dee said. 'I don't know how it got there.'

'It's a complete fucking mystery,' John said.

'You are one sick little klepto,' I said.

There was no yelling. There was no further interrogation. There was no apology. Dee Dee's expression didn't even change. That was more upsetting to me than either losing the cash or even the idea that my bandmate would steal it. For all Dee Dee apparently cared, this could have been the baggage carousel at LAX. I counted the money a second time, put it back in my wallet, and we continued rehearsing.

We rehearsed at SIR for a second day and a third. I took my bag to the bathroom every time I had to go. When we resumed the sessions at Gold Star, I took a good look at Larry Levine. He looked okay. There was a rumor going around that Larry had suffered a minor heart attack. To me, 'minor heart attack' was an oxymoron. If it was true – and we definitely weren't going to ask Larry or Phil – it had to have something to do with stress. Specifically, the stress of being used as a whipping boy over the past few weeks or the past couple of decades. The more you held it in, the more it came back to bite you. But I didn't want to play doctor or psychologist. I was just glad Larry was alive and well. In the studio, it was business as usual.

Business as usual for the Ramones included wearing leather jackets on the album cover, but there was now talk of doing away with them. The photographer, Mick Rock, had us shoot it both ways: one set with the jackets, the other without. The shots without the jackets were above the waist only and featured each of the four of us in a different, solid-colored T-shirt: black, yellow, red, and blue. Now that we heard through Danny Fields that Sire was considering putting the T-shirt shot on the cover, it was time for a band vote.

I thought we should keep the coats on for the cover. First of all, it was punk. Second of all, we looked better in the jackets. Third, and not necessarily last, with Phil Spector at the helm, *End of the Century* was in all likelihood going to have more of a pop sound than our audience were used to, so I felt that keeping the jackets on would reassure our fans. The place for the T-shirt shots, I thought, was the inside cover. *No jackets inside the jacket, get it?* It was good bonus material, but not an album cover.

John agreed. He had been wearing the same exact jacket the whole time I had known him, and to him it was a family member. But Joey and Dee Dee liked the T-shirt shots, so the vote was two to two. The record company would have to serve as the tiebreaker. It didn't matter much right now. The album wasn't due out for a while. The project was winding down, and there wasn't much left for John, Dee Dee, or me to do. I wanted to get back home and relax for a little while before we started touring again in June, and it seemed John and Dee Dee couldn't get out of LA fast enough.

Though it was also premature, we talked about what song or songs might become singles. 'Rock 'n' Roll High School' seemed like an obvious choice, but the lyrics were over-the-top anti-school. 'Do You Remember Rock 'n' Roll Radio?' seemed like another obvious choice, but that one broke an even more sacred rule: don't bite the hand that feeds you – or plays you. The song took a clear shot at commercial radio of the day, blasting stations for generic playlists and predicting the imminent death of rock and roll.

We wouldn't know for sure for a while still, but it looked like 'Baby, I Love You' would be the first single off the album, given its history. I didn't mind that Phil had Jim Keltner play drums on 'Baby, I Love You'. Jim was one of the best session drummers around. His massive résumé included extensive work with John Lennon, George Harrison, and Ringo Starr on their various solo projects. George and Ringo even put notes on their album covers asking people to join the Jim Keltner Fan Club. For me, having royalty fill in once in a while was an honor.

The guitar work on 'Baby, I Love You' was being done by David Kessel. He and his brother Dan were sons of Barney Kessel, session guitarist extraordinaire and charter member of the Wrecking Crew. If you took people like Barney Kessel and Hal Blaine out of the picture, the *Billboard* charts of the fifties, sixties, and seventies would look like a wall full of holes.

The background vocals on the original version of 'Baby, I Love You' had a strange history of their own. Even though the Ronettes were scheduled to tour at the time, Phil Spector held back his future wife

Ronnie Bennett to work on the lead vocals. While Ronnie's cousin Elaine filled in on tour with the other Ronettes, the background vocals in the studio were performed by Darlene Love and a seventeen-year-old Cher. They were the best fill-ins available on the planet.

Whoever Phil Spector had in mind to sing background vocals this time around, it wasn't going to be Dee Dee or, for that matter, Johnny Ramone. They were flying over the Rocky Mountains by now. I wasn't far behind.

Before he took off, John reflected for a moment on Three Mile Island. He had no use for all the fairy rock stars and the No Nukes concert they were already talking about putting on. In fact, John said, we needed more nuclear plants – a lot more, and fast – to put an end to those long queues at the gas pumps and to destroy those Arab towel-head fucks and their oil fields. I didn't bother arguing. If nothing else, it was good to see John feeling like his old self again.

12

TRICKLE-DOWN
ECONOMICS

The building at 29 John Street where Marion and I lived had been around for about seventy years but was no match for my 500-watt stereo system. It was a tall converted loft building in the financial district, a few blocks north of Wall Street. The building was originally commercial but was now 'mixed use', in this case about half commercial and half residential. I managed to disturb both halves.

When we had a few days off from touring, I led the life of a king – or at least a punk prince. I would get up in the late morning and order in. In my case, ordering in consisted of calling the liquor store across the street from our building. The owner would usually make the trip up in the elevator to the ninth floor himself. He loved me. And why wouldn't he? I spent hundreds of dollars on wine, champagne, vodka, and anything else that seemed appealing with a late brunch, or instead of it.

Once I had a few drinks to wake up, the afternoon concert began. I blasted a wide variety of great music: the Kinks, the Who, Miles Davis, Charlie Parker, the Beatles, Blondie, Little Richard, the Ronettes, and this other great band called the Ramones. There were complaints from the left and complaints from the right. From upstairs and from downstairs. There were complaints from jewelry wholesalers, law offices, and residential loft dwellers who were having trouble dwelling. Apparently, the pipes carried the sound up and down through the building to a degree where my neighbors could tell whether I was playing the studio version or live version of *Tommy*.

I didn't give a shit about the complaints. It was business hours, and this was my business. But they did have a point. It was getting a little too loud. One afternoon, side two of Jimi Hendrix's *Electric Ladyland* cracked the glass in one of our cabinets.

For the first time in my life, I was making really good money consistently, and there was nothing wrong with that. When I first joined the Ramones, the arrangement was done on a handshake, and it was great to get that regular paycheck from Ira Herzog. But I asked for a more formal agreement, and John resisted.

I called my father one day while we were on tour and told him how disappointed I was. He told me not to let them screw me. My dad got me a lawyer, and we asked for a piece of the record royalties and merchandising. Our offer seemed reasonable to me: about half of what John, Dee Dee, and Joey got starting with my first Ramones album, *Road to Ruin*, and thereafter a slightly increasing percentage with each album that followed. The Ramones camp held out for a long time, but my father told me to stay cool because eventually they would cave. And that was exactly what happened.

Meanwhile, John was excited because his man, Ronald Reagan, was gearing up for the 1980 presidential race. Reagan promised to cut taxes for the rich as a way to benefit the middle class and the poor. My father said the right wing had it all backward. I agreed although I wasn't an economist. I was a musician having a few vodka martinis.

But I was capable of doing my own kind of research. I kept stacks of cash around to pay the liquor bill, tip the pizza delivery guy, or thank the super. A stack typically was an even mix of a few dozen singles, fives, tens, and twenties. By lunchtime, I usually had a few in me and I was up for adventure. John Street was pretty narrow and packed around noon with business suits shoulder to shoulder. I wasn't sure what would happen the first time I did it, but that's what experiments are for. I took a stack of cash, opened the window, and tossed it out.

It was feeding time. For a second or two, as the first few bills hit street level, there were simple reflexive reactions. It could have been litter. Or it could have been shredded paper. We were a block from Broadway and the Canyon of Heroes, so a tickertape parade for astronauts, returning war veterans, or John's beloved New York Yankees was always in the back of people's minds. But as the bucks dropped out of the sky in clumps, the suits saw green and foamed at the mouth.

It was survival of the fattest. Overfed middle-aged men in suspenders climbed over savvy women in gray wool business attire. Young virile executives threw themselves over the hood of a parked car to retrieve a ten-spot stuck in a windshield wiper. Law-school grads looking to make partner laid out the elderly on the sidewalk en route to an Andrew Jackson on a manhole cover. I took notes. It was a jungle out there. It was bedlam. But I finally understood trickle-down economics.

When the excitement died down in the early afternoon, it was time for a shower. The only problem was, we didn't have one. As far as we knew, none of the residential lofts had one yet. We had an old claw-foot, cast-iron tub, but, after a long, hard morning of boozing and tossing cash out of the window, there was nothing like a good hot shower. So a bunch of the tenants chipped in and created a shower room on the fourteenth floor.

I didn't dress up to take a shower. I walked down the hall in slippers and a bathrobe with no pants or underwear beneath. Sometimes, when I was dying my hair black, my head was wrapped in tinfoil. I shared an elevator with VPs and accountants who wondered which floor the half-naked space alien was getting off at and why. Sometimes I ran into punk kids in the elevator. Some were spike-haired, others were Ramones clones, but they had one thing in common, and it wasn't that they were pricing out the open loft space on the eleventh floor. They were there to catch a glimpse of me. So I signed a few autographs and took my shower.

About a mile uptown, Joey and Linda moved in together. A studio apartment opened up in the building where Joey's mother lived on East Ninth Street, and the happy couple took it. Joey and Linda were getting serious. They were engaged and shopping for a diamond ring. Aside from wishing them happiness, we all hoped Linda would do wonders for Joey's hygiene and punctuality. If nothing else, she could take some pressure off Monte.

A block north on East Tenth Street, John and Roxy were still playing house, with Roxy slipping a few drinks and John hitting her a few shots. The Ramones' women took breaks from the action now and then. Not every venue or club was a preferred destination like London or Berlin. Places like West Orange, New Jersey, and Allentown, Pennsylvania, needed to be seen only once.

When they stayed behind, Marion would sometimes hang out with Roxy. Roxy liked some new wave with her vodka. Adam Ant and Bow Wow Wow, two upstart bands, were among her favorites. When the Ramones got back from Staten Island one night in late June, Marion told me her night with Roxy was a brief one. They went to the Mudd Club to see the bands, but inside of an hour, Roxy was falling all over herself and then all over some cute guy. She used one of the best pickup lines in the history of the downtown music scene: 'Do you want to see Johnny Ramone's apartment?' The answer would have been yes 99 per cent of the time if Roxy was sober and had two heads. As she was drunk and provocatively dressed, it was 100 per cent.

There was no way I was telling John or Marion was telling on Roxy. We didn't really know what happened once Roxy and Mr. Whoever hopped into a cab, and it was none of our business. Aside from that, we had a band to keep together.

It was early summer and before heading up to Toronto to play the Canadian World Music Festival we did something purely for fun. *The Uncle Floyd Show* was the brainchild of Floyd Vivino, a local comedian about our age whose act and clothing came out of the burlesque era. *Uncle Floyd* was a throwback to *The Pinky Lee Show* of the fifties and *The Soupy Sales Show* of the sixties – kids' shows at first glance but with a subversive adult sense of humor just beneath the surface. If you listened closely, you could hear things no one was supposed to get away with saying on public television. Comedian Andy Kaufman was making a career using the same approach. There was a fine line between silly and sick, and, the more it could be walked like a tightrope, the better.

Floyd was a Ramones fan, and we were *Uncle Floyd* fans. We weren't alone. *Uncle Floyd* had a cult following. John Lennon watched the show. So did David Bowie. That wasn't bad for a show broadcast on Channel 68, the far end of the UHF dial. If you lived in Manhattan, at least you could get 68 clearly on cable. If you lived in Brooklyn or Queens, you had to hold on to the rabbit-ears antenna, stand on one foot, and use your other hand to play with a metal clothes hanger. For lots of viewers, it was worth it.

The WBTB-TV studio in Newark was tiny. We lip-synched to 'Sedated' in a space the size of someone's living room. There was a plain blue background that gave the room an amateur hour feel, and that was no accident. That was ambience. It was hard to keep time with the record because there were no monitors. The song bounced around the room and sometimes we were off by a beat, or live Joey stopped mouthing lyrics a moment before canned Joey stopped singing them. But no one cared. It was *Uncle Floyd*.

Once or twice a minute, we were interrupted by one of Floyd's weirdo in-house characters. There was Scott Gordon, the crook who wore a woman's stocking over his head and tried to mug Joey for his pants. There was a guy in tights calling himself Captain Amazing who looked as if he could barely lift Dee Dee's Fender Precision bass if his life depended on it. The cast of misfits were getting smiles out of John, which was really saying something.

When it was time to go to break, Floyd Vivino asked each of us for a more interesting way to say, 'We'll be right back after these important words.' My suggestion was 'See ya later.'

'I knew yours would be cymbal-minded,' Floyd remarked, adding, 'That is the worst drummer joke. It's really beat.' *Ba-dum-bum. Ching.* That was what made *Uncle Floyd* goofy and addictive. Getting a round of applause from two dozen people in a shoe box in New Jersey never felt so good.

A few days later, on 2 July, we were getting booed by fifty thousand people. The Canadian World Music Festival was being held in Toronto's Exhibition Stadium. The stadium was an odd-shaped sort of rectangle with an Astroturf field. First built as a fairgrounds, then adapted to Canadian football, it had recently been reconfigured to serve the Blue Jays, Toronto's expansion Major League baseball team. John told me it was horrible for baseball. The viewing angles sucked. The left-field bleachers angled off to nowhere. The place had an identity crisis.

So did the festival. We were opening for Ted Nugent, followed by Aerosmith. John quoted Yogi Berra, who once said it was *déjà vu* all over again. It really was – just like opening for Sabbath in Atlanta. There were pockets of kids getting into it, but then came the booing and, by the sixth or seventh song, the artillery. It was coins, cans, and whatever debris was solid enough to chuck from the crappy baseball seats. By now, we were as good at using our middle fingers as we were with picks, mikes, and drumsticks.

Before we could pack it in and start heading back down to New York, Steven Tyler, Aerosmith's lead singer, showed up in our dressing room. The Boston band's albums including *Toys in the Attic* and *Rocks* were FM radio staples and had gone platinum again and again. Aerosmith was rumored to be having heavy drug problems at this point, but Tyler seemed sober and sincere. He told us he was a Ramones fan, and he was very sorry for what had just happened out there. He said we were ahead of our time and one day a lot of those kids would be buying Ramones albums and bragging they saw us kick ass in Toronto years ago.

Those words really helped cool off John, Joey, Dee Dee, and me. Not many people understood how much work it took just to take that stage when it was your turn. It was hundreds of miles of traveling and thousands of feet of cable before you played one note, one beat. We were sick of getting pissed on. Having someone like Steven Tyler reach out like that – when he didn't have to and might never even cross our

Top left: My grandfather, the chef, relaxing in Florida.

Top right: Hurrah for the Beatles.

Below left: At the top of the Empire State Building with Fred and Mom.

Below right: Mom and Dad.

Top left: Dust.
  (*Courtesy of Alan Weinstock*)

Top right: Early
merchandizing.

Centre: Dust playing
live.
  (*Courtesy of Alan Weinstock*)

Right: Dust at the New
York State Theatre.
  (*Courtesy of Alan Weinstock*)

Above: The Backstreet Boys.

(*Copyright © by Leee Black Childers*)

Left: Showing support for Wayne County.

Above: My better half.

Below: Me and Johnny Thunders, both born on July 15.   (*Copyright* © 2015 *by Eileen Polk*)

Above: Wayne County – Man Enough to Be a Woman. *(Copyright © 2015 by Eileen Polk)*

Below: Me, Arturo Vega, and Sid and Nancy at CBGB. *(Copyright © 2015 by Eileen Polk)*

Right: Richard Hell and me in New York.

Below: The Voidoids *circa Blank Generation*.

Left: The infamous Ramones van.

Below: Guess what Marion's doing?

Right: Me and my car
'Bully' at Coney Island.
The Hornet had the same
ride – a Chrysler Imperial.

Below: My work is play.

Left: With the Queen of Punk, Debbie Harry.

Right: My friend, Phil Spector.

Left: In New York with Roger Daltrey.

Left: Tony Bennett – Tony's cool. Washington, DC.

Right: KISS and my friend Mark Neuman.

Left: My childhood idol Dave Clark has the best snare drum sound.

Left: Talking Beatles with Ozzy Osbourne. (*Courtesy of Aimee Osbourne*)

Right: In England with Robert Plant.

Left: The night Bono presented me with MTV's Lifetime Achievement Award.

Left: Lemmy the Great.

Right: Hanging with Green Day in Italy.

Left: With Joan Jett, a big Ramones fan.

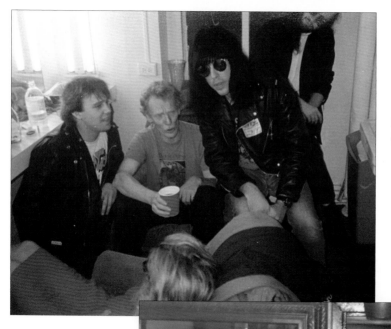

Left: Ginger Baker (centre)…

Right: … and Charlie Watts are two of my drum idols.

Left: Seymour Stein, the headman at Sire Records. A great guy.

Right: Joking around
with Eddie Vedder,
Los Angeles.

Left: My man
Anthony Bourdain.

Right: Andrew
W.K. is the King of
Party.

Above: Me and the best fans in the world.

Below left: Hey Ho.

Below right: Visiting my handprint at the Rock Walk in LA.

Left: Chaos to couture
– dressed to kill for the
Met Gala.

Below: The beat goes
on…

paths again – meant we could cross the border back into the US without feeling like we needed to start an international incident.

We left before getting a chance to meet Ted Nugent. The Motor City Madman's albums hadn't been selling as well as *Cat Scratch Fever* a couple of years earlier, but he was still tearing it up Nugent style. Everyone in the Ramones loved 'Journey to the Center of the Mind' by his first group back in the late sixties, the Amboy Dukes. Only John, however, liked Nugent's political and personal beliefs, which were basically to kill and eat everything that moved. It would have been almost worth the price of coming to Toronto and getting booed off the stage to see Ted and John discuss how Ronald Reagan was going to sweep into office and send welfare cheats to forced-labor camps, but that would have to wait for another tour or for never.

Our biggest difficulty getting out of Toronto was not Joey having to cross the US–Canada border several times. It was Monte and his attaché case. Dee Dee and I hid it on him. We did that a lot just to see Monte freak out. This time we hid it in a bathroom stall. It was only the tenth or fifteenth place backstage he searched. We went easy on him this time.

It was a long ride home from Toronto, and John was already driving us crazy an hour or two east on US Route 90. When John popped open his second can of sardines in the space of fifteen minutes, Joey shook his head. We could almost see him rolling his eyes behind the sunglasses. The rest of us didn't appreciate the cuisine much more. John and his sardines stunk up the van. But Joey believed John did it to piss him off in particular and he was probably right.

'Could you stop with the fucking sardines already?' Dee Dee said. 'You're fucking killing us.'

'Hey,' John said. 'Leave me alone. It's good for you.'

It was good for his wallet. Like the rest of us, John got a *per diem* that included meal expenses. But the less he spent, the more money was left over for his ever growing bank account. John bragged that he never made a withdrawal. Not once. Ever. He also kept stacks of cash in his dresser drawers. They weren't for tipping delivery guys, much less for tossing out the window to throngs of businessmen.

John's culinary preference was any 7-Eleven off of any highway. There, he stocked up on milk and Pepperidge Farm cookies. He drank too much milk too quickly, to the point where he snorted a lot to keep it down and we feared it was coming up his nose any minute. Marion told John he ate too much dairy, but that was like telling him he saved too much money.

During the warm months, like now, John liked to listen to baseball games on the radio, but we told him we didn't want to hear three hours of play-by-play and Midas Muffler commercials. So John used his earphones and a transistor radio. We took votes on what to listen to on the radio but found over time that no one objected to rock-and-roll oldies. So we tuned into whatever oldies station was strongest on the FM dial, and when we got within about fifty miles of New York City that was always WCBS-FM.

The bigger shows we had been playing lately allowed us to lease a new Dodge van. It was burgundy and silver and held fifteen passengers. The van came with a new feature that provided not just convenience but one more way to fuck with Monte. Behind the right-hand captain's chair was a second set of digital controls for the radio. It allowed someone in the first passenger row to change stations and adjust the volume. Monte didn't know it was there. So with John in the captain's seat, I sat behind and started messing with the dial. I quickly found a disco station.

'Hey, Monte,' Dee Dee said. 'Turn that shit off!'

'I didn't do anything,' Monte said. 'I dunno what happened.'

'C'mon, Monte,' I said. 'Stop fucking with us.'

I moved the dial to an opera station and cranked the volume.

'We gotta listen to this shit all the way back to New York?' John said.

'And I can't even listen to the Yankee game?' John shot me a smile. He was in on it.

'You saw me!' Monte said, reaching for the dial and trying to get back to the oldies station. 'You saw my hands! I didn't touch a thing.'

'Are you just pissed off at us because we hid your attaché case?' I said. 'Oh, we're sorry, Monte. We won't do it again.'

We kept the joke running till we picked up Route 81 South. Monte finally figured it out and asked us why the hell we had to drive him so fucking crazy all the time. And we told him – boredom.

Just south of Syracuse, we found a Cracker Barrel and pulled off the highway. Other than hitting the stall and ordering half the food on the menu, the first order of business was to hide Monte's attaché case again. He brought it in with him, which was good, and placed it under the table, which was also good. What wasn't good was that he had it handcuffed to the center leg of the table. I didn't know if he was carrying the handcuffs with him just for this reason, but I hoped so. In any case, I asked Dee Dee for a piece of the gooey eggplant parmesan he was eating and then smeared it all over the handle of the attaché case.

When we got outside, Dee Dee asked me if I'd had dessert. When I told him no, he pointed to the front of the van. It was a hot, muggy summer night in upstate New York, and that usually meant a variety of bugs flattened on the windshield.

'How much?' I asked.

'Twenty-five bucks,' Dee Dee said.

'Twenty-five bucks each,' I said.

'Oh, no,' John said. 'I'm not chipping in for this one.'

'I got twenty-five of that,' Joey said.

'I can't watch this shit,' Linda said.

'No one's making you,' I said.

I picked a crushed horsefly off the glass on the driver's side, put it in my mouth, and swallowed.

'See what I do for you?' I said to Monte.

'Oh, God!' Vera said.

'Okay, Marc,' Marion said. 'Let's call it a night.'

'Gotta get my protein,' I said, putting number two in my mouth.

'You're gonna get sick,' Linda said.

'No, *you're* gonna get sick,' I said. 'I just made seventy-five dollars.'

With that, I put dead horsefly number three in my mouth, swallowed, and climbed into the van.

We attended a preview of *Rock 'n' Roll High School* as a band in Texas, but the film made its limited premiere in movie theaters on 24 August. That night, with a friend, I went to see it in disguise. The 8th Street Playhouse in the West Village was the kind of movie theater that made New York what it was. They ran indie movies, art movies, classic horror flicks, and anything they wanted to. The 8th Street Playhouse put *The Rocky Horror Picture Show* on the map and made it a midnight institution.

I wore shorts, a tank top, and sneakers with no socks. I had on regular glasses and a fisherman's hat. I wanted to have a good time like anybody else. I wanted to experience the film like someone who didn't watch Dee Dee Ramone pop dozens of greenies in an LA schoolyard. It seemed to work. We sat in the back and no one said a thing.

It was surreal. As a band we looked like a bunch of aliens inserted into a real movie. The only thing missing was the tinfoil on my head. There it was – sunny California plus four leather-jacket-clad hoods representing the gritty East Coast. It wasn't something I thought about while shooting the movie, but now it was clear as day and hysterical. You could have dropped us into another new movie, such as *The Warriors*, almost seamlessly, but we sort of fitted in there, so who would have cared? *Rock 'n' Roll High School*, however, worked on its own terms. It was outrageous. The audience laughed and clapped. They weren't flattering the incognito lone Ramone in the audience. They really loved it.

For an hour and a half, we were giants. Not in the filmmaking sense like Elia Kazan or John Huston. We were on a huge screen, where a head of long hair was a black forest and a pimple was Mount Vesuvius. Joey could have been a monster in a Japanese movie crushing little toy cars. When the four of us came strutting up the street to the Rockatorium to the beat of 'I Just Want to Have Something to Do', the crowd at the 8th Street Playhouse clapped along. I looked even sillier than I thought I would walking along clicking my drumsticks, but that worked, too. I heard feet stomping in the theater. We were *their* guys, and for a little while we all had something to do – something really ridiculous – together.

When the closing credits rolled, my friend and I slipped out the back.

I didn't know if *Rock 'n' Roll High School* was the next *Rocky Horror Picture Show*, but I could imagine Dee Dee's face appearing on the screen and the midnight audience throwing fists full of pills. Or spitting milk at John. The movie had cult classic written all over it.

On 17 October at Marietta College, Ohio, we crossed paths with the Police. It was the band, with a capital *P*, which was good because the other police might have been interested in what was in Dee Dee's pockets and socks.

We were opening up for them. 'Roxanne' and 'Can't Stand Losing You' saw some chart action, and their forthcoming second album, *Reggatta de Blanc*, had a lot of buzz going. We were always made to feel very at home in the UK and wanted to extend the same courtesy to British bands on our soil. So John and I walked over to their dressing room to say hello to the Police and wish them luck.

Sting was looking in a mirror and preening his hair. We walked up to him and John made the introduction.

'How are you? Johnny from the Ramones, and this is our drummer, Marc.'

'Pleasure.'

Sting reached out to shake John's hand. 'Shake' is an exaggeration. He grabbed it limply and released. He never made it to my own extended hand. Sting eyeballed the Ramones presidential-seal pin on John's leather jacket.

'Where did you get those pins,' Sting said. 'Woolworth's?'

We were stunned. It didn't seem as though he was kidding around. There was no hint of a smile on Sting's face. Maybe we were being tested, but we were the Ramones and we didn't take tests. We had already graduated rock 'n' roll high school.

'You know what?' I said. 'Fuck you.'

'Yeah, fuck off,' John said.

We turned and walked out without waiting to see a reaction. Better to go out there and blow them off the stage. As we walked down the hallway, we let out some steam.

'What an asshole,' John said.

'It's no big deal,' I said. 'It's just peroxide reggae.'

I thought about the Ramones logo Gordon Sumner – a.k.a. Sting – had just taken a potshot at. It featured a bald eagle with a baseball bat. The bat was there to beat on a brat. A brat very much like Sting. *With a brat like that what can you do?*

It was a long drive from Marietta to Detroit that night. We didn't have the benefit of the Phil Spector album being out yet, but the release of *Rock 'n' Roll High School* was definitely doing something in terms of where we could play and what we could ask. The Midwest crowds were larger now, so the movie must have had legs.

It was around two in the morning, and we were in Ohio, headed west on US Route 90. Monte was fading. We could see it. He never quite fell asleep, but he was battling. The van would drift ever so slightly, and he would quickly blink, grunt, and shrug his head.

'Okay, that's fucking it,' John said. 'You're gonna get us all killed. We're taking over.'

At that point, we pulled over and rotated. John took the driver's seat, I took John's regular seat up front, and Monte took my seat behind. We weren't back on 90 more than five minutes before Monte was out cold. He snored like a lawn mower.

John liked steering the van. He liked steering everything. It wasn't the happiest summer or fall for him. He was having the usual problems with Roxy and her drinking. A Yankees catcher and one of John's favorite players, Thurman Munson, had died in a plane crash in early August. It had happened in Canton, in the very state we were now driving through. I wouldn't have known the significance of the location, but John mentioned it four times. He also complained that for the first time in four years the Yankees hadn't even made the playoffs.

Of course, John was driven by all sorts of things I didn't understand. I didn't really get the obsession with baseball, and I didn't quite get the fixation on money. When you put them together, I was totally lost. John collected baseball cards in his early thirties the same way he collected them as a kid. That sounded nice until you understood what he actually did. A normal kid would rip open the wrapper, stuff the gum in his mouth, and then look at all the cards. After that, the cards would get flipped, traded, stuck in notebooks, and pinned to bulletin boards. To John, that was sacrilege.

John would open the wrapper carefully at one end, maybe even steam it off if the situation called for it. He would then take tweezers and surgically remove the stick of gum. It reminded me of the board game Operation we played as kids. John did for baseball cards what Roxy did for minibars. From there, John would reseal the wrapper to protect the baseball cards for posterity. Because even though as a kid John had no idea what he would eventually do for a living, he knew he would one day resell his mint-condition packs with a huge mark-up.

These days a guy John called his baseball 'dealer' would come over to his apartment on East Tenth Street and buy mint-condition packs, individual mint cards, and autographed cards. From there John could either reinvest by buying sought-after movie posters – fifties horror and sci-fi – or simply add to his impressive collection. Buy or hold – it was a tough call, but, as Vivien Leigh said in *Gone with the Wind*, tomorrow is another day.

Someone else once said it takes money to make money, but for John it didn't take too much. When we were off the road, it seemed like he lived at the post office. His business model was simple – buy an inexpensive eight-by-ten publicity photo, send it to a celebrity with a nice note, and wait for it to come back in the mail autographed in a self-addressed, stamped envelope. John had phone books worth of signed head shots.

If it was Sophia Loren, he threw in a few words about how much he enjoyed *It Started in Naples*. If it was Whitey Ford, he would write about how much he enjoyed watching him throw eight and two-thirds innings of shutout ball in the fourth game of the 1950 World Series against the Phillies. Even if John was two years old at the time. It didn't matter. The important things were that John knew more trivia than a TV network's weekday line-up of afternoon game shows and that those eight-by-tens came back signed.

If he knew a little too much about celebrities and what their autographed publicity shots fetched in the collectors' market, John knew way too much about the personal lives of the postal workers who served him. He knew Joe in Customer Service and his wife just had twins but that the slightly smaller one was colicky. He knew Marsha over in Sorting had a nineteen-year-old enrolling at NYU.

'How could she afford that?' John asked us. 'She's only making about twelve-five. That's nine grand after taxes. But I think her husband just got a new title over at the Board of Ed.'

I had to wonder whether the folks down at the post office knew how many bugs I had eaten off a windshield for money or what Godzilla posters were selling for at auction these days. In the end, none of it mattered. What did matter was that Monte's snoring now sounded like an eighteen-wheeler with a loose axle. We were getting close to Toledo and I told John I thought it was time. He agreed.

'*Holy shit! Watch out!*' I screamed for dear life, and Monte popped up like a zombie.

'What . . .? What the fuck happened?'

'Nothing, Monte,' John said. 'Go back to bed. Looks like you were having a nice wet dream.'

'Nice one, Sloth,' I said. That was our nickname for John.

'You're sick,' Monte said. 'You're all fucking nuts. I really thought we were dead.'

'Close,' I said. 'We're going to Detroit.'

The State Theatre in Detroit was a classic old brick building that seated about twenty-three hundred people. We had already done the sound check and had an hour or two to kill before dark. John and I took a walk down Woodward Avenue. The area was kind of blighted. It had been a rough decade for the country, and Detroit in particular took it in the crotch. But the city was trying to bounce back.

About half a block from the State Theatre we stopped at a construction site. There was an opening in the chain-link fence. There were a couple of excavating vehicles on site, but it looked as if digging hadn't begun. The lot was mostly covered in gravel and loose rocks. This really was Detroit rock city.

'Hey, check this out,' John said. He picked up a rock about the size of a baseball and, with a two-step running start, threw it overhand into the lot. It wasn't a bad toss – probably just shy of three hundred feet.

'What do you want me to do?' I said.

'See if you can touch that.'

'Yeah, okay.'

I wasn't known as a jock growing up. I played baseball and basketball about as much as the other kids, mainly when it was required for gym class. But I had some talent when it came to throwing rocks. One time I threw one clear over PS 217, which was five stories but really at least six by normal standards. By the time I got to Erasmus, I was completely absorbed by the drums, which undoubtedly gave me additional arm strength.

I picked up a rock a few feet from where John had taken his and about the same size. I stepped in hard and let it fly. It landed about thirty feet beyond where John's had landed and bounced a few times.

'Almost,' John said.

'Almost what?' I said. 'I won.'

'No, you didn't.'

'Give me a fucking break, Sloth. Yours landed out by that cone. Mine easily cleared it. Get your eyes checked out.'

We went three more rounds. The results were about the same. I could see it really bothered John. He would tell us how he was a star in Little League. How he almost won a batting title and might have gone pro if he hadn't pursued music. He just couldn't leave it alone.

'You know what?' John said. 'You picked the smooth rocks. That makes a big difference. It's the aerodynamics.'

'Yeah, it's definitely that. And your arm sucks.'

We started to walk away, but then John ran the fifty yards or so back to the lot, grabbed another rock and threw it as if it were the last play in the seventh game of the World Series. I let him have the last throw. We had a show to do. I took a look at where it landed. He did a little better this time. It skipped in front of a big pile of sand. I thought that was fitting. We were like a bunch of kids in a sandbox.

On 6 January 1980, Monte picked me up in front of our building at 29 John Street. We had played New Year's Eve at the Palladium in New York City and nothing since. We were starting off the new decade by heading up to play Port Chester, New York. It was cold outside and not exactly breaking new tour ground, so the Ramones women weren't coming along.

Monte parked as usual by the fire hydrant off the corner of Ninth Street and Third Avenue and went upstairs to get Joey while we waited in the van. People who followed our band very closely knew if they had some business or music to discuss we would be right here in the late morning before a show. Lester Bangs had joined us a few times as had other music critics, merchandise people, and promoters. It was the closest thing the Ramones kept to office hours. But this time we were having a closed meeting and would even find another parking spot if we had to.

Monte brought Joey down pretty quickly. Maybe Monte was getting better at the whole routine. Maybe Linda was helping Joey. She was, in fact, keeping him from drinking too many beers from time to time. Or maybe for once Joey took the elevator without the usual up and down to hear what we all came to hear: the final mastered version of *End of the Century*. John popped in the cassette tape. It was the entire album in final form.

A DJ introduced the song 'Do You Remember Rock 'n' Roll Radio?' When the band came in, along with a loud keyboard none of us had ever heard before, it was a bit of a shock. It wasn't a Ramones sound as we knew it or as anyone knew it. At this rate, it was going to be a very long twelve-song experience sitting on a corner in a van with snowflakes falling and a band in a state of confusion.

But the song settled in very quickly and so did the rest of the album. The sound was bigger than we were used to. The core Ramones sound was not as upfront as usual, but it was definitely there. The more my ears adjusted, the better I liked it. 'Rock 'n' Roll Radio' was powerful. So were 'I Can't Make It on Time' and 'I'm Affected'. 'Danny Says' was actually a moving experience. I thought of the Beach Boys during the *Pet*

Sounds era. The music was nicely layered. Not every song was a winner. 'The Return of Jackie and Judy' may have been my least favorite, but that had at least as much to do with the song itself as the production.

I felt good. I felt relieved. If this was an experiment – a huge Phil Spector experiment – it was a successful one, studio drama and all. I thought once it was released to the public, we would definitely pick up many new fans, and the old Ramones fans – or at least the large majority – would come to appreciate the album.

John and Dee Dee weren't among those Ramones fans. You could tell from their body language. Joey and I were rocking our heads to the beat. John and Dee Dee were staring into space with almost no expression. John told Monte we needed to get moving, and Monte pulled out of our office spot. The ride up to Port Chester was nearly silent. We listened to WCBS-FM, oldies 101.1.

In the dressing room at Port Chester, John finally broke his silence, but just barely.

'Not good,' John said, shaking his head. 'Not good.'

The album on which he himself had played some great guitar deserved a more thorough review, but there was as much point in arguing with him about this as about the rocks we threw in Detroit. Punk wasn't a religion. Music wasn't a religion. You tried new things and they worked or they didn't and you went on. We opened up some new doors, and it was time to look around on the other side. We never really surrendered our sound, but I couldn't see us ever going back to exactly the format and production the Ramones had used in the past. As Joey sang in 'Rock 'n' Roll Radio', it was definitely the end of the seventies.

13

PUT ME IN A
WHEELCHAIR, GET
ME ON A PLANE

Joey didn't want to get off the plane at Heathrow Airport. We had twenty shows to do in twenty cities over twenty-four days in England, plus at least two major BBC appearances – *The Old Grey Whistle Test* and *Top of the Pops*. The list of cities read like roll call in the House of Commons: Brighton, Leicester, Cambridge, Norwich, Exeter, Aylesbury, and so on. The UK loved the Ramones, and if we had a real chance for a Top Ten album, it was here. We came to conquer, but it would all go to shit unless Joey set foot on British soil.

Monte climbed the aircraft stairs and reboarded the Boeing 747. Joey looked kind of sad and pathetic in the little window of seat 23H with his long legs scrunched up toward his chin. As usual, John was the most pissed off. If someone had handed him a dozen large Grade A in a carton, John would have egged Joey. At first we thought if we all got off the plane, Joey would follow, but we were now past a half-hour of waiting. It seemed like ten hours and it was no bluff. Our lead singer was dead serious about wanting to go back to JFK. About *having* to go back to JFK.

Monte was armed with every subtle and not-so-subtle tactic. This was not a door or an elevator. This was not even a crosstown trip back to the airport. This was a trip across the Atlantic. The Ramones had already landed and planted a flag. There was no turning back. It didn't matter what Joey had to tap back in Queens. The Queen herself was waiting. So were all her subjects. So was British Airways.

In the end, what Monte and the Ramones had on our side was time. Somewhere near the forty-five-minute mark Joey got his head together. We had no idea what was going on inside that head. But we knew from experience we could wait it out just a bit longer if we had to. And we had to.

The band ended the tour in London in February. We had a day off before an afternoon of filming at BBC Studios. Although England wasn't known for great food the way France and some other European countries were, Marion and I loved it. That night, we went to the hotel restaurant and treated ourselves. We ordered cod fillet and, as expected, the chef came to our table to debone the fish. It was a big production, like a TV cooking show without the cameras. It was all done cleanly and quickly with precision.

At BBC Studios the following day, we told John about our evening. He was appalled and dumbfounded. It was hard to tell what puzzled him more – why we would subject ourselves to the deboning ritual or why we would spend all that money. From listening to him rant, you would have thought we'd taken all our tour money and then some and plunked it down on the crown jewels. We explained that we were in England – not Queens, Brooklyn, or da Bronx – and it was all part of a great experience. John summed it up for us with two words – he said we were 'nigger rich'.

But we did have something in common with John – seafood. While we were eating fillet, he was dining on canned tuna and sardines he bought at a London discount market. John traveled in style. He always packed his can opener on transcontinental flights. As far as we knew, he had never once in his life ordered room service. If he was feeling really flush, he might eat at the hotel cafeteria.

Top of the Pops made its debut in January 1964. The first show ever, on New Year's Day, featured the Rolling Stones performing 'I Wanna Be Your Man', the Dave Clark Five with 'Glad All Over', the Beatles with the number-one hit at the time, 'I Want to Hold Your Hand', and several other huge acts. Considering that the Ramones were going to be performing Phil Spector's 'Baby, I Love You', we were in royal company all around. *Top of the Pops* could have been compared to America's *Ed Sullivan Show*, but there were major differences, not the least of which was that on *TOTP* you played live.

Not just the band played live. Every backing instrument on the recording had to be played live as well. There were strict union rules in the UK when it came to radio and television. Whereas in the US we could have played live to a soundtrack featuring a string arrangement or just lip-synched the thing entirely, on *TOTP*, they brought in a half-dozen professional violinists and assorted other musicians to represent the recording on a one-for-one basis. This was not *The Uncle Floyd Show*.

Our lunch break in the studio cafeteria was an event in itself and not just because John got to eat for free. There were dozens of actors dressed up in period costumes – Shakespearean, Victorian, Knights of the Round Table. It was like a scene out of *A Hard Day's Night* and representative of English entertainment as compared with the American kind. English entertainment was *theater*. Even English music was theater.

The twenty-something actor with a green leotard at the next table eating pudding might not have been so imposing while wiping his chin, but in an hour he would be completely convincing stealing from the rich and giving to the poor as Robin Hood. Two tables over to the left, the middle-aged man dabbing ketchup on his forearm might have been enhancing a fake wound while playing Jack the Ripper. At least we hoped he was preparing for a scene.

We performed 'Baby, I Love You' in front of a live studio audience. The stage was clean and sparse and illuminated by huge oval overhead fluorescent lights. Nicely dressed English kids swayed in front of the stage. Farther back, some more nicely dressed English kids danced slowly beneath a checkerboard ceiling lighting system. There was no mosh pit. We sounded big, smooth, and produced, just like the Phil Spector record. Joey sang with feeling that belied any personal problems he was having. Dee Dee's background vocals were spot-on. I played for real, doing the part Jim Keltner performed on the album. My drums were a bit drowned out by all the orchestration, but this, of course, was a wall of sound.

Those nicely dressed English kids bought records. The single of 'Baby, I Love You' was at number eight on the British charts. Across the Irish Sea, it stood at number five. The album was at number fourteen in England. Back home the album was peaking at forty-four on the *Billboard* chart, though the single had failed to chart entirely. The glass was half full and of course half empty. From a sales point of view, it was as high as we had ever gotten on either side of the Atlantic. In a few short years, the Ramones had gone from downtown nuisance to international sensation, from inventing punk to helping make it a viable force in commercial music. We played to larger crowds for more money and with more media coverage.

On the half-empty side, there was no runaway hit, no forthcoming triple-platinum status, and no tour headlining American baseball and football stadiums. I heard John and Dee Dee make a few comments to the effect that not even the great Phil Spector could do it for the Ramones. I pointed out that he had done more than maybe they realized, and the song we had just performed for the BBC proved it. Not that I had the world figured out, but I had been in many band situations and knew that success was dangerous because it whet your appetite for more success, even when you didn't know exactly what that meant. Being proud of what you achieved wasn't a poor substitute for success. It was what made any form of success worth it in the first place.

I did see the rest of the band grasp that idea to a degree, even if it wasn't exactly spoken. As we rode the vans, buses, and planes, we talked about getting back in the studio soon to make another album. We made plans to keep touring the US and the world. We even had new management in the form of Gary Kurfirst.

Gary Kurfirst grew up in Forest Hills and knew John from the neighborhood. Kurfirst was a rock-and-roll mover and shaker right out of high school, booking large shows at the West Side Tennis Club and Singer Bowl in Queens and jumping across the East River to innovate in Manhattan. He started the Village Theater, which became Bill Graham's Fillmore East. That club had deep personal history for me. And, as a young kid, Marion had gone to see Janis Joplin, the Doors, and Jimi Hendrix at Kurfirst's open-air festival in Flushing Meadows Park, an event some people claimed paved the way for Woodstock. We knew from the grapevine that Gary used to print up three or four hundred extra tickets for those early shows in Queens and pocket a small fortune, but that was show business.

More recently, Gary Kurfirst had taken on Talking Heads and the B-52's as manager. He had an office of eight or nine people on the corner of Fifty-Seventh Street and Broadway, a building which downstairs was home to the famous Coliseum Books and upstairs was home to a different kind of book – the kind kept by most of the respected accountants in the music business. Gary wasn't our buddy, but he was thoughtful and businesslike, and got things done. I respected that. Together with our booking agent, Frank Barsalona of Premier Talent, who handled virtually every major act a game show contestant could name in sixty seconds, the Ramones were set to keep doing what we did, which was spread Ramones music.

On 6 June 1980, we played Six Flags Great Adventure in Jackson, New Jersey. Playing an amusement park was not up there in the rock-and-roll stratosphere with playing, say, a soccer stadium in Italy. But, in defense of Great Adventure, it was not your average amusement park. Located inland of the shore on what Bruce Springsteen might have been referring to when he sang about 'the swamps of Jersey', the park was built on about five hundred acres and included an animal safari that dwarfed anything Disney ever built. I loved animals, especially if they were Ramones fans. Towering over this city in the swamps was the Giant Wheel, the tallest Ferris wheel in the world. It was probably the tallest manmade structure in the Garden State, and, once we spotted it from Route 195, Monte could toss the directions.

Our dressing room was a trailer surrounded by trees and grass. We thought it was the safari dressing room. The natives were restless. Dee Dee was on something, maybe coke. The roadies were on something, too. Joey was drinking one beer after another. Normally, he wouldn't with Linda around, but Linda was not around. Not immediately, anyway. She and John had stepped out of the trailer and hadn't come back.

With Monte's help, we gathered up the troops and walked over to the outdoor concert grounds to do the sound check, but the doors were locked. We were actually early, which was unusual for a rock band, but, then again, we definitely weren't your average rock band. How to kill time in an amusement park wasn't exactly a difficult proposition, especially since we all had free day passes to the rides.

We walked toward Rolling Thunder, which was the mother of all roller-coaster rides. As we stood on line, fans began to come up to us and ask for autographs. Joey wasn't quite as tall as the Giant Wheel, but he towered over the other patrons. Dee Dee and I were pretty conspicuous, too. Even without our leather jackets in the warm sun we had our long dark hair and our attitude. Suddenly we were one of the attractions at Great Adventure.

Joey decided to sit out Rolling Thunder. That made sense because once it pulled away, it was five minutes of terror and no going back to touch something. Dee Dee told him there were plenty of kiddie rides in a place like this. He was joking around, but Joey wasn't happy about it. He didn't seem too happy about anything. After Rolling Thunder, Dee Dee and I did the Lightnin' Loops, then called it a day. We stood out like sore thumbs. It was like the amusement park version of *Rock 'n' Roll High School*.

The grounds were packed for the show, and the crowd enjoyed the ride. We went up and down through a twenty-seven-song set, from the highs of 'Blitzkrieg Bop' to the soft refrain of 'Here Today, Gone Tomorrow' and back up again to 'Pinhead', finally closing with the dysfunction smorgasbord of 'We're a Happy Family'.

At night, as we got ready to board the van, I grabbed a small safari souvenir, a frog. I probably could have made a solid hundred bucks eating it, but I had bigger plans for my little green friend. I walked up to Dee Dee and put my cupped hands out near his belly. Then I released the Ramones' new mascot. The frog jumped about a foot and a half onto Dee Dee's chest. He completely freaked out. So did the frog. Dee Dee jumped back and swiped at it a few times in a panic like a detox patient having DTs.

'What the fuck? What the fuck?'

'Sorry,' I said. 'I didn't think you'd go crazy. It's just a frog.'

'Are you fucking serious? You almost gave me a heart attack.'

'Give me a break, Goon,' as I called him sometimes. 'Don't blame that on the frog. Blame it on whatever you're on.'

'Really? What am I on?'

Dee Dee pulled his switchblade out and flicked it open. It was the six-inch Springer switchblade he carried around these days, even at theme parks. He held it steady and pointed it at me. I grabbed his wrist with my right hand and bent his thumb back in one quick motion. The knife fell to the ground. My grip on his wrist was like an airbrake on a sanitation truck. I released the grip and pushed Dee Dee hard. He stumbled back, looking dazed.

'Do it again, ever,' I said, 'and the knife's going into you.'

The ride back to the city was quiet except for the oldies on WCBS-FM. I knew Dee Dee wasn't going to stab me. But I had to teach him a lesson. It was for his own good. This wasn't a forgiving world, not like that. The next guy Dee Dee tried it with might kill him. I thought about all the shit that went down when I was growing up and how it seeped into who I was. These were my bandmates. I had their backs and hoped that they had mine. I never brought up the Brooklyn-versus-Queens issue, but it was always there. Dee Dee, John, and Joey were a lot of things, but they weren't tough guys.

There was never a time in my experience when John and Joey would talk much on the van or, for that matter, anywhere. But now it was down to zero. Joey was sullen, even when he was sitting next to Linda.

During lunch, Marion and I had seen John rub Linda's leg. Chances were that others in our group had seen it, too, and, even if they hadn't, there were nonetheless a bunch of incidents like that one lately.

I was a realist. People got together and people broke up. That was, unfortunately, part of life. However, doing it this way was stupid. Doing it in a situation where we all lived together on the road and had to depend on each other was even stupider. But there was nothing to do about it. There was nothing to say. So we listened to oldies. We were not a happy family.

On 28 June, we were doing the middle of three shows in Tokyo kicking off an ambitious tour of the Pacific Rim that would have been unthinkable a few years earlier. Being in Japan was really being away. In the UK, I knew the language. In Europe, many people spoke English, and I could make out a lot of the foreign words. In Germany, we had Dee Dee. In Japan, though there were exceptions, we were dealing with a much more complete language barrier and a cultural one to go with it. But we knew they loved the new Ramones stuff. The publicity poster was the cover of *End of the Century* with all Japanese writing over it.

The venue was impressive but definitely a change of pace. The Seibu Theatre was an auditorium seating several thousand situated on the top floor of a large modern commercial building. Where we came from, auditoriums either occupied an entire building or, like a swimming pool, were at the base of one. But the Japanese were innovators.

The Tokyo faithful packed the Seibu Theatre and flipped over the Ramones. Once we were up there blasting out twenty-eight songs, we were all speaking basically the same language. The Japanese fans dressed like us, knew the lyrics, and applauded wildly on cue. But on the way back to the dressing room, we knew something strange was going on in the Land of the Rising Sun. There were cracks along the concrete walls. They weren't wide cracks you could stick a finger in – more like hairline cracks. There were still more along the staircase. I knew we played loud, but this was ridiculous.

A few people who looked as if they worked for the venue were trying to tell us something but weren't getting through at first. It was Little Matt whose words first penetrated my brain.

'We just had an earthquake.'

We hadn't noticed a thing while playing. Ramones noise and vibration covered the noise and vibration from moving tectonic plates. It wasn't like the Japanese disaster movies we grew up watching. This was a minor earthquake. Someone said it was not quite a 5.0 on the Richter scale. The Japanese, they explained, built their modern structures to withstand a much larger quake. They learned that the hard way. But, we were told, we had to vacate the premises immediately as a precaution. Sometimes the aftershock was worse than the initial earthquake. I thought about one of the songs we had just performed – 'Gimme Gimme Shock Treatment'. This was a different kind of shock, but, if you weren't used to it, it was still scary.

There were no fatalities outside, as far as we could tell. The reaction everywhere was very orderly. Dee Dee and I had made loose plans to go sightseeing, but tonight definitely wasn't the night. I had a drink or two or three, and Marion and I decided to get some sleep back at the hotel.

I woke up startled at about four in the morning thinking maybe I was having a bad dream. Marion was not quite awake. As the bed lifted off the ground, I thought somebody – maybe some gigantic sumo wrestler – was underneath. I dragged my body to the edge of the mattress and stuck my head under the frame. There was nobody there.

'That was the aftershock,' Marion said.

'Holy shit!'

Tremors were a lot more jarring when you weren't in the middle of a punk-rock show. I wasn't looking forward to the after-aftershock. I drank a glass of wine and tried to fall back asleep.

In the morning, Marion made sure to put two more kimonos in our valises. The hotel provided psychedelic-looking robes every time they cleaned the room in much the same way Holiday Inn provided new little soap bars and tiny bottles of shampoo. We weren't like John, who we suspected had a closet full of hotel hand wipes back home, but for the psychedelic kimonos we made an exception. They would be perfect for the shower runs back at 29 John Street. The rest of the band and crew were pilfering kimonos, too.

We had an off day on 30 June before traveling to another show in Nagoya. We did a television interview show in the afternoon. When Dee Dee and I got back to the hotel, we were going to take Vera and Marion out for dinner and sightseeing, but they had gone out shopping earlier in the day and never returned. So we started our own little tour in the hotel lobby and ordered some sake. Sake is made with rice and often served warm. It's a clear liquid that's not really wine because it's brewed. But sake is also not a beer, as beer is about 5 per cent alcohol and sake can be as high as 20 per cent.

Dee Dee and I had different tastes when it came to booze, but we had at least one preference in common – more. We had five or six cups of sake apiece and had a nice little buzz going. It was time to hit the streets of Tokyo.

We didn't know the streets around the InterContinental Hotel, and it wasn't like Chicago or Detroit or Houston where you were basically in another version of a big American city. We knew we were near some sort of highway, and that was about it. We walked and laughed and looked at one Japanese face after another. It was like a dream. There were, of course, Asians all over New York, but there was everybody all over New York. This was just Asians and us, and we felt like we were the Ramones dropped into another film, this time a monster movie. We also realized that we had underestimated the sake. It hit you hard and fast. The nice little buzz had been crushed by a forty-foot dinosaur. We were drunk out of our minds. Dee Dee approached a mid-forties businessman in a suit.

'Hey! Hey! You see that? Godzilla's coming! Look out, it's fucking Godzilla!'

The poor guy hurried away. He had, in fact, seen a monster. I saw a neatly dressed young woman and made the next play.

'Where is Hirohito? Where is Hirohito? Please, take me to your emperor! Take me to your leader!'

She walked away, too, but not as fast as the guy before her. And she looked kind of insulted.

I didn't know exactly where we were when the police surrounded us or if we were now in the second movie of the double feature. But I had an urgent message for Tokyo's finest.

'We are Ramones! We are Ramones! We come in peace!'

'We play rocky-rolly,' Dee Dee screamed. 'We drinky sake, go pee-pee. We rove you velly much. We rove Nippon! Rong rive Hirohito! We no droppy bomby!'

There was now a language barrier the size of Mount Fuji. Maybe that was good. When I heard the things we were saying, I knew the less they understood, the better. I wasn't sure they knew we were Ramones, but they definitely knew we were Americans and a pain in the ass. One of the police said something and motioned for Dee Dee and me to get into the car. I wasn't sure if this was how an arrest was made, politely, in Japan, and I didn't want to find out. I had to think fast, which was hard because at this point I couldn't even think slow.

I pulled the hotel keys out of my pocket and handed them to one of the officers. He looked at the key chain with its InterContinental logo and had a moment of recognition. Dee Dee saw it, too.

'Ahso! Ahso! You see key? Ahso! You takey to hotely!'

The officer showed the keys to his partner, who nodded and said something. This time when they motioned for us to get in, we did it.

Instead of just dropping us off in front of the hotel, the officers walked us into the lobby. That was the right move. We were staggering.

'Don't forget to write!' Dee Dee said as the police walked back out the front entrance.

We took the elevator up to our floor and went back to our respective rooms. I checked my pocket to make sure I still had the keys. I opened the door, walked a few more drunken steps, and collapsed on the bed.

In the morning, Marion told me it had taken her and Vera half the day to find gifts for everyone back home. When they got back to Vera's room and opened the door, Dee Dee was crawling around the room on his hands and knees like a dog. He was barking a bit, too, but in Japanese. Vera prepared him his favorite: a bubble bath. Once he was in the tub, he started demanding more bubbles and then quickly nodded out. Vera drained the tub and Dee Dee stayed there for the night.

The Ramones' summer tour of the Pacific hopped south to Australia and then east to New Zealand. I turned twenty-eight in Sydney. The final show of the tour was in the city of Christchurch, New Zealand, on 24 July. New Zealand was primarily two large islands. Britain had adopted New Zealand as a colony the previous century, making English the official language. As in Australia, the police understood every word Dee Dee and I said except for the ones we slurred.

Christchurch, like the rest of New Zealand, had the kind of beauty that many of the Scandinavian destinations had. You would think you'd died and gone to heaven if you didn't know better – and if John and Joey weren't carrying on a transcontinental cold war. As the name said, there were churches, and, whether they were old-fashioned or modern, they were classic. Looking east, you saw a perfectly blue Pacific Ocean. When you looked west, you saw the Canterbury Plains stretching out to a ring of snow-capped mountains. But, like any city on the planet, they wanted to hear 'Go Mental', 'Pinhead', and 'Beat on the Brat.'

Christchurch Town Hall held about twenty-five hundred people. It was a modern, artistic steel-and-concrete building set up for theater-in-the-round with a high platform in the center. To avoid architectural boredom, there were irregular heights between various seating areas. Marion and I were road weary, strung out on some hash we had just smoked, and wandering around the building like kids in a corn maze. The opening band were already onstage. We found our way back to the dressing room and had a rude awakening.

There were journalists everywhere. They were excited as if the Queen herself were visiting, which was great, but I was in no condition or mood to answer questions. Worse, the entire backstage was illuminated by extremely bright fluorescent lights that penetrated our already dilated pupils. It felt like waking up from a pleasant dream and then waking up again. We had to get out of there.

The contrast between light and dark was sudden and overwhelming. The opening band were maybe in their third or fourth song, and we figured we would watch from the side of the stage. We went up a staircase, decided we were too close, and figured we'd be better off on one of the nearby landings. Even though I couldn't see it or much of anything at that point, I figured there was another staircase on the opposite side of the stage. But I was wrong.

I plummeted about eight feet. When I was about halfway through the free fall I didn't know if I was about to hit the ground or if I still had a long way to go. So when I hit the auditorium floor, as bad as it was, I was relieved. I had survived. My right ankle was badly sprained, and my knee was banged up. Before I could think about whether I would be able to play a show in less than an hour, Marion landed on top of me. It was the blind leading the blind and the stoned leading the stoned. I might have broken something, but at least I broke her fall.

No one seemed to notice the two near casualties limping up the aisle. No one in the dressing room seemed to care. We had a show to do. Marion got me some ice and we tried to reduce the swelling. Before the ice could melt, two and a half thousand New Zealanders were yelling, 'Hey Ho, Let's Go!'

The hashish must have killed a third of the pain and the adrenaline another third. The remaining third I felt, but I played through it. I hobbled back to the dressing room, and, when Monte saw how swollen my right leg was, he freaked. He and Marion had to cut my pants off to get me out of them.

The next day, we were homeward bound. New Zealand was so far east, you flew east to get to America's west. It was cold at the airport. This was winter Down Under and we wanted to get up and over. We would be flying to Singapore, changing planes, and then flying to Hawaii, Los Angeles, and, finally, back to New York. Monte had called ahead to the airport in New Zealand to get me a wheelchair. When we pulled up in the bus, one of the flight attendants met us and helped me into the chair. Sometimes life really did imitate art. I thought, *Put me in a wheelchair, get me on a plane.* Not only that, I really did want to be sedated.

Having already copped everything else along the Pacific Rim, Dee Dee copped an attitude. He told Monte that I was getting special treatment.

Monte didn't even bother to answer. Then Dee Dee took it up with me directly. I told him he was fucking nuts. 'What part of "I have a busted leg" do you not understand?' It took a special kind of maniac to be jealous of a guy in a wheelchair. Of course, Dee Dee needed one, too, but for different reasons.

Dee Dee and I continued our stupid argument on the flight over to Singapore. We were in first class with an open bar, which for the Ramones' rhythm section usually spelled trouble. Dee Dee said something about what Marion was wearing, and I said something about Vera. Dee Dee was done pulling knives on me, but he wasn't done calling me an asshole. Our women for the time being were done with both of us. There were open seats scattered throughout the plane. Marion and Vera found a couple of them at the other end.

Dee Dee was making a pyramid out of beer cans. The pyramid was five wide at the bottom, which is impressive enough on an airplane in flight. The fact that every can was empty because the two of us guzzled the contents made it even more impressive. I was considering starting my own pyramid with shot glasses when I accidentally elbowed one of the bottom-rung beer cans and the whole stack came toppling down midflight. This bothered Dee Dee a lot more than it should have.

'What the fuck is your problem?'

'What are you gonna do about it? You pack your switchblade?'

We were loud and menacing. We were a terror in the sky. Suddenly the copilot, a big Australian-looking guy, popped out of the cockpit, walked down the aisle, and confronted us.

'I can radio ahead to Singapore and have you both arrested,' he said. 'Have you ever been to jail in Singapore?'

'Okay, sorry,' Dee Dee said. 'We'll be good.'

We had about another thirty hours till we hit New York, and crossing the international date line wasn't going to help. I just wanted to get home.

Joey had problems with his feet. We didn't know all the details and we didn't want to know. He had infections and toe fungus. His nails got so infected that they couldn't be trimmed with a regular nail clipper. It took a large shear. After we played Central Park in New York, Joey went to the hospital for one of his feet and we had to cancel a bunch of shows.

A lot of his problems were related to hygiene. He wasn't changing his clothes much lately, and maybe that had something to do with Linda. Not that Joey didn't have problems before he ever met her. I told him that whatever else was going on, he had to change his socks. If not daily then at least every other day. The feet are very unforgiving. Walk all over them, suffocate them, never care for them, and they will eventually take their revenge.

If I'd shared an apartment with Joey, I would have changed his socks myself rather than see him go through that. But these days his fiancée wasn't even much of a roommate. Joey was tapping things and twirling his hair at a record pace. The band's open secret had become Joey's open wound – literally.

Hygiene at 29 John Street was no problem. We now went to the shower in style dressed in our psychedelic hotel kimonos. Other members of the entourage had given us theirs, so we now had a couple dozen. We were all set for the eighties as far as Christmas gifts were concerned and had already given some out to our neighbors. We walked the halls and rode the elevators in kimonos. Word actually got out that 29 John Street was taken over by Japanese tourists.

Joey was back on his troubled feet in time for our next tour of Europe, which began with five cities in Italy. Picking a favorite Italian city is like picking a favorite Beatles song, but Milan was right up there. Located near the foot of the Alps in northern Italy, Milan had everything a great city could have – great fashion and art, breathtaking churches, and ancient history. There were canals dating back to the Roman Empire. Milan was also the industrial engine of Italy. The brief tour we took on the afternoon of 13 September barely scratched the surface.

Milan had one more thing it could have done without: political unrest. On the streets, outside museums, on pavilions – wherever the tour bus brought us – we saw police. It was nothing like seeing the relatively friendly police in New York or even in Tokyo. In New York especially, the police usually had an air of being relaxed on the job until you gave them a real reason not to be. The year before, the Ramones had done a very successful benefit at CBGB to raise money so the New York cops could get bulletproof vests. We were criticized by some people for doing that, but it wasn't just John who was for it. Of course, there were exceptions, but for the most part New York cops were New Yorkers protecting New Yorkers.

The police in Milan did not blend in. It was hard to blend in when you were looking for terrorists and had a submachine gun slung over your shoulder. When we walked along the pavement, we could feel their penetrating watch. Sometimes the police held their submachine guns ready for use and marched toward us. Once they were past us, we felt relieved but never completely.

Despite that, Milan wasn't running a police state. The intense police presence was a reaction to terrorism from within that had been going on for at least ten years. The Red Brigades were probably the most notorious of all the violent radical groups. They were a pro-communist faction so left-wing that even the far, far left in Italy condemned them. They started out as a vocal pro-worker organization but quickly moved on to murdering pro-fascist figures. Then they moved on to killing legitimate labor leaders.

In 1978, the Red Brigades committed the highest offense when they kidnapped and assassinated Aldo Moro, the former Italian prime minister. At the time, Moro was negotiating a peaceful compromise between the Communists and the Christian Democrats. No matter how beautiful Milan was, reality was clear. Once a political group proves it will stop at nothing, the state will do anything to stop it.

The vibe outside the Velodromo Vigorelli before our sound check was tense. The police and their submachine guns were out in full force. There were demonstrators with armbands and a Nazi aura about them. It wasn't a joking matter even for John, who for months on end was ranting about how we should nuke Iran for holding Americans hostage. It wasn't a simple issue of good guys versus bad guys here. It was an issue of not knowing what was going to happen next.

The Velodromo, originally built for bicycle racing, was an oval stadium with regular seating of about nine thousand and an even larger capacity for festival seating. There was excitement as in any Ramones crowd when we opened with 'Blitzkrieg Bop', but everything changed about midway through the set when we launched into 'Commando'. I didn't use my cymbal a lot in that song, but suddenly there was a crash that didn't come from my stick. A large rock hit the cymbal and fell to the ground. It was bigger than a baseball. If it had hit me, it would have knocked me out at best or killed me at worst.

I didn't give anyone the finger. This was about saving lives, not saving face. I was a sitting duck behind a Rogers drum set. I got up and walked offstage. 'Commando' was such a rhythmically driven song that John, Joey, and Dee Dee didn't notice for about twenty seconds that they had lost their drummer. The words still rang out.

The band joined me backstage soon. I was loud and clear about not going back out. I had read about Buddy Miles, whom I had met once, almost getting his eye put out onstage by a BB rifle. You couldn't say it would never happen to you. *It almost just did happen to me.* If we went back out, they could finish the job by nailing me or any of the other Ramones. Once one of us was out of commission, we were all out of commission. It was as simple as that. John, Joey, and Dee Dee agreed. The promoter did not.

While we saw red, the promoter saw green. He was freaked out. The thought of refunding sixteen thousand tickets was scarier to him than the thought of someone losing an eye or a limb, as long as it was someone else's eye or limb.

'Donna worry. We got the man who did a-this.'

'Yeah?' I said. 'Where is he? Prove it. Bring him in here.'

'I assure you the police have-a this man.'

It was bullshit as far as I was concerned. Even on the outside chance that they had a suspect in custody, if there was one psycho in the crowd there could have been twenty more. Meanwhile, we could hear and feel the crowd stomping their feet. It was literally louder than a medium Japanese earthquake.

Joey told me about a riot that had occurred in this very stadium in the summer of 1971. Led Zeppelin were playing, and a disturbance in the audience grew out of control. There were hundreds, then thousands, of kids fighting, throwing everything they could get their hands on, and destroying the band's equipment. Police with riot gear charged into the crowd and shot as many canisters of tear gas as they could fire off. The members of Zeppelin barely made it out of there with their lives.

Between the earth-rattling stomping and Joey's story, I had a change of mind, if not heart. I had two choices: I could stay out of the line of fire and start a riot or walk into the line of fire and stop one. I figured it was time to take one for the team, but only figuratively.

Before I sat back down behind the kit, I stood there for a moment, turned my head left, right, and center, and shot a look out to the audience. It was a look I still carried with me from Brooklyn that said *Don't try it again*. We launched into 'Here Today, Gone Tomorrow', which ended with the famous last words 'Someone had to pay the price.' Fortunately, no one had to this time. At least none of us. Milan screamed and shouted its appreciation even as the police combed the crowd.

Unfortunately, at the end of the show, Joey started his neurotic back-and-forth routine while exiting the stage. The promoter was fooled. Milan was confused. And we had had enough. There was never a good reason for a riot at a concert, but obsessive-compulsive disorder was the worst one possible. Monte grabbed him, and the show was over.

Rome was where gladiators fought to the death in front of bloodthirsty crowds, but, for the Ramones, being there was a relief. The atmosphere was calm compared with Milan. The biggest problem we had was not being able to get something to eat during the afternoon siesta when stores closed till five and people closed their metal shutters to take a nap. The second-worst problem was being taken out to dinner by the promoters. The Italian food was the best in the world, but the meal was a dozen-course event dragged out until two in the morning, at which point we really understood why the Italians needed their siesta.

The sound check at Castel Sant'Angelo was a short study in contrasts. In the daylight, we played 'Cretin Hop' against the backdrop of the ancient fortress built two thousand years earlier by Emperor Hadrian. The walls of the castle had deflected bombardments of flaming arrows and withstood battering rams, but no one in the Roman Empire ever expected four guys in T-shirts shouting, 'Four five six seven, all good cretins go to heaven.'

The show at night was tight. A song like 'Rock 'n' Roll Radio', stripped of everything but bass, guitar, drums, and vocals, sounded pure and hard and distracted us from recent rocks, riots, tear gas, police, submachine guns, temperamental producers, and stolen girlfriends.

Traveling to Spain was like going back in time. The joke on *Saturday Night Live* for a couple of years was that Generalissimo Francisco Franco was still dead. But sometimes it was hard to tell. In Barcelona, the hotel was utilitarian at best. If you wanted to see a first-run movie, you had to cross the border into France. Rock albums were available only on the black market. Even though as a dictator Franco rejected communism, what was left after his death felt a lot like the Soviet Union. The roads were horrible. Going from point A to B was a misadventure.

We figured out quickly that rock and roll was still new and the Ramones were a novelty. We stopped at a little café for sandwiches. When we looked at the menu, there were just a few locals sitting at the tables and the bar. By the time we ordered coffee, there were maybe a hundred people in and around the establishment gawking at us. No one mentioned our band's name or asked for an autograph. Apparently, the punk fashion – the guys in leather jackets and the girls in tight, bright miniskirts – was as new to them as color TV.

Spain was transitioning to democracy and determined to move forward. Joey was having a hard time moving forward. The Ramones plus wives and girlfriends had just been dropped off and were walking to a TV studio to do an interview. We crossed a busy intersection as a pack. Joey was right behind me and Marion. As we reached the opposite curb, the light turned red, and I heard a collision. It was the screech of car tires and a dull thud, and that was never good. I turned around to see Joey flying over the hood of an Alfa Romeo.

No explanation was necessary. Joey had done an about-face to touch the opposite curb and then run out of green time. In Barcelona, as in New York, drivers had no time to waste. Crossing the street normally wasn't a round-trip ticket unless you were the lead singer of the Ramones. We had our hearts in our throats as Joey twirled through the air and hit the street still spinning sideways. Barcelona came to a halt at least at this one corner. We surrounded our frontman, who sat up dazed but thankfully much more alive than the Generalissimo.

We played in front of about 250,000 people on the stepped side of a hill known as Montjuïc. Someone told us in all seriousness Montjuïc in old Spanish translated to 'Mount Jew'. We hoped this information didn't get to John so we could be spared dozens of horrible jokes. But Joey, true to form, did tower over the huge crowd, which was much better than being sprawled out on the pavement.

As we packed it in backstage, we heard Mike Oldfield's band playing *Tubular Bells*, featured in *The Exorcist*. It didn't follow 'Pinhead' that smoothly, but the audience loved all of it. It was a nation still getting rid of its demons.

The last leg of our tour was Great Britain, starting with London on 2 October. The week before, while we were closing out Spain, John Bonham of Led Zeppelin died after drinking what was reported to be the equivalent of forty shots of vodka. It was doubtful the band would continue.

Everyone was seasick as we took the ferry across the Irish Sea to Dublin. Everyone but me. My strong stomach went beyond the ability to swallow bugs of various types and foods barely fit for human consumption. But on this cloudy afternoon afloat, my head was the problem. The frenzy of a tour combined with my hyper nature would usually distract me from thinking too much about mortality. Now, for a little while, there was time.

Mortality naturally wasn't a favorite topic, but, when someone in rock passed away, it hit a little closer to home than I might have liked. If he was a legendary drummer who inspired me, it hit closer. And, if it was alcohol related, it was a bull's-eye. Like most musicians, I went through ups and downs doing what I had to do. Feeling invincible served a purpose. It was a useful tool. But for a few quiet moments at sea I felt vulnerable.

Reflection time was over when we arrived at Dublin Port. It was a homecoming of sorts for Marion with her Irish roots. It was also a homecoming for the Ramones. We had played here two years earlier and put down some Irish roots of our own. The recent success here of 'Baby, I Love You' watered the tree.

The Dublin punks were out in full force. They were in their leather jackets and swarmed us as we got off the ferry. It felt like they had hung out by the docks for two years waiting for our return. The Irish warmth and cheer was contagious, and we invited about a dozen of the kids to board the charter bus taking us to the hotel. They helped us with our bags and even navigated a bit. They were all taught about the next world in catechism, but this was apparently punk heaven on earth.

They got a little more than they bargained for. John, also of Irish descent, played big brother on the bus and asked them every question that popped into his head. Are you in school? What are you studying? What's your favorite subject? What kind of job are you looking to get? What does it pay? What's rent like over here? You would have thought he was at the post office.

For every punk on the bus, there were fifty waiting outside the hotel. Each of the band members got a nice round of applause as we disembarked. The real applause, however, was saved for the women. It started when Marion stepped off with her long strawberry-blonde hair and black miniskirt. It continued when Vera followed with high leather boots and a black lace top. Roxy and Linda brought up the rear with an array of pink leggings and brightly painted, studded leather jackets. The kids went wild, transforming the bus steps into a fashion show runway.

Not all of the kids were welcoming. Word was the skinheads had been attacking punks as well as each other in Dublin, and there had been some violence at past concerts. There was a local political push to ban rock concerts of any type at the Grand Cinema, the sixteen-hundred-seat converted movie theater where we were playing. The fans were frisked on their way into the show, which we definitely didn't like.

There was no trouble when we played. These were good kids looking to have a little fun. John could have told anyone that.

There were two negative things about Ronald Reagan's election as president of the United States. One was an agenda of letting corporate interests run wild while pulling a lot of the social safety net out from under the poor. The other was having to listen to John's one-man band play 'Hail to the Chief' for at least the next four years. I wasn't sure which was worse. It might have been a three-way tie with our spotting John and Linda together in the Village all the time.

Later in November, Bruce Springsteen released the single 'Hungry Heart'. Sometime earlier, when Joey met Springsteen in Asbury Park, New Jersey, he'd asked Bruce to write the Ramones a song. 'Hungry Heart' was it, and it had a classic rock-and-roll-meets-doo-wop feel plus a great hook that was perfect for the Ramones. But Springsteen's manager, Jon Landau, had seen Bruce give away hit singles to Patti Smith and the Pointer Sisters and persuaded him to keep this one. It quickly rose to number five on the *Billboard* singles chart.

That wouldn't have bothered us if we were getting airplay, but we weren't. At least not much. We were the band almost everyone said they loved, but the radio time wasn't there to back it up. So Joey wrote 'We Want the Airwaves' as a direct shot at corporate media. He didn't pull any punches, rhyming 'programmer' with 'hammer' and threatening to smash his own radio.

We would be going back into the studio soon to record 'Airwaves' along with a full album of new material. In the meantime, Joey was having health problems for reasons we could largely guess.

Marion and I went to bed late on the night of 8 December. No TV or radio – just music on the stereo. For us it was a quiet evening. In the morning, I heard John Lennon's new song 'Starting Over' wafting up through our ninth-floor bedroom window. I drifted in and out of sleep and heard 'I'm Losing you', another song from the new Lennon album *Double Fantasy*.

I was now awake enough to realize it was coming from the record store downstairs at street level. The owner had to be blasting it out the window to be this loud this high up. I couldn't understand it. The album was doing well and definitely didn't need to be promoted this way. I grunted to see if Marion knew what was going on, and she didn't. 'Watching the Wheels' was next. Someone knocked on our door, and Marion got up to get it. I heard a neighbor's voice. When Marion returned to the bedroom, she told me John Lennon had been shot and killed.

The kind of depression I experienced over the next few days was supposed to be reserved for the death of family and close friends. Obviously, I was not alone. This was the harshest of all ways for millions of people to discover that John Lennon *was* family. He was a close friend. If you looked at a calendar, the seventies had ended a while ago, and the sixties were already ancient history. But they both ended for real right there, and along with it the little kid in so many of us that thrilled to a Beatles song. The music kept us young.

Beyond that, this was personal for me as a New Yorker. Most of us were born here and made the best of it. John Lennon had picked this city out of a planet's worth of cities and wore it proudly on his T-shirt. Where we took New York's liberties for granted, Lennon fought to stay here. I understood that one insane man took his life, but, on another level, I felt that New York City let him down.

I let in a friend at the door for a couple drinks of our own. He told me to look out the window because on the sidewalk below was a shit-faced Wall Street-type businessman in a three-piece suit with an attaché case. He was sprawled out facedown. It was time to spread the yuletide cheer. I took a plastic garbage bag, filled it with water, and tossed it out the window toward the businessman. It landed on him and burst, making a sound like a car tire exploding. He was so bombed, he didn't even move. I knew what that was like.

14

THE M&M BOYS

The Ramones' sandbox was getting harder to play in. John and Joey had both dug in deeper. When they pissed in the sandbox, we all got wet. Our trip up to Ithaca, New York, on 28 February 1981, was the last show scheduled until July. We would be taking a break to record our next album, *Pleasant Dreams*, and then resume an intense touring schedule once the record was released.

Everyone in the van wanted to be released as we traveled north along Route 81. The Ramones women took a rain check on this dreary trip. I caught a little sleep in the first row but woke up and started a conversation with Joey about a couple of movies I wanted to see once we had a little time off the road. *Altered States*, a sci-fi flick about schizophrenia, was at the top of my list. Joey had heard great things about Martin Scorsese's new film, *Raging Bull*.

Our guitarist wasn't exactly a raging bull, but he wanted to charge whenever I talked to Joey. That's how bad it had gotten. After I mentioned to Joey how Robert De Niro had gotten himself into amazing shape for the movie, John sneered.

'So now you're *his* friend?'

'Yeah,' I said. 'What's wrong with that?'

'If I have to tell you . . .' John shook his head and looked out the front window.

He didn't have to tell me. In John's world, I had to choose between the two of them. I was never going to live in a world like that even if I happened to be stuck in the sandbox. Joey wasn't much better. When I hung out with John, Joey gave me dirty looks. He didn't elaborate, but I knew he disliked John to the point where my talking to him seemed like a betrayal. Joey would then give me the cold shoulder. That might last a day or two. I was damned if I did and damned if I didn't, and sometimes I just put my head back on the damned seat and went back to sleep.

Sometimes I had to play messenger. Like most messengers, I didn't want to get shot. Monte was a messenger, too. The reality of a band on the road is that sometimes the guitarist has to tell the lead singer about a change in the set list. And sometimes the lead singer has to approve that change. Though our guitarist and lead singer were sitting in the same van, they needed an intermediary for something as simple and easy as that. The thing about insanity is that when you're around it long enough you become part of it. So, after a while, carrying messages back and forth in the van like a foreign envoy seemed really normal.

Just north of Binghamton, we pulled off of Route 81 to stop and eat at one of our favorite Cracker Barrels. This one looked like the rest, with the long country porch and wood columns with sway braces. But they cooked a mean plate of chicken and mashed potatoes at this outpost. On the way in, just before the porch, Dee Dee picked up a beetle and told me there was fifty bucks in it for me if I made this my appetizer.

'We're not doing this now,' Monte said.

Maybe we were and maybe we weren't. With the whole band watching, I took the beetle from Dee Dee in my right hand. It was sluggish but not quite dead. I noticed right away it had a few little bumps stuck to it, which I identified as eggs.

'They're actually called larvae,' Joey said.

'Go for it, Marc,' Dee Dee said.

I thought about it. I had an iron stomach. How bad could this really be? Jet-setters paid thousands to eat caviar, which was just a bunch of fish eggs. And here, in front of Cracker Barrel, someone was paying *me*.

'Forget it, Marc,' John said. 'Not before the show. You could get really sick.'

'I'm sick just thinking about it,' Monte said.

John flicked the beetle off my hand and it fluttered to the ground. I would have to settle for something on the menu.

We always got stares when we ate out, and this afternoon was no exception. People would look, look away, and look back again. On this day, a nice elderly couple a few tables over had trouble with the looking-away part. That sort of thing, for lack of a better word, usually egged us on. We kept talking about the beetle and the larvae and how maybe it was still waiting outside, hoping to be dessert. Joey was tapping away with his fork.

I ate fast, but no one ate as fast as Monte. Maybe he thought the faster he ate, the less time we would have to prank him. That strategy wouldn't work this time, since I had already smeared maple syrup on his briefcase handle. All that syrup made me hungry again, and I noticed at the next table someone had left without touching a stack of blueberry pancakes. So I got up and helped myself. I did this once in a while, but I never ate leftovers if someone had already taken a bite. I had to draw the line somewhere.

When the band finished eating and walked out of the restaurant, Monte was already waiting out front warming up the van. When we got in and took our seats, Monte told us he had finally gotten some of the credit he deserved. The nice elderly lady had approached him in the parking lot and told him what he was doing was absolutely wonderful.

'Aren't you the nice man who's with those mentally disabled boys?'

'Yes,' Monte said. 'Yes, I am.'

'They're lucky to have you. You're very good with them.'

There was no denying that. We didn't know where we'd be without him. He made us a better band. In fact, tonight this mentally disabled group was performing for Cornell – an Ivy League institution.

Graham Gouldman wasn't the Ramones' first choice to produce the album *Pleasant Dreams*, but he was Sire's choice and that was that. Graham Gouldman might have had something to say about second choices and second chances. As a nineteen-year-old in the English group the Mockingbirds in 1964, he submitted a song called 'For Your Love' to the band's label. Columbia Records turned it down, but, when the Yardbirds recorded it the following year, it became a massive breakthrough hit. The song also took on a life of its own in a different way, prompting the Yardbirds' lead guitarist Eric Clapton to leave the group in favor of more bluesy, less pop-oriented music.

More recently, Graham Gouldman was a founder of the band 10cc, who produced such pop hits as 'I'm Not in Love' and 'The Things We Do for Love'. In the mid- to late seventies, there were stretches of weeks, even months, when you couldn't go an hour without hearing one of those songs on your local light-rock FM station. That's what Sire wanted for the Ramones.

We wanted that, too, but on our own terms. Joey and I were very happy to be working with Graham. That was less the case for Dee Dee and John. John wanted a return to the raw punk sound of earlier albums and was afraid that *Pleasant Dreams* would become Phil Spector, part two. There was no chance of that, and not just because no other top-of-the-line producer in the world packed a .38. If there was a similarity in the approach, it was just that we were going for a big, clear sound. For all we knew, the second time could be the charm.

In March, when we loaded into Media Sound on West Fifty-Seventh Street in Manhattan, I had good memories from when we recorded *Road to Ruin* in the same studio. Media Sound was once the Manhattan Baptist Church, and the acoustics in what was originally the sanctuary were huge. The state-of-the-art studio was built in the late sixties with the help of young financiers John Roberts and Joel Rosenman and caused a buzz in the music industry. Roberts and Rosenman were soon asked to build a second studio, this one in upstate New York. Those plans morphed into a giant outdoor festival: Woodstock. When you thought big and pursued your ambition, big things happened even if they were nothing like plan A.

Graham was easy to work with. I liked to think I was easy to work with, too. I was getting comments about my drinking, but I came into the studio sober and ready to go. The drum sound was powerful and tight, the way I liked it. I had my tracks done in less than four full days.

There was obviously a lot of work left to do after the drums were done, but I didn't hang around for much of it. Russell Mael from the innovative band Sparks was scheduled to come in and sing background vocals. So was Debbie Harry. So were Kate Pierson and Cindy Wilson from the B-52's. But I didn't feel like hanging around the sandbox drama on my best behavior for weeks just for a cool highlight here and there. After my part was done, I basically shut off everything in my brain that had anything to do with the band. I had heard Joey was scheduled to go back to England to work on vocals at Strawberry Studios, where Graham Gouldman had produced so many hits in the sixties. My thought was, *Bon voyage*.

Pleasant Dreams was released in July without much fanfare and without a single in the US. The album quickly peaked at fifty-eight on the *Billboard* LP chart. Criticism was mixed, with the common denominator that it was too clean a sound to really be classified as a 'punk' album. One of the harshest critics was our own guitarist, who felt the Ramones had let down their punk fans a second time in a row. But our collective cage wasn't that rattled by any of it. We had definitely been down this road before, and it wasn't the road to ruin – literally or figuratively.

My own reaction wasn't mixed. I loved the sound, and I loved a lot of the songs. 'It's Not My Place (In the 9 to 5 World)' sounded radio ready, even if radio wasn't willing. I loved the Bo Diddley feel of the drums and the change to a straight beat in the break, which gave it the sound of an early Kinks or Who song. Motown and Wall of Sound imprints were all over 'Don't Go', 'You Sound Like You're Sick', and 'She's a Sensation'.

At the same time, there was plenty of darkness in the lyrics for anyone who bothered to listen. 'The KKK Took My Baby Away' was an ode to a young black woman Joey had befriended when he was institutionalized as a teen and who one day just disappeared. Dee Dee's 'All's Quiet on the Eastern Front' was an insomniac's twisted love song to New York penned by someone who definitely had his share of sleepless nights. And beneath the doo-wop of 'This Business Is Killing Me' was Joey's unapologetic lament about the life we were in: it was making him a sick, sleepless train wreck running around trying to please everyone – as if Joey didn't have enough problems.

Not one of us was having many pleasant dreams. But we knew what came next: wall-to-wall touring to support the album. It was time to run around.

Lunchtime on 7 August, I made sure to sit near the front window of the Howard Johnson's right down the block from the hotel we were staying at in Austin, Texas. We were finishing a swing through the Lone Star State before a day off to drive all the way up to Denver. The coffee I was sipping was helping with my hangover, but what I was seeing out the window was not. Joey and Dee Dee were arguing. I couldn't hear what it was about through the thick plate glass. It was very animated, like a Ramones silent movie.

But I had to keep looking out the window because Aaron Cohen was going to show up any minute. I had gone through first through ninth grade with Aaron, who was now living in Austin. I thought it was great that he had followed my career through Dust, Wayne County, and the Voidoids, right through my transformation to Marky Ramone. When he reached me on the phone, he was looking forward to catching up. He sounded excited, which was flattering but nothing new for Aaron. He was a hyper kid. Of course, so was I, but, between the two of us, I was always the one telling him to chill out, and that really said something. Aaron also had a lazy eye, which didn't help a lot with his social life.

Things were gearing up outside between Joey and Dee Dee. They weren't in full Ramones regalia. Joey had on his prescription sunglasses, but otherwise just jeans and a striped, collared shirt. Dee Dee was wearing jeans and a wife-beater shirt that might have been more fitting for John. They were waving their arms around and making heated points right in each other's face. I hoped no one identified them as Ramones, because this was a scene.

Into this chaos walked Aaron Cohen. I waved from inside the Howard Johnson's, but his lazy eye didn't see me and his good eye was on Joey and Dee Dee. By the time I saw what was about to happen and waved my own arms, it was too late. Aaron Cohen walked straight into the plate-glass door.

It was a powerful but dull thud. It shook the door but not enough to give Aaron much of a break. He bounced off and fell backward, stunned. I bolted from my table and ran out. So did a waiter and a couple of customers. Aaron was on his back and a bloody mess. His nose and forehead were badly cut, and he was out of it. I put my hands behind his head to make sure he didn't bang it again, and a manager came out with a towel and a pitcher of water. I heard someone say they were calling an ambulance.

'Take it easy, Aaron,' I said. 'You're gonna be okay.'

When we were in grade school, they used to give us these worksheets that featured a drawing and a caption that said 'What's wrong with this picture?' The idea was to find something that was out of place. It wasn't hard to spot in front of the Howard Johnson's. What was wrong with this picture was that Joey and Dee Dee were still going at it.

'Don't tell me you didn't say it!' Dee Dee shouted. 'Vera told me everything!'

'Really?' Joey said. 'What if I told you Vera was full of shit?'

With no hesitation, Dee Dee punched Joey in the mouth. It was a bit of a reach, but he landed a solid blow. Joey fell to the pavement and his sunglasses popped off. More patrons were pouring out of the Howard Johnson's for the main event. The only positive thing I could think of was that an ambulance was already on its way.

From the moment I noticed Joey and Dee Dee fighting, through Aaron's horrible accident, to our bassist's KO of our lead singer, very little time had elapsed. The whole thing was about two and a half minutes – about the length of a good Ramones song.

Our tour swung back through New York, and on 1 September, we stopped in at 30 Rockefeller Center to appear on NBC's *The Tomorrow*

Show. We were fans of the show and its host, Tom Snyder. Tom was a good-natured Midwestern guy who'd made his way out to Los Angeles to be a newscaster en route to becoming a major talk-show personality. We liked *The Tomorrow Show* because an interview with Tom was not standard fare.

Tom sat you down like a guest in his own living room and plunged headfirst into your situation like a half-journalist/half-shrink. If three or four million people happened to be watching, so be it. He laughed hard, he scoffed hard, and he set the bar for a good interview right around the bar for good sex – nothing short of sheer exhaustion was acceptable. Once Dan Aykroyd of *Saturday Night Live* had captured the manic flap of the head and arms in his brilliant impression, Tom Snyder was permanently etched into the brain of everyone who stayed up past eleven thirty.

The official name of *The Tomorrow Show* was *Tomorrow with Tom Snyder*, but that applied to tomorrow, not today. Tom was out, so for our afternoon taping we were getting the substitute host, Kelly Lange. Lange had done the news with Snyder out in Los Angeles and was a fairly regular stand-in, but she was no Tom Snyder. We didn't care. We were happy to get a national spot.

I was really excited that afternoon to meet Ed Asner, who was backstage with us waiting to go on the show. Asner played Lou Grant on *The Mary Tyler Moore Show* along with one of the best supporting casts in television history. He was currently playing Lou Grant in a top-rated show of the same name, making the jump from comedy to drama seamlessly. Anyone who knew Ed Asner strictly from those series thought of him as a gruff, short-tempered character, but in real life he was smooth and gracious, a testament to terrific acting.

Asner's politics were also not so obvious from the characters he played. He was president of the Screen Actors Guild and outspoken on behalf of progressive causes. Asner spoke out against US support for right-wing governments in Latin America and advocated for universal healthcare. My dad would have especially enjoyed shooting the breeze with him.

My friend Richard was with us backstage, and I asked him to grab me something to drink from the dressing room. My mouth was getting dry from talking up a storm with Ed Asner and letting him know I was a big fan. So when Richard handed me a can of club soda, I thanked him. I quickly opened the top and almost the whole can shot all over Ed Asner. I knew the prank was meant for me, but, unlike *The Tomorrow Show*, this was happening live.

Asner was drenched – jacket, shirt, tie, and pants. Makeup was running from his cheeks. I said I was very sorry and almost called him Lou. He looked flustered, and for a split second I thought he was going to call me Ted and tear me a new one. But a couple of assistant producers were there in a flash with paper towels. It wasn't a great omen for the show. The studio audience loved our two-song set of 'Sedated' and 'KKK'. It would have been good to walk off to that applause, but, once Kelly Lange had the four of us sitting in front of her, she fired away.

'You don't give your real names because you don't want your mothers to be subjected to that.'

'To be disgraced,' John said.

The audience laughed at John's comeback. It was completely sarcastic, and they picked up on it. Kelly Lange was not physically unattractive, but she came off like a schoolmarm. She was the true-life version of Principal Togar from *Rock 'n' Roll High School*. We could see Lange was already reloading, but she didn't seem to understand that we prepared well for our roles. Not just in the movie – our entire lives.

'Can you see?' Lange asked Joey while moving his hair from his eyes.

'I was meaning to get a haircut,' Joey said. Laughter.

'What do you guys do all day?' she asked.

'Nothing,' John said. More laughter. Then Joey dropped the bomb.

'We really feel cheated that Tom isn't here.'

Touché. The roof caved in. Ramones humor, like Ramones music, was best served stripped down.

Kelly Lange proceeded to back off a bit and ask some legitimate questions, which led to a half-decent though not quite Tom Snyder-caliber discussion. Joey explained that the Ramones had stuck to their original idea but that there were no hard feelings toward bands that were heavily commercial. There was room for everybody. Dee Dee talked about how the kids in Detroit and Ohio identified with the Ramones because they had the same problems, which was too bad for the kids in Detroit and Ohio.

As the group continued discussing the Midwest, my left foot, sitting atop my right knee, began to vibrate visibly as if it had a little motor in it. John's steel-blue eyes fixated on the vibrating foot until he couldn't stand it a moment longer. He grabbed my left Chucky-T sneaker and stopped it cold, to the delight of the studio audience. Then he let go and without missing a beat it started vibrating again. I hadn't said anything to that point. But somehow, without really trying, I had made a deeply personal statement.

MTV launched on 1 August 1981, and, in the two full months since, no one we knew had caught a glimpse of the video for 'We Want the Airwaves' that we'd shot on the roof of Joey's building. We couldn't personally watch all the time, but we had a lot of eyes out there, so, unless they slipped it in at 3:53 a.m. one night between the Police and Styx, we were now being ignored by a completely new medium. We wanted the airwaves *and* the signals sent through coaxial cables, but we weren't getting either.

On the night of 8 October, we played a show in Columbus, Ohio, and had a day off to travel to a show in Virginia Beach on the tenth. Our hotel was a place called Swingos Celebrity Inn in the Cleveland area. Swingos had serious rock-and-roll party credentials. Elvis once booked more than a hundred rooms for his extended entourage. Keith Moon stayed there, dressed up as a cop, and handcuffed guests together. Ian Hunter of Mott the Hoople was quoted as saying, 'Swingos is a place you remember checking in and out of, but you can't remember anything in between.'

I did remember the fan who came by the table to sit with me and Dee Dee. I didn't remember her name, and I didn't recall exactly where and when we first ran into her, but it all seemed real enough, and the important thing was she remembered us. I was drinking shots of Bacardi 151 one after the other. Dee Dee was drinking blackberry brandy. Our fan was having some of both. So was Danny, my drum roadie. A great local tradition weighed heavily on our shoulders, so we did the best we could.

Monte came over to the table to remind me that we were getting up early and driving all the way to Virginia Beach. I told him to go ahead without me because our fan had promised me a ride in her friend's car and with the day off there was no big rush. Monte asked me if I was sure. I was, and that was that.

I had a vintage Swingos hangover in the morning and finally made it out to the dining room for lunch, which would include as many coffee refills as the staff could bring me. Another thing that took my mind off the heavy feeling in my head was spotting Roger Maris. The retired baseball hero was in town for a convention. I introduced myself and sat down. He had heard of the Ramones.

Although I wasn't a big baseball fan growing up, my father was, and he had given me, of all things, a Spalding Roger Maris glove. I was familiar with a few of Maris's career highlights: the sixty-one home runs in 1961, the two consecutive MVP awards, and the seven trips to the World Series, five with the Yankees and two with the Cardinals. So we hit it off in the Swingos dining room and talked memories. *If John could only see me now.*

Maris talked about how, when he and Mickey Mantle were battling to see who could break Babe Ruth's single-season home run record, the feud between the two players was all media hype. In reality, Mickey had moved in with Maris and outfielder Bob Cerv to their two-bedroom apartment in Queens. There, Mickey slept on the couch and Bob and Roger tried to look out for him. They weren't always successful. Mickey would come to the ballpark tanked and see three baseballs pitched to him. He would always swing at the one in the middle. One time, Mick was nursing a hangover and tried to strike out so he could sit back down in the dugout. By accident, he hit a home run and cursed as he barely made it around the bases.

Roger didn't look well. I didn't imagine I looked so great either. But Roger looked kind of pale, as if there could have been a real health problem. I definitely wasn't going to bring it up. I was just enjoying the conversation and the fact that I could relate to these classic stories. For a little while, I felt like one of the M&M Boys. I even had the right first initial.

When our fan from the day before, my ride, came over to our table, I was ready to introduce her to Roger and then excuse myself, since we had a long trip ahead of us. But she told me her friend couldn't give us a ride. For the first time since waking up, I felt genuinely sick. The ride by car from Cleveland to Virginia Beach was about six hundred miles – around nine hours if you did it nonstop. I started to see a disaster in the making. I had never missed a show in my life. I quizzed our fan about her friend and got a whiny response. Who knew if there ever was a friend or a ride? I was upset.

I ordered a couple of drinks and calmed down. I remembered that today was a day off and the show the following day was at night so I would have tomorrow to deal with all this. As for today, I wanted to keep drinking and talking to Roger Maris.

When I went to sleep after another night of partying, I was sure I could catch a flight out the next morning. The next morning, I was no longer so sure. Monte called my room panicked to say he was at the hotel in Virginia Beach calling everyone and there were no direct flights. Not only that, but the connections were going to involve three, maybe four, layovers and weren't going to get me there in time for the show. I told Monte to keep trying and hung up.

As I hobbled to the front desk of Swingos, I kept telling myself that, if I could rent a private plane, the flight would be only about three hours, leaving me plenty of time. Or maybe there was a bus or a train that would get me there.

There was no bus. There was no train. There was no plane. I enlisted every employee of the hotel I could find. They were all making calls. It looked like the Jerry Lewis telethon back there. Meanwhile, Monte was calling them asking to speak to me. He was freaked out. I told him to calm down. There was a private airport on the outskirts of Cleveland, and one of the hotel managers was calling it this very minute to hook me up. Monte told me to call him the second I knew.

I was having a couple of shots at the hotel bar when the desk manager walked in and told me Monte was on the phone with potentially good news.

'They may have a private plane for you,' he said.

So I followed the desk manager back to the front desk and took the receiver from the young woman who normally did check-ins.

'Listen,' Monte said. 'It's a Beechcraft. A two-seater.'

'Okay,' I said. 'I'm ready. I'll take a cab to the airport.'

'But wait a second,' Monte said. 'They're going to call you at the hotel first.'

'Fine, whatever.'

I hung around the front desk, and a few minutes later the phone rang. The check-in clerk handed me the receiver and nodded her head.

'This is Marc.'

'Yes, I'm calling about the charter flight to Virginia Beach.' He was either the pilot or the airline manager or both. He had a slightly high-pitched Southern drawl.

'Did you speak to Monte? I'll take it. Let's go.'

'Sir, we may not be able to have the craft ready in time.'

'C'mon,' I said. 'How much? Name your price.'

'Mr. Ramone, I assure you this is not a matter of cost.'

'I'll fly it myself if I have to. I need . . . Come on, fucking help me out here.'

'Mr. Ramone, we will call you back at the hotel and let you know the flight status.'

I handed the phone back to the clerk and told her to direct all calls to my room. I needed to put my head down. Just as my head hit the pillow, the phone rang. It was Monte. He sounded as if he was calling from a funeral.

'Marc, they can't put you on that flight. The guy could hear you were drunk. From your voice.'

'Give me a fucking break, I wasn't serious about flying it.'

'It's a very small plane,' Monte said. 'It's not like you were gonna be back in coach somewhere, out of sight. I guess they felt something could happen.'

'Now what, Monte?'

'I'm here in Virginia working my ass off is what! I have six calls in to every private airport in Ohio! I have a call in to one in Michigan and another in Pennsylvania! I'm losing my mind here!'

'Well, call me when you have something. I'm tired.'

'But—'

I put down the receiver and looked at the clock radio on the night table next to my head. It was 4:07. In less than an hour, I would miss the sound check. That left me with a little more than three hours to fly in, have Monte pick me up and get me to the venue, and get onstage. It was going to take not just one miracle but two. My head was as heavy as a steel drum riser. Time was slipping away on the clock radio. My main concern was not to be bothered again just to be told about another flight that wasn't happening and was too late in any case. I reached over, took the phone off the hook, and blacked out.

The next day, the Ramones had a show in Washington, DC. Monte had booked me on a regular commercial flight from Cleveland to Dulles Airport. On the van ride from Dulles to the venue, Monte warned me what lay ahead. I was going to have to reimburse everyone for everything. That included not just the contract fee for the cancelled show but any related expenses. When I asked what related expenses that actually meant, Monte told me that, when the kids heard the show was cancelled, they went nuts. They broke windows, chairs, and anything they could get their hands on in the club. When they were forced out the door, they vandalized cars in the club parking lot. So the punks of Virginia Beach were getting an all-expenses-paid riot on me.

Backstage I got the cold shoulder. John and Joey were no longer communicating through me – *or to me*. Dee Dee, my partner in crime, was aloof. John finally broke the silence.

'You fucked up.'

'Yeah, I know. It won't happen again.'

'That's right. It won't.'

The show was on automatic pilot. It was always much better to have some eye contact and body language to keep it as tight as possible, but, with countless thousands of road miles behind us, we could do it in a vacuum if we had to.

I felt bad, of course. Contrite. In baseball terms, as John or maybe Roger would see it, this was worse than striking out with the bases loaded. It was like being too wasted to step up to the plate. But the more I thought about it, the more I thought the treatment I was getting was out of proportion. I had never missed a single show. What I did was stupid but not intentional. I agreed, without a hiccup, to pay everyone back. Meanwhile, our lead singer had cancelled entire tours without any penalty. So the cold shoulder really seemed like overkill.

I had tried really hard to stay dry on the flight into DC that afternoon. I had one beer and that was it. Fortunately, this was the last stop on the US tour before we took about a week off and flew to London. I would have a chance to drink and unwind after the show and was already looking forward to it.

15

UP IN FLAMES

When we were growing up in the fifties and sixties, we were told that one day computers would take over the world. As of 1982, it hadn't happened. Insanity had taken over the Ramones' world, but no one we knew owned a computer.

Steve Wozniak was out to change that. The US (pronounced 'us') Festival was his brainchild and a big, loud, elaborate, expensive way to bring together computers, electronics, and music under the California sun. It was a showcase of the future, and we were glad to be a part of it.

The US Festival in San Bernardino was a far cry from Woodstock. Woodstock was about peace and love. US was about dollars and technology. Woodstock was disorganized but virtually without incident. US was highly organized, but on this Friday of the Labor Day weekend, we were hearing about numerous arrests. At Woodstock half a million flower children shouted in unison, 'No rain!' At US there was a high-tech rain machine to provide relief in the 110-degree heat. The order of bands appearing at Woodstock was more or less stream-of-consciousness. Here at the US Festival each of the three days had a theme: punk/new wave, rock, and country. The Ramones were band number two on day one, following Gang of Four.

As a musician, ideally, you want to perform the same whether it's in front of ten people or ten thousand. But, when it's in front of a hundred and fifty thousand you can't help but take notice. It was by far the largest audience we had ever played for in America, and we wanted to kick ass. Things out onstage happened so fast. We were led on as Gang of Four were led off. The sound check was a minute or two testing levels with cameras – stationary and mobile – all over the place. It was like a behemoth multimedia experiment, and we were the next guinea pigs.

Before we launched into 'Rock 'n' Roll Radio', I whipped off my leather jacket. I could take 110 degrees, but 130 was pushing it. John was in a T-shirt, and so was Dee Dee, who was also keeping cool these days with short hair. Only Joey kept the leather jacket, and, while his personal, psychological, and, more recently, substance abuse problems were growing, he was undaunted in the blazing sun. The only obstacle, ironically, was a technical one. In the middle of 'Shock Treatment', Joey's microphone failed. It was out for about a minute, but if we had learned anything over the years, it was not to panic. We played through it while one of the roadies swapped out the mike.

As we blitzed through 'Rock 'n' Roll High School', 'Sedated', and 'Beat on the Brat', I looked out at the audience from time to time. It was spectacular. You could see way off in the distance where the crowd melted off into the open field, but that was farther than John or I could throw a rock. In between us and the horizon was a sea of kids. They were into it, and a lot of them were dancing shirtless. We felt really good up there. In about twenty-two minutes it was all over.

The US Festival was prepared for almost anything. Backstage was an oxygen tank connected to tubes and face masks. Dee Dee and Joey went right for it. They really didn't seem anywhere close to passing out. Knowing them, they probably just wanted to try something new. It was probably the cleanest thing either of them had breathed in since the late sixties.

Joey was hospitalized on 12 September with another foot infection, which resulted in weeks of cancelled shows and a lot of time on my hands. Our next-door neighbor at 29 John Street was a little older than we were and the mother of three young kids. Marion and I were both friends with her. She was fun to be around. Meanwhile, we had the Mudd Club just north of city hall, which became my home away from home. Closing time there usually meant calling a cab for a ten-block ride, which was a lot better than staggering a half-mile. When I chose to make the walk, fans would literally follow me home. Marion was on my case about the drinking, but this was a long-running soap opera to me, and I basically flipped the dial when I got tired of listening.

One afternoon Marion left to go shopping. Within ten minutes, the woman next door knocked on the door. I knew she would have something with her. This time it was a bottle of champagne. When that ran out, we had whatever was left over from the night before, and when that ran out, we had the liquor store downstairs. Infinite room service. We ordered a bottle of vodka and a bottle of 151 and cranked the stereo. Fred dropped by with a bottle of Fleischmann's whiskey. It was an average day.

When Marion walked through the door around five o'clock in the afternoon, she looked different. She closed the front door hard, walked over, and turned off the stereo. There was quiet for the first time in hours and it hurt my ears. She looked around at the cans, cups, and bottles strewn all over the living room, and then looked at our next-door neighbor.

'So where are your kids?'

'They're . . . home.'

'Are you sure?' Marion said. 'You better go check. Now.'

When our friend left, Marion told me she couldn't take it any more. We were living in a twenty-four-hour party zone populated with enablers. The party was now officially over. We were moving back to Brooklyn.

Decent rentals were hard to find in New York, but Marion opened the Sunday *New York Times* real estate section and found a bunch of two-, three-, and four-room apartments available in Sheepshead Bay, a good family neighborhood by the water.

If they were any good or even if they were not, apartments in New York didn't remain available for long. You could measure it in hours. So Marion went out to Brooklyn first thing Monday morning. When she got back, she told me there were two apartments available at the rents listed and they were both horrible. They sounded like the apartment I shared with Bruce before I moved upstairs with Joel. But the landlord, on cue, explained that he had something much nicer a couple of blocks away. It was the oldest trick in the landlord's playbook: bring in a prospective tenant with a low-priced 'teaser' apartment and then rent them something a lot more expensive.

It worked. Marion had put down a deposit on a one-bedroom apartment in a newly constructed two-story concrete-and-brick condominium-style building. The landlord wore another hat, as a developer, and this type of development had become a gold mine in Brooklyn and Queens. They would buy an old Victorian house, tear it down, and build a four- or six-unit building on the same lot. Then they would take the profit and do it again, this time with two or three lots.

The process sucked a lot of the charm out of the old neighborhoods. But we needed the apartment. It was clean, utilitarian, and came with a garage below. Each apartment had a concrete terrace barely big enough to actually use, but who cared? It was very far from the Mudd Club and our alcoholic next-door neighbor.

Our landlord at 29 John Street wasn't happy. He was a friend of ours and a jeweler who had years before carved out some extra space from his ninth-floor workshop. That space was our apartment. When we moved in, it was basically a loft with a bathroom. We poured money into improvements including finish work, an air conditioner, a refrigerator, and a police dead-bolt lock for the front door. We didn't expect a dime in return then or now.

But our friend the jeweler told us we were basically leaving him high and dry. On the contrary, we explained, the apartment would take all of one minute to rent and he could pick up a key fee, which is basically upfront money in the landlord's pocket. So we were leaving both him and the apartment in great shape. High and dry did not apply. Except that the rent would be high and Marion wanted me dry.

It was hard to give up downtown and the Mudd Club, but the move to Avenue X in Sheepshead Bay came with a nice perk. I bought a 1960 Cadillac Coupe de Ville and restored it. It was a work of art with its big tail fins and dual bullet taillights. I liked to think of it as the pride of the neighborhood. The neighbors included a Mob family in a big brick single-family home across the street. Frank admired my Caddy and had one of his own, a 1958. When we saw each other out front or ran into each other at the little market down the block, we traded Cadillac stories like a couple of doting parents.

In late October, the Ramones were rehearsing for our upcoming album, *Subterranean Jungle*, which we would be recording in December. With the 1960 Coupe I had my ride into Daily Planet studio in Manhattan. Little Matt, John's roadie, lived four blocks away from us on Ocean Avenue. So with Matt, I had a co-pilot. And with a shot or two in my stomach, I had a smile on my face. What I didn't have was a driver's license. I did, however, have an insurance card with my insurance agent's name on it.

One afternoon Little Matt and I were riding along Ocean Avenue on the way to rehearsal a little on the fast side. With the horsepower of a 1960 Coupe, it was hard not to go fast. Matt preferred to sit in the back. Not that he was playing Phil Spector, but Matt was a big smoker and preferred the rear.

I suddenly felt intense heat on my back and asked Matt if he had dropped some ashes down my back. He told me absolutely not. I knew what the problem was instantly. I slammed on the brakes, put the car in park, and jumped out.

'Get the fuck out!' I said.

Little Matt followed. The car sat in the middle of the street and small visible flames licked the front seat. We stood on the curb between Avenue T and Avenue U. Behind us was St. Edmund, a Catholic high school for girls. A few girls in their uniforms stopped to look and stood near me and Matt. Within five seconds, the flames were shooting out of the windows. Within another five seconds, the flames were twenty feet high and had engulfed the front end of the car. There were now closer to fifty Catholic girls in uniform watching the spectacle like the Second Coming.

I didn't say anything, but I kicked myself for not taking care of the wiring under the seats. The car had electric seat controls, and I had a hunch when I bought it that the wiring was brittle. But, lately, I wasn't following up on details the way I might have. Just getting up and getting to rehearsal was an accomplishment.

Little Matt took gravel from the front yard of St. Edmund and threw it on the car. That slowed the fire down a hair, but the car didn't stand a chance. Within a few minutes, Ocean Avenue was a sea of fire engines and police cars. The firemen doused the flames with a chemical spray and followed it up with water from the hydrant on the corner. Smoke engulfed the street. It was a while before we could see the Coupe again. It was a goner.

The cops asked a few questions and, fortunately, one of them wasn't 'Can I see your license?' They just wanted to know what happened, and I told them. They were sympathetic. The firemen were even more sympathetic. 'I feel bad for you,' one of them said to me. 'Man, that was a beautiful car. That's gotta hurt.'

It did hurt. I looked around, and there along the front façade of St. Edmund was a four-story-high crucifix. Smoke billowed up around the cross and then cleared for a moment. I wasn't a religious person, but I knew whatever was coming next wasn't good.

The tow truck came and brought the Coupe back to our building on Avenue X. Little Matt and I jumped out of the tow truck cab, and I took a better look at the car. It was a concentrated fire. The rear was basically intact, but the interior and roof were fried. It had gotten so hot inside that the key melted in the ignition. I asked Matt to call the rehearsal studio and let the band know what happened.

John called me later at the apartment all pissed off that I missed rehearsal.

'You fucked up,' he said. 'And you fucked up my day. Don't you think there were other things I would like to do today? You could have told me you weren't coming. I have a fucking life.'

'John, my car caught on fire with your roadie in it. Didn't he tell you what happened? I wanted to rehearse as much as anybody. What was I supposed to do?'

I could tell from John's voice he didn't believe me. To him I was either lying or stretching the truth. There was doubt in his mind that probably started with the Virginia Beach fiasco and grew with every drink I took. It was a boy-who-cried-wolf situation, and I thought it was totally unfair.

Three days later, the Coupe was still in front of our building and smoldering. I popped the hood and couldn't find the source. The wires were probably still hot under the seats. I thought about taking the car apart, but now I had another problem.

Over the three days, Frank had never once walked across the street to ask me what happened to my baby. He waved a couple of times and didn't look happy. Then he went inside. His uncle and a couple of associates shot me a few dirty looks. If there was one thing in the world the Mob didn't want, it was attention. And, if there was one place in the world they didn't want it, it was on the block where they lived. I knew I had to dispose of the body. So I had it towed to a scrapyard in Bensonhurst. They gave me fifty bucks for the car. It was an offer I couldn't refuse.

By December, when we started recording *Subterranean Jungle*, I had bought a 1968 Cadillac and carefully checked the condition of the wiring under the front seat. Little Matt and I headed out to Kingdom Sound in Syosset, Long Island, enjoying a little speed on the Northern State Parkway. I was looking forward to recording. The demo we did sounded almost good enough to be an album. The songs themselves were, for the most part, a bit of a return to the Ramones' punk roots. 'Psycho Therapy', 'Outsider', and 'Time Bomb' could have been recorded in 1977 and would have fitted right in. The guitar was aggressive, and the lyrics, largely thanks to Dee Dee, were sufficiently warped.

While Dee Dee himself was perpetually warped, there was a concerted effort by those around him to straighten him out at least a bit. He was medically diagnosed as bipolar. We knew he was on psychotropic drugs, but exactly which ones were the subject of speculation. Lithium, a time-honored conventional drug for treating mood disorders, was likely. After that, it was anyone's guess: Tofranil, Stelazine, Thorazine, Antabuse. It could have been a whole category on *Jeopardy!*. And, as far as we knew, he was still using cocaine. How all those substances, legal and illegal, interacted was a stretch even for a PhD in pharmacology. But I could definitely see one change in Dee Dee: he was starting to gain weight.

When Little Matt and I arrived at the studio, I went right to the men's room. I pulled a bottle of vodka out of my bag, took a swig, and placed it gently into the metal garbage can with a flip top. The trick was not to put it in the garbage bag but between the bag and the wall of the garbage can. As I pulled my hand out of the can, I knew this was a departure for me. I had never drunk before or during a recording session in my life. But I thought, *Compared with the grab bag of shit Dee Dee is on, this is nothing.*

As usual, the drums came first. Ritchie Cordell, the producer selected by Gary Kurfirst, got my sound going as I warmed up. Cordell was a noted writer and producer who had success in the sixties with Tommy James and the Shondells. He co-wrote 'Gimme Gimme Good Lovin'' for the one-hit wonders Crazy Elephant. Most recently, he had produced Joan Jett and the Blackhearts' version of 'I Love Rock 'n' Roll', which hit number one in the US. I understood we were still after that one huge single and that Ritchie Cordell was supposed to get it for us.

There was one problem: the drum sound he was getting was horrible. He had his own way of tuning, which made each drumhead sound as if it had a towel over it. There was no bite, no hit. No balls. I had never stayed silent about anything important musically, and I wasn't about to start now.

'This is no good,' I said.

I saw Ritchie Cordell frown through the control room glass. He shrugged his shoulders and then pressed the monitor button for me to hear in the headphones.

'It's fine. What's wrong with it?'

'Well, to begin with, the whole thing sounds like shit.'

'Just go with it for now, please.'

I went with it for one song. It was a cover of 'Little Bit o' Soul'. It was a solid hit song from the sixties, though I thought choosing to do three cover songs for the album was a mistake. But that wasn't my call, and I played the song while John and Dee Dee laid down scratch tracks. After a second take, Ritchie Cordell asked me into the control room to listen back. To my shock and surprise, it sounded even worse than it did in the cans.

'What do you have on this?' I said.

'What do you mean?'

'You know what I mean,' I said. 'What kind of effects are making the drums sound like you wrapped them in a paper bag and flushed them down the toilet?'

'I have a noise gate on and some compression.'

He seemed defensive. He pushed a few control panel buttons off and then on again. He looked over at John, who said nothing. There was no way I was backing down for something this important.

'You need to get rid of the fucking noise gate and lose the compression,' I said. 'It's cutting off the cymbal crashes. You're fucking with the Ramones' sound. This is basic stuff. I shouldn't even have to mention this. You're the producer. You're responsible for the drum sound. You need to do your homework.'

'Okay, Marc,' Monte said. 'Why don't you take a break?'

Monte was playing peacekeeper, and I figured a break couldn't make things any worse. I went to the men's room, first for a piss, then for a drink. With no one else in the bathroom or, for that matter, wanting to be anywhere near me, I reached down into the garbage can and found my friend. As I drank from the bottle, I thought about how in a normal situation the producer would listen to what the drummer had to say and at least try to make a few adjustments. A few compromises. But I wasn't being given an inch.

On my way back from the bathroom, Monte stopped me and asked me if I was okay, and I told him of course. I was sticking up for the band's sound and would have appreciated a little help. I settled down when I got back and tried just to do my job. We were working on 'Outsider'. I knew the song well from the demo. Right now, I was clearly the outsider.

I felt a bit more on the inside the second day. Our old friend Walter Lure of the Heartbreakers was with us getting ready to do some lead guitar work later in the week. As with our other albums, by the time we went out and played the songs live, John would eventually sort of get the few leads we ever used. For the leads in the studio, we got a pro. Walter was still using heroin and nobody questioned it. He did his thing.

And I did mine. I had a fresh bottle of vodka in the bathroom and a few shots already in me plus a few I'd done before I'd got in the car with Little Matt. I was feeling good and wanted to spread it around. It was a perfect time for Chicken Beak Boy. I put my hands under my armpits and stuck my elbows out like wings. I arched my back, stuck out my ass, and started strutting around the sound room.

'Chicken Beak Boy! Chicken Beak Boy! Is he human? Is he a chicken? No, it's Chicken Beak Boy! Strange visitor from another planet!'

I jumped up on a couch and squawked around. Walter laughed. John put his guitar down and walked out of the room. Dee Dee popped a handful of pills.

We worked on a few songs, including 'Time Bomb'. The song had a great hook and a manic straight-ahead beat but the same problem as all the other songs: the way it sounded on tape. I threw down my cans and stomped into the control room.

'Can I ask you something?' I said, looking down at Ritchie Cordell, who was seated at the board.

'What?'

'Am I alive?'

'Marc, what kind of question is that?'

'It's a good question,' I said. 'Because on that tape I sound like a drum machine. And not even a good drum machine. One of the really cheap ones at Sam Ash.'

'I'm not here to argue with you.'

'This isn't an argument,' I said. 'All you have to do is listen back, and you'll hear it. You know something else? Lemme say something else.'

'Marc,' Monte said. 'Come on, take it easy.'

'No, let me finish,' I said. 'The demo we did sounds better than this album. Okay? And it's not even that close. I hear a live drum sound on the demo.'

Monte and Walter calmed me down, and I resigned myself to playing and shutting up the rest of the day. If they wanted me to treat it like just a job, I could do that. And, as with any job, there were bathroom breaks. As I reached into the garbage can, I wondered if *I* was the time bomb. I wondered if Dee Dee had written these songs specifically for me.

That night, Monte called the apartment, and Marion picked up. Monte asked her to ask me to bring it down a notch. Not to be silent when it came to my opinion but just lower it in tone and aggression. Like the recording of my drums.

'Ritchie Cordell is afraid of Marc,' Monte said. 'That's the point it's gotten to. And I think he's talking to Gary about it. Just talk to Marc and ask him to cool it, that's all. Please.'

On the ride over the next day, I thought about leveling out just to help Monte. It was not right that he had to clean up our mess all the time. One of the songs coming up was 'Time Has Come Today'. It was a big hit for the Chambers Brothers in 1968 but wasn't right for the Ramones. It was too flower-power and psychedelic and at four and a half minutes dragged on way too long for a Ramones song. But I figured I'd play ball and do it anyway.

Even with Oldies 101.1 playing on the radio, there was an awkward moment of silence in the car. Little Matt broke the silence with a question.

'Hey, Marc, if you weren't in the Ramones, what would you do?'

'I don't know,' I said. 'Tell you what, I wouldn't be trying to cover "Time Has Come Today".'

After I planted my bottle of vodka in the men's room, I walked toward the sound room. I passed John in the hallway, and he looked right through me without saying anything. I saw Joey coming out of the control room, and he stopped me.

'You all right, Marc?'

'Yeah, I'm fine,' I said. 'You all right, Manny?' That was my name for him sometimes.

'Yeah, of course, whatever.'

He didn't smell all right. Nothing did. I couldn't stop thinking about what Matt had said in the car. It wasn't his style to ask me an abstract question about life. It was a reaction to something he had heard. I could imagine what that might be.

I had never before met the drummer from Walter Lure's band. But now as I walked in he was sitting at the kit getting sounds up with Ritchie Cordell. They both looked at me as if I had interrupted something really important. The drummer got up and walked out of the room. Ritchie Cordell followed him.

I did a take of 'Psycho Therapy'. Then another. I no longer needed to hear it back in the control room. Whatever they were going to do, they were going to do. It was time for a bathroom break. As I walked down the hall, I saw Walter Lure coming out of the bathroom and Dee Dee going in. Walter was in on my secret and was sharing the bottle. The only rule in this club was, put the bottle back where you found it. I figured I'd wait a minute or two till Dee Dee came out.

Dee Dee came out with the bottle of vodka in his hand and a big grin on his face like a kid at an Easter egg hunt or a narc after a raid. I had to give him credit. It was a righteous bust. He had to smell the liquor on my breath, figure out where I was drinking, size up where I might hide the bottle, and stick his arm not just into the garbage can but also into my secret compartment. He had to think like an addict. That wasn't a stretch. By comparison, I was an amateur. There was no one in the world better than Dee Dee at the art of stashing. All those years of burying pot in exotic countries had finally paid off.

'Look what I found. Look what Marc was hiding in the bathroom. Merry Christmas and Happy New Year!'

I heard the door to the control room open as Dee Dee continued showing off his catch. There was no bottle waiting for me any more, but I went to the bathroom anyway because I had to. When I got out and walked back into the sound room, there was no tribunal. No one was stunned. Everyone knew what I was doing. Only now they had hard evidence.

I worked on the drum tracks for Dee Dee's song 'Somebody Like Me'. There was nobody like Dee Dee. He knew that. We all knew that. And that, I figured, was why he ratted me out. His substance-abuse problem was a runaway train. Pointing at a little flatbed car on the side of the tracks was a great way to get the attention off himself.

I wasn't saying anything about the hypocrisy of all this. Still it pissed me off. This guy was busting *me*? I finished the last original drum tracks for the album and told Monte I was going home. There was no way I was doing 'Time Has Come Today'. They could get whoever they wanted to do it.

For the album cover shoot, we visited the real subterranean jungle – the New York City subway. The photographer, George DuBose, had the idea to use the stop at Fifty-Seventh Street and Sixth Avenue in Manhattan. It was the end of the line for the B train. At night, there was about a twenty-minute layover before the train left on its next run. It was a lot cheaper than renting out a station or building a set.

The B train had some personal significance for me. It linked the Prospect Park area of Brooklyn, the East Village, and Midtown where I had done so much studio work and equipment shopping over the years – now decades. The cover concept was simple – the Ramones on a train. The station was nearly empty except for us. There was no issue over what to wear this time. Ramones plus subway equaled leather jackets.

A photographer and his willing subjects could go through quite a few rolls of film in twenty minutes if they put their minds to it, and we did. There were shots of us sitting in a row in the car, standing up and strap-hanging, and standing in the open subway car door staring out onto the platform. It was hard to tell if George suggested it or if I did it instinctively, but either way it seemed like a good idea when I scooted over to a window seat. While John, Joey, and Dee Dee stood and looked out the door, I looked out the window like a lonely commuter. George took half a roll with us like that, each click recording a slightly different nuance of the same somber mood.

One of the first things a visitor, tourist, or transplant to New York learned was that the subway wasn't for having conversations with strangers and making new friends. You barely even talked to your old friends. And so the shoot for us came naturally.

The jukebox in my Sheepshead Bay bedroom was playing and a *Kojak* rerun was on in the background one weekday afternoon in January 1983 when the phone rang. It was Joey.

'Marc,' he said. 'I gotta tell you something.'

Not that I hadn't known for some time. Not that not even being called to rehearsals for the upcoming tour hadn't underscored it. But the tone of Joey's voice was the one people reserved for informing you about a death, breaking up with you, or firing you.

'You can't be in the band any more. I feel bad about it, but there's nothing I can do. These guys feel they just can't handle you any more.'

'Listen,' I said. 'I had a feeling this was coming.'

I told Joey not to worry about it. Just to do what he had to do. What I had to do now was answer Little Matt's question from the car ride – if I wasn't in the Ramones, what would I do? The answer was easy. I would do exactly what I was doing now – having fun. I would have more time than ever to do it.

On the TV screen, another question was being asked. It was Telly Savalas's famous line, 'Who loves you, baby?' That answer wasn't as easy.

16

DOG DAYS

They used the shot of me alone in the window of the B train. 'Ramones' was written in graffiti on the side of the subway car. It was a special effect. The spray paint wasn't really there. I was there but just barely.

I was relieved. I was disappointed. I was angry. As the spring of 1983 began, and for the first time in a long time I wasn't touring with the Ramones, there was a lot of stress I no longer had to face on a daily basis. John couldn't stand Joey. Joey couldn't stand John. Joey couldn't stand Dee Dee. Dee Dee couldn't stand John. John could just about put up with Dee Dee. And their solution was to throw me out. Me!

I could understand it to a degree as a cutthroat business decision. Dee Dee and I were a team. We partied hard and became toxic when we were together. The team had to be broken up. As valuable as I felt I was, Dee Dee wrote most of the songs and was indispensable no matter what he put in his mouth. Still, I had thought we were brothers. Sure, brothers who fought, but that was most brothers. The fighting was supposed to make you stronger as a unit, not rip you apart over a problem. I didn't expect to be thrown overboard. If anything, I thought I deserved the chance to clean up for a month or so and come back. But there was no lifeboat waiting. There was no rope. I tried to let it all go.

When I thought about the recording sessions for *Subterranean Jungle*, I regretted the tone I took with Ritchie Cordell. That was the alcohol talking. But I didn't regret the content of what I said. It needed to be said one way or another. I couldn't understand the point of spending your whole life building your chops as a musician – or as anything, for that matter – and then putting out something you couldn't be proud of. The Ramones' approach of getting it over with quickly in order to divvy up the leftover advance money had driven Phil Spector to Manischewitz in a Dixie cup and me to vodka in a garbage can.

The way I saw it, I had nothing to apologize for. There were plenty of guys I knew hitting their thirties who were still wondering what to do with their lives. I had had my nose to the grindstone – or to the skins – since my teens. I had been a professional musician for almost fifteen years, paid all my dues and then some, and been an integral member of three, maybe four, groundbreaking bands. The Johnny Shines album I recorded was in the Library of Congress. I had money in the bank. I had earned the right to sit back and enjoy life.

One Sunday morning in the late spring, Marion and I did what couples all across America had done almost for ever – go for a nice drive and shop for a few things. We were cruising down Sheepshead Bay Road in the 1968 Caddy at about forty miles an hour when I slammed on the brakes.

'Holy shit!' I said to Marion.

It was John and Linda standing on the sidewalk outside a drugstore.

'What the hell are they doing here?' Marion said.

I had no idea. They had been sneaking around together for literally years, but why here? Why now? They both lived in downtown Manhattan. A secret rendezvous might have brought them to the Village or Midtown, but Sheepshead Bay, Brooklyn, was across a river and a borough and had seemingly nothing of interest to them, including either of us. The attraction couldn't have been the drugstore they had just walked into. It was a perfectly nice little family-owned drugstore, but there were at least a dozen Duane Reades in Manhattan that blew it away.

'What are you doing, Marc? No.' Marion put her hand on the wheel.

I had to do it. I parked the car and got out. Marion got out, too. Stupid as it was, it was hard not to. We walked into the drugstore. John must have seen us, because I saw him hiding in the back behind a large cardboard nail polish display. He must have thought I wanted to kick his ass. Linda darted over to the bath-supplies aisle. Suddenly Marion and I had the urge to shop for deodorant, toothpaste, hand lotion, and anything else we might be running low on. We took our sweet time. Every so often, I spotted John's bowl haircut peering out from behind the Maybelline sign.

We checked out with enough stuff for the medicine cabinet to last through the summer, then headed for the door. We burst out laughing when we hit the sidewalk and the fun continued in the car. Coincidences like this one had been happening for a while in Manhattan, but certainly not out here. It wasn't as if we were stalking John and Linda. We had moved out to Brooklyn to get away from the craziness, not run toward it. If anything, they were stalking us.

John and Linda had become a little sickening. The way they ran around on Roxy and Joey was part but not all of it. They would do these cutesy little things that drove us all crazy. On a given Monday, John would have on a red T-shirt, and Linda would have on a short red dress. The next day, he would wear a green T-shirt to match her green sweater and skirt. It was color-coordinated torture. Part of the torture was that we couldn't say anything to their other halves, who were our friends. We couldn't rock the boat or sink it. But, now that I was out of the band, all bets were off. Or, as John might have said, it was a whole new ball game. We rushed home.

Marion called Roxy first. The idea wasn't to build a federal case. It was just to report what she saw and leave it at that.

'We saw them together. In Sheepshead Bay, of all places.'

'Are you kidding me?' Roxy said. 'Are you sure?'

'Roxy, either one of them is unmistakable. Together they're one of a kind.'

I called Joey next. Joey accused me of lying to stir up trouble now that I was no longer in the band. He was in denial.

'Joey,' I said, 'I'll bet all the money in the world she's not home with you right now. How would I know that?'

Joey said that didn't mean a thing, and we got off the phone. Marion and I had done our duty and it felt pretty bad.

When the phone in our bedroom woke us up, the digital clock read 1:48 a.m. Marion picked up the receiver, and I could hear Roxy hysterical on the other end. She wanted Marion to repeat the content of their conversation Sunday morning, including where we spotted John and Linda and exactly what Linda was wearing. For a moment, I wondered why Roxy needed to hear all this again, but then I woke up a little more, and it dawned on me this wasn't for her ears only. No sooner did I realize that then I heard John's voice shooting out of the receiver like darts.

'Why are you upsetting her?' John said.

'Why are you doing what you're doing?' Marion said.

'Why don't you stay the fuck out of my life?'

'Why don't you stay the fuck out of our neighborhood?'

'I wasn't even in your neighborhood,' John said.

'Oh, really?' Marion said. 'So I happen to know you were wearing a gray shirt and walked into a drugstore on Sheepshead Bay Road because I'm psychic? You're a disgusting liar!'

'You need to find something to do with your life now that Marc's not in the band.'

'So, John,' Marion said, 'who were you hiding from in the drugstore? Who were you so scared of?'

The fight escalated into the kind that can happen only when things have built up for a long time and when you no longer care because you think you'll never see the other person again. Marion and John unloaded, and I couldn't tell who hung up first.

Early in the summer, I got a call from Little Matt. He had parked the Ramones' equipment truck overnight in the street in front of his apartment on Ocean Avenue and awoke in the morning to find the vehicle had been burgled. Everything was gone – amps, monitors, mixing boards, lights, cables. Even John's leather jacket had been stolen, so he was really pissed off. I told Matt I was sorry to hear it, and then he let me know the other reason he was calling. John thought I might be behind the robbery. He wasn't sure, but, when the Ramones were discussing the incident, my name came up. John's reasoning was that I was getting back at him for firing me and that I lived in the neighborhood.

I had to laugh. I hardly had to remind Little Matt who else lived in the neighborhood – the same people who just a few years earlier had successfully planned and executed the Lufthansa heist, the largest robbery of cash in the history of the United States. By comparison, the Ramones heist was probably easier than sniffing glue. But somehow, in John's paranoid mind, in a few short weeks I had gone from stalking him and Linda to casing out the band's equipment truck.

When Little Matt called again on the night of 14 August, he had bad news about John. He had just gotten out of the van and was walking to his apartment on East Tenth Street when he spotted Roxy in front of the building with a guy named Seth Macklin. No one else in the band or crew witnessed it, but, whatever happened next, John and Seth Macklin got into a fight. John was severely beaten and, once he was down, kicked in the head with a steel-tipped boot. A witness had seen John defending himself by swinging his travel bag. Macklin was in police custody, and John was in St. Vincent's Hospital undergoing surgery for a fractured skull. Matt said everyone expected John to pull through.

In the morning, the story was splashed all over the newspapers including, of course, the front page of the *New York Post*. There was no more information than what we had the night before. In fact, there was less. But the basics weren't hard to figure out. I had heard that Roxy had been bringing guys home for years. When John saw Roxy and her friend together, he charged. He was probably looking to assault Roxy but instead wound up running into Seth Macklin and a steel boot.

A few days later, I heard from Little Matt that John was expected to make a slow but full recovery. His relationship with Roxy, however, was not expected to recover. The night of the incident, while John lay in St. Vincent's, Roxy invited the police and the press into their apartment and handed out personal photos of John and herself that were on the cover of the *Post* the very next day. When John got out of the hospital, he read Roxy the riot act. There was nothing more upsetting to a control freak than losing control. In this case, he had lost control of both Roxy and the information coming out of his own home. Word was that John was looking for another apartment and that, presumably, Linda would join him.

Joey was ecstatic that John got his head handed to him. Any time the world did to John what Joey himself couldn't, he was happy. I was sad for John. I really didn't like seeing anything like that happen to anyone, especially someone I was friends with for so long. But I wasn't shocked it happened. John set himself up for it. Eventually your lifestyle catches up with you.

I didn't want to wake up. I was having a nice dream and knew the world I was waking up into wasn't going to be nearly as nice. But the tapping noise wouldn't stop. I reached out my right hand as if to silence some sort of alarm clock, but there was no alarm clock. I was inside my Caddy. There was a New York City cop on either side of the car. The tapping was the sound of their service revolvers against the windows.

'Unlock the door! Now! Unlock the door!'

The cops were pissed off, and there were other people, civilians, around them. These other people were pissed off, too. They all seemed to want me out of the car. I noticed upholstered chairs, dressers, and beds flipped this way and that surrounding the car. I had an idea about the furniture, but it was only an idea. I thought about opening the lock on the driver's-side door, but I knew that, as soon as I did, life would never be the same.

It was one of those hot, sticky days in late August when summer smothered you and made you pay through the nose for the pleasant days only a month earlier. My plans were to stay inside the apartment on Avenue X with the air-conditioning on. But my old friend Paul Baxter called me around lunchtime to ask if I would give him a lift to the traffic court on Atlantic Avenue so he could pay a bullshit speeding ticket. I said sure, as long as on the way we could stop at a grocery store and pick up a six-pack of Newcastle Brown Ale.

We picked up two six-packs – one for the road and one for the road back. We drove north on Ocean Parkway, and by the time we hit Flatbush Avenue we were working on the six-pack for the road back. Paul threw another empty bottle into the backseat and told me to drop him off at the corner of Flatbush and Atlantic Avenues. He wasn't sure how long it would take. A half-hour if he was lucky. Maybe more. I pulled up to the curb and told him I would circle around and look for him a little later.

I made a left onto Fourth Avenue, a left onto Pacific, and a left onto Flatbush, completing my first circle. I was blasting WNEW-FM on the car stereo, but they were playing too many commercials. Circling the block got boring fast, and I was quickly out of beer. The air-conditioning was humming, but the traffic was driving me insane. Everybody and his uncle was converging on these streets to pay a ticket, pay a fine, get a license, see a judge, enter a plea, shop, fight for parking, and get in my fucking way.

I spotted a bar on the corner of Atlantic and Flatbush. I didn't know how I missed it the first four times. My problems were solved. There was even a parking spot right in front of the bar. I pulled in nose-first. As I slammed the door of my 1968 Coupe, I took a look at the perfect silver paint job I had just had done and realized I was parked in a bus stop. I didn't think I'd be too long and really needed a drink. The sweltering downtown August air made my lungs feel like a couple of wet paper bags.

The bar was the right place to be. It was air-conditioned, and WNEW-FM was on the radio, so it was like being in the car again with a fresh supply of beer and no traffic. I took an open seat near the bartender, an old-time Brooklyn guy, and ordered a Newcastle Brown. That was becoming as boring as circling the block, so I switched over to shots of Old Grand-Dad. George Thorogood's version of 'One Bourbon, One

Scotch, One Beer' was blasting out over the barroom speakers, and I figured if George can mix it up, so can I.

When the song was over, I switched back to beer, this time Pabst Blue Ribbon, which was a brew connected to summertime, baseball, and bars just like this one. There were a few guys scattered in the barroom hiding from the world at midday, and I was hiding with them. There was a ball game on the overhead television, and two of the guys were arguing. One of them was saying the Yankees had no pitching and had to rebuild. The other said the first guy didn't know what the fuck he was talking about. And I couldn't care less. I was chasing whiskey with beer and beer with whiskey and having a good time doing it. The only problem was the Miller Beer clock on the wall, which said five past three. Paul was probably done, so I downed my last shot and left.

My car wasn't towed or ticketed. When you're lucky, you're lucky. I put the key in the door, got in, put the key in the ignition, and took a quick look out the driver's-side window. I saw a cop. He looked like one of the old-timers in the bar and was tapping the window with a bottle. I blinked: it wasn't a bottle. It was a service revolver, but it was the same cop. I saw the chairs, dressers, and beds again and realized for the first time I was in a furniture store. There was glass all over the showroom floor and the showroom window looked like someone had driven a tank through it. Someone *had*.

'Unlock the door! Now! Unlock the door!'

I did. The cop on the driver's side grabbed me and spun me around while the other one handcuffed me. Like anyone in America, I had the scene in my head from countless movies and news shows. The perp is led away surrounded by mothers and fathers, sons and daughters, neighbors, salesmen, clerks, each one yelling. Each one wanting a piece. Only this time I was the perp.

'You ran over my daughter's foot, you piece of shit!'

If I did, what are you doing here screaming at me?

I was fingerprinted and booked at the 78th Precinct. It was a large brick fortress of a building just two blocks away. When they took my mugshot, one of the cops told me to smile for the camera. Just what I need to show a judge – that I was so crazy I could laugh it off. I stared deadpan into the lens. It came naturally.

Bail was set at ten thousand dollars. The charges included driving under the influence and first-degree reckless endangerment. I called Marion, who called a friend. My friend had an attorney friend of his come down to the precinct. He was a middle-aged guy who knew the system. He took off his glasses, stared at me carefully for a moment, and told me I was as lucky a man as he had ever seen in his life.

No one was killed. No one was injured. Not inside the store and not outside, where a bunch of kids waiting for the bus scattered to either side of my Caddy. The father who claimed his daughter's foot was run over never took her to the hospital and was not pressing charges. If we ran the same scenario a hundred times, my attorney said, ninety-nine times we would have at least one fatality and a few critical injuries. But the charges were serious, and I was looking at up to seven years behind bars. If I was really lucky – and, as far as he was concerned, I had used up all of my luck for this lifetime and the next – I could get probation. That would mean getting sober, staying sober, and proving it. That was what we were shooting for. But my lawyer was making no guarantees.

As we walked out of the precinct, I spotted my 1968 Coupe parked across the street. There were dents on the front right side and scratches all over the hood and the roof. I had just finished restoring it and felt like a schmuck. I told myself I would get it into the body shop the next day, or at the latest the day after. I knew the guy there and would ask him to turn it around as fast as he could. As I walked around the car one last time for the moment, I realized it was maybe a two-day job with a new coat of paint and realized it could have been a lot worse. For the first time since the accident, I felt a sense of relief.

My hearing was at Kings County Criminal Court on Schermerhorn Street. I wore a gray suit and combed my hair. My lawyer was with me and told me to look as serious as possible when the judge addressed me and not to say a word unless I was asked to.

'Do you understand the seriousness of the charges?'

'Yes, Your Honour.'

'Do you understand this court can order a criminal trial?'

'Yes, I understand.'

The judge explained I was being given a suspended sentence pending treatment. I was released under the watchful eye of my attorney, whose responsibility it was to see to it that I entered a licensed rehabilitation facility. From there it was up to me to complete the program successfully. I was to appear before the court in six weeks, sober and with a letter verifying treatment. If I failed to do so, I could count on going to jail. The judge asked if I understood everything he had just said.

'Yes, Your Honor. Absolutely.'

My lawyer turned to me and told me again how lucky I was. But I didn't feel lucky. My immediate reaction was frustration that I had to waste the next six weeks of my life.

I spent the next couple of days at home drying out while Marion called around and looked for an inpatient rehab facility. There was one in Freeport, Long Island, that came highly recommended by other people we knew in the music industry. I figured that, if they could do it, I could do it.

Around dinnertime, the downstairs bell rang and I heard my father's voice over the intercom. Marion buzzed him in. I hadn't heard from him since the hearing; this was a surprise visit. He walked in and asked me to have a seat in the living room. He grabbed a kitchen chair, placed it a few feet away, and sat down facing me. When you're a kid, your father looks gigantic, especially if he's a six foot three, 230-pound longshoreman. As you get older, he seems a little smaller every year. At this moment, my father assumed his full stature from my childhood. In fact, he looked even bigger. He took up all the air and light in the room.

'What do I have to do to get through to you?' he said.

'Nothing,' I said. 'I'm going to rehab. Next week probably.'

'That's not what I mean. How do I make you understand where you're headed? How you're hurting me. How you're destroying your mother. *Destroying her.* You don't want to know what kind of shape she's in. What you've done to her. You don't even seem to know what you've done to yourself.'

'Look, I don't know what you want me to say.'

'It doesn't matter what I want you to say. The problem is if you really understood the position you've put yourself in, you would know it. I would know it. We would all know it. But I don't see anything like that. What I see sitting in front of me is a guy who wants his car back. I see a guy who sees all this as a pain in the ass. Let me ask you something. Do you know what happens if you kill someone?'

'I didn't . . .'

'It means everything is over. Everything is gone. For ever. You never get it back – your freedom, your life, your conscience. And that . . . that is the moment you understand for the first time what you actually had. When that door closes . . .'

My father put his head in his mammoth hand and wiped a tear before looking at me again. I tried to recall the last time I had seen him cry and realized this was the first time. It didn't last long. He got up, walked out, and slammed the front door. The building shook. I was shaken.

Falling asleep that night wasn't easy, and not only because I had been dry for about a day. The episode with my father had me freaked out. I went over it in my mind again and again. He was unbreakable, but I had nearly broken him just by not giving a shit. That was the last thing in the world I wanted to do. I wished he could just ignore my misadventures, but for better or worse, that was never going to happen. Because he cared, I was stuck with the power to destroy.

The threshold with most people was low. That included my mother. She showed her concern the old-fashioned way, by getting upset easily and raising hell. As I lay in bed staring at the ceiling, what came to mind was the time I was practicing on the drums in our old apartment building and a bottle sailed through the window, soared over my head, and hit the far wall of my bedroom.

I knew who it was instantly. The guy who lived across the alleyway worked the nightshift and slept during the day. My room faced the alleyway, so the sound traveled right out my window and into his. He felt like he was living inside a snare drum. He had complained before, but throwing the bottle took it to the next level.

My mother confronted him right out in the open at the Ditmas Avenue F train station near McDonald Avenue. She spotted him on the platform atop the trestle and let loose. When a woman screams at a man in a crowded public place, it's a public shaming. And my mother could scream.

Any number of things could bring any number of reactions from my mother. My father, however, was slow to anger. He thought things through on a deeper level. In his mind, there was a big gulf between a real crisis and every run-of-the-mill nuisance in life. When my father confronted you, you could be sure you had crossed a serious line and were staring out over the edge.

I had crossed that line a couple of times back in school. On one occasion he told me calmly we were going to the barber. There was no point in resisting. He could have dragged me there with one hand, so I just walked along. It was like walking the plank except that he was walking it with me. The only way to get through to me was a haircut. If I lost that big head of hair, maybe some of the arrogance and stubbornness would go with it. And here we were again walking the plank – a real plank with death and destruction at the other end. We were way past haircuts.

Marion wasn't in the apartment in the morning when I woke up. As I walked to the bathroom in my kimono, I felt jittery but hopeful I could make it through the day without a drink. Everything alcoholic was out of the house. That alone made me anxious. A splash of cold water on my face would go a long way. I opened the door and turned on the light in one motion and felt a colder sensation than any splash of water. Standing in the tub was a man in his thirties. He looked like he was from India and he was wearing a suit. He could have been waiting for a train. He was not surprised to see me. But I was surprised to see him.

I thought of one move and one move only – turning away, then looking back again. Then maybe he would be gone. So I turned away. Then I looked back again. But the train hadn't arrived at the station. The Indian was still there. And I was gone in a flash. I was in my pants and a T-shirt and out on the pavement in under a minute. The nearest bar was three blocks away, and that's where I was headed on foot. I just hoped I could make it without seeing the Indian along the way.

I made it to the bar like a desert wanderer to a watering hole. I couldn't stand another mirage. I ordered a shot of Bacardi 151 and greeted it like a long-lost friend. I leveled out quickly. But I knew I was far from okay.

I had heard of delirium tremens, or the DTs. Your brain became so chemically dependent upon alcohol that, without it, reality and the imagination collided. But knowing about something didn't mean you were prepared for it. As I walked to my parents' house on a warm late-summer day, I felt I just needed to keep moving, and, as long as I did, I would be okay. It was when I stopped that the problems started.

I wanted my mother and father to see that I was sober for a few days and was fine. If I could convince them, then maybe I could convince myself. I walked in, said hello, and went to the kitchen to pour myself a glass of water. Before I could put the glass to my mouth, my jaw dropped. There was something large and fuzzy moving slowly through the backyard.

It took on more definition as I stared. There were scales, a large tail, and three long pointy horns. It was a dinosaur – specifically a triceratops. *A fucking triceratops.* He was thirty feet long and fifteen feet tall, towering over my parents' garage. His movements were powerful and intimidating. He had one eye right on me through the kitchen window. I looked away and looked back again. He lumbered toward me, treading heavy on the grass. I wanted the Indian back.

I bolted out the front door without closing it behind me and ran through the streets of Brooklyn back home as if the triceratops were right behind me. I didn't want to look. I made it home, ran upstairs, closed the door behind me in the bedroom, pulled down the shades, turned off the lights, and got under the covers.

I remembered how much as a kid I loved seeing dinosaurs in sci-fi movies and at the Museum of Natural History in Manhattan. My mind was getting cleaned out like an old stuffed closet. Whatever was in there was coming out in no particular order. I had absolutely no control over it and didn't want to see what was next.

I did, anyway. They followed me under the covers. There were weird winged one-eyed creatures flying around my head. There were bats with the heads of lions. There were two-headed lizards flicking out their tongues. I thought, *This is it. I'm Ray Milland in* The Lost Weekend. *I'm Jack Lemmon in* Days of Wine and Roses. *But I can't turn off this movie.*

We are a recognized leader in the field of alcohol addiction treatment. We have built a reputation for excellence by providing world-class care in a surrounding of compassion and respect. Flexible start dates are available to ensure the most convenient transition into treatment. Regular contact with family members is encouraged, and the utmost privacy and discretion are always assured. While your primary focus needs to be on your recovery, if you own a business or have similar obligations, we can work with you to ensure you are able to fulfill essential duties during your stay.

The facility in Freeport, Long Island, was like a country club. I had a clean private room with a TV. The cafeteria was more like a dining room, and we were given menus. We had our choice of a dozen entrees and another dozen main courses. The staff let us know the chef would prepare special dishes if we asked. They probably would have done anything I asked, including setting up a riser with a twelve-piece drum set in the recreation room.

I did go to the meetings. There were three a day. I barely said a thing the first week. I mostly sat and listened. One woman started drinking when her kids were old enough to go to school and she was alone in the house. There was a guy whose father got him started. I appreciated their honesty in sharing their stories and the details, but very little of it seemed to have anything to do with me. I did go on binges and become loud, obnoxious, and even dangerous sometimes and wanted to put an end to that. But I also had periods where I barely drank at all. *I had a problem, but I wasn't like these people.*

'Hello. I'm Marc. And I guess I'm an alcoholic.'

That was as far as I would go. I was trying to be polite.

I kept to myself. The cable service included a movie channel. With all the meetings I was already going to, I didn't want to beat the thing to death. Whenever I shut off the tube and had time to think, my mind drifted back to things that upset me. Getting ratted out by Dee Dee was near the top of the list. He was not only my best friend in the band but the person who really got me into the Ramones in the first place. We were like brothers on the road. Life wasn't perfect, but we had a great time most of the time and had each other's back. I had Dee Dee's back even when he pulled a knife on me. So the idea that a friend like that would rat me out hurt – especially when his problems were clearly worse than mine. There was a code, and he broke it. He sold me out. If anyone should have been in here, it was Dee Dee.

The two weeks had gone slowly but were almost over. I was sober. I did it and would walk out with a certificate to prove it. My lawyer would show the certificate to the judge, and the judge would have to let me go. My father would stop crying, and my mother would stop yelling. Marion would stop worrying. Maybe I could start playing music. It all sounded pretty good. But I wasn't that interested. What I really wanted was a drink.

A few days after I got home, we adopted a dog. He was a half-Labrador mutt and still a puppy. I thought the dog would help with my sobriety. Labs were known as assistance dogs and even therapy dogs. They were man's best friend and then some. Besides, responsibility was important at this point in my life. I wasn't going to three AA meetings a day, but walking the dog three times a day seemed doable.

My first drink was at a neighborhood bar. It was a beer on tap. Just one, and I walked home. As far as I was concerned, I proved something that night. I earned my way back and was in control. There were a lot of rules I was supposed to be following, but in my mind they were for weaker people who used them like a crutch. It was much better to be your own boss.

Boss's orders were to hang out in the Village a few nights later. It was a shot here and a shot there. Nothing too serious. I worked my way down to CBGB, which was like a homecoming. It was good to be somewhere where you were appreciated and treated like an adult. The only problem, however, was quickly apparent when I stepped outside. I no longer had an apartment downtown.

I had to call Marion and let her know I'd be taking a cab and would be home soon. Around one in the morning, I spotted a payphone at the corner of Bowery and Bond Streets. When I got a little closer, I noticed there was a guy already in the booth. I needed to make a call and told myself I'd give him five minutes. I knew Marion was already upset with me and, when I called, she'd probably give me a hard time about the dog. But it was better to call ahead than to get hit all at once when I got home. I looked around at the first real signs of fall – a few leaves and loose newspaper pages blowing around in circles. The streets were nearly empty. I thought about going back into CBGB.

Five minutes were up. If not six or seven. I tapped on the glass of the phone booth. The guy on the phone inside glanced back at me for a split second and shook his head. I didn't like that. Now all I could see was his blue corduroy jacket pressed up against the glass, in my face. He looked like he thought he owned the phone booth. He blabbed and blabbed into the receiver, leaning into the payphone, and now refused to make any eye contact with me as I hovered around to the other side of the booth. Then he reached into his pants pocket and pulled out some change. He didn't know it yet, but the call was already over.

I opened the door with one hand, grabbed the collar of his jacket with the other, and yanked him out of the booth. As he stumbled on the pavement, I stepped inside the booth and shut the door. It was all one easy motion, like a drum roll. He pounded on the door, and I flipped him the finger. By the time Marion picked up on the other end, he was gone.

Marion was all pissed off. I was out too late, I was obviously drinking, and I hadn't walked the dog since the morning. Why did I get a dog if she was going to have to walk it all the time? It wasn't fair to her and it wasn't fair to the dog. I told her not to worry. I would be home soon, and we'd talk about it then.

I hailed a cab up the block from CBGB, but a guy about my age dressed in a business suit caught it from the other side and got in at the same time I did.

'Guess what,' I said looking straight at him from the other end of the backseat. 'You're leaving, not me.'

'Really?'

'Yeah, really.'

'I don't think so.'

'Who cares what the fuck you think?'

I reached across with one hand, leaned on the door handle, and pushed it open. With the other hand, I pushed the guy out of the cab before slamming and locking the door. Another drum roll. The cab driver looked back at me.

'Can we go now?'

'Definitely,' I said. 'Go down to Canal and over the bridge.'

Marion was working in the city when I got up late the next morning with a slight hangover. My first step out of bed was a rough landing. My second step was even worse. I felt the ball of my right foot in a pile of something slimy and knew right away the dog had shit on the rug. He had probably waited there all morning for me to wake up till he finally couldn't wait any longer. I felt bad for him. It wasn't like he could just yank me out of bed like a guy in a phone booth. But I felt worse for myself because I had to clean up his mess. By the early afternoon, he was already barking at me because he had to go again. I was in no mood to get dressed and start walking around the neighborhood at this hour. So I took him up to the roof to shit.

I waited a few more nights to go back to Manhattan. At CBGB, I ran into a couple of friends I had known since before the Ramones. We always drank a lot back in the day, and it seemed natural to pick up where we left off. One of them had an apartment a few blocks away, so we continued the party up there. He had an annoying little

Chihuahua that wouldn't shut up. When I drank I liked loud music, not loud barking. This was high-pitched and penetrated my eardrums like a drill. Then the dog started climbing up my leg and jumping around like some kind of wind-up toy. I shook it off, but it came right back. The dog belonged wrapped up in some rich lady's mink coat, not near my crotch. I needed to drink my vodka in peace. I picked up the dog and put it in the refrigerator.

'Hey, what the fuck are you doing?' my friend said.

'Let him cool the fuck off.'

My friend laughed a little bit. Then he poured us all another round. As we continued drinking and laughing, I could hear the dog through the door still barking in the refrigerator. *Good*, I thought. *Let him learn a lesson.*

After about ten minutes, the barking was fainter and inconsistent. I put my shot glass down on the coffee table and went into the kitchen. When I opened the door to the refrigerator the Chihuahua was shivering between a container of Parmesan cheese and a six-pack. I reached in, grabbed him, and placed him down on the linoleum floor. He pedaled out the door, frazzled but somehow calmer. The treatment worked. Except now I was shaking.

I slept it off at my friend's apartment. When I put the key in the door of my own apartment in the late afternoon, I knew I was in the doghouse. It was a bad month for dogs, period. But, when I opened the door, there was something different about the air inside. It was calm and stale, like in a funeral parlor. When I found Marion in the kitchen sitting at the table going through some mail, she told me I had to leave.

She was expressionless. She told me absolutely nothing had changed since I went to rehab. In fact, it was worse. I had a piece of paper and the consent of the court and was living a complete lie. She knew the longer I stayed, the more she was enabling me to live that lie. Most of all, she was exhausted. On any given night, she didn't know if I was going to come back wrecked or if I was going to come back at all. There was no point in going over it again and again. I didn't argue. I knew she was right.

I called a couple of days later to tell Marion I was staying in Brooklyn at my friend's apartment. Freddie Anselma could be a pain in the ass, and that was what I needed. He was a Vietnam veteran and a recovering alcoholic. He was going to meetings, and when it came to getting me to go, he was like a drill sergeant. If I did anything stupid, he collared me. The leash was short. I wanted Marion to know I made a good decision by moving in. She wasn't all that impressed. *And why should she be?*

Over the next couple weeks, my thoughts started to come together in a way they had not before. I happened to hear 'Sedated' on the radio. I liked what I heard. The drumming was good. Everything was good. When music was honest, it changed your trajectory. Even if you were having a bad day. *Especially* if you were having a bad day. I was glad to have been a part of it and that it lived on. *I knew I wanted to live on.*

There were times when music became a job. There were times when music became a burden. But I understood now, maybe for the first time, that *playing* was not a job. *Playing* was not a burden. I lived to play. I was born to play. The elements that surrounded playing could be hell. But, once I took that seat, all the bullshit dropped away. When I drank, all the bullshit *seemed* to drop away, even while it got worse. For so many years, I drank and I played but never at the same time. Both activities calmed me down. One gave me a purpose. The other was destroying me.

There was no doubt alcohol was destroying me. I was able to kid myself for a long time, but even for the most stubborn among us there came a time, and mine had arrived. I lost my band. I was twenty pounds overweight and looked puffy. My brain was filled with images that sent me running. My mother didn't want to speak to me. My father, the Rock of Gibraltar, was broken. I left shattered glass, scattered furniture, and shrieking people in my wake. Worst of all, the person I cared about most in my life had nothing left. I had drained her. As if calling her and telling her I was dry for a few days was supposed to make her do cartwheels.

Anyone can be told anything they want to hear. I had gotten good at it. Like alcohol, it just made things worse. The two went hand in hand. I had brought both those arts, those skills, into rehab at Freeport and polished them a little more. There were more people to convince. More people to impress. Some wore nice coats. Some wore gowns. No matter what impression they walked away with, I was the same. I was doing something for them. Not even. I was *pretending* to do something for them.

It was a game. I could see how the game had turned out so far. And I could see how it was going to end. Today one thing was different. I wanted to change. But I didn't know how.

17

I took the Staten Island Ferry alone. Getting dropped off by a car service in front of the rehab facility would have been self-defeating. If you really wanted it, the very first step and the very last step had to be hard, like the ones in between.

A few weeks earlier, I ran into my old friend Anthony, a good wholesome Italian boy from Brooklyn. When you looked at Anthony, it was hard to imagine he had once hit rock bottom, but he had. I told him where I was in life, and his eyes lit up. They didn't exactly light up with joy. It was more like he saw what I would have to face and was glad it was already behind him.

Bayley Seton was the hard-core drug and alcohol rehabilitation facility of New York. According to Anthony, it was the polar opposite of what I experienced in Freeport. At Freeport, no one wanted to ruffle your feathers. At Bayley Seton, you were stripped down. I was ready. I had only one change of clothes. The facility had once been run by the United States as a military hospital but had been taken over by the Sisters of Charity, a Catholic organization. They named the hospital after New York's Saint Elizabeth Seton. It was hard to imagine a saint coming out of New York.

The New York I knew, with its imposing downtown skyline, looked small and distant now. The St. George area of Staten Island seemed as a whole like a campus or an institution with smaller, stately brick buildings lining the shore. Bayley Seton was one of them. I walked about ten minutes south along Bay Avenue, made a right, and walked in the front entrance. When the door closed behind me, it was as close a feeling to final as I had ever had. It could have been the marines. But that would have been too easy.

I was nameless and faceless in Bayley Seton. Where my days used to be marked by tour destinations and scheduled interviews, they were now marked by floors washed and toilets cleaned. There were no doors on the bathroom stalls. I knew there was a practical reason for that. The effect was to rip away any remaining arrogance.

I slept with the other male patients in a long, open room with a row of about forty army cots. A security guard was posted at every door. There was no TV to watch. No tapes to listen to. No phone calls to make. No magazines to flip through. No midnight snack to grab. I was alone with my thoughts. Every last thought – about why I was here, what I could learn, what was that strange spot on the ceiling – was coupled with the only lasting thought I had. I wanted, more than anything I ever wanted, to get out.

Along with the close quarters I shared with dozens of men in the other cots, we all shared at least one distinction. We were not in the other wing. The other wing, across an interior hallway, was for alcoholics whose relationship to life was touch and go. These were men who had been drinking heavily for thirty or forty years. Wars and eras had come and gone, and they were all strung together by a bottle from which these men were now being weaned. Throughout the night, we heard screams and moans that were seared into our dreams.

It was much worse than the movie version of a sanitarium. In the movie version, the sounds of agony came from a speaker in the cinema and were always just a little bit fake. Here agony bounced off the four walls and came from the bowels. Every few minutes the screams were punctuated by fierce, vicious ranting and raving as these men fought a cockfight with whatever demons the cruel detox process happened to release. Just like the missing bathroom stall doors, the nearness to these deathly sick men had a purpose. We were listening to our future.

I kept to myself during the day. I didn't want a close companion. I was just getting to know myself, and that was more than enough. I had brief conversations with people, mainly speaking when I was spoken to. I saved my speech for the meetings. There were three a day. The idea wasn't to go to meetings just because we were in here. The idea was to go to meetings wherever we were or might ever be, from now on.

This time I really listened to what other people said. Whatever and whoever I thought I had outsmarted in the past, there was no outsmarting these people. They had seen it, done it, and gone down the same drain to wind up in the exact same place I was. They had thought of the same excuses, wrecked the same friendships, hurt the same parents, worn out the same girlfriends and wives, and crushed the same dreams. Only the details changed. One thing was no longer hard. When I got up to speak, I knew exactly what to say.

'Hi, I'm Marc. I'm an alcoholic.'

I was not guessing.

It was the longest month of my life. No other month came close. No other year came close. With only three nights to go, staring at the ceiling and trying to shut out the screams from across the hall, I noticed another change in my thoughts. I still wanted more than anything to get out. But now I had a plan for when I did. It wasn't a very elaborate plan, but it was a start. I swore to myself I would never take a drink again.

My last breakfast at Bayley Seton was different only because I knew it was my last. When I finished, I gathered the few items I had brought, put them in my bag, signed a few papers, and checked out. I walked up Bay Avenue, took the ferry, and headed across the bay back to Brooklyn. I sat out on the top deck and let the cold crisp air hit my face. Based on when I took the ferry the other way it had to be getting close to Thanksgiving.

I took a subway to Sheepshead Bay and rang the bell to our apartment. Marion had let me back in before Bayley Seton, but this time when she opened the door and welcomed me, I knew I had earned it. I had a new craving lately: to sleep in my own bed. But first, I had something else to do. I pulled out the pamphlet from my bag, made a few phone calls, and went to a meeting that night.

I carried my Alcoholics Anonymous pamphlet with me wherever I went. In it were the addresses of morning, afternoon, and evening meetings throughout the city. Wherever I happened to be, I made sure to make a meeting. Sometimes there was a meeting within walking distance of our apartment. Other times the next one was farther, so I rode my bicycle. I would chain the bike up to the gate of the church, temple, Lions Club, or VFW hall. If I had someplace to be during the day, I would map out my route around these meetings. I was on tour again – a different kind of tour.

Alcoholics Anonymous was an organization like no other. Started in the thirties, it had no political affiliation, no restrictions on the type of person who could join, and accepted no money from outside sources. The organization eventually acquired millions of members across dozens of countries and stuck to the principle of its name. It was truly anonymous. AA wasn't out there trying to make news, do the talk show circuit, or win awards. Its focus was simply and quietly helping people to stay sober the only way it could be done in reality: one day at a time.

Over time, AA developed the Twelve Steps, which, if followed seriously, could lead to sobriety. The full Twelve Steps were a life's work. I had gotten through the first one, admitting that I had become powerless over alcohol. I was an addict. The next steps were believing that a power greater than myself could restore my sanity and acknowledging that I had to turn my life over to the care of God *as I understood Him*. The last part was problematic for me. I wasn't religious and didn't believe in a little old white-haired man sitting in a chair ruling over the universe. That, to me, was just another form of insanity. But I understood in my bones that the important things were to go to meetings and take sobriety seriously. The rest would have to work itself out.

The meetings were definitely the core of the program. With the meetings, sobriety was a struggle. Without them, it was nearly impossible. The idea that an alcoholic was a homeless guy sleeping in a box on skid row had begun to leave my mind weeks earlier; now it was gone for good.

The people at meetings were doctors, lawyers, teachers, sanitation workers, housewives, students, businessmen, and even one punk-rock drummer. Some had lost the respect of their partners, others had lost everything – houses, cars, jobs, their life savings. Some had plummeted from tremendous heights, others had quietly slipped through the cracks. The details of their stories – the agony, the denial, the humiliation, the stripping away of things they didn't know were important till they were gone – were different. Some had been to jail. Many were divorced. Some had gone through their child's education savings. Others had suffered tragic accidents. Regardless, these people were all basically the same – lucky to be alive, and sick and tired of being sick and tired. I was one of them.

It was an incredible relief to me to know I wasn't alone. I spent many meetings just listening to other people talk, learning whatever I could, knowing someone else had been to that terrible place, seeing there was hope. And there was hope. Some of the speakers had been sober for weeks or months. Others for five, ten, fifteen years. Just the fact that these veterans of the program kept coming was an amazing thing to consider.

Gradually, I began to share my own story. The more I shared, the more comfortable it became. I started to mingle with other people after meetings and continue my story and theirs. The stories were always evolving because every day sober was another obstacle. You didn't know what might set you off or set you back. The bottle was always waiting in the wings, powerful as ever. But knowing that in an hour or two you would be talking to someone who really understood gave you the power to fight back. And that tremendous resource was how I got through Steps Two and Three. I didn't look up in the sky for my higher power. My higher power was the collective miracles of the people in the room.

In AA, a sponsor is someone who has had more time sober than you have, and is willing to be a friend, teacher, mentor, and above all someone you can just pick up the phone and talk to about what's going on in your life at that moment. After a few months sober, I was lucky enough to get my sponsor. He was a New York Italian guy who worked as a jeweler on Forty-Seventh Street in Manhattan. He was very good at what he did. We had a lot in common. We were around the same age and liked a lot of the same music. Of course, I had a lot to say about music. And he had a lot to say about our addiction. He had already been sober over six years.

Sometimes I would meet my sponsor for lunch in the Diamond District. Sometimes he would meet me if I had an appointment in Manhattan. When we met at night, it was usually to go to a meeting. Everything centered on meetings. It was the reverse image of the picture when I was drinking, when everything centered on alcohol and wherever it was served. My sponsor's approach on a tough day was usually exactly what I needed to hear. Keep it simple. Think of the positive things in your life. Do something constructive at the moment. Make a meeting. Of course, my sponsor and I didn't go to every meeting together. My sponsor had his own sponsor.

Although meetings gave life rhythm, there needed to be music in between the beats. As far as actually playing music was concerned, at least in a band situation, I was counseled against it. A psychiatrist I saw at Bayley Seton strongly suggested that I not jump back into the lion's den until I had, at the bare minimum, a full year sober. My sponsor agreed. So the music would come from the spokes of a bicycle wheel.

When we were kids, we biked everywhere. The subways took us from Brooklyn to Manhattan but not from neighborhood to neighborhood. Bikes gave us freedom. Bikes gave us mobility. Bikes gave us accountability, because we had to take care of our transportation for it to take care of us. In my thirties, it was about to happen all over again.

I became a bike messenger. I knew the territory from a short stint many years before. Most of the action was in Manhattan. I would get up at five thirty in the morning, eat a big breakfast, ride the subway in with my bike, and report to the dispatch office on West Twenty-Seventh

Street. I wore sweatpants and bicycle shoes. I tucked my hair into a baseball cap. When I showed up at the bare-bones office around 7:15 a.m. and approached the dispatch desk, I was Marc. People may have known who Marky Ramone was, but that was not me. This was Bike Messengers Anonymous.

Not much had changed. Delivering packages by bike in New York may not have been a lion's den, but it was definitely a jungle. Cars, taxis, trucks, and buses were predators, and we were prey. Intersections were like swamps. You hoped you and your backpack were going to make it out alive. But I liked the jungle. It was survival of the fittest, and I was getting fit. I had a feel for how to cut through traffic and where to take an alternate route. I felt the rhythm of the city in my arms and legs.

There were moments of peril. You never knew when the door of a parked car was going to swing open in your face. You never knew when a yellow cab was going to run a red light. But as long as it was only a scare or a scrape, I wasn't going to start a confrontation. The streets of Manhattan were a strange kind of proving ground for my sobriety. If there was anything in the world that could drive you to drink, it was New York traffic.

The money was okay. Not that I needed it. I was lucky. We were paid by the parcel. But there was another bonus that I hadn't counted on: every day was filled with pickups and deliveries, and, with every one, I dealt with someone outside my usual walk of life. There were secretaries and clerks, concierges and bellhops, designers and fabric cutters, editors and advertisers. Every one of them had a backstory and a deadline of some type, and, with my success or failure to traverse Seventh Avenue in under ten minutes, I had the ability to make or break their day. After being driven and flown for so many years, now I was the driver and the flier. I was relearning a work ethic from the ground up.

No one impressed me more than the other bike messengers. On a hundred-degree day in mid-August, when sweat poured off me like from a car wash, I could fall back on the idea that I wanted to do this but didn't need to. For most of the other bike messengers, that wasn't the case. They were paying bills with three dollars here, four-fifty there, one mad run at a time. But these guys and gals lived like brave bombardiers with every new mission, not knowing which one might be their last.

One afternoon the supervisor asked me to deliver a bunch of packages on a dolly. So I loaded up the dolly and rolled it into the freight elevator. As I walked west along Twenty-Seventh Street and pulled the dolly behind me, I blended in seamlessly with the mid-afternoon crowd swelling the sidewalk. It was business as usual. Then I heard a familiar voice.

'Hey, Marc!'

It was a friend of mine from high school who had been walking in the opposite direction. If my cover was eventually going to be blown, it made sense that it wasn't someone from the music scene. My friend held out his hand, and I shook it.

'Hey, man,' I said. 'What's going on?'

'Why don't *you* tell *me* what's going on?' he said. 'I thought you were playing all over the world. Where are the other Ramones?'

'Yeah, well, I think they deliver for another messenger service.'

'Seriously. What the fuck are you doing?'

'Can you keep a secret?' I said.

'Yeah, you know me.'

'I'm in recovery,' I said. 'This is part of the program. Part of staying sober.'

'Holy shit. That's great. Really. People aren't recognizing you.'

'You're the first,' I said. 'I gotta run. So give me a call.'

'Bah-bah-bah-bah, b-bah-bah-bah-bah! I wanna be sedated!' he sang, and smiled as I walked on. Then he waved.

A couple of weeks later, I was given a small package to deliver by hand. That happened when occasionally the pickup and delivery were both close to the office. As I walked west on Twenty-Ninth Street, a familiar face came into focus from about fifty yards. He had black hair hanging straight down in bangs and a wide angular chin. There was no question: it was Dee Dee.

I was in my usual all-purpose nondescript messenger outfit with the baseball cap. Dee Dee's mind was usually not at street level unless he was copping. I knew the only way he would recognize me was if I made a move and got right in his face. As it was, I barely recognized him. It wasn't just that he had aged more than I might have expected. It was more a matter of his gaining about another twenty pounds. It had to be all the psychotropic drugs he was still taking. They altered your whole metabolism.

I made my move, in the other direction. I turned away at just the moment Dee Dee might have seen me and had a clue. I wanted to talk to him. I had more to say than ever. But I just wasn't ready.

Winter in New York is cold enough. Winter on a bike nine hours a day pedaling directly into the wind is like living in the Ice Age. I hung up the bike for a while. But I had logged hundreds and hundreds of miles, lost fifteen pounds, gotten into great shape, and maintained my sobriety even while riding between lanes on Broadway during rush-hour traffic. I also felt a lot more connected to the people around me. My sponsor encouraged me to find another occupation for a while and keep the momentum going.

It so happened our downstairs neighbor knew a locksmith who had just secured a big city contract and needed to staff up. The contract called for sealing off abandoned buildings by installing wrought-iron security gates in the windows. The locksmith turned out to be a really sweet guy when I met him, and he hired me on the spot.

The buildings were concentrated in the Bedford–Stuyvesant area of Brooklyn, a largely blighted neighborhood with potential for a comeback. Most of the buildings had been crack houses, and Mayor Ed Koch wanted to make sure the addicts didn't return. So he hired an ex-addict to seal them off. By the time we got there, the squatters had been cleared by the police. But I got to see in plain daylight the remains of the lives they were leading.

There were empty crack vials all over the floors. Crack had taken over entire communities in the mid-eighties. It was cheap, easily smoked, and available almost everywhere. But the vials and needles were just the beginning. There were utensils and hotplates. There were plastic bags with ratty clothing and makeshift beds of newspapers and old blankets. There were a few books, sometimes neatly arranged inside a milk crate.

Once in a while, I would spot a wire draped in through a window and jumped to a light pole outside. Like most people, I would have believed that life inside a crack house was completely chaotic and random, but there was lots of evidence that these people, even in the middle of their horrible addiction, were incredibly resourceful. Sounded like somebody I knew.

One thing their ingenuity couldn't overcome was the lack of adequate bathroom facilities. Whether we were working in a narrow three-story walk-up or a sizeable six-story building, most of the plumbing fixtures had been ripped out, and, even where they remained, there was no active plumbing. The stench was overwhelming. Everyone at one time or another had been to a gas station bathroom that hadn't been cleaned in a while. This was different. This was the smell of death.

Using an acetylene torch was a new experience for me. The only thing I had ever torched was an ashtray filled with Bacardi 151. The first thing I did with the acetylene torch was make sure my hair was tucked completely in my cap. There was a lot more than I thought to installing a window grate. The opening had to be made stable so you were anchoring the bars into something solid. The opening sizes and shapes varied a lot, so we were always cutting and fitting. But I was always good with my hands, and within a few weeks I was like a pro.

Whereas at one time I was freelancing in the music business and got jobs by word of mouth, I was now freelancing in the construction business. The job installing window security gates led to a job doing interior demolition in Manhattan. The condo craze had hit New York. There was Wall Street money all over the place and property values were soaring. High-income people wanted to own luxury apartments, mortgage rates were pretty low, and the tax write-offs were great. Old rental buildings with small, basic apartments were being converted into condominiums with large spaces, granite floors, marble kitchen islands, and central air. The first step was to knock down walls, and that's where I came in.

Demo work wasn't one of the Twelve Steps, but maybe it should have been. Demolition was the most I ever sweated without riding a bike or hitting a snare drum. And it was by far the dirtiest. Knocking down walls was just the beginning. I cut down wood beams and steel beams. I cut the thick wire lath on the old plaster walls. I stripped off half a dozen coats of paint from old metal doorframes. It wasn't all brute force. Demolition was an art. Without the right tools and technique you were just fighting a losing battle. Sledgehammers, reciprocating saws, drills, and heat guns all became my friends.

Before you did anything, you had to make sure you weren't removing a load-bearing wall or you would be demolishing yourself as well. The debris had to be cleared constantly to keep the floors from collapsing. The dust had to be controlled to keep us breathing. All of it had to be collected and brought to the main dumpster so the Mob could cart it away.

The whole process made me think. By the time the Mob got the waste, it was all neatly packed. By the time the carpenters, masons, and electricians got to the job, all the really nasty work was done. Demolition represented the trenches. I had surprised myself by surviving, living, even thriving in the trenches. I could stay there if I had to. I had gotten my AA medallion with the Serenity Prayer for six months sober, a year, then two years.

Life was good. Marion and I were good. My parents were good. The only thing was, I missed being in the band. With time, I understood on a gut level what I really missed about it. I missed the feeling of playing music. I missed the friendships that formed in a band. And I missed giving people the gift of music.

I didn't miss drinking. At least I thought I didn't. I had talked to my sponsor about it many times. I thought it was time to go back into the lion's den. Clubs and bars were where the music was. They were also where the alcohol was. You could have one without the other, even though it wasn't always going to be easy. What I had done was put myself through what I thought was enough physical, mental, and spiritual training to recognize the danger and deal with it. Regardless,

I'd be going to many more meetings than clubs and had no illusion that I could go it alone. I was not afraid of the lions.

The Cat Club was the home of glam metal in New York. Located on East Thirteenth Street in Manhattan, the club had among its management Roy Webb, who ran the Electric Circus back in the day. The Cat Club was a bit of a circus, with everyone from Joey Ramone to Billy Idol to Dee Snider of Twisted Sister hanging out. The New York scene had changed while I was delivering packages and knocking down walls. Hair bands such as Cinderella and Poison were huge. My friends and I couldn't stand much of it, and if there was a next big thing it was likely to come out of a place like the Cat Club.

My band, King Flux, were ready to be that thing. We played a hybrid of punk and metal with lots of stops and high-pitched vibrato singing. The group were started by Richie Stotts, a founding member of the Plasmatics, who, with Wendy O. Williams fronting the band, blew minds and blew up TVs and cars onstage. Also on guitar was Billy Hilfiger, with his brother Andy on bass. Billy and Andy were younger brothers of the fashion designer Tommy Hilfiger and were truly stand-up guys. The lead vocalist and frontman was another stand-up guy, Anthony Nicholas.

We rehearsed in a building near the Port Authority, and sometimes Tommy would come down and take us along with his brothers out to eat. Tommy had just started his own line of clothing, was extremely generous, and living proof that you could still make it in America if you had vision and the willingness to back it up with a lot of hard work.

There was plenty of drinking going on at the Cat Club, but none of it by me. I had been in King Flux for a few months and had proved to myself it was safe to go back in. There were so many positive things going on, and alcohol didn't have a place at my table. We had sold out the Cat Club a few times, and it was a fairly large room. Our 'following' included some of my favorite musicians and people in the world – Joey and Dee Dee, and Steven Van Zandt of Springsteen's E Street Band.

Joey was probably happier than anyone to see me. Even years after the fact, he was still apologizing for having to let me go. The important thing, I always told him, was that getting the boot was the beginning of my getting sober. I was still sober, and if anything, I owed him a thank-you.

There was a buzz around King Flux, and we were given an industry showcase at the Ritz on East Eleventh Street, a sizable venue. There were at least three record companies interested in signing us, with Elektra the lead among them. The A&R guys came to every show and told us how much they liked the act. That was great, but I had been down this road before. It was as if each of them were waiting for the other one to make a move, and none of them did. We did a great show at the Ritz, so once a few days had passed and there was no phone call, it seemed the writing was on the wall.

We heard through the grapevine that the record companies thought, despite all the money they were still making, that hair bands were on their way out. We weren't a hair band, glam metal, or even metal, strictly speaking, but we were the baby thrown out with the bathwater. The industry was looking for the next big thing and, as far as it was concerned, we were part of the previous big thing.

In theory, a band forms to create music and continues as long as the music is good and they enjoy playing together. Reality can be something very different. The experience of nearly being signed can tear a band apart. When disappointment replaces anticipation, the steam can go out of the engine quickly, and that's what happened to King Flux. You could argue that it's better to build a following slowly without any record company interest, but it's not as if you can control what happens in the wide world. It's hard enough to manage anything *inside* the band.

The aftermath of King Flux was a side project called the Richie Stotts Experience. Since the rise and tragic early fall of Jimi Hendrix, his original band more or less owned the name 'Experience'. Not legally, but for all practical purposes. Taking on that surname was like taking 'Zeppelin'. 'Stones', or 'Sabbath'. You didn't do it unless you were a tribute band, e.g. Dread Zeppelin, Bowling Stones, Crack Sabbath. But the Richie Stotts band were not a Jimi Hendrix tribute band, and Richie Stotts was no Jimi Hendrix. No one was.

I agreed to play drums, anyway. It was a good little band. Daniel Rey, who had both produced and played lead guitar on the Ramones' latest album, *Halfway to Sanity*, was our bassist. Richie decided we would do a warm-up gig for a bunch of invited friends at the Pyramid Club on Avenue A between Sixth and Seventh Streets.

As we loaded in my drums on a hot, sticky summer night in early August 1987, I had an uneasy feeling. It wasn't because the Pyramid Club was almost a textbook hole-in-the-wall. It was a cool hole-in-the-wall. It was a well-known venue for the drag and gay scene in the East Village. RuPaul had done her first New York show at the Pyramid Club, and celebrities such as Debbie Harry, Madonna, and Andy Warhol dropped by every so often.

My problem was subliminal, but, once I was inside the club, I understood. The flyers for the band, both outside the club and in, made no mention of Marky Ramone. I didn't even get a tiny 'with'. Maybe this oversight or snub shouldn't have bothered me, but it did to a degree. Even as a simple matter of promoting the band, it made no sense. Marky Ramone was a name with far more recognition than Richie Stotts. There should have been a 'Marky' somewhere.

The show went okay. We played a set of both covers and originals for about a hundred people, which was about what the room could hold. We talked for an hour or so with our friends and supporters, and I drank a 7-Up. But once the drums were back in the van on Avenue A, I told myself no more of this. I deserved a better Marky Ramone experience.

A few weeks later, I was home in Brooklyn when Marion handed me the phone. It was Monte. I wasn't exactly expecting this call, but at the same time I wasn't entirely surprised. The drummer who had replaced me in the Ramones was named Richie. I knew his girlfriend, who wrote for the music magazine *Spin* and who had given King Flux a good review. She had let me know that her boyfriend was unhappy with the money he was getting in the Ramones and wanted a cut of the merchandising revenue. He was considering walking out on the band to drive home his point, but his girlfriend warned him to be careful because the Ramones might call Marky back. Richie's response was that would never happen.

It was happening. Monte explained that not only did Richie quit suddenly on 12 August after a show in East Hampton, but he did it with zero notice and in the middle of a full touring calendar. The Ramones had quickly rustled up Clem Burke of Blondie to assume the name Elvis Ramone and fill in at a show in Providence, Rhode Island, then another one in Trenton, New Jersey. We all loved Clem and his drumming, but it was not the fast-handed, frenetically pounding, trademark Ramones style. After two shows, he was out.

Monte and the gang were up against it. September was jam-packed and included a full tour of California. The following month was a massive tour of Europe. The potential lost income was enough to make John walk to the precipice, and the penalties and potential litigation were enough to make him jump. The whole band, right down to Dee Dee and his devil-may-care attitude, were desperate. So, after Monte gave me the gory details, he laid it on the table.

'Marc, we need you.'

So it went back to where it all started – a meeting with John. This time it was just me and John, without the women in our lives. We met at Daily Planet rehearsal studios, where history ran deep. As before, there was an audition in name only. John knew through Monte, who knew through Joey, that I had been sober for four years. It seemed like John just needed to see for himself. As we settled into the studio and John plugged in his guitar, everything felt about the same. John even looked about the same except that, as he tuned the strings, he stopped every now and then to touch the side of his head. The scar tissue from where he was kicked four years earlier probably still bothered him.

We launched into 'Commando' and that was that. I saw John nod his head as he whirled around as if we were onstage. I felt a smile come across my face. John called out a few more songs – 'Blitzkrieg', 'Affected', 'Shock Treatment', 'Sedated'. Nothing came close, at least musically. We were locked in. It was as simple as that. It was like a dry run backstage before the show, minus Dee Dee for the moment. It was like coming home. Or in my case, like riding a bike.

After ten songs we wrapped it up and for about a minute I saw a side of John I didn't often see. A side hardly anyone ever saw.

'Marc,' he said, 'it's like you never left.'

Even though I had lived a lifetime – a different kind of lifetime – over those four years, I knew what he meant. But then John threw me a curve. He told me he was grateful. Not just for the small fortune I would be saving him and the band over the next couple of months. John confided that until he walked in the door of the rehearsal room and played the first few chords of 'Commando', he was seriously considering retiring. That was really something coming from John. Whatever his faults, he was always a very goal-oriented person. He was one of the few people – *let alone musicians* – around our age who even thought in terms of building up a nest egg to fall back on. If he was ready to the pull the plug, he was really at the end of his wire.

I could appreciate the feeling of despair. I could appreciate a lot of things I was unable or unwilling to feel just a few years earlier. One of those things was how small a world it was. It was a cliché, of course, but also a reality. Not just with all the 'Richie' trouble on both sides of the fence lately. Not just with the intertwined circles of people in the world and how somehow everyone knew everyone, and everything you did eventually came back to you in some strange way.

The most amazing thing was how a longstanding difference could just evaporate like a little moisture on a drumhead. When I was asked to leave the Ramones, I needed their help and didn't get it. When I considered over the years how any of this could ever possibly be resolved, I never imagined it would be this way – *through my helping them.*

There was a higher power at work here. The collective miracles of people could unfold even in a well-worn rehearsal room. So I thought I'd share with John, for a minute, a side of myself he had probably never seen. I told him getting back in the band was the third best thing that ever happened to me. And getting kicked out was the second best thing.

18

When you look at a photo of a US president at the beginning of a term and another photo near the end you'll see a difference. Same face, but the aging is obvious. Gray hairs replace brown or black. Skin sags and creases. There is a weary look in the eyes that says this was harder than I thought it would be. *To you it was four years. To me it was a lifetime.*

Monte's four years in my absence were all over his face. He mediated civil wars and prevented international incidents. He served as diplomat, negotiator, and counselor. He was a friend, confidant, and psychologist. Not to mention driver, tour manager, and den mother. There was no retreat to Camp David for Monte. There was just another trip in the van.

John was still in the front, and he still didn't talk to Joey, who also didn't talk to John. If anything, the wall between them was thicker and taller. Not even a word slipped through. Any absolutely necessary communication went through Monte, who also served as a messenger and translator. John still had the band's affairs mapped out. Joey still tapped things. But now Dee Dee rapped.

'I'm a Negro! I'm a Negro!'

Dee Dee shouted it out from the rear of the van on our way down to Washington, DC, my second show back.

'I'm a Negro! I'm a Negro!'

'No, you're not,' John said. 'You're a fucking white guy who can't rap.'

Dee Dee was heavy into Run-DMC and Public Enemy. He was dead serious about hip-hop and working out rhyme schemes in the van between popping Thorazine and Stelazine. Once he figured out he could rap and annoy John at the same time, Dee Dee was off to the races. He was a funky man, and he let his funk flag fly.

Linda was gone from the van. She was gone from sight. The long awaited and inevitable had happened. She had left Joey and moved in with John. John assured me she would never be a problem. She would never go on tour again and would only come to an occasional show and remain in the audience to avoid any drama. Switching apartments was one thing, but switching seats in the van was another. Linda was not to be seen. That was simple, understood, and one more line in Monte's face.

In spite of everything, I made meetings on the road wherever I could, and the shows were on the money. In DC, Long Island, the Ritz in Manhattan, San Diego, Los Angeles, and San Francisco, I spotted signs in the audience that read 'Welcome back!'; 'We love Marky!'; 'Marky's back!' I was back for sure.

I always thought the Ramones had the best fans in the world, but now there seemed to be more of them, and they included a lot of younger faces in the audience. There were fourteen- and fifteen-year-olds jumping around and singing the words to 'Sheena'. They were barely walking when the first album came out. But somehow, watching *Rock 'n' Roll High School* on video and listening to *Rocket to Russia*, *Road to Ruin*, and *End of the Century* had gotten into their bones. They brought a new energy to the shows and a new energy to me.

It took no time at all to remember how great it was to perform in the Ramones. The insanity, neuroses, arguments, feuds, innuendos, and mishaps were all worth it the moment we stepped onstage. There was an excitement and a bond with the audience that trumped all the bullshit before and after. It beat any substance, hands down. I especially wanted Dee Dee to feel that way. Sometimes it seemed he got that. Sometimes it didn't. When the encores were over, I knew it would soon be time for parts two, three, and four of whatever lunacy was going on before the show. But I would drink a seltzer and not let it bother me. These guys were crazy, but they were my brothers.

Steps Four, Eight, and Nine of the Twelve Steps had to do with making lists, making amends, and taking personal inventory. Those weren't altogether easy, but at least musically speaking they were enjoyable. I was focused and wanted to be the best I could be. I was determined to be on the money and eradicate any memory anyone might have of my onetime flakiness or inconsistencies.

My spare hours were spent rehearsing. I enabled myself positively by planting drum kits all over the city. I had one in my friend's loft and another in a studio. I had my main kit at SIR in Lower Manhattan. My drum pads were always with me. I played three hours every day, sometimes more. I was addicted to playing. Getting back to my earlier peak in the Ramones was not the goal. It was the starting point. When the fans at a show waited for the drum fill on 'Sedated', I didn't want to disappoint. I wanted it to be like it was on the record *or better*. I made sure I could do the roll with just my left hand.

The Ramones weren't models or model citizens. They made a living on music and attitude. Punk ethic and all, they were well aware that not every comment, problem, or prank was for public consumption. They generally didn't want cameras around. So I brought one along to Europe. It was a Nikon Hi8 analog video camera. The tape looked a lot like a smaller version of VHS, but the quality was better. The way I saw it, if someone in their inner circle was filming, the band's guard would be down. The footage would be honest, funny, and preserved for posterity. Not to mention, filming would give me something constructive to do in transit.

On the flight to Copenhagen, Dee Dee, Vera, Marion, and I occupied four of the five middle seats in one row of a wide-body jet. We were a little jammed in and it probably seemed even more crowded than it was with Dee Dee rapping away. One of the stewardesses walked over and told us we didn't have to squish in. There was plenty of room in the rear and we were more than welcome to go back and spread out.

'No, thanks,' Marion said. 'But we appreciate it.'

She didn't look back, but for good measure I did. Joey was sitting in one of the rear five-wide rows. There was no one on either side of him or in front. Or behind. Two or three rows in front, a few passengers were scattered. It was like a ripple effect, when you tossed a stone into a lake and concentric circles formed. No one wanted to sit near Joey because of his body odor. He was having a bad-hygiene day. Maybe a bad-hygiene week. He was drinking and doing cocaine, and I wanted to help him just as I wanted to help Dee Dee.

Things weren't all bad with Joey. While I was out of the band, he'd had a girlfriend named Angela. She and her sister, Camille, hung around the Tropicana in Los Angeles. Angela moved in with Joey and the sister moved in with Monte, so Joey and Monte became practically brothers-in-law. Angela was pretty and sharp. They made a good couple, and a big part of that was the great job Angela did taking care of Joey. By the time I came back, they had split up. Joey was a handful again.

But they were still friends. Not in the clichéd sense of a cheap consolation prize. They really liked each other. Taking all that into consideration, Angela was the best thing that had ever happened to Joey. As for Camille, she was a wild one and a drug addict. Monte came back one day from a tour to find his computer, stereo, camera – everything – gone. She had taken and sold it. When I heard that, I was very sad for Monte.

The next show after Copenhagen was Hamburg. The tour bus picked us up from the ferry across the Great Belt Strait then took us south along the peninsula that was Denmark. Dee Dee showed up that morning in a red Adidas warm-up suit with black stripes. He had a spiky haircut, multiple rings on his fingers, and a large, gold Mercedes-Benz medallion hanging from his neck on a chain. He looked like a white Flavor Flav.

'What about the gold teeth?' John said. 'Where are those?'

'I'm working on it,' Dee Dee said.

'Don't even think of setting foot onstage looking like that,' John said with his icy blue-eyed stare.

'We'll see how I feel,' Dee Dee said.

How he felt was like working on his rap project all the way to Germany.

It was quite a homecoming. He took the stage in Hamburg without the warm-up suit and medallion. The spiky hair remained, but if that was punk enough for Richard Hell, it had to be good enough, just barely, for Johnny Ramone. Backstage Dee Dee was all pissed off. He told us somebody in the audience, remarking on his weight, had yelled, 'Hold in your gut!' We didn't know if it was shouted out in English or German, but Dee Dee could be insulted in two languages. He stood in front of a mirror in the dressing room with his shirt half up and gazed straight ahead.

'Do I look fat?'

'Yes,' John said matter-of-factly as he walked by.

A few minutes later, Dee Dee disappeared into the bathroom. We could hear him retching. It was a universal language, but through the stall and the wall it sounded guttural, like his native tongue. It was hard to listen to. Dee Dee had all the bases covered. He was overweight and bulimic at the same time.

When we finished the tour in London and got ready to board at Heathrow, I needed a different strategy as far as my camera was concerned. Terrorism was spreading around the world, especially in Europe. Security was intense and everyone had to go through a metal detector. When we first arrived in Copenhagen, I reviewed the tape in my video camera and received an unpleasant surprise. The tape was erased. It had evidently been demagnetized going through the metal detector. I couldn't let that ever happen again. Especially not now. I had too much good shit on those tapes.

I walked up to the head guy at the security gate and explained that I was on tour filming my band and would cooperate with any reasonable security procedure so long as he didn't run the tapes through the metal detector. My plea aroused more suspicions than it relieved. They patted me down, front and back. They went through my bag thoroughly. They opened the camera case and eyeballed the battery as if it were hooked up to a bomb. But in the end, they let me through and ran my tapes around the metal detector. I breathed a little easier. I now had an effective MO, and the images of Dee Dee in a jumpsuit were safe for the ages.

Dee Dee was dressed normally when I met him at his apartment in Whitestone, Queens, on a chilly day in early March 1988. I had a strategy. I drove my Cadillac Seville to the apartment and got Dee Dee to drive us to the meeting in his Camaro. Before we got into the Camaro, I spent a few minutes talking to Vera. I wanted to help her maybe even more than I wanted to help Dee Dee. Vera was pretty much the nicest, warmest person Marion and I had ever met, and she suffered tremendously through Dee Dee's addictions. If there was a punk version of the country song 'Stand by Your Man', she could have written it.

My strategy was to get Dee Dee to the meeting nearest to his apartment. That way, if there was a second meeting he ever wanted to go to, it would be convenient. By the same token, if he took the driver's seat in his own car maybe it would be the beginning of a good habit.

Dee Dee was hyper but in a reasonably good mood talking about his record deal. Seymour Stein had signed him to Sire/Warner for a one-album deal as a solo rap artist. Seymour's eternal encouragement and long leash with all of us meant total creative freedom for Dee Dee. And strictly as a business venture, Dee Dee's writing ability had not only been very successful in another genre – it helped launch the genre. So from Seymour's point of view, it was worth a shot.

Dee Dee would need help, and he was getting it. Vera was managing the project behind the scenes and developing the artwork. We had deep resources in the musicians department. Dee Dee asked me to play drums, but I preferred just to advise him on the beats to use and quietly take an acknowledgement. I was a rocker, not a rapper.

The kind of help I was trying to get Dee Dee was up ahead in the First Presbyterian Church on 149th Street. The large wooden structure had a sanctuary with a steeple on the left and the entrance to the rectory on the right. Dee Dee rolled his Camaro right up onto the neatly manicured front lawn.

'Dee Dee,' I said. 'You can't do that. You can't park on the lawn. People go to church here. A minister lives in there. People pay money to maintain this place.'

'How long is the meeting?' he asked.

'That's not the point,' I said. 'This is not the way to come to a meeting. You have to show some respect. Plus, you're gonna leave tire tracks.'

I got Dee Dee to pull out slowly and repark in the lot, which I supposed for him was Step One. The moment we walked into the meeting room, he asked me where the coffee and donuts were.

'Dee Dee, you're not here for coffee and donuts. You can have coffee and donuts at home. You're here because you want to get off the shit you've been taking for years and years. And, if you want to do that, which I hope you do, you've gotta keep your ears open. You've gotta listen.'

'I'm hungry.'

'Be hungry to learn something,' I said. 'This is the first day of school as far as you should be concerned. These people have been through a lot of what we've been through. If you listen, something might really click. You can't do this on your own.'

'Okay, Marc. I'll sit there and listen. But I'm not getting up there and making a speech.'

'That's fine,' I said. 'Do what you want. If you learn something – *even one thing* – you're ahead of the game.'

We took two of the few dozen chairs set up. The room was packed with men and women in their twenties, thirties, and forties. It made sense that there were no senior citizens. This was NA – Narcotics Anonymous. When the meeting leader asked me if I'd like to introduce myself, I got up and spoke as I had hundreds of times.

'Hi, I'm Marc, and I'm an alcoholic. I've been sober for almost five years.'

'Hi, Marc.'

The other attendees were polite but clearly not thrilled to see me. NA meetings were open to AA people and vice versa, but many people in either camp considered the other to be another world. Yes, there were cliques even in the world of addiction. To me, this was a little crazy. It was like the difference between hardcore and thrash – not all that much. Whether you were addicted to drugs or alcohol, you were dealing with a substance that took control of your life and made you a hostage. But whatever my opinion might have been, there was no doubt that Dee Dee had come to the right place.

'It's good to be here,' I said. 'I've been working very hard to stay sober and stay focused. I'm a musician, and focusing on my music has been very positive for me in funneling my excess energy. And I'm very excited tonight because a good friend of mine is here.'

Dee Dee was sitting next to me and stood up as I sat down. He looked around for a moment, and I had some of the same anticipation I always had when he counted off a song . . . one, two, three, four . . .

'Hi. I'm Dee Dee. And I'm checking it out.'

That was it. There was no other intro. No verse. No chorus. I understood exactly where he was in life. I had definitely been there. He couldn't admit to the other people in the room that he was an addict. He couldn't admit it to himself. Step One would have to wait at least a little longer.

But my afternoon wasn't wasted. I made sure he knew where to go and what to do. I made sure he took a pamphlet listing all the upcoming meetings – morning, midday, and night. I told him the next time he picked up something he was better off keeping out of his mouth, nose, or arm, he could also pick up the phone, call me, and maybe I could talk him out of it. I left the door open. The door was always open.

The Ramones had by now officially been around long enough to make a compilation album. The working title was *Ramones Mania*. This wasn't to suggest Beatlemania. There could probably be nothing like that ever again. But, as we neared the end of the decade and played bigger shows to wilder audiences, we could see and feel we were at least reaching another level of appreciation.

We were on tour in California in the summer of 1988, and on 9 July took a day out of our schedule to film a video for 'I Wanna Be Sedated'. In the early days of MTV, a video and a song were usually released more or less simultaneously. Sometimes when a song became popular, the video would follow a few months later to capitalize on sales. It had been ten years since 'Sedated' was released. It was hard to believe.

The song, like the band, had steadily picked up steam even as an entire era came and went. It was the Ramones song most likely to turn up when we were just randomly flipping through the radio dial. There were probably millions of casual listeners who were familiar with the song and the 'ba-ba-ba-ba' at the end who couldn't even identify the band. It was amazing what a talented singer and bass player could come up with one night while bored in a London hotel room.

The video was being shot to promote the compilation album. The director, Bill Fishman, had a simple concept for the video. The Ramones would be sedate while everyone around them was in a frenzy. That would be a first, but this was Hollywood.

We filmed in the hallway of a hospital. Dee Dee, John, Joey, and I sat at a table in the middle of the hallway, ate breakfast, and read while dozens of actors dressed for every walk of life dashed up, down, and across. It was a nice payday for extras. We had a ballerina, a young bride, a nun, a pinhead, a guy on a unicycle, a cheerleader, a doctor, a nurse, a bagpipe player, and many other folks from central casting. It was a real mental ward. We felt right at home.

The trick to the shoot was that the band had to move in slow motion while the extras moved at normal speed. The film would be sped up later to make our motions appear normal and everyone else's appear frenetic. It was the slowest I had ever eaten a bowl of cornflakes in my life. Dee Dee turned the pages of the comic book he was reading in the same time he would usually take to empty a medicine cabinet. This was either the challenge of a lifetime for our hyperactive band or some sort of bizarre therapy.

Meanwhile, the loony bin was getting loonier by the second with cereal, crackers, potato chips, hors d'oeuvres, and party streamers flying around the hallway. Just another day in the nuthouse.

On the flight up to San Francisco the next day to play the Fillmore, Marion and I sat behind Joey. It wasn't his worst-smelling day and it wasn't his best, but the flight was full and this was the luck of the draw. Somewhere over San Jose, Marion pointed out something bizarre. Because of Joey's height his head extended well above the top of his headrest. Stuck in his large mop of hair were bits and pieces of food – chips, crackers, cereal, plus a few bits of paper. Each shard was a small souvenir from the shoot the day before. It was a new low in personal hygiene. Even grubby frat boys cleaned up the day after a food fight.

I felt fortunate to have every last fan, and being sober made me appreciate the upside of the Ramones' world even more. There were people I was a fan of, too, and of course, I always hoped to be treated with respect. One of the rare and special occasions was when we discovered someone we were a fan of was also a fan of ours. Stephen King, it turned out, was a huge Ramones fan.

John and I were into science fiction and collected sci-fi posters. Ramones songs were, in some cases, musical sci-fi. Ultimately, science fiction wasn't about the special effects, however good they were getting lately. It was about the power of a story – with the help of the outer limits of knowledge – to probe your darkest fears, deepest insecurities, and wildest fantasies. In a movie like Stephen King's *Carrie*, a homely girl gets picked on by the brats in her high school, which happens every day in real life. What doesn't happen every day is that girl's rage triggering her telekinesis and creating a vengeful bloodbath. We were all outcasts sometime, somewhere. We just didn't get to torch and decapitate the school bullies by blinking our eyes.

During a brief Ramones swing through New England, Stephen King invited us up to his home in Bangor, Maine. The house was a classic Victorian structure with a slightly haunted look. King had piercing eyes you could tell had read and written a lot of books. He was really friendly and happy to meet us. He served us a big dinner in the basement, but the real treat down there was all the props and memorabilia, mostly from sci-fi and horror movies, and not just the ones based on his books. *Godzilla, Night of the Living Dead, The Blob, The Texas Chainsaw Massacre* – it was a museum of some of the best gore ever splashed across the silver screen. John's eyes became as piercing as King's.

During a break in the friendly Yankees–Red Sox debate between John and King, the legendary author handed Dee Dee a copy of his bestselling novel, *Pet Sematary*. It was the story of a graveyard where cats and dogs were resurrected and humans inevitably followed. The problem was, they became ghoulish and bloodthirsty. As the baseball and movie trivia session continued, Dee Dee disappeared for a while. That usually meant trouble. But, in less than an hour, he came down the stairs, book in hand. In the other hand was a piece of typing paper with some words scribbled on it. Dee Dee had written a song called 'Pet Sematary'. He had condensed the book into a concise, hooky, three-minute song in which he pleaded that he didn't want to live his life again.

I could see why he didn't. Dee Dee's life had gotten hard. But when it came to writing songs, he had definitely done it again. Dee Dee hummed it for King and the rest of us, and a title track was born. *Pet Sematary* the movie was set to begin shooting the following month, and Stephen King wanted the song, as long as it was recorded by his favorite punk band of all time.

Out on the front porch a little later I asked Dee Dee why he wanted to quit the band, as good as he was at what he did. He had heard this question from me at least a dozen times, and I had the answers memorized. He wanted to be Dee Dee King the rap artist, not Dee Dee Ramone. He was past the point of no return putting up with John and Joey's long-running cold war and sick of being looked upon by everyone as a problem child. As a liability. He was a toxic-waste dump site, as far as he was concerned, for blame. He wanted a life free of control by the Ramones, by Vera, by his doctors, and the medications they prescribed.

Whenever I heard this laundry list of complaints, I told him the truth – that I not only sympathized, I empathized. I told him that, if he got out from under the control of the drugs, the control by everyone else would become a nonissue because *he* would then be in control of his own life. I told him maybe the psychotropic drugs were masking the symptoms of whatever dope he was still using but that what he really needed to do was get clean of all substances, legal or not. I told him the band would probably wind down over the next couple years, and there was no reason the two of us couldn't hang on, hang out, and have a few laughs while socking away some decent money.

This time, on a front porch in Bangor, Maine, having just witnessed what I had witnessed, I figured I would try a different approach. I explained to Dee Dee that he was among maybe a handful of people who could pick up a book, skim it, and write a catchy song about it in under an hour. I told him he had done for punk what Stephen King had done for fiction: create, from scratch, images, themes, and stories that drew people in because they could relate. Because the songs penetrated to the curiosity, fears, and insecurities people carried around with them but couldn't put into words. I told him it was great to play Dee Dee King for a while, but he was really the *Stephen* King of punk. With a gift like that, he had a basic, fundamental need to use it. Dee Dee listened and stared silently into the dark New England woods.

For a guy with one foot out the door, Dee Dee contributed a lot to our next album. The foot that was still in wrote at least half the songs, including the straight-ahead rocker 'I Believe in Miracles', the punk-metal song 'Zero Zero UFO', the anthem 'Punishment Fits the Crime', and of course the movie ballad 'Pet Sematary'.

It was a struggle for John to play the arpeggios and chords in 'Sematary', even with Dee Dee coaching him. The style was a bit of a late-eighties rock ballad with a lot of tasteful picking. After a while Daniel Rey laid down both the rhythm tracks and then the lead, which John was never going to do in the first place. Daniel also helped with the structure of the song. Jean Beauvoir of the Plasmatics produced, and gave it a commercial feel to make it radio and movie friendly.

The Ramones were way past craving a so-called hit, having experienced repeated disappointments over many, many years creating a sort of Zenlike approach to the recording process. High expectations were a way to set yourself up for another fall. But having a song in a major motion picture couldn't hurt.

Our main producer, Bill Laswell, had an avant-garde background. He had worked with Brian Eno and Herbie Hancock. He was jazz-influenced, which I liked, and he had even worked with my friend and Voidoids bandmate Bob Quine. Bill experimented with my sound by placing my drums up against a brick wall. The intention was to generate a lot of slap-back into the drum mikes.

It definitely did that. The effect was to make the drums very loud and up front. The snare in particular seemed to jump out of some of the songs instead of sitting nicely in the middle. I figured if a drummer like myself who enjoyed big drums thought they were too loud, we were likely to turn off just about everybody else. But this wasn't Ritchie Cordell in 1982, and I didn't have a bottle stashed in the bathroom garbage pail or anywhere else. I gave my thoughts to Bill Laswell calmly and politely, and we went about our business. For the first time on a Ramones album, my business included contributing lyrics, which I did on 'All Screwed Up' and 'Learn to Listen'.

There was more to like than not to like on the project. 'Can't Get You Outta My Mind' had a classic Ramones feel to it. I thought we played 'Miracles' a little too slow and the early-sixties cover 'Palisades Park' a little too fast, but *Brain Drain* was not a drain to record. If anything, it was energizing and moving us into the next decade.

The sound of rock radio was changing, and the record companies that passed on King Flux might have been on to something, whether or not it was a self-fulfilling prophecy. Guns N' Roses was all over the airwaves, and you could hear the punk influence on almost every song from their breakthrough album, *Appetite for Destruction*. Bands like the Red Hot Chili Peppers, R.E.M., Suicidal Tendencies, Jane's Addiction, Sonic Youth, and the Cure were getting heard. They were different from the Ramones and from one another, but all shared a sort of do-it-yourself attitude that started with sixties garage bands and, a bit later, punk.

FM radio was starting to play songs with eclectic mixes of sounds that defied easy categorization. There were more genre names than bands, but the one name that seemed to provide an umbrella for all of it was 'alternative'. We were hearing the word dropped here and there. The Ramones' music was diversifying, too. I didn't spend a lot of time wondering whether we were influencing these younger bands or they were influencing us. Clearly, both things were happening at the same time.

In the middle of all this evolution and progression, the final song on *Brain Drain* was Joey's 'Merry Christmas (I Don't Want to Fight Tonight)'. Going back to Irving Berlin, nice Jewish boys had a knack for writing catchy Christmas tunes. Ours had enough of a Ramones feel not to be a campy sellout and enough of a doo-wop holiday spirit to actually get cued up during the Yuletide season.

Our breath looked as if it had been produced by fog machines. That was fitting for a video being shot in a graveyard. But this fog came naturally. It was January 1989, and we were shooting the video for 'Pet Sematary'. As in all horror flicks, even three-and-a-half-minute ones, the scariest scenes were shot at night. The temperature was twenty degrees Fahrenheit and falling, and Joey, Dee Dee, John, and yours truly were all freezing our asses off. Sleepy Hollow wasn't any run-of-the-mill cemetery. Located just north of Tarrytown, New York, near the Hudson River, Sleepy Hollow was the setting for Washington Irving's short story 'The Legend of Sleepy Hollow'. In it, the lovelorn Ichabod Crane gets chased through the graveyard by the fabled Headless Horseman. At the moment, the Ramones had another graveyard occupational hazard to worry about. We were getting lowered into an open grave by a hydraulic lift. The lift was in the hole, hidden from the camera, so all that would be seen were the Ramones, slowly disappearing into the grave as we played 'Pet Sematary'.

I stood next to Joey, who sang as I pounded a drum kit just big enough to play a dirge. We both had prescription sunglasses on, which are ideal for reading tombstone inscriptions in three-hundred-and-fifty-year-old cemeteries. Dashing and dancing around us were a couple dozen ghoulish characters who could have been the 'Sedated' video extras refitted with funeral garb. But a few – like Debbie Harry, Chris Stein, and members of the Dead Boys – were stars in their own right.

This video wasn't pretend slow motion. The lift dropped ever so slowly, giving plenty of time for the bone-chilling winds to penetrate our leather jackets. The cast placed a large headstone over us with 'The Ramones' written on it. That was take one and probably the closest we were ever going to get to dying on a set. The problem was take two. And then take three. Dee Dee had written he didn't want to live again. The real horror was dying again.

When the klieg lights were turned off and the crew disappeared, all who were left were Dee Dee, me, and my friend Mike. The three of us had driven up together in my silver two-door 1979 Cadillac Coupe de Ville. Mike brought along Max, his 120-pound Rottweiler, who was getting anxious and seemed a little spooked. The darkness had closed in quickly. With the darkness and the quiet came faint sounds of leaves, trees, and night owls you would never notice in the commotion of a video shoot. This was not a set. It was a real graveyard.

We made it to the Coupe by the partial light of the moon and the distant glow of the town of Sleepy Hollow. There was some relief as I flicked on the headlights, but we just wanted to get the hell out of there. We pulled away and made a left at something called Cataract Hill. We drove for a while, laughed as we warmed up a little in the car, and swung a gradual left around a site called Monticello.

'You sure this is it?' Mike said.

'This is the general direction,' I said.

I kept veering right, past headstones, ancient arches, monuments, mausoleums, and old stone walls built before there was such a thing as the United States and that would probably still be here afterward. Finally, we got to a clearing. It was the same place where we shot the video, and it now looked more desolate than ever.

'Do you know the way out of here?' Dee Dee asked.

'Do you?'

'I'm asking you,' Dee Dee said. 'You're driving.'

Mike was smart and said nothing. But Max was literally howling at the moon. I tried driving in the other direction. Even in a graveyard, streets have names, and Sleepy Hollow was no exception. Forest, Terrace, Lincoln – the one sign missing was the one that said 'This way out'. I tried a left on Pleasant Avenue. There was nothing pleasant about it. Sleepy Hollow was apparently arranged in a series of interconnected circles. We started recognizing headstones, which was never a good thing. As we tried another winding road Dee Dee looked out the front window, then the sides, panicked.

I didn't believe in ghosts but I believed in the DTs, and this was the closest I had come to seeing things since drying out. My mind, like every mind, was filled with movie scenes and random phobias, and a place like this was a mirror to every fear you could dig up. The Headless Horseman may or may not have been right around the next towering headstone, but he was definitely in our collective minds. Besides, dogs had better sensory perception than humans, and this dog, now growling in the backseat, was picking up on something frightening. I hoped it was only Dee Dee.

'I'm freaking out,' Dee Dee said. 'I just saw something with like a horn on it, Marc. And wings. We've gotta get the fuck out of here.'

'Dee Dee,' I said, 'how do you think we all feel? Do you think any of us want to be here?'

I stopped the car and idled near a little footbridge. Off in the distance I saw a bright stream of light and heard a gentle whoosh. That had to be Broadway, otherwise known as Route 9, which went all the way back to the city. A little closer, I saw an interior road that seemed to head straight out to Broadway. The problem was I didn't know how to get from here to there except to drive straight through, which is what I did. I put the Coupe in gear and rolled over a curb, then onto some grass and over a little hill. I swerved around one headstone then another and thought I missed them both. In the end, it didn't matter. They were already dead and we were just trying to stay alive.

We hit the pavement and tore out the front gate. It was like the end of our own little bonus Ramones horror video without the soundtrack. I wished I had brought along my Hi8 camera, but getting out was reward enough. I had never seen Dee Dee so desperate to get out of anything. *Almost* never.

On a sunny afternoon in April 1989, the Ramones held a press conference at the Hard Rock Cafe a little north of Times Square. *Brain Drain* was out and so was the movie, *Pet Sematary*. The song 'Pet Sematary' had hit number four on the *Billboard* Modern Rock chart. *Number four!* In the United States of America! I sipped my seltzer and glanced at Dee Dee, who was sitting next to me and shifting around in his seat. Then I thought about a song he had dashed off in another restless moment and how every time from here to eternity the movie ended and the closing credits rolled people would hear our song. The chart success wasn't the reason we were still together after all this time. But it was nice.

I picked up my seltzer again, put it to my mouth, and gagged. Some of the liquid dripped to the tablecloth but some went down my throat. Whenever something went down that wasn't supposed to there was a shock to the palate while the brain tried to identify the substance, fast. It took about a second. It was an old friend and enemy – vodka. Dee Dee grinned and took credit for the prank.

'Now I have more sober time than Marc!'

'Dee Dee,' I said, 'I wouldn't get too proud if I were you. It's a little early.'

Dee Dee had just over thirty days sober. He had shown all of us his one-month medallion. We were glad for him. But this was not a prank worthy of the Ramones. It was like tripping someone in the last mile of a marathon. Or pushing a Flying Wallenda off a high wire. It was low-class, low-rent, low-mentality. If there was anything I wanted Dee Dee to compete with me in it was sobriety. This was not the way to go about it.

Dee Dee's rap album, *Standing in the Spotlight*, had flatlined. There was no chart action. While looking to do a solo album of his own, Joey was actually rooting for Dee Dee. John was rooting for the opposite. I was in Dee Dee's corner as much as anyone. A cover song like 'Mashed Potato Time' was silly to begin with and too ridiculous to put on an album competing with N.W.A and artists who had already been at the rap game for half a lifetime. But a song like '2 Much 2 Drink' could have been sold to the Beastie Boys and done well.

There were other songs on the album I thought Dee Dee should have saved for the Ramones. In a thumbs-up/thumbs-down world, I hoped Dee Dee had a little perspective on the album's flopping, but at this point I wasn't sure if he had much perspective on anything.

I looked up at the 1960 Cadillac Coupe hanging from the Hard Rock Cafe ceiling. It was my car. Not simply the same model. It was my *actual* car, salvaged from the scrapyard and put on display like an Eric Clapton guitar. I thought about my state of mind when the car caught on fire on Ocean Avenue. More than a car was going up in flames back then. Every single day these days, even a simple uneventful one at home, was a tribute to being sober and healthy. A day like today was even better. When you're sober, you can truly appreciate what you've done and what you have. That's what I wanted for Dee Dee.

On the flight back east from our California tour, Dee Dee told us the 5 July show we had just done in Santa Clara was his last. He had been saying that for a few weeks, but, in Dee Dee's case, we took things with a grain of salt. More like a truckload of salt. Still, we had to give him credit. He had proven he could make absolutely horrendous decisions and follow through on them. The previous month, he had left Vera. Dee Dee was off his medication, Vera insisted he go back on, and Dee Dee decided to ditch them both.

On the plane ride back, he proudly showed us a new pair of boots he had picked up in LA for his new girlfriend. He was pretty thoughtful for someone completely out of his mind. Even the punks knew that Dee Dee had blown it. When we were walking together on the Sunset Strip, a couple of spiky-haired kids with nose rings shouted from across the street, 'Go back to Vera!'

John was one of those punks, at least in theory. He was outraged that Dee Dee left his better half and told him to his face he couldn't treat Vera like an old pair of shoes. This was more than a little ironic coming from someone who had left more than one pair of shoes behind. It was still more ironic considering that back in 1978 John was dead set against the marriage. If he had shown up to the ceremony – and he did not – John might have been the one standing up in the back and telling the priest why this union should not take place.

John's concept of rock-star marriage was a page out of the early Beatles playbook – don't do it, and, if you have to, hide it from the fans, especially the young girls. They wanted their knights in shining leather eligible. That's what Brian Epstein had John Lennon do with Cynthia, and that's what Johnny Ramone wanted to do with Dee Dee Ramone. Worse yet, over the years Johnny Ramone took potshots at Dee Dee and Vera Ramone whenever he could. It was a little late in the game to be a marriage counselor.

A few days later, John called me at our apartment in Brooklyn. Gary Kurfirst had called him to say that Dee Dee's quitting was 100 per cent real and we needed to have an emergency meeting. If this was an emergency, it was like Venice sinking. Even the dead flies on the van windshield knew Dee Dee was looking to quit. But I went to the meeting.

John said it was fine that he quit. *Let him*. John had a master plan to find a young Dee Dee without the drugs. Nothing was going to stop John. And anyway, he said, Dee Dee was still going to write songs for the Ramones. I agreed we should continue as a band. That was the practical, business side of me talking. In the rear of my mind, I was trying to make a mental adjustment and not getting very far. Dee Dee's quitting the Ramones was like Paul McCartney's quitting the Beatles. Talk about brain drain! I tried to remind myself that the Ramones were not a person. We were a band made up of people, and one of those people was very unhappy and had serious problems to deal with. He was Dee Dee Ramone for almost twenty years. He was Dee Dee King for about a day. But he was Doug Colvin his whole life, and I hoped he would find some real joy in that life.

19

You could advertise for almost anything in the *Village Voice* and get at least a few responses. The *Voice* readership could not be shocked. But at least a few people had to be surprised to spot a musicians-wanted ad in mid-July looking for a bassist to replace Dee Dee Ramone. We rented out the big room at SIR downtown for auditions.

On the first day, at least fifty guys lined the hallway. They came in all shapes, sizes, and colors. I didn't recognize anyone, but they definitely recognized us. There was a buzz in the hallway and any time John or I poked our head out of the rehearsal room, they looked like fans waiting to get a peek backstage. And that's basically what they were – Ramones fans hoping to get that once-in-a-lifetime shot, sort of the punk version of the movie *Rocky*.

Gary Kurfirst had his office make some calls, and there was no one of any punk or hard-rock notoriety available. They were all in their original band or in their next band or the one after that. It was just as well. The Ramones started as the ultimate do-it-yourself band, and here we were, still doing it ourselves and by the seat of our pants. Besides, you never knew who you might find out there.

At first, with each auditioning bassist, I missed Dee Dee a little more. Then things started to get a little better. A couple of auditions looked like they weren't going to melt down from nerves. Then a few showed some chops. Nothing amazing. Promising, maybe. But John wasn't so much listening as looking. There was a guy with a long beard who was decent, and once he left the room, he became 'Rabbi Ramone' to John. A capable black bassist was dubbed 'Spook Ramone'. A Chinese guy auditioning was 'Li-Li Ramone'.

John was having the time of his life not only coming up with names but also knowing how much I hated it. What I hated even more was sending talent out the door. The Chinese guy was really good. He had a nice, clean, powerful attack on the strings. When he played 'Sedated', I didn't have to make little adjustments for his timing. We started, and he was right there all the way through.

'That's not our image,' John said.

'John, the ad didn't say we were looking for a Dee Dee clone.'

A few more bassists came and went, but then John lit up. A long-haired guy named Chris from Long Island played an okay version of 'Sedated', but Johnny Ramone looked as if he had just seen a young Jack Bruce. John went over and spoke to Chris for a while and made sure we had his correct home phone number. The kid looked as if he had just talked to God.

After the last audition closed the door behind him, John told me Chris was it. I didn't see it, and I told John so. Chris seemed like a finger player who wasn't experienced at using a pick. His downstroke wasn't as strong as Dee Dee's, and some of the fast eighth notes weren't all there. His hands weren't as big, and so his left hand didn't have the control over the frets I was used to hearing. The strings not being played at any given moment were supposed to be muted, but that wasn't happening consistently. The overall effect was a lot of clicking in the bass sound.

John told me I was getting way too technical. The kid had a youthful look, John said, and a lot of energy. Most important, he could be molded. I knew John would be doing most of the molding, and that scared me.

Chris came back for a second audition, did a decent job on 'Blitzkrieg

Bop' and 'Rock 'n' Roll High School', and got the job. His situation was apparently all systems go. He had been in the marines but explained he was honorably discharged and living with his parents in Deer Park. He was free to hit the road and dine in a wide variety of Cracker Barrels. Monte told him the first thing he needed to do when he got back to Deer Park, even before he called all his friends, was apply for a passport. We were headed to England, Australia, and New Zealand in October.

Chris's full name was Christopher Joseph Ward. 'Chrissie' rhymed with 'sissy' and was already the first name of Chrissie Hynde, who fronted the Pretenders for many years. So we took his first two initials and C. J. Ramone was born.

A little later in the summer, Marion and I were invited to dinner by Dee Dee and his new girlfriend. Dee Dee had moved into a large loft on Broadway just south of Houston Street. When we arrived, we realized that Dee Dee and his girlfriend were two of six people living in the loft. I traded a few quick startled glances with Marion. It wasn't that Dee Dee was bouncing off the walls. He was, but we were used to that. Either he was on his medication, off his medication, or on some new combination. What was strange was seeing Dee Dee transplanted into a whole new apartment, crowd, and context. I wanted the old Dee Dee Ramone back. At this point, I would even take Dee Dee King.

Dee Dee told us his girlfriend was going to be the next big thing. She was a folk-rock singer, and he was her bandleader and cowriter. We were all invited to see them play. I pulled Dee Dee aside, out of earshot from everyone.

'Do you know what you're doing?'

'Does it look like I know what I'm doing?'

'No. Not really.' I was being honest.

The following week Marion, Monte, and I went to Dee Dee's show at a dive bar downtown. Dee Dee's girlfriend had kind of a Marianne Faithfull thing going on. Dee Dee apparently was looking to be her Mick Jagger. We were supportive and polite, but Monte couldn't hold back a comment or two under his breath.

'Don't quit your day job. Oh, wait a second – you already did.'

C.J.'s day job was not only to learn a lot of Ramones songs. It was to learn to be Dee Dee. It was a tough job, but somebody had to do it. The assignment was for the stage only. John did his best to make sure C.J. was clean. John also put him to the test a lot like you would a Broadway understudy. C.J. was responsible for learning Dee Dee's performance moves – the jumping, midair splits, bouncing, the half-crazed 'one-two-three-four . . .' I had to admit C.J. had a great attitude. He did what we asked him and didn't complain, and in that sense was as far from Dee Dee as you could get.

Then, one night in August, I got a call from C.J. and freaked out. He was calling from a military prison. I got the story in bits and pieces. The story I was told was that he had asked his commanding officer to be released so that he could help his mother, who had been diagnosed with lupus, and also deal with a couple other unfortunate family situations. It was complicated, and C.J. was rambling, but the bottom line, I was told, was he left the base before receiving his papers. When it came to learning that you were military property, there was a hard way and a harder way. The harder way was to wake up to your mother screaming that the military police were at the door. I knew what C.J. was thinking even before he said it. It was what any at least half-sane person in the same position would have feared. He was almost in tears.

'This was a once-in-a-lifetime opportunity,' he said. 'I want you to know I appreciate it, and I'm sorry. But I blew it. I fucking blew it.'

'Hold on,' I said. 'You didn't blow anything. Do you have a lawyer?'

'Yeah . . . yeah, my parents are getting one for me.'

'Okay,' I said. 'Good. If you have any trouble with that or need another referral, call me. In the meantime, if what you said is true, that you did inform your commanding officer, you may have a way out of this. We don't have to leave till the end of September, and you already know most of the songs. So hang in there, okay?'

'Thanks, man. Thank you.'

I tried to handle the phone call the way my father would have – calm things down, put everything in perspective, and make sure there was legal representation. I had been given a second chance and everyone, including C.J., deserved one – especially since he hadn't really had a first chance. I told him to make sure he talked to John. C.J. was nervous about that, but I assured him it would be no problem. John was his number-one fan and wasn't crazy about military school back in the day.

C.J. was released within a couple of weeks with an official discharge. His first real day on the job was doing the *Jerry Lewis MDA Telethon* on Labor Day. C.J. was more grateful to be there than Jerry or any of his kids. The only problem was, the prison barber had given C.J. a military buzz cut.

We had to wait so long to go on, C.J.'s hair grew back a little. When we told people we were doing the telethon, they seemed to think we were flying out to Las Vegas to hang with Jerry and Ed McMahon. Maybe Frank Sinatra would drop by and bring Dean Martin along for a surprise visit. But we were in WWOR-TV studios, Nine Broadcast Plaza in Secaucus, New Jersey, with the other New York performers.

We watched Jerry on TV like everyone else. He looked drained and by two in the morning complained of a migraine from the phones not ringing enough. Around two thirty, he looked wearily into the camera and said, 'It's the right hour. Get off your ass, for crying out loud.' Around three, the Ramones got off their asses and played. We were not making our national debut as a skinhead band. C.J. wore a bandana.

Our tour of Germany brought us to Berlin on 27 November. The Ramones were happy with C.J., who brought a ton of energy to the shows. He had learned a lot of moves from old tapes of the band. His playing was getting better. His backup vocals were solid. He was as grateful to be in the band as anyone had ever been to be anywhere, and his attitude was good. His hair was even growing back quickly.

But I had one problem with C.J. It wasn't that he gravitated toward John. That was natural. John was his biggest advocate. The problem was that he started to sound like John. I had to hear it in monotone for so many years. Now I had to hear it in stereo.

I was watching a transformation take place slowly in vans, buses, airplanes, and dressing rooms. It was exactly the kind of 'molding' I hated to see. Without a doubt, there was some brown-nosing going on, and at least for me, viewing it that way made it more understandable. He was the new guy in the band aiming to please and being led down the wrong path.

Personally, I was definitely not there to be a killjoy. I was still pranking people and being pranked. I was still eating an occasional windshield bug. But there were times when I couldn't let the 'schooling' continue without a pushback. Some shock treatment was needed.

The Berlin Wall had started coming down earlier in the month. It wasn't done all at once or because of a government decree. The people of both sides had just worn down the system. East Germany had been grudgingly selling 'day passes' to its people to visit West Berlin. West Berlin was allowing trips in the other direction. German citizens from both sides started showing up with picks and sledgehammers and busting through the concrete. The guards had orders but just gave up. They probably would have joined in if they were off duty.

When I visited the wall near the Brandenburg Gate, it was still serving its official purpose, but there were holes and cracks all over and more being made as I watched. People were hacking at the wall, smiling, taking pictures, and walking away with little concrete souvenirs. We were living in the true-life version of Martha and the Vandellas' song 'Dancing in the Street'. I walked over to a hole about a foot and a half in diameter and put my hand clear through to the other side. Someone in East Berlin – not more than two feet away – shook my hand. I shook it back. Two thoughts flashed through my mind. One was what an amazing way this was to experience history. The other was I definitely missed Dee Dee.

We were back in Secaucus in the summer of 1990, this time for an appearance on *The Howard Stern Show*. Stern had rewritten the rules of talk radio in the 1980s and became the poster boy for the new term 'shock jock'. Part of his reward was a weekend TV show on WWOR. Another reward was getting to hang out with some of his favorite rock bands, and the Ramones were one of them. We were Howard Stern fans, too. Whenever we did the radio or TV show, Howard would mention how much he looked like Joey, and he had a point.

They ran a skit we had taped for the show. In it, Joey and I played golf with President George Bush. The Bush impersonator was top-notch, almost on Dana Carvey's level. The president kept calling us Dee Dee, and we kept reminding him Dee Dee quit the band. Between drives with a 3-iron, Bush tried to recruit us to write a pro-war song to get the kids involved. The best we could come up with was 'I don't want to be buried in an Iraqi cemetery'. It was one time we really needed John's help with lyrics.

We had the whole crew laughing – Robin Quivers, Jackie 'The Joke Man' Martling, Fred Norris, and the producer Gary Dell'Abate. For me, the most entertaining part was the interview that followed. Howard and Robin were really interested in our sobriety, and I gave them the *Reader's Digest* version of my experience. Joey announced that he was seven months sober.

I had seen enough not to believe it, but I wasn't there to argue. Joey went on to explain that he never even had a real problem. He just enjoyed drinking and partying. He was sober on the road, he said, but found he was partying too much off the road. He didn't need to enter a program like Marky. Instead, he just decided to stop. Howard and Robin didn't challenge Joey on this. Instead, they told him he never looked healthier. I happened to think he looked white as a sheet. But even if I had wanted to offer a differing opinion, there was no time. The whole segment devolved into a pitch for Snapple.

Unfortunately, life wasn't as simple as a Snapple commercial. Two days before New Year's, we were backstage getting ready to play a major show at the Ritz in New York. Two guys I had never seen before were hanging around Joey. One of them said, 'Um, Marc, I hate to ask you this, but can you leave the room for a few minutes?' As if I didn't know what for. As if this didn't come straight out of an addict's playbook. I left the room anyway.

When I walked back in, Joey was wiping his nose and snorting. It was like a modern version of the old story where the king says he can't stand to see his subjects suffer so he tells the guards to torture them in another room. This wasn't *The Howard Stern Show*. I wasn't going to let it go.

'Joey, can I ask you something? Do you think I'm stupid?'

'Why do you say that, Marc?'

'Because it was obvious that you guys were using from the moment the two of them walked in here.'

'I just figured you wouldn't appreciate seeing that.'

'Listen to me,' I said. 'I'm your drummer and your friend, but I'm not your parent. I'm not an enforcer, and I'm not a babe in the woods. I'm not here to tell you what to do. It's your life. It's none of my business.'

A few months later, though, I made it my business. Joey wasn't any more eager to go to a meeting than Dee Dee had been a couple years earlier. Monte had all my respect for getting Joey out of his apartment over the years for shows. But on this day I deserved a tip of the cap for getting him out to go to AA. My MO was similar to before. I found a meeting on St. Marks Place, not far from his apartment. Joey was already complaining about it on the walk over. At least he wouldn't be driving his car up on the front lawn.

I made the usual introduction.

'Hi, I'm Marc. I'm an alcoholic.'

The other people at the meeting were fairly young and hip, and given the location that made sense. They told stories of how they were helped by friends, family, God, self-discipline, and self-respect. Some were stuck on this step or that. Joey was stuck in his seat sneering. On the walk back to his apartment, he avoided stepping on the cracks in the sidewalk and complained.

'Look, *Merk*, I'm not into this God crap.'

'No one's telling you you have to be.'

'Oh yeah, right,' Joey said. 'That's all I heard in there was God did this and God did that. What a bunch of shit.'

'Joey, that was a few people – not everybody. It's not about God in there. It's not about religion. It's about using whatever you can focus on to help you get sober. There's no written rules. The Twelve Steps are guidelines. They're suggestions. As time goes on, you learn what works best for you. And you learn from other people.'

'C'mon, Marc, it's like a cult.'

'You're totally wrong, Manny! That's bullshit. A cult has a leader. Someone no one even questions. There's no leader in there. Didn't you notice that? It's just people helping each other. It's you and your sponsor figuring things out. It's a program. If you can just deal with the program and deal with yourself, you can conquer a lot of your problems. But I guess you just don't want to.'

'I'm gonna stop on my own.'

He did stop. Then he started again. Then he stopped. And so on. He was a recreational drug user and a dry drunk. Millions of people were. When he was dry, it was an addiction on pause. His attitude, anxiety, stress, and fears were still in full force. His overall train of thought was the same. I knew from experience that there was only so much you could accomplish by dealing with your addiction. *What you had to deal with was life, on life's terms.* Without a change in approach and a real support system, you were always one bad day, one bad break, one bad conversation, one bad thought away from the next drink.

Having a drink is not the same as selling a drink. In 1991, the Ramones were offered a good sum of money by the Anheuser-Busch Companies for the use of 'Blitzkrieg Bop' in a Budweiser commercial. There was no conversation within the band as to whether to accept. We weren't the Doors debating whether or not to allow General Motors to produce a jingle with the line 'Come on, Buick, light my fire.' The Ramones were capitalists. We had our capitalists from the right and our capitalists from the left, but we all spelled it with a capital C.

Like a lot of Ramones songs, 'Blitzkrieg' was loud, fast, and catchy, so we weren't exactly dumbfounded by the offer. It didn't take a lot of imagination to see a song like that helping sell beer to a bunch of guys on the couch watching football. But we were curious as to why now. The answers were hitting us in the face and in the eardrums every day. So-called grunge bands such as Nirvana and Soundgarden were breaking. Hardcore and thrash bands such as Biohazard and Anthrax were selling millions of albums worldwide. There was a buzz surrounding a Bay Area pop-punk band called Green Day.

These sounds were beginning to take over MTV and even push their way into commercial radio. It was called 'new' music, but very little of it was really new to us. In almost all of it, we could find bits and pieces and sometimes whole chunks of things the Ramones and our fellow punk bands were doing fifteen years earlier. Through some strange process of percolation and osmosis, the sound the Ramones helped pioneer and then stuck with out on a limb for many years was going *mainstream*.

At the same time the mountain was coming to the Ramones, the Ramones were coming to the mountain. We had one more album to complete to fulfill our contractual obligation to Sire/Warner and decided it would be a live album. *Loco Live* was recorded in Barcelona, Spain, and included old, not so old, and new songs from the Ramones catalogue. *Loco Live* was recorded live, sort of. The live tracks were taken into a recording studio so that the guitar, bass, and vocals could be overdubbed. Essentially only the original drum tracks remained.

Those drum tracks were faster than I would have liked. It wasn't an issue of playing songs a little faster live than on the studio albums. This was a conscious decision being pushed by John, not just for Loco Live but also in our live shows, period. John's argument was the Ramones had developed a younger audience who were also listening to hardcore and thrash. The Ramones had an incentive and even a duty to deliver the goods.

That reasoning sounded nice on paper but not quite as nice on a CD. A song like 'Do You Remember Rock 'n' Roll Radio?' speeded way up lost a lot of its soul. Joey's phrasing suffered when certain words were squeezed in while others were squeezed out. It was not 'Do You Remember Hardcore Radio?' Or, as I reminded John, in the words of the great Chuck Berry, if you try to play it too darn fast, you lose the beauty of the melody.

Even John's guitar phrasing suffered. He couldn't play true eighth notes with a downstroke at those tempos. No one could. But no one else even bothered to try. Hardcore and thrash guitarists were strumming faster, up and down. In a breakneck race to 'keep up' on his own terms John was sometimes fudging fours by using a triplet and letting the third chord ring a little longer. I didn't think we needed to put ourselves through the grinder.

Whether it was John's way or just the way of the future, something felt different in April when we got off the plane in Buenos Aires, Argentina. As the name said, the air was good. So was the vibe. We were used to fans following us around here and there in twos and threes and small groups. In Argentina, a group of maybe three hundred were waiting for us at the airport. There were more kids hanging around the hotel, so the hotel staff had to work a little harder, showing us alternate exits from the building. The venue held about four thousand. We were playing more shows lately of that size in venues like the Roseland Ballroom in New York and the Brixton Academy in London. But these four thousand fans sounded more like fourteen thousand.

It was more of the same in São Paulo, Brazil. The chants of 'Hey Ho, Let's Go!' were even louder than we were used to. They started well before the show and continued well after the second and final encore. The fans spoke primarily Portuguese, but when it came to singing out the lyrics to 'Sedated', 'Sheena', and 'KKK', their English was great. The singalong wasn't just an oldies show. They nailed songs like 'I Believe in Miracles' and 'Pet Sematary'. That proved a lot of things, among them that these kids were buying albums. And, if the speed of the music cramped Joey's phrasing a bit, it definitely didn't bother the kids.

We tried to take that spirit into the studio in early 1992 when we recorded *Mondo Bizarro*. It seemed like the timing was right and that our time had come. Nirvana had taken over the airwaves. Labels were signing bands just for wearing flannel and being able to pronounce the word *Seattle*. Green Day's album *Kerplunk* was making a sound more like *cha-ching*. If we had somehow opened the door for these bands, we now wanted them to hold the door open for us a little longer so we could walk through a second time bigger, better, louder, and faster than ever.

Some things would be the same as many times before. We had Ed

Stasium producing. Dee Dee, who was wandering the city and the globe like an ex-punk messiah, had contributed three songs. We made a conscious effort to go back to a classic Ramones sound. What's old is what's new.

Some other things were not the same. For one, we were no longer with Sire/Warner. Gary Kurfirst had persuaded us to sign with his label, Radioactive, a division of Chrysalis. As a manager, Gary had secured us bigger venues. There was no argument there. But leaving Seymour Stein and Sire – even as a stepchild of Warner – felt more bitter than sweet. Seymour was an uncle to us, and one who let us do whatever we wanted in the backyard. He gave us the creative freedom that most artists could barely dream of. We were leaving that for something else, but who knew exactly what?

The other issue was a lot more concrete. Gary was still and would remain our manager. One of a manager's jobs – though a job he never bargains for – is to push the record label for the best possible recording situation and promotion. As good a manager as Gary was and as good a label president as he could be, could we rely on Gary to push Gary? Was there a fox anywhere born to guard a chicken coop? We would find out. While John and I wanted to stay with Seymour, Joey wanted to go with Gary. So did Gary. Case in point.

The early favorite for a single was Dee Dee's 'Poison Heart'. Musically, it had the commercial appeal of an R.E.M. track but the lyrics read like a page from Dee Dee's diary since he left the band to roam the streets. There were Dee Dee sightings on the Bowery, in West Hollywood, and across the Continent. In truth, he was involved with new musical projects like the short-lived Spikey Tops. But, whatever else the Ramones represented to Dee Dee, they were also a payday, and we were glad.

'Censorshit' was Joey's answer to Tipper Gore and the PMRC, who had been labeling albums for several years. The most quotable line was 'Ask Ozzy, Zappa, and me. We'll show you what it's like to be free.' It was good company to be in, even if Joey had to point it out himself. They were like an unholy trinity of rock and roll.

Joey's most memorable and hummable track on the album might have been 'Touring', a tribute to surf music left over from *Pleasant Dreams* eleven years earlier. It reminded us of the Beach Boys' 'Shut Down'. The hook was 'Touring, touring, never boring.' That was why I took my camera along.

I also took my notebook. When I wrote the lyrics to 'The Job That Ate My Brain', I was probably thinking of every job anyone ever had that on one hand they loved but on the other hand drove them a little crazy – like the job I had. The sci-fi title was in keeping with the finest Ramones tradition. In fact, the music itself could have been dropped in pretty easily to any of the early Ramones albums. I wanted to see more of that on *Mondo Bizarro*, but I was just one voice.

The cover song on the album was 'Take It as It Comes', from the Doors' first album. We got an able assist on the keyboard from Joe McGinty. There were lots of ways to do a cover, but basically only two ways – your own way or the original artist's way. Ours in this case was a fairly faithful version. We took it as it came. Joey did his best Jim Morrison, which was pretty good. It was the older, fatter, rough-throated Jim Morrison. Joey had been taking that approach more frequently both live and in the studio. He wasn't just the singer on 'Rockaway Beach' any more. And it wasn't much of a stretch.

Joey was getting a little fatter. Not like Jim Morrison *circa L.A. Woman*, where if you gave the Lizard King an axe he could have passed for a lumberjack. Joey was getting a little porkier around the hips. It was the same thing that happened to Dee Dee for the same reason.

As a medical diagnosis, OCD had been around for many years. As an FDA-approved drug, Prozac had been around for only a few years. What was even newer was prescribing one to treat the other. Psychiatrists were handing out Prozac prescriptions as if they were Lotto tickets. The results varied, but, in Joey's case, they seemed to be good. He was less moody and more outgoing. He seemed to be drinking less, though we couldn't be completely sure. He even displayed less tapping and fewer re-entrance problems. His mondo had gotten a little less bizarro.

Monte, of all people, deserved the break. Joey had moved into a one-bedroom apartment that opened up on the same floor as his studio. The new view included the large old-fashioned dial clock atop the Consolidated Gas Company Building on Fourteenth Street. That meant a ploy Monte had used for years was now, for all practical purposes, obsolete. On his way over for a pickup, Monte would tell Joey the current time was an hour or two later than it really was. Joey now had a local landmark to know otherwise. But Monte now had Prozac.

20

HELLO, WE MUST BE GOING

No one second-guessed Gary Kurfirst when he sent us down to South America in September to promote the just-released *Mondo Bizarro*. It was four consecutive shows in Buenos Aires, one in São Paulo, one in Rio de Janeiro, concluding with two shows up 'north' in Mexico City. Nirvana, our fourth cousin once removed, had virtually taken over North America. *Mondo Bizarro* had some decent reviews, and Dee Dee's 'Poison Heart' had topped out at a respectable number six on the *Billboard* Modern Rock chart. As in the previous eleven Ramones studio albums, there was no single runaway hit. It felt as if for a moment we had been suckered into believing it could still happen for us so late in the game. But at the same time, it really didn't matter. We were home. Sort of.

Saying South America was our home was no insult to our roots. It was just the way we felt at that very instant. How could we feel any different? We were greeted like returning conquerors. The kids at the airport were greater in number than before and held up more signs. The kids at the hotel were more determined and better at eluding security. In between the airport and the hotel, fans chased our van – sometimes in cars, sometimes on foot. And we hadn't played a note yet.

'Hey Ho, Let's Go!' was the international phrase for a Ramones encore. They were like the code words for getting into an after-hours club. In Buenos Aires, we got the 'Hey Ho' from the get-go. It echoed like thunder off the back wall of a twenty-thousand-seat soccer stadium. Even with a natural amplification of twenty thousand, we could pick up the Spanish accent. It was still more apparent when they chanted the band's name – 'Ra-mon-es . . . Ra-mon-es . . .'

They knew more than our names. They knew the lyrics to 'Poison Heart', which had been out all of a few days. This was just one more thing Dee Dee should have been around for. Joey could have done the cheesy eighties arena-rock thing, stopped singing, and pointed the microphone out over the audience. But that was never us. Neither were hugs, high fives, clowning around onstage, or long speeches about how great it was to be in country X. As far as we were concerned, that was all a waste of time. If we were really happy to be in country X, we showed it by playing.

It seemed in Buenos Aires that was all understood. It seemed that even with a language barrier, the fans 'got' everything we were about. Not to look a gift horse or a gift nation in the mouth, but I had to wonder why. There were at least a few obvious answers. In a class-conscious country like Argentina, where for centuries there was a caste system, the Ramones might have represented a leveling of the playing field. All you needed were sneakers, jeans, a T-shirt, and a leather jacket and you were one of us. Membership may not have been free, but it was certainly cheap.

We weren't experts on South American politics, but we knew that Argentina had lived through one oppressive military regime after another with a few breaks in between. The current government was democratically elected, but even the younger members of the audience had some memory of the last 'reorganization' in the late seventies and early eighties. In 'reorganization', anyone perceived to be a political threat might be taken away in the middle of the night and never heard from again. That meant mothers, fathers, aunts, uncles, brothers, sisters, and friends.

I thought about that when the Buenos Aires crowd sang 'The KKK Took My Baby Away'. They loved that song. They sang it louder and clearer than any other. Maybe they related to it in a way we couldn't possibly understand when Joey wrote it as a goof. A song that was supposed to hit the funny bone instead struck a deep chord.

The best explanation for our popularity below the equator was perhaps the simplest. The young people spent most of their lives dealing with shitty governments, shitty jobs, and shitty surroundings. A rock show – any good rock show – provided a short but huge relief from reality and sent a booming message to authority. A good rock band were a bunch of antiheroes. Maybe, just maybe, the Ramones – with our street look, loud obnoxious songs, and no-bullshit stage presence – were the perfect antiheroes.

Rio was just as crazy in its own way. Kids in Ramones T-shirts waving handmade 'Hey Ho, Let's Go!' banners were camped out night and day in the street outside our hotel rooms. They not only knew where we were staying, they figured out which rooms by watching the windows attentively from below. We didn't feel stalked. We felt flattered. Eventually we gave them what they wanted. We walked out onto the balcony, smiled, and waved. Their response was more than just screaming hysteria. From two or three stories below, they tossed up Ramones T-shirts. We knew what to do – catch them, sign them, and throw them back down.

Getting from point A to point B in Rio required planning and coordination. Monte's already full-time job became double-time. Every movement outside the confines of the hotel had to be squared with our security, who were big, beefy South American guys. Leaving the hotel was like a getaway, with fans swarming the driveway and then the van itself as we pulled away. It was tempting for the driver to tear out, but with fresh young Brazilian faces pressed against the windows on all four sides, that might have meant killing someone. There was an art to accelerating gradually and slowly shedding loyal fans. Our driver had mastered it.

His job was never quite done, at least not till we flew out of town. There was the trip from the airport to the hotel. Then the hotel to the sound check. Then from the sound check back to the hotel. Then back to the venue that night for the show. Then back to the hotel at the end of the night. Everything was choreographed. Forget about leaving the hotel on your own to see a few sights. You might disappear, South American style.

Mexico City sits about a mile and a half above sea level, which makes the air thinner. Marathoners from sea-level countries became light-headed and in some cases even fainted during the 1968 Olympics. Playing drums for a full set in the Ramones was like a marathon, but there was no chance my energy was going to let down. In Mexico City, what the air lacked in oxygen it made up for in sheer excitement. Besides, your lungs got used to it by the second day.

In Mexico City, as in the other great Latin cities we were playing, the fans wanted a piece of you. Not literally, but the next best thing. They wanted a souvenir. Signed T-shirts were cool but not the pinnacle. For most fans, nothing beat a drumstick.

But the simplest thing in the world wasn't that simple. In my mind, quantity did not equal quality. I had seen other drummers bring dozens of pairs to a show and throw out to the crowd sticks they never used. I took the opposite approach. I signed a few pairs of sticks opposite the label before the show. I waited till the right time during the show, usually when there were a few moments between certain songs, and threw the pair one at a time out to the audience. Then I picked up the next pair. The souvenirs were genuine and personal Marky Ramone drumsticks. Not everyone could have one. This wasn't Bat Day at Yankee Stadium.

I had on occasion in my earlier days thrown sticks overhand like a fastball. Not a good idea. You could put out a fan's eye that way. I never did, but the possibility concerned me. Over time, I developed a gentle but very accurate pitch. I could put a drumstick in row R, seat 15, most of the time. These considerations might have seemed like minutiae to a lot of people, but they were important to me. I felt lucky to be playing such large venues far from home. We were no longer just a band. We were ambassadors.

In June 1994, we were on tour in Europe, leaving Brussels. Traveling from city to city by rail in the US would have been beyond unthinkable for a band. Europe's rail system, however, was excellent and getting better. Just the month before, the Chunnel, linking France and Great Britain via rail tunnel, had opened after many years of work. Later in the year, all the connections would be complete and a passenger would be able to travel from Brussels to London in two hours without ever lifting off the ground.

The Ramones had to fly this afternoon, but with our feet. The promoters had done their job by dropping us off at the Brussels Eurostar station, except at the wrong end. We had a couple of kilometers to walk and less than a half-hour to pick up our tickets, board, and leave. The mezzanine at the station in Brussels was an endless array of columns in perfect square patterns. Outside, the arches and trusses gave the station a grandeur we rarely saw back home. Most remarkable of all was how incredibly clean everything was. That might have been the beginning of Joey's problem.

When the rest of the Ramones finally arrived and took our seats in the first-class compartment, we still had some time to settle in. The stewards took our coats and bags and offered us drinks. We were not as comfortable as we might have been because Joey and Monte were nowhere to be found. When Monte finally showed up he was huffing, puffing, and sweating bullet trains. Joey was being detained.

We couldn't blame Belgian rail security for wondering. Joey's medication wasn't perfect. He still tapped here and there. He was still Joey, still unkempt, and still attracting attention. To boot, he was seeing a wacky homeopathic chiropractor who saddled him with aloe juice and a wide variety of herbal pills. When Belgian security frisked Joey and went through his bag, they found a massive stash of salves, concoctions, and prescription medications, at least one bottle of which they were convinced was ecstasy. Monte, as always, was doing his best to be in two places at once. There was still a little time to broker a deal.

'Don't worry about it, Monte,' John said. 'We don't have a show till tomorrow. He'll catch up with us.'

He did, and, with Monte's hostage-negotiating skills, it was only a matter of minutes. Once we were shooting through the fields of Belgium at 280 kilometers per hour, Joey and Monte cooled down and settled in. To everyone's amazement, Joey turned around and asked John a question.

'So, do you think the baseball players are gonna go on strike?'

John was startled. There was in fact a Major League strike looming, and John probably would have loved to talk about it, but he would have been more prepared to answer a talking horse.

'I dunno,' John said. 'I dunno.'

John stared blankly and Joey turned back around to face forward. He went out on a limb and was rebuffed. It was kind of sad, but we all knew it was the Prozac talking. Even Joey seemed to know that. It was like that weird, bold moment at a party when you're so buzzed you walk up and talk to the prettiest girl there and ask her to marry you. Even sadder was the fact that John and Joey really did have something important to talk about, and it wasn't whether a bunch of baseball players were going to stop playing. It was whether the Ramones were going to stop playing.

Both John and Joey were talking about it a lot, just not to each other. Green Day's album *Dookie* had gone platinum and then gone platinum again. That was bittersweet for the Ramones. Songs like 'Basket Case' and 'Longview' were catchy, powerful pop-punk. Anyone with half a working ear could hear the Ramones influence not just musically but in the attitude and the warped, self-deprecating lyrics. 'Basket Case' was the new 'Shock Treatment', and 'Longview' was the new 'Sedated'.

Personally, I felt energized by the new prominence of punk, though we weren't reaping the rewards on our home turf. Even that wasn't exactly true. We played all sorts of significant shows at home, and American rock icons like Eddie Vedder of Pearl Jam were our friends and fans. It was an honor and a thrill for them to wear the pinhead costume at a Ramones show. Slash could usually be seen wearing a Ramones T-shirt. Across the ocean, Bono invited us to play a huge show with U2 in Oviedo, Spain, and his biggest thrill seemed to be finally meeting us. Bono told us he had seen one of our shows in Dublin in the late seventies, gotten inspired by our sound and attitude, and never looked back. These tributes made me want to go right out there again and do even more. But John and Joey didn't feel the same way.

John was well into his forties and had his eye on a house in California. He had reconciled himself to the Ramones having achieved cult status and to the idea that the sky was no longer the limit – time was. The band's legacy had already crystallized in his mind, and he was okay with it. He wanted to relax, enjoy spending time with his friends, and maybe produce sci-fi and horror films like he had always talked about.

Joey was also in his forties. He liked Green Day, but the band's commercial success irked him. He and the other Ramones, after all this time, deserved better than being patted down in a Brussels train station. They deserved a real piece of the pie they had put in the oven so many years before. He still had music in him. Behind the prescription shades, his eyes lit up every time he talked about his solo project. But for the Ramones, maybe it was time to start winding down. And there was something else. Joey was sick. It wasn't discussed, but we all knew it.

John and Joey had played over two thousand shows together. Whether they liked it or not, the decision to call it quits was also going to have to be made together.

Adios Amigos was an appropriate title for our final studio album. We still had some gas left in the tank, but the goodbye was well thought out. Our amigos were everywhere, including Iggy Pop, the forerunner of everything punk was about. Our amigos were all over the world and growing in number even as we prepared to wrap it up.

For a supposedly dysfunctional family, we functioned really well and sometimes bordered on being a happy family. Daniel Rey produced and played lead guitar wherever necessary. We covered a Tom Waits song called 'I Don't Want to Grow Up', which was the answer to the question 'Why are you still playing in the Ramones?' We even covered the Motörhead tribute to our band, 'R.A.M.O.N.E.S.'

And Dee Dee wrote half the album. Who else could have written 'Born to Die in Berlin'? When I slipped my hand through the wall years earlier, I knew for sure he'd make it back to Berlin. I just hoped he'd make it back to the States again.

There was an expression on this side of the Atlantic called 'phoning it in'. It meant not putting in anything close to your best effort. Strangely, we set up a phone in the studio so Dee Dee could call in and sing the third verse of the song in German.

The back cover of the album was a photo of the band lined up against a wall, hands tied behind our backs, preparing to be executed by firing squad. In reality, we had a much better exit planned. We were going out in style.

A lot of being in a band feels like pushing a cart up a hill. Record, tour, record, tour – left, right, left, right. There is the fear that if you let go, the cart will start to roll backward and pick up steam. But, if you're really lucky, there comes a time when the cart is rolling downhill forward and all you have to do is enjoy the ride.

We didn't know exactly what had happened since we flew down to Rio de Janeiro the year before. But in March 1996, something was definitely different. The itinerary was pretty much the same. Sleeping on the long flight down was the same. As far as we knew, the Brazilian government was the same. But from the moment we touched down on the tarmac it was bedlam. The fan base had grown incrementally with each visit, but this time it was more than a quantum leap. We were going off the deep end.

Once we made it to the hotel alive, it was incredible to think we were going to have to leave again soon for the sound check at the stadium. That felt like swimming through shark-infested waters to a life raft and being told you had to swim back to shore. When we looked outside our balconies down into the parking lot, we saw thousands of kids. When they saw one of us step out, they pointed up and shrieked as if they had spotted a shooting star. A simple wave from above would drum up more hysteria. It was the closest a kid from Brooklyn or Queens could ever come to feeling like the Pontiff. We would soon be surrounded by the masses.

Less than an hour later, we sat in the van in the hotel garage as it prepared to venture out into the streets. A half-dozen members of the tour security force stomped around the foot of the driveway trying to keep the crowd at bay. Any moment we would have to roll through that crowd, and the last thing in the world we wanted to do was hurt Ramones fans. We were about to walk the plank. Or they were.

'Very well-organized, Monte,' John said.

'Jesus!' someone in the back of the van said.

'He's going to clear a path,' C.J. said.

'Yeah, right,' John said.

While we waited, a few girls had run up to the side of the van and were desperately pulling on the locked doors.

'What do these kids want?' John said.

'They want the band,' I said. 'They want T-shirts . . .'

'They want to tear you limb from limb,' John said. 'That's what they want.'

As the van began to push forward, the sea of youth swarmed us. We moved slowly and steadily as if through a car wash of stray arms, legs, and torsos. The pressure of hands, heads, and elbows seemed enough to break the glass and flood the cabin. There was a moment of relief as the sea parted slightly and we hit the street. But it was just a moment. As the van picked up a little speed, the throngs of fans in the street saw their chances fading and went to more desperate measures. From behind, they chased us on foot, one or two making it onto the rear bumper, riding along for a few seconds before dropping off.

Many more fans were able to press their flesh against the doors or even go for an extended ride before falling by the wayside. Healthy but temporarily insane young Brazilian faces were smashed up and contorted in the windows like monsters in a fun-house mirror. A lone daredevil threw his whole body onto the front windshield and bounced off, never to be seen again. We were traveling only about twenty miles per hour, so we were optimistic he would live to see another day if not that night's Ramones show.

Red lights were our enemies. They gave the delirious fans a chance to catch up to us and begin the process all over again. Whenever we shook off some of the swarm, there were reinforcements waiting along the route to the stadium. Their campaign was mapped out like a battle. Even other cars rolled up alongside us to see how long they could stay abreast, wave, yell, gawk, stalk, stare, and catch a Ramone in his natural habitat.

After the sound check there was an award ceremony with a sea of media. We were presented a Brazilian gold record for *Mondo Bizarro*. It wasn't too little too late. It was a great feeling to sell so many records any time, anywhere. It wasn't the only album selling, either. Earlier albums from the Ramones catalogue had finally paid back the advances and were starting to pay royalties, including in the US. When we had economized on studio time to control costs and pocket the savings, we never planned on this happening, but it was happening. With *Mondo Bizarro*, it was just happening much faster and very far from home. All this had taken only about twenty years and a couple million miles on the road. It was definitely a bizarre world.

Brazilian MTV was a lot like MTV back home. A twenty-something fast-talking hip kid in a T-shirt asked questions, waved around a microphone, and smiled at the amazing job he somehow landed. The VJ interviewing John, however, seemed more elated than his American counterparts. He was only a few feet from the great Johnny Ramone. The VJ wanted some inside stories from the CBGB days but had come to the wrong person.

As was his style, John was brief and borderline polite, listing a bunch of bands from the early days and leaving it at that. But he did have a very thoughtful answer to why the Ramones had decided to hang it up. John explained that a decline was on the horizon and the band wanted to be remembered for playing at a certain level. It sounded like something Joe DiMaggio might have said.

We called for a police escort back to the hotel. It was four or five police cars in front of us and a pair of police motorcycles on either side. The Ramones had been using the presidential seal since almost the beginning but this was our first presidential motorcade.

Even as we caught our collective breath at the hotel, Ramonesmania reached out to us from the TV screen. Brazilian CNN was doing a story and we could see the word 'Ramones' across the bottom of the screen. Above was clearly some sort of riot involving fans. A hotel waiter explained to us that there had been a promotion for a Brazilian cola where the inside of winning bottle caps could be redeemed for tickets to tonight's Ramones concert. The problem was, there were about seven hundred winners and only about two hundred tickets. That left around five hundred cheated kids breaking windows and burning cars on the streets of Rio de Janeiro.

The soccer stadium we played at that night held about forty thousand people. Every seat was taken, although few were ever actually used. The Brazilian fans liked to stand, sway, and sing along the entire show. There was a constant roar, half human, half jet engine. They were electrified by 'Shock Treatment' and bouncing to 'Do You Wanna Dance?' One young long-haired male fan had his moment in the spotlight when he jumped up onstage and stood triumphantly next to Joey during 'Spider-Man'. Fittingly, the next song was 'The KKK Took My Baby Away'. The kid was gone, too. The encore was six songs, ending with 'Beat on the Brat'. We were a little beat, as well. We could have done another six, but we had to save something for the rest of South America.

We wound up the tour in Buenos Aires, where it was more of the same bedlam. We had a night off before the final show, at River Plate Stadium. John's fantasy was for the band to make a side deal and slip in an extra stadium show without management's knowing. In this fantasy, the local promoter would bring cash in a suitcase. Instead, we were spending a quiet night in.

We soon found out that would be impossible. Across the street from the hotel was a building under construction. There was a building boom in South America throughout the nineties, and here was another piece of it – a tall concrete frame structure with just the bare bones. No walls. No windows. But plenty of fans. Somehow they had hopped the tall fence surrounding the lot and climbed up the scaffolding to catch a glimpse of their favorite band.

They were camped out all night on the open concrete slabs and looking our way. At least a dozen fans occupied the fourth floor directly opposite my room. They were on the lookout for Marky. I felt good, bad, ambivalent. Closing my curtain seemed like a snub. Opening the curtain seemed to encourage them, and for all I knew, one of those kids could get excited and take a fall. So I opened and closed the curtain a few times until the police finally came and escorted the kids off the premises. I hadn't gotten a wink of sleep. It was our second-to-last curtain call in South America.

Eddie Vedder was our special guest the next night. Iggy Pop opened for us. River Plate Stadium held about sixty thousand people. Iggy had a rapport with the fans and had them standing. But the fever pitch went nuclear when the Ramones took the stage. Outside of festivals, where the band really shared the crowd and the energy with other bands, this was the largest *Ramones* audience we had ever played for.

We launched into 'Durango 95' with the 'Adios Amigos' letters standing tall on the huge faux brick wall behind the drum riser. The crowd noise sounded like a 767 taking off in our ears with a high-pitched frequency numbing our hearing. I had the sound crew turn up the volume in my monitors. I rarely did that, but this was sink or swim. I looked over at John and he looked back at me. We were in for a long, loud ride. Our job was to keep it all together. That never changed.

Over the next hour and fifteen minutes, we gave Buenos Aires everything we had. That included a 'We're a Happy Family' too fast for Joey or anyone either above or below the equator to keep up with. Joey's voice was suffering here on the very last leg of the tour, and who could blame him? During the last gasps of the encore – 'Brat', 'Chinese Rock', and our Creedence cover 'Have You Ever Seen the Rain', the entire audience stood and rocked back and forth. Some lucky fans, including a few kids not more than ten, surfed atop the crowd or rode on their fathers' shoulders.

It sounded a little sappy when I repeated it to myself silently, but the love coming back at us from the audience was something we could never forget. It was like that rock-and-roll saying about the love you take being equal to the love you make. Coincidence or not, this was the closest I had ever come to feeling as if I were in the Beatles.

Finally, when there were no more encores left in us and the houselights went up, we knew our time here was over. Still, the audience shook the stadium so that we could feel a dull and slow bounce in the concrete floor as we walked backstage. From the first crazed fans at the airport in Rio to the last hurrah in Buenos Aires, it had been an experience we could never have dreamed up. And I had it all on tape.

With only a matter of days to go before our final show, 6 August 1996, it was a little strange to be playing Lollapalooza. The alt-rock festival started in 1991 by Jane's Addiction frontman Perry Farrell had drifted away from its offbeat freak-show roots and gone sort of mainstream. For a lot of critics, the presence of Metallica underscored that point. Metallica came and went via helicopter and spoke to almost no one in between. It was a far cry from the exhibit tents of a half-decade earlier, where a performance artist demonstrated how heavy a weight he could hang from his nipple by a clothespin.

But the rest of the bands got along well, and for the Ramones, as had become our unspoken mantra, it was again better late than never. A show on Randall's Island – long home to a New York prison and sanitarium – was perhaps appropriate to be the last ever in our own backyard. Bands such as Soundgarden and Rancid were eager to hear stories and hang out with us. This, too, was a relatively new experience for John, but it was an easy cherry to pop. He was admired and respected. A guy like John who had grown up idolizing John Wayne was now, after all these years, practically the Duke himself.

Between sets, Chris Cornell of Soundgarden as well as Lars Frederiksen and Tim Armstrong of Rancid followed us back to where we were parked. They were not alone. At least a dozen members of various bands – Rage

Against the Machine, Screaming Trees, Ben Folds Five – all wanted the same thing: to get in the Ramones' van. Just to sit there and soak it in for a few minutes. It seemed, given its storied history, the van was the greatest place in the world to be. If they only knew.

John's house in Southern California was nothing Phil Spector would write home about. But it was nice, quiet, and, finally, after 2,262 shows, John's piece of the American pie. He was proud as he showed me and Marion around. It was a suburban ranch house with a swimming pool. There were classic movie posters and celebrity autographed publicity photos all over the place, so it was definitely home. Some punk purists would have picked CBGB for our final performance, but America had gradually moved west, and so had Johnny Ramone.

The Palace Theatre on North Vine Street in Hollywood was a classic Art Deco building renovated in the late seventies. There was a large balcony and the main floor that had been long ago cleared for dancing, which we hoped to see Ramones fans doing one last time in a couple of hours. This type and size of venue had been our bread and butter for many years. So except for the special guest stars we had brought in and the movie cameras all over the place, it seemed like just another show.

Even Dee Dee was up to his old tricks. He was in town to help send off the band he had cofounded a generation before. As always, Dee Dee had his needs. He knew that my friend Barry and his girlfriend Karen lived in the area, that they would be coming to the show, and that Barry always had some of the best pot this side of the Sierra Nevada. Dee Dee asked me and Marion to ask Barry to pack along some of that choice California weed.

When we all met up backstage and Barry handed Dee Dee what he came for, the next thing out of his mouth was more bizarre than any song he had ever penned on the back of an envelope filled with Acapulco Gold.

'I know you want to have sex with me and your girlfriend.'

Barry and Karen looked stunned. It was so out of left field, it wouldn't have even made it to an album as a bonus track. And this was before he got high.

Onstage, we had a good set. Lars and Tim from Rancid helped us out with a few songs, including Dee Dee's famous '53rd & 3rd'. Chris Cornell and Ben Shepherd of Soundgarden gave us an assist on 'Brat'. Eddie Vedder pulled off his pinhead mask and sang lead on a cover of the Dave Clark Five's 'Any Way You Want It'. Motörhead's Lemmy, a true friend and supporter going way back, sang his tribute, 'R.A.M.O.N.E.S.'

Then we said good night to an appreciative audience.

Backstage there were no goodbyes and no pats on the back. We just went about our business in the dressing room. There was too much to say and no reason to try to say it. I thought ending with a tight, workmanlike set was very Ramones. Playing to a medium-sized crowd was very Ramones. Doing what we loved among friends and not getting dramatic and campy about it was very Ramones.

And there was one more thing. At Lollapalooza, we had been approached by a major promoter from South America. He carried with him a huge roll of paper containing thousands of signatures demanding that the Ramones play one final, *final* show in Brazil. He also carried with him a firm offer for that show: $1 million.

John wanted to do it. Joey didn't. John had his reasons – a million of them – and no one had to ask. Joey had his reasons, and we knew they were health-related. Joey hadn't disclosed to us exactly what was wrong with him and why his energy as of late was so sapped. But we knew something was not good. His skin was sallow and his eyes, even behind the prescription shades, a little dim. When you're around someone for so long, you just know.

I wanted to do the show and made my case to Joey. It was six weeks away. That seemed like enough time for him to go home, chill out, get his health together, and do one last monster of a set. The price was right, and the people of South America deserved a killer lasting impression. We were talking legacy.

Joey said no. The health issues were real, but he was not by any means on his last legs. John was on one side, and that made Joey's position final. Over the years, John had tipped the scales and they weren't tipping back for anything.

There was an old joke about the sadist and the masochist. The masochist says to the sadist, 'Beat me!' The sadist says, '*No.*' When it came to making John twist and turn, Joey was willing to take a hit. Even a million-dollar hit. For better or for worse, that was also very Ramones.

21

A WONDERFUL WORLD

Joey and I weren't talking like old times, but at least we were talking. When the Ramones were winding down, Joey had a short fuse. Once the band ended, Marion and I weren't running over to his apartment every night to have dinner. The hundreds of dinners over almost two decades at Cracker Barrels and random diners across the US were enough for a while. When Joey asked me to play in his new band, Joey Ramone and the Resistance, I resisted. I did a couple of shows and told him that was it. I had my own band and wanted to focus on that.

By the late nineties we had all cooled our heels to a degree. Joey was very excited about his solo album and was working with a variety of top-performing artists on the project. He was still tight with his former girlfriend Angela, and had even written a song about going up to visit her in South Fallsburg in upstate New York. Angela had married someone else, but Joey was crazy about her kid and mentioned he was setting up a college fund for him.

Perhaps most important, Joey had been sober for a while. It wasn't through the approach I advocated – working a program – but sobriety was a good thing no matter how you got there. So I was happy to take his call and agreed to work on his album where my touring schedule permitted. The fact that Daniel Rey was on board as both guitarist and producer would definitely make things easier in the studio and reduce any remaining friction between me and Joey.

Joey did have one serious problem, however, and it was getting worse. He had been diagnosed with lymphoma while the Ramones were still together, and by now we all knew the details. He was receiving chemotherapy on a regular basis. We could only assume treatment was effective, but, at the very least, the side effects were horrible.

He was losing weight, and Joey Ramone didn't have a lot of weight to lose. He had good days and bad days, and on the bad days he didn't leave his apartment. He was seeing a holistically oriented nutritionist. Knowing his condition, we now understood why Joey was so quick to bite in the final days of the Ramones. If only we had known then.

Seeing what Joey was going through made me appreciate my own health even more. The world was filled with great things to do, and I was getting a chance to do them. I had started my own band, the Intruders, when the Ramones were coming down the homestretch. I had begun writing songs fairly prolifically by then, and it continued well past our final show. What also continued was the steady rise in popularity of Ramones music both at home and abroad. I was connected to punk music for life and wasn't running from it. Just the opposite – I was running toward it. With the Intruders, I had the opportunity to promote the music I loved into the next millennium.

The Intruders' sound had some similarities to the Ramones' but had a second guitar and was a bit fuller and heavier, a little bigger on the bottom. The crowds were also getting still bigger at the bottom of the world. By having bands like Motörhead and Iggy Pop open for the Ramones, we had effectively opened doors for them, and, like the Ramones, they had a chance to extend their audience and legacy to the far reaches. When I first took the Intruders to Argentina, Brazil, and Chile, my own band members were initiated into the thrill and power of it all. The South Americans loved our songs – 'One Way Ride', 'Telephone Love', and especially 'Three Cheers for You', my punk tribute to South America.

The Brazilians were highly appreciative when the Intruders opened for the Sex Pistols in Rio de Janeiro in front of more than forty thousand people. The Sex Pistols weren't as fortunate. I loved the band and their music, but it was obvious they weren't well rehearsed. They had recently gotten back together for a few big shows and it came off like they were just doing it for the money. The Rio audience must have thought the same thing because they started pelting the Pistols with cups, cans, and bottles. Forget 'God Save the Queen'. God save the Sex Pistols.

There were no hard feelings. At least as far as I could tell. I hung out backstage in the Pistols' dressing room with bassist Glen Matlock and singer Johnny Rotten. Glen was the friendliest guy in the band and the one who, in my opinion, held them together. But, when the guitarist and bass player from my band knocked on the door, Johnny Rotten wouldn't let them in. On one hand, I understood the Sex Pistols didn't know my band members from the halcyon days of punk rock. Still, I thought the no-admittance was very unpunk. It seemed that Johnny Rotten took the name 'Intruders' a little too literally.

Reuniting to make money and play in front of huge international crowds was the farthest thing from our minds when Dee Dee and I started the Remains. When I picked up Dee Dee and his second wife from JFK Airport in my 1996 Chevy Impala SS, I had the pleasure of meeting their cute Airdale terrier, Banfield. Dee Dee was relaxed and in a relatively good mental place. Not that he hadn't expressed regret to me on several occasions over having left Vera, but at least Dee Dee seemed comfortable with who he was and the iconic punk status he would have for the rest of his life and beyond, whether he wanted it or not.

We decided to make music just to have fun. No pressure, no expectations, no worries over money. We had money. We had fame. What we hadn't had enough of when Dee Dee's days wound down in the Ramones was a good time, and there really was nothing to stop us now. We decided to do a few shows, perform a few Ramones songs, maybe write a few new ones, and see what happened.

Dee Dee played guitar and sang lead on some of the songs. While that might have surprised a few people, in the Ramones Dee Dee was always writing songs on the guitar and then showing John exactly how to play them, right down to the fingering. Dee Dee was a good downstroke rhythm player who could also play lead. Dee Dee's second wife played bass and did some of the singing. It was a blast playing clubs like the Continental. Performing at a little club with tables like the Long Island Brewing Company, where the band played at the same elevation as the audience, was not only a chance to reinvent classic songs like 'Sheena' and 'I Don't Care'. It was also a way to exorcise a few demons. It had to be therapeutic for Dee Dee. On that particular night, Joey was supposed to come out and join us, but he wasn't up to it. So Joan Jett joined us as a guest and helped out on vocals. It was like a revival meeting.

Another band by the same name got wind of us and we had to change our name to the Remainz. Inevitably, the booking agents got wind of us, too, and wanted to book the Remainz all over the country. We turned them down but did agree to play out in LA. It was our second home and now John's permanent one. I had no hesitation traveling with Dee Dee. He had leveled out. He was coherent. And he was doing it all with marijuana.

Dee Dee was more of a pothead now than ever before. This wasn't the perfect solution for Dee Dee's addictions, but it was better than almost any other. I commended him on it. Relying on pot instead of the endless revolving pharmacy of chemicals he had been on for so many years was a vast improvement, and it showed in his behavior.

Of course, he was still Dee Dee. He tried almost obsessively to cover his tracks. He would go to a department store, buy an air purifier the size of a small TV, and set it up in the hotel bedroom to mask the pot odor. Whenever we left a hotel, he left the unit behind and bought a new one for the next hotel. But the owner of one of the hotels could smell the Colombian Red through the HEPA filter and knocked on the door.

'Yeah, what's up?' Dee Dee said.

'You cannot have marijuana in there. Do you read the rules?'

He was a Vietnamese gentleman who had probably stared death in the face on more than one occasion, so staring Dee Dee in the face didn't faze him. And he didn't faze Dee Dee.

'Hey, chief,' Dee Dee said. 'I don't know what you're on, but I'm clean and I'm trying to get some sleep.'

'I'm calling the police. You hear me?'

'Call the police,' Dee Dee said. 'You think that does anything for me? All over half a joint that's already been smoked? This is LA. Don't you guys have some rapes and murders to worry about?'

'You must get out today.'

'Go fuck yourself.'

But Dee Dee came to his senses once the owner walked into the stairwell. If we weren't looking for publicity, we definitely didn't need this. We packed up our clothes, toiletries, and the pot. The air purifier was the only remains.

I dropped by John's house and was glad to see he was enjoying a peaceful life. He had his LA friends, who showed him everything from respect to worship. John had become more accepting in his views of people and situations. He still collected movie and sports memorabilia and of course kept up with the business end of the Ramones, which over the years had taken on a life of its own. The one thing John didn't want to do was go somewhere and play guitar – not in an arena or in a club Dee Dee and Marky were playing that night. The way John saw it, when the Ramones hung it up, he hung up his guitar, period. The more time away he spent, the rustier he got and the less he wanted to expose himself to any sort of comparison.

I understood all of that. What I didn't understand, even after all the animosities of the past, was why he didn't want to give Joey a call once in a blue moon. We all knew Joey was struggling with the chemotherapy, and, as much as we believed he would beat his illness, I had to remind John that a simple thing like a three-minute phone call could sometimes do more for a person than all the IV tubes in the world. John told me no, flat out. He and Joey had nothing to talk about.

One early morning in late 1999 Joey and I had lunch a couple of blocks from his apartment on East Ninth Street. Joey looked pale and weak, but I had gotten used to seeing him that way recently. If anything, today was a great day simply because he was up and around on his own two feet and moving about town. Joey had been in and out of the hospital lately, getting more chemo and trying to build back some strength. Lately, we had been meeting under very different conditions.

Working on his solo album seemed to work a lot better than chemo. The recording studio was in New Jersey, and Joey insisted on being there whether he was having a good day or not. That included days when he had to be driven directly from the hospital. The album was his baby and he was going to see it through, no matter what.

I already had my roadie get my drums out of the rental space and load them into the studio. I was there to do half a dozen songs or as many as I could before I left to go on tour with my own band, the Intruders. Daniel Rey and I tried to make it as easy as possible for Joey in the studio. I came in having learned the songs off of a demo tape and was ready to lay them down. Joey would usually sit and record a scratch vocal for us to follow. He could lay down a polished vocal on whatever day or days he happened to feel strong.

The project had a good, solid sixties rock-pop feel. Some of the songs reminded us a little of the early Who. 'What a Wonderful World', originally recorded by Louis Armstrong, was about the most positive take on the beauty of this earth ever put forward in song. When I heard Joey sing it breathily in the studio, I pictured him singing it much more sweetly and smoothly, in his mind, as he looked out the window of a hospital room. I thought about the title track on the album: 'Don't Worry About Me'. I tried not to. But I did.

The 31st of December was normally a good day for the Ramones. We were usually playing a New Year's Eve show at the Palladium or somewhere else special. On that day in the year 2000, however, Joey was leaving his apartment in the morning, and there was snow on the ground. He slipped and went down hard. Something popped, and he couldn't get up, so he lay there in the slush moaning and groaning. A young woman walking along looked down, looked back up, and passed him by. Then an old man. Then a few more pedestrians. They might have thought he was drunk, homeless, or both. Regardless, no one reached out to help the legendary Joey Ramone until a woman police officer on foot eventually stopped and radioed for help.

Joey was taken to the Rusk Institute of Rehabilitation Medicine on East Thirty-Fourth Street near the FDR Drive. His hip was broken, possibly because the chemo had weakened his bones. I called him as often as I could and followed his progress. He was transferred from this hospital to that one and back again for various complications. He had hip surgery in one facility and rehab in another. Then back out for cancer treatment. Somewhere along the line, Joey had picked up a hospital infection that was giving him a high fever, compromising his immune system, and wreaking havoc with the cancer.

When I pulled my car up to the Rusk Institute on a cold snowy evening in late February, I was lucky to get a spot. There was never enough sidewalk in New York, especially around hospitals. I picked up a pass at the visitors' desk and went up to the fourth floor to see Joey. He was on his back looking emaciated, but he smiled when I walked in. I was bearing gifts.

Joey always loved Marion's cooking, especially her oatmeal and her chocolate-chip cookies. I sat down on the edge of the bed and placed a tin of cookies on the night table. Then I pulled a boom box out of the Styrofoam packing and set it up next to the cookies. Joey looked excited like a kid from Forest Hills on Hanukkah and asked me if I brought any CDs. Of course, I said. I showed him a handful of sixties rock and pop albums, and Joey's eyes zeroed in on a Dusty Springfield CD.

We started to talk, but I was distracted for a moment. I looked around the room, and there was very little. When I had picked up the boom box and the CDs I thought it was a nice gesture but that I would basically be adding items to the pile. There was no pile. There was no other boom box. That to me was startling and sad. Leaving Joey without music was like leaving Linus without a blanket.

We discussed his solo album and how it was going. I told him I thought it kicked ass and that we were all looking forward to his getting the hell out of the hospital soon enough and holding a release party.

Joey smiled and then stopped to consider something. Out of the blue, he asked me if I thought there would ever be a Ramones reunion. I told him that, like everyone else, I was having fun doing what I wanted to do, but if anything like that ever came along, all he had to do was pick up the phone and call me.

I thought it was a strange question considering not only how we ended but also the fact that he and John hadn't spoke even once in years. Maybe, I thought, the idea of a reunion, however improbable, gave Joey a little more hope and strength lying here in a hospital bed. Wherever the notion had come from, Joey then asked me a question that caught me far more off guard.

'Where is everyone else?'

I knew what he meant. Where are the other Ramones? Regarding John, a telephone call was a long shot and a visit was a moon shot. Dee Dee owed him a visit, but it seemed like he just didn't want to deal with Joey's mortality. Tommy was a mystery. I couldn't figure it out. Ultimately, I couldn't worry about it. I was here. What I also couldn't do was let Joey down any further, so I changed the subject.

'You know they still love us down in Buenos Aires.'

'Yeah?'

'Definitely. They still go fucking wild over "Sheena" and everything else.'

'That's cool.'

At that moment, Joey's nurse walked in. She was a pleasant-looking African American woman of about forty. She stood close enough to the bed so that her knee almost brushed against mine. She tilted her head down slightly, and we made eye contact.

'I'm sorry, sir. Can you move over just a bit?'

'Sure,' I said. 'No problem.'

'It's time for his bath.'

I slid down toward the foot of the bed and turned my body to allow clearance for Joey's long legs. As Joey leaned his head forward slightly, the nurse slipped her left hand under his thighs and her entire right arm under his back. She was an average-size woman, not particularly powerful-looking, but our lead singer was lifted right up off the mattress and gently into the wheelchair alongside the bed.

As the nurse pushed the wheelchair, I followed them a few steps out into the hallway and then stopped. She continued pushing the chair as I stood and watched. Just as they prepared for a left-hand turn around a corner, Joey managed to swing around to face in my direction. It was a struggle, but he waved to me. I waved back. Then he disappeared.

I stepped back into the room for a moment to get my jacket off the back of a chair. As I grabbed the jacket, I glanced out the window and saw my car. I didn't know it at the time, but I had parked directly below Joey's window. In some small way, we were in tune. The frequency coming from him was very faint.

I called John the next day.

'You need to visit him. The window is closing.'

'Let it close,' John said.

'C'mon, John.'

'I'm out here on the West Coast, anyway.'

'Don't tell me that. We spent half our lives on this flight and that one. You can get on a plane an hour from now. And I'm sure you can find plenty of things to do while you're here in New York.'

'He's not my friend,' John said.

'Who cares if he's your friend?' I said. 'That's not the point. We're past that now. He's dying. So you don't like him. Big fucking deal. How about the fact that you practically grew up together? How about the fact that you were in a band together for twenty-two years? How about all the songs he wrote that helped you in your career? How about the fact that without Joey you wouldn't have *had* a career?'

'Look,' John said, 'I hope he beats the thing.'

Joey passed away a few weeks later, on 15 April. In life, death and taxes were assured, and this time they came on the same day. No matter how much you prepared mentally for a thing like this, you never really knew how you were going to feel until it happened. Even then, you weren't sure because the shock was just setting in.

The first thing I felt was sadness over how he wouldn't get to see his album released. Then I considered how many other things he would miss, and the album seemed like just a speck of sand. My mind drifted past any of the events, honors, and awards that had been discussed lately. As both Louie and Joey sang, it was a wonderful world. But I had a hard time imagining a world where Joey wasn't somewhere quietly listening to a Dusty Springfield song and smiling.

One thing that never changed about John was his methodical thinking about how to get the Ramones to the next level. Our first year of eligibility for induction into the Rock and Roll Hall of Fame was coming up in 2002. Gary Kurfirst had just let John know that the Ramones were invited to receive an MTV Lifetime Achievement Award on 6 September 2001. In John's baseball mind, that was a warm-up – a bullpen session – before the Hall of Fame voting.

John actually made two calls to the bullpen – one to me, and one to C.J., whom he wanted to accept Dee Dee's award. We were the only Ramones he wanted alongside him at the MTV awards. He had thought it out. Joey was obviously gone, and Dee Dee might embarrass us and screw up the Hall of Fame voting. John pointed out Dee Dee's erratic behavior at the final Ramones show in Los Angeles. I told John without Dee Dee's erratic behavior there would have been no Ramones.

Besides, Dee Dee and I were playing in the Remainz. Dee Dee had leveled out. Dee Dee *was* the Ramones. He deserved to be there. John explained it was too late. The arrangements were made. I told John that as much as I disagreed with the decision, I would be there. When I put down the receiver, a strange thought occurred to me: *No one had even mentioned Tommy.*

The event organizers had us enter through the Lincoln Center garage rather than on the red carpet to keep the lifetime achievement award 'a secret'. But, after many years of being shoved aside, the plan felt oddly like a snub. And after going along with the Dee Dee snub, maybe somehow we had it coming to us.

Among other things, Dee Dee missed a cocktail hour and Britney

Spears parading around in a diamond-studded jungle outfit with a boa constrictor wrapped around her neck. He missed Johnny Ramone's new entourage – Lisa Marie Presley, her fiancé Nicolas Cage, and their contingent of bodyguards. He missed Johnny Ramone and his dark Elvis shades, which looked as if they'd been for $5.95 at the Graceland gift shop. It seemed John and his wife were now very age-conscious and were maybe hiding a few wrinkles.

When it was time to talk to the press and take photos, I started walking toward the media room on instinct. But my instinct and John's sense of control were two different things. He grabbed me and told me I needed to wait for C.J., who was lingering back near the bar. At that point I drew the line.

'John,' I said, 'this isn't 1978. I'm not Joey. I'm not Dee Dee. I'm not Monte. We're not in the van. News flash – the Ramones are over. It's nice that we're here. But the band is over.'

The award presentation took place in the Metropolitan Opera House. There was probably no building on the planet less appropriate for giving the Ramones a lifetime achievement award, but there we were – John, C.J., me, and Bono, who was presenting the award – exiting a Plexiglas tube worthy of the movie *This Is Spinal Tap*. As my feet touched the stage I unconsciously began dancing to 'Blitzkrieg Bop'. I wasn't sure exactly why, but I was sure Dee Dee would have liked it.

Lisa Marie Presley sprang for a reception at the elegant Hudson Hotel a few blocks away. Bodyguards, including the massive southern dude assigned to me and Marion, ringed our table like a force field. Lisa Marie, Nicolas Cage, and even the punk god Johnny Ramone seemed perfectly comfortable inside. But Marion and I were suffocating. Just beyond the force field were our true people – Monte, Arturo, and Danny Fields, who was getting very emotional about missing Joey. They were literally barred from entry. So Marion and I made our move. We busted out of the cell to talk to our friends. Then we busted out of the hotel. It felt at least as good as getting the award.

In one sense John was right about Lincoln Center being a warm-up. Leather jackets and the Waldorf Astoria never really went together, but then again neither did punk rock and anything you might call a hall of fame. None of that mattered on 18 March 2002, when the Ramones were inducted into the Rock and Roll Hall of Fame. The doors to the Hall opened on cue – just over twenty-five years since the release of the first album. As far as individual eligibility was concerned, the voting members elected Joey, Johnny, Dee Dee, Tommy, and me.

John made sure he was seated at a different table from Joey's mother, Charlotte, and her other son, Mitchell. Before we were called up to the podium, John avoided any kind of contact with either of them. I thought that deserved an award for callousness. They had recently lost a son and a brother and were there to celebrate what that person had accomplished. I wasn't a believer in life after death, but animosity after death was very real.

Tommy spoke first and in doing so redeemed John and the entire band. 'Believe it or not, we really loved each other even when we weren't acting civil to each other. We were truly brothers. The honor of our induction into the Hall of Fame means a lot to us. But it really meant everything to Joey.'

John thanked Seymour Stein, Danny Fields, Gary Kurfirst, and Ramones fans. He ended his brief speech by proclaiming, 'God bless President Bush and God bless America.' In a room filled with progressives, this got a lesser round of applause but a decent ovation just the same. The wounds of 11 September were still fresh, wide open, and only blocks away.

The attacks were deeply personal if you were an American, a New Yorker, or a downtown person. We were all three. As I looked out from our twentieth-floor apartment window through binoculars and watched the plumes of smoke rising from Ground Zero, I knew what everyone else knew: that things would never be quite the same. But a public gathering of any sort in New York was a celebration and reaffirmation of the city's and the country's resilience. For the time being, political differences were suspended just like personal differences in the band should have been.

'Hi, everybody,' I said. 'I'm Marky Ramone, and I want to thank

Johnny Ramone for asking me to join the Ramones. And especially Tommy Ramone, who started that drum style that I had to work very hard to duplicate. Thank you very much.' A complete list of the people I wanted to thank would have bumped Tom Petty and the Heartbreakers, Talking Heads, and all the other deserving artists being inducted that night. Besides, everyone wanted to hear what Dee Dee had to say, and as usual he did not disappoint.

'Hi, I'm Dee Dee Ramone, and I'd like to congratulate myself, and thank myself, and give myself a big pat on the back. Thank you, Dee Dee. You're very wonderful. I love you.'

Maybe John at that moment didn't agree Dee Dee was so wonderful. Whatever he thought, John and Dee Dee were, now and for ever, members of the same hall of fame.

Before we left the stage, I gave a shout-out to Charlotte and her son, Mitchell. No one else had bothered to. I wasn't sure whether they were told not to join the rest of us onstage or decided not to, and it didn't matter. They needed to be acknowledged, so if by keeping my acceptance speech brief, I had a coupon for a few more words, I cashed it in at the right time.

Once we had all taken our seats, Hall of Fame statues in hand, we noticed something strange. There was a single statue still standing on the podium. I said to Dee Dee, 'That must be Joey's.' It seemed like a prearranged symbolic gesture, but it was simply a mistake. It was not Joey Ramone going back to the stage one last time to tap something. Seymour Stein told Charlotte's assistant to retrieve the statue and give it to Charlotte. But, when he hand-delivered it to Charlotte, she noticed it said 'Dee Dee Ramone'. Dee Dee then realized his said 'Johnny Ramone'. Tommy and I had the ones engraved for us. That meant John's statue read 'Joey Ramone'. That alone was worth my trip to the induction ceremony.

Ten weeks later, Dee Dee was dead of an overdose in the apartment he shared with his second wife. She found him hunched over the couch with a needle in his arm, not quite at rest. He was never quite at rest, at least not while he was alive. He created songs, poetry, books, and paintings to try to find that elusive peace, and anyone who cared about him hoped that in utter tragedy he had somehow found it.

We were supposed to be grieved, not shocked, at Dee Dee's death, but I was both. Dee Dee had been clean for a long time other than smoking pot. Potheads lived to a ripe old age, and that was what I was hoping for with Dee Dee. He had moved into an area of Hollywood where dope was readily available, but that was for artistic inspiration, not to cop. I heard through the grapevine that, when he finally did cop, it was very pure stuff. The combination of that and the fact that he had been clean so long caused the overdose. The jolt to his system was too much. It was bitterly ironic that sobriety – though with a large asterisk – killed Dee Dee. The old Dee Dee had so many substances coursing through his veins the heroin might have gone into shock.

As the next few days passed, I thought about how strange it was that I would never be able to pick up the phone and call Dee Dee. Coupled with that thought was the phone call he never made to me. Even after our first little fiasco in Whitestone, I had taken him to more meetings – AA, NA, whatever was available. Over time, he went back to meetings on his own, and the program became part of his life. Dee Dee never did anything conventionally, but he was as dedicated to it as anyone ever would have had a right to expect of him.

I knew there would come a day when the opportunity to cop again would be staring him in the face and he would be staring right back, ready to surrender. I always told him when that day came – or even when he thought that day was a week or a month away – to call me. *Let me know how you feel. Let me know what your urges are. We'll talk it through and figure it out together.*

But I never got the call. I never had the opportunity. Dee Dee did things on a whim. He would say things on a whim, buy things on a whim, move to another country on a whim. He would cop on a whim, then write a song about it. Only he never got to write that last song, and we never got to hear it.

The streets in Lower Manhattan had names such as Washington, LaGuardia, and Astor. They were named for founding fathers, beloved mayors, and members of the aristocracy. When we were overgrown kids running around downtown checking out band flyers taped to lampposts, our craziest fantasy was to have a sneaker named after us. But on Sunday, 30 November 2003, the powers that be were about to unveil Joey Ramone Place. A sixteen-year-old fan from Staten Island had gotten the ball rolling with a petition, the ultimate do-it-yourself campaign for the ultimate do-it-yourself rocker. Sadly, Arturo Vega told me, the fan's parents wouldn't let her come to the unveiling.

It was the corner of Bowery and East Second Street, right up the block from CBGB. The club was still there, still owned and operated by Hilly Kristal, and bands still showed up seven nights a week to try something old, something new, and maybe pick up a following. But the area was becoming gentrified, and the rents were getting high. Not that everything in the world needed to stay exactly as it was. Not even punk made a demand like that.

Still, this was an appropriate place for Joey's sign. The music he helped create made this once grimy, sleazy, drug-infested block the center of the creative universe. People gazing at the sign as they walked by needed to remember that the movers and shakers in this world didn't all have to have money, wear suits, or bathe regularly.

A young guy from the crowd who seemed connected to the media spotted me and asked me if my view was okay. I told him it was fine. He pointed to a lift used for telephone repairs and let me know he could put me up there to get a better view of the proceedings. I told him no, thanks. If I wanted a better view, I could just walk a few feet and stand on the roof of my Caddy parked on Bowery.

There were a lot of Lower East Side has-beens and wannabes milling about. Not that there was anything wrong with has-beens. But a lot of these has-beens and wannabes were trying to get into the act in the vein of the old Jimmy Durante line. Anyone who had ever had a little too much to drink and puked in front of CB's thirty years earlier wanted to give a eulogy and develop a screenplay. I just wanted to take in the moment by myself.

I clapped like everyone else when the veil came off. The name 'Joey Ramone' loomed large over the word 'Place', and the green and white sign sat just above the one for East 2nd Street. It was way up there, towering well above where Joey's big head of hair would have been had he been watching from below, and hopefully high enough to prevent theft by memorabilia – and thrill-seekers.

I paid my respects to Dee Dee by visiting his grave site whenever I was in Los Angeles. The Hollywood Forever Cemetery near Paramount Studios was crowded with such legends as Cecil B. DeMille and Rudolph Valentino. Dee Dee helped invent a genre of popular music and fit right in. Not far away the voice of Bugs Bunny, Mel Blanc, was interred. Appropriately, his headstone read 'That's all folks'.

Dee Dee's headstone was rock-and-roll, but tasteful. At the top was the Ramones presidential seal but with the lyric 'I feel so safe flying on a ray on the highest trails above.' The stone was modest in size. Not to be outwitted, at the bottom it read 'O.K. . . . I gotta go now.'

Which reminded me I had to go visit John. I was an agnostic standing in a cemetery talking to my friend and, at best, skeptical that my friend could hear a word I was saying. But being there gave me some peace.

Beliefs, in my mind, were all fine, as long as the person was sincere. But I never went in for superstitions. Superstitions were a way of avoiding confronting an issue. They were a substitute for thinking. They limited what you could do in the world, what you could strive for, and what you could hope to change. But lately one of the stupidest, most annoying superstitions was ringing in my ears. *Bad luck comes in threes.*

John had been quietly battling prostate cancer for years. He had been in and out of Cedars-Sinai Hospital many times for chemotherapy and treatment of complications. John kept it quiet, and we respected his wishes. Of all the orders he had fired off for so long, this one had the most authority behind it. Lately, he was clearly getting weaker to the point where he sometimes had trouble finishing a phone conversation. I tried to call him once a week on average. But now, as much as I was hoping for a turnaround, phone calls alone weren't enough. The doctors believed the cancer had spread.

When I visited John from time to time, he would usually take me for a drive. We would just check out the California sights and shoot the breeze. On this visit, he hesitated when we got out to the front lawn, and I could see he was wary of his own car. I knew he was too weak to drive so I asked him if he would do me a favor and let me drive. He handed me the keys to his Cadillac.

As we headed up Mulholland on a sunny day, the conversation was the usual: music, movies, cars, collectibles. But suddenly he straightened up in the captain's chair as if we were back in the van, looked straight ahead, and issued a warning.

'You're gonna have to watch out when it comes to business.'

'I understand.'

'I don't know if you do,' John said. 'I mean, if I'm not around . . . to run things.'

'My eyes are always open.'

'All I'm saying, Marc, is just make sure you never kiss anyone's ass.' I was a little stunned. And the last-will-and-testament part was the least of it.

'John, you know me. Do you think I would really ever kiss anyone's ass?'

'No, but just a word to the wise.'

John's stamina even as a passenger was fading. He was self-conscious when we got back to the house and I opened the car door for him. He had always projected a physical presence. Whether it was hopping in and out of the van or striking a Punk Rock God pose onstage, he had a proud self-image and didn't want to be seen when he couldn't measure up to it. Inside the house, he walked into the bedroom to take a nap, and I left.

My next visit was to Phil Spector's castle in Alhambra. Phil had been charged with murder and out on $1 million bail. In February, he had met B-movie actress Lana Clarkson while she was working at the House of Blues on Sunset Boulevard. About an hour after they got to the castle,

Phil's gun went off in Clarkson's mouth, killing her instantly. A media circus ensued that hearkened back to the O. J. Simpson trial. But Phil Spector didn't try to escape in a Ford Bronco and had a substantial amount of evidence on his side.

Whenever Phil and I got together, it was to get away from the circus. So we talked about music even as we walked past the exact area where Lana Clarkson had been found slumped over in a chair. Phil asked me how touring was going, and I told him about the amazing fan base we had built in South America.

Phil was incensed over how the Rock and Roll Hall of Fame had botched the Joey situation at the induction ceremony the year before. I told him living well was the best revenge, and maybe dying well could be the second best. Our music was all over the planet, and that meant a billion times more than a statue or a speech. Those words gave Phil Spector little comfort. He was still pissed off over what the government had done to Lenny Bruce.

I let Phil arrive at the subject of Lana Clarkson, and he eventually did. He looked me in the eye and said without blinking that she put the gun in her mouth and pulled the trigger. She was simulating a sex act, and it went off. Phil explained that she was down on her luck and had asked him for a $100,000 loan. He turned her down, pointing out that he had met her just a few hours earlier. 'Marc, why would she even ask?' Phil looked as if he was still trying to make sense of the whole thing.

We continued talking as we walked into the billiard room. The solid and striped balls lay scattered across the pool table and looked inviting, but I knew not to touch. Phil was intent upon keeping the table exactly as they had left it the very last time he and his good friend and billiards coach Willie Mosconi played. Mosconi had died in 1993, ten years earlier.

There was nothing I could do for Phil Spector but visit or call once in a while and wait till the trial. And there was not much I could do for John until I noticed the rumors running wild on the Internet. MySpace was huge at that particular moment. A friend got me on, and I could see instantly why it was so addictive. Suddenly anyone had a quick and convenient home in cyberspace and could interact easily with anyone else on the site.

As with any form of communication, especially one where no physical presence was required, some people fired missiles. MySpace and other forums were filled with speculation and misinformation about Johnny Ramone. The most popular fiction seemed to be that he was dying of Alzheimer's disease like Ronald Reagan. HIV was also near the top of the list. As I read and read, I saw clearly that it went beyond a bunch of fans hungry for the truth. The lies were being spread viciously by people who claimed to know first-hand. It wasn't hard to read the small minds firing off these shots. They didn't like John's politics, so they condemned him to the same fate as his hero. Or they implied he was using needles, messing around, whatever. As if they had any right.

My friend John couldn't fire back. So I fired back for him.

'Stop your shit. You don't know what the fuck you're talking about.'

'Who the fuck are you?'

'I'm Marky Ramone, and you're full of shit.'

'Yeah, right, asshole.'

'My friend and guitarist has a problem called cancer. He's fighting it bravely. Who are you to belittle him and spread lies?'

'So now you like Reagan, too.'

'Tell you what, if you're the left, I don't want any part of it. Learn some basic respect.'

A few days later, *Rolling Stone* called to ask me what Johnny Ramone was dying from. The paparazzi were already hanging around Cedars-Sinai and John's friend Lisa Marie Presley was seen coming and going. Now they wanted a statement from Marky Ramone. The way I saw it, I had two options. One was to lie about John's condition and be really no better than the anonymous bloggers out there. The other was to tell the truth. From where I was sitting, neither option looked very good, but there wasn't much choice in the end.

'Prostate cancer, unfortunately. Johnny's been a champ confronting this, but at this point I think the chances are slim. I've been getting so much email from people and from papers and magazines wanting to know what was up, I had to take it upon myself to say something . . .'

The shit hit the fan at the speed of a microprocessor. John's wife threw a fit. I heard the static through everyone still around in the Ramones camp. The sharpest arrow slung was that I did it all for the publicity. That was as false as the rumors being spread about Johnny Ramone. I was in the Rock and Roll Hall of Fame. I was touring all over the world to large crowds. I needed publicity, especially this kind, the way Tiger Woods needed another endorsement deal. I just wanted to stop the nasty rumor mill. That shouldn't have been hard to understand. But, in the craziness that had developed over the decades and now threatened to outlive most of the Ramones, it had unfortunately become business as usual.

Johnny was too weak to attend the tribute concert held for him at the Avalon in Hollywood on 12 September. It was a star-studded charitable benefit with Eddie Vedder, Rob Zombie, the Red Hot Chili Peppers, the Dickies, X, Rancid, and essentially a Who's Who of John's world and rock music in general. The house band for the Ramones songs was Daniel Rey on guitar, C.J. on bass, and me on drums. The one low point came when Rob Zombie whipped out a cellphone, called John at his home, and put his voice over the PA system. It was done with the best of intentions but just underscored how ill John really was.

John passed three days later when I was on my way to Prague. I had lost a close friend and bandmate, again. For me, the tribute concert was the memorial. I had a permanent image in my mind of John playing guitar, and that was good enough. Months later, they unveiled the large black statue at the cemetery.

Everyone could have taken a lesson from Dee Dee's humble monument, which, as it turned out, was only a stone's throw away in Hollywood Forever Cemetery. The proximity would make visiting my old friends in the Ramones – a very difficult task – a little easier. The walk from Dee Dee's to Johnny's would be a little more than two minutes – about the length of the Ramones song 'I Remember You'.

When I appeared on Sirius Satellite Radio's *The Wiseguy Show* one day in late 2004, it seemed like a natural thing to do. Hosted by Vincent Pastore, who played Salvatore 'Big Pussy' Bonpensiero on the HBO hit series *The Sopranos*, the show was ideal for a Brooklyn guy with something to promote. I had just released the DVD *Ramones: Raw*, which featured behind-the-scenes footage I had shot all around the world. Sirius occupied an entire floor of the McGraw-Hill Building. It was an island in the sky of studios, glass booths, and cubicles churning out programming that otherwise couldn't be found on the airwaves. It was a new kind of fraternity. I felt strangely at home there, as I did with the wise guys.

It was about to become even more of a home. A few days later, I got a call from one of the top executives at Sirius. He asked me to perform another natural act – appear on skateboarding champion Tony Hawk's show. I knew this would be a bit like my first time playing with the Ramones – an informal audition. And, like the earlier informal audition, this one would be a perfect fit. Tony was a punk-rock fan. Talking about music, skateboarding, the do-it-yourself approach, and everything else connected to the punk world came as naturally to me as banging on a cheap snare drum for the first time. I wasn't polished but all I needed was a shot.

Sirius offered me one. They liked my New York persona, my tone of voice, and the knowledge I brought to the table. They asked me to pitch them a show. When someone asks you to pitch them a show, you're basically in. I threw a fastball down the middle. My idea for *Marky Ramone's Blitzkrieg* was simple and straightforward: to create a place, a universe, where listeners can hear their favorite punk-rock songs and learn a bit about where they came from.

I gathered together my entire collection of punk-rock albums, EPs, and singles and hauled them into the studio. When it came to punk, my stash was the Library of Congress. The first few shows were carried by the music. As I learned my craft, the emails started pouring in. Where else could someone go to hear 'Born to Lose by Johnny Thunders or 'Live Fast, Die Young' by the Circle Jerks? Nowhere but here.

I got up at seven in the morning to go to Phil Spector's retrial. The first one had ended in a hung jury. It was March 2009, and I headed to the United States District Court in downtown LA on the 101 in my rented Chrysler 300C. A true New Yorker is always a little disoriented driving in Los Angeles. I got off at the exit and spotted the courthouse parking lot just a moment too late. When I veered off toward the lot entrance, I saw two lanes of traffic coming right at me and realized I was going the wrong way. There were dangerous times in life when you just had to follow through because turning back was far worse. I had to be there. I was Phil Spector's friend.

I met Phil, his wife Rachelle, and Phil's two massive bodyguards in the courthouse lobby. They were hard to miss. Phil asked me what took me so long. With the traffic in Los Angeles, it was basically a rhetorical question. I told him I needed to go to the cafeteria and that I would meet him upstairs in the courtroom.

After eating a granola bar and sucking down a cup of coffee, I made my way through the metal detectors and security personnel, who went through my bag and frisked me. I had on a pair of black jeans and a leather jacket. I didn't look like your average courtroom curiosity seeker, but that was really all relative. In any case, I was eyeballed thoroughly up and down. In a post-9/11 world, the only venue more security-conscious than an airport was a celebrity murder trial in LA.

When I got to the third floor, I knew it might be a long morning so I asked a young woman in the hallway hacking away at a laptop computer where the men's room was. She pointed farther down the hallway and I thanked her.

As I entered the courtroom, the first thing I noticed was that Lana Clarkson's side was packed with friends and relatives. The other side was just Rachelle and now me. Phil Spector preferred mono to stereo, and he had gotten it. As I settled in, I noticed one of the jurors – a white guy probably in his early thirties – had on a Ramones T-shirt. It was the first positive experience of my morning.

I listened as the district attorney presented evidence. It didn't seem like much. They had a sport jacket with a little bit of blood on it. It seemed anyone firing a .38 from that range would have been absolutely drenched in blood. They had no motive. Instead, they presented accounts of the legendary producer waving and sometimes firing a warning shot in a recording studio many years earlier. It was famously eccentric behavior. And, as I knew only too well, famously exaggerated. What it had to do with putting a gun in the mouth of a forty-year-old struggling actress you had just met and then pulling the trigger was beyond me.

Every so often Phil turned around, looked right at me, and gave me a smirk. It was like Gold Star studios, where we were pretty much in synch. I knew exactly what he was thinking. *Is that all they got?*

I was upset the next day in court. The harmless-looking woman who had pointed me to the men's room was a blogger who stalked celebrity criminal cases. She posted that she had covered a lot of trials in her time but on that day spotted the two most evil-looking people she had ever seen walk into a courtroom: Phil Spector and Marky Ramone. She went on to describe every item of clothing I was wearing, making a case even weaker than the DA's.

I thought about the metal detector I had just gone through for a second straight day. Through that metal detector over the years had undoubtedly passed rapists, child molesters, and mass murderers. Compared with that, you had a legendary record producer and a punk rocker in what she called Converse. She had even gotten the shoes wrong.

But, as I calmed myself down, I realized I was distraught over something else, too. The juror with the Ramones shirt from the day before was gone. Disappeared like a political enemy in Argentina. Someone from 'the people's' side figured out that Phil Spector, over a quarter century before, had produced a Ramones album. That album, as it turned out, had over time become the biggest-selling record the seminal punk-rock group ever had. But it didn't help Phil Spector much then, and it wasn't helping him at all now. It was well past the end of the century. And perhaps the only person who stood between Phil Spector and another hung jury had been taken away by the KKK.

On 29 May 2009, Phil Spector was sentenced to nineteen years to life after being convicted on a second-degree murder charge. The last time I saw him, he was awaiting sentencing. He drove up with Rachelle and the two behemoth bodyguards in his Roll-Royce Silver Shadow to one of his favorite restaurants in Pasadena, where Marion and I were already waiting. When we sat down, Phil seemed relaxed. The impending sentencing barely came up. Instead, he told stories about Joe DiMaggio, Mickey Mantle, and his longtime bodyguard, George. Phil asked us to come to the castle after dinner, but I told him we really just needed to get back to the hotel and sleep. I hugged Phil and his wife, wished them well, and that was the last time I saw him.

When I heard about the sentencing on a cable news channel, it hit hard. Maybe the DA's office went after Phil Spector with such a vengeance after striking out in high-profile fashion first with O.J., then Robert Blake. Maybe Phil Spector's defense had blown it. Whatever the case, I thought back to the time we were all made to listen to the opening of 'Rock 'n' Roll High School' again and again and again. The principal players in the studio that afternoon were now all gone in one way or another. And I thought, *Maybe bad luck comes in fours.*

Good luck, I've learned, comes in thousands, maybe millions. I'm still very happily married to my childhood sweetheart. I've been sober for more than thirty years. My show on SiriusXM goes out via satellite to all fifty states and Canada and is entering its tenth year. Fans keep coming to the concerts in thousands, and giving them what they want is what I love.

There are different ways to accomplish that, but my way is to put together a very professional band and take it over the top. We spend a good part of each year in far-flung hotels and go to places that not long ago were entirely off the punk map – Vietnam, Dubai, Serbia, Colombia, the Philippines, China, and even Russia. *Rocket to Russia*, a tongue-in-cheek title, became a reality. A whole new generation is discovering the bold, unpolished beauty of the punk song – two minutes to convey your message of love, hate, anger, joy, frustration, fun, sarcasm, war, politics, or sometimes just an inside joke among you and your friends.

When we played Beijing for the first time in 2007, waving the punk flag high, the culture shock was mostly mine. At first I noticed a few people on bikes and on foot wearing respirators over their faces. They reminded me a bit of the masks I'd sometimes worn when I'd done demolition work. I thought these folks were perhaps fighting off some kind of new Asian flu until I realized there were thousands and thousands of city dwellers wearing these masks. They couldn't all be sick or on their way to a construction site. Then someone explained to me the masks were to protect them against air pollution.

Fortunately, punk was in the air, too. At an outdoor stadium packed with nineteen thousand screaming kids and former kids, even the hip-hop group Public Enemy were infected. They played 'Blitzkrieg Bop' along with my band as the fans went crazy behind tall security fences and rows of police wearing white gloves. In China, chaos is a very controlled affair. And I thought, *Given how unlikely it was for these kids to adopt this music in the first place, the future really is wide open.*

When we traveled to play Vietnam not long after, a bunch of government officials woke us up at six in the morning the day of the first show to review our songs. We faced five solemn-looking bureaucrats behind a long table. They pored over CDs the way they once pored over US military propaganda. After a while, however, they gave us the green light. I had to wonder whether they really understood the New York-bred cutting sarcasm of songs like 'Commando' and '53rd & 3rd'. Probably not. But, if ever one day they did, we would know Vietnam was truly free.

It's been said that if everyone who claims they were at Woodstock really was there, Joni Mitchell would have sung about half a billion rather than half a million people. Sometimes it seems like it's getting that way with the Ramones. Major acts who back in the day would sooner have had a ventriloquist open for them sometimes make it sound like they were headbanging in the first row at CBGB *circa* 1976.

Sometimes it seems the 'half a billion' fantasy may actually become a reality for the worldwide punk nation. When we tour, it's no oldies act. More than half of the audience are under twenty-five, and about half of them haven't reached sixteen yet. These kids are just discovering punk rock, and they bring more friends back with them every year. We went from playing a hole in the wall to playing stadiums. And there is no end in sight. We always knew we had the greatest fans in the world, and now there are more of them than ever.

Not that our generation has gone away. Far from it. While punk back in the day was thought of as in the moment, it's now the stuff of legacies. I recently received an email from a couple throwing a *Rock 'n' Roll High School* pajama party for their kids. The parents wanted to know if Marky could call the house around 9 p.m., when the movie was about midway through. It's not important that I happened to be catching some shuteye on tour halfway around the globe. What is important and kind of unexpected is that sometime between the seventies and today, the music we made by the seat of our pants against all odds somehow became 'timeless'.

The requests I get never cease to amaze me. I'm often asked to sit in with multiplatinum bands covering Ramones songs. And who would ever have thought the lyrics from 'We're a Happy Family' would come true? I recently found out Pope Francis and President Obama are Ramones fans. Every day is an adventure.

I see countless people around the globe wearing Ramones T-shirts. That's a good thing, but I often wonder if it's like the Che Guevara T-shirts worn by people who don't know who Che Guevara is. Or if they can name the guys on the shirt.

If I had more time I'd be happy to tell them who these guys really were. The significance of John's politics was overblown. No matter how bossy he sometimes got in the van, the America he loved was ultimately about freedom. Dee Dee was a poet trapped in a punk body. He never quite found the freedom he was looking for on earth, but the ride he gave the rest of us was liberating. Joey was a punk hippie who found an odd, self-styled freedom down in the basement of his mother's art store, wrapped it up, and gave it to the world as a gift.

John, Dee Dee, Joey, and all the wonderful people we worked with in the Ramones as well as our friends in other bands were blessed and cursed by the same thing: they were way ahead of their time. I am incredibly lucky to have known all of them and to have lived long enough to realize something very important. The time they were looking forward to is now.

ACKNOWLEDGEMENTS

Special thanks to Mark Neuman. And thank you to Gertrude Bell, Meyer Rossabi, Francis Vitello, Charles Carpenter, Matthias Prill, David Riu, Andres Vignolo, Bonnie Slifken, Ray and Daang Goodman, Andrew Hilfiger, Tommy Hilfiger, Karen Mamont, Linda Aroz, Harvey Leeds, Cheryl Neuman, Andrew Wilkes-Krier, Linda Spinner, Bryan Cullen, Steve Leeds, Seymour Stein, Daniel Boulud, Anthony Bourdain, Peter Criss, Vera Ramone, Roy Rosenthal, Steve Lewis, Nancy Sayle, Vinny Damino, DJ Ringo, Doug Mustang, Angel Nokonoko, Andrea Rock, Steve Blatter, Gary Diaz, Jim Bessman, Larry Kilroy, Eddie Clark, Steve Leeds, Will Pendarvis, David Chiedkel, Stacy Creamer, Paul Carpenter, Stephen King, Chip Ruggieri, Andrew W.K., Graham Vanderveen, Monte Melnick, Kim Dillard, Tim Siedelbach, Gary Borres, Phil Spector, and Trigger.

Gone but not forgotten: Linda Stein, Bob Quine, Frank Barsalona, Gary Kurfirst, Ira Herzog, Kenny Kerner, Dee Dee Ramone, Joey Ramone, Johnny Ramone, Tommy Ramone, Leee Black Childers, Peter Bell, Arturo Vega, Charlotte Lescher, Bob Fitzpatrick, Neil Bogart, and Justin Leitner.

Additionally there have been an incredible amount of influences on my life beyond the music and here are some of them:

Drummers: Ringo Starr, Keith Moon, Hal Blaine, Mitch Mitchell, Buddy Rich, Dino Danelli, John Bonham, Dave Clark, and Benny Benjamin.

Bass players: Jack Bruce, James Jamerson, Paul McCartney, Kenny Aaronson, Carol Kaye, John Paul Jones, John Entwistle, Chuck Rainey, and Bill Wyman.

Guitarists: Jimi Hendrix, Johnny Thunders, Jimmy Page, Dave Davies, Bob Quine, Buddy Guy, George Harrison, Pete Townshend, and Wes Montgomery.

Producers: George Martin, Shadow Morton, Tom Dowd, Bob Crewe, Snuff Garrett, Mickie Most, Shel Talmy, Jimmy Miller, and Eddie Kramer.

Singers: Dion DiMucci, David Ruffin, Steve Marriott, John Lennon, Darlene Love, Mick Jagger, Frankie Valli, Eric Burdon, and Levi Stubbs.

Movies: *Alien, Angels with Dirty Faces, On the Waterfront, Godzilla* (1956), *The Maltese Falcon, Raging Bull, A Hard Day's Night, Giant, Man with the Golden Arm,* and *Bullitt.*

Cars: 1963 Corvette Stingray, 1964 Aston Martin, 1968 Dodge Charger, 1965 Jaguar XKE, 1964 Buick Riviera, 1965 Pontiac GTO, 1967 Austin-Healey, 2014 Dodge Challenger, 1989 Mercedes 560 SEC, and 1963 Facel Vega II.

INDEX